CANADIAN CARNIVAL FREAKS
AND THE EXTRAORDINARY BODY, 1900–1970s

In 1973, a five-year-old girl known as Pookie was exhibited as "The Monkey Girl" at the Canadian National Exhibition. Dressed only in her diaper and on display for just one day before complaints closed the exhibit down, she would be the last of many children exhibited as "freaks" in twentieth-century Canada.

Jane Nicholas takes us on a search for answers about how and why the freak show persisted into the 1970s and offers a sophisticated analysis of its place in twentieth-century culture. These exhibits survived and thrived because of their flexible business model and government support, and remained popular by mobilizing cultural and medical ideas of the body and normalcy.

Canadian Carnival Freaks and the Extraordinary Body is the first full-length study of the freak show in Canada and is a significant contribution to our understanding of the history of Canadian popular culture, attitudes toward children, and the social construction of able-bodiness. Based on a foundation of impressive research, the book will be of particular interest to anyone interested in the history of disability, the history of childhood, and the history of consumer culture.

JANE NICHOLAS is an associate professor in the Department of History and Department of Sexuality, Marriage, and Family Studies at the University of Waterloo.

CNE Midway 1920? City of Toronto Archives, fonds 1244, item 2015.

JANE NICHOLAS

Canadian Carnival Freaks and the Extraordinary Body, 1900–1970s

UNIVERSITY OF TORONTO PRESS
Toronto Buffalo London

© University of Toronto Press 2018
Toronto Buffalo London
utorontopress.com

ISBN 978-1-4875-0265-2 (cloth)
ISBN 978-1-4875-2208-7 (paper)

___

Library and Archives Canada Cataloguing in Publication

Nicholas, Jane, 1977–, author
Canadian carnival freaks and the extraordinary body, 1900–1970s / Jane Nicholas.

Includes bibliographical references and index.
ISBN 978-1-4875-0265-2 (hardcover)   ISBN 978-1-4875-2208-7 (softcover)

1. Freak shows – Canada – History – 20th century. 2. Sideshows – Canada – History – 20th century. 3. Carnivals – Canada – History – 20th century. 4. Entertainers – Canada – History – 20th century. 5. Freak shows – Social aspects – Canada – History – 20th century. 6. Sideshows – Social aspects – Canada – History – 20th century. 7. Carnivals – Social aspects – Canada – History – 20th century. 8. Entertainers – Canada – Social conditions – 20th century. I. Title.

GV1835.56.C2N53 2018   791.3'50971   C2017-906322-7

___

This book has been published with the help of a grant from the Federation for the Humanities and Social Sciences, through the Awards to Scholarly Publications Program, using funds provided by the Social Sciences and Humanities Research Council of Canada.

University of Toronto Press acknowledges the financial assistance to its publishing program of the Canada Council for the Arts and the Ontario Arts Council, an agency of the Government of Ontario.

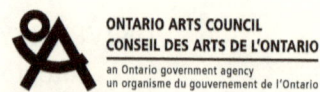
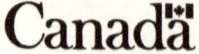

For Karl and Sebastian

Contents

Illustrations ix

Acknowledgments xi

Introduction: Pookie's Story 3

1 Monsters and Freaks: Exhibitionary Culture and the Order of Things 22

2 The Carnival State: Protests, Moral Regulation, and Profits 42

3 The Carnival Business in Canada: Paternalism, Belonging, and Freak Show Labour 78

4 The Twentieth-Century Freak Show: Medical Discourse, Normality, and Race 115

5 Not Just Child's Play: Child Freak Show Consumers and Workers 149

6 The Spectacularization of Small and Cute: Midget Shows and the Dionne Quintuplets 174

Epilogue: "I guess it really is all over" – The End Which Is Not One 201

Notes 205

Bibliography 263

Index 283

Illustrations

Frontspiece: CNE Midway 1920? ii
1.1 World's Fair Freaks at the Canadian National Exhibition 39
2.1 Johnny J. Jones Freak Show, CNE Midway, 1913 45
2.2 Crowded midway in front of sideshows, 1940 46
2.3 Girl performers ca 1920. 54
2.4 Skid Road attractions, 1919 64
3.1 Photograph of carnival workers setting up the midway, July 1953 85
3.2 Map of Coop and Lent Circus's route for 1916 89
3.3 Map of the James Patterson Trained Wild Animal Show and the Gollmar Bros. Circus, 1917 91
3.4 Map of Polack Bros.' "Twenty Big Shows" Route, 1920 92
3.5 Map of the Ringling Bros. and Barnum and Bailey Combined Shows route, 1922 93
3.6 Possibly James Gibson at the Canadian National Exhibition, 1930s 110
4.1 "Nature's Mistakes" performers in midway carnival ten-in-one sideshow, 1940 134
4.2 'Ubangi savages' at the Canadian National Exhibition 143
4.3 Eskimoland at the Canadian National Exhibition 144
5.1 Freak performers, CNE 152
5.2 "Ernie and Len: Two Living Brothers with One Head," CNE, 1937 167
6.1 "Midget City," Canadian National Exhibition 181
6.2 Postcard featuring the Quints, age 3, with their stuffed dogs, 1937 194
6.3 Dr Dafoe accepting his honorary degree of "Doctor of Litters," New York, 1939 197

Acknowledgments

Historical research is time-consuming and often dependent on funding to facilitate trips to archives and provide time to write. As a Canadian historian, the research for this book took me into unique areas and provided for some new and interesting experiences. I might be the only Canadian historian to be peed on by a lion in the course of her research. For all of this (except perhaps for the lion pee experience), I am especially grateful to the Social Sciences and Humanities Research Council for the Standard Research Grant that made this research possible. In addition to much-needed research funds, it also provided less tangible support in making me think I wasn't the only one who thought this was a story worth telling. Additional funds from Lakehead University, in the form of a sabbatical, which gave me necessary time to write a full first draft, and from St Jerome's University in the University of Waterloo were essential to its completion. I am grateful to the Federation of Social Sciences and Humanities for the Aid to Scholarly Publications award, which helped to fund the publication of the book.

Research funds also made possible the hiring of undergraduate and graduate research assistants. Sabrina del Ben, Ulysses Patola, Jordan Lehto, Jamilee Baroud, Teaghan Koster, Whitney Wood, Meg McLeod, and Rachel Christian provided research assistance, and I thank them for their work. For many of us who attempt to balance teaching, service, and research, research assistants keep projects moving forward when our day planners are filled with teaching and new course preparation and meetings. At times, I also needed to call on the assistance and skills of professional researchers, and for this I thank Paul Jasen and Alice Cox Phillips. Reg Nelson at Lakehead University's Geospatial Data Centre made the wonderful maps.

Researching the history of the freak show has proven challenging. I have been supported in my efforts by a number of archivists and institutions that have assisted me in tracking down and accessing archival sources. In particular, I thank the Pacific National Exhibition for providing permission to access their collection held at the City of Vancouver Archives, and the archivists there for facilitating that access. I also thank the New York Public Library for permission to use the material in their collections. Linda Cobon at the Canadian National Exhibition and Peter Shrake at the Robert L. Parkinson Library and Research Centre at Circus World Museum have been especially helpful. My thanks to Alicia Cherayil of the CNE Archives for assistance with the images. Many thanks to Glenn Charron and the late Jennifer Walker for their assistance accessing the material at the North American Carnival Museum and Archives. Jim Conklin spoke with me about the collection, and I appreciate all of his time and energy in preserving Canada's carnival history. The Library and Archives of Canada processed my requests for access to information quickly and efficiently, and I thank them. At Lakehead University, Monique Johnson and Tracy Zurich in the interlibrary loan department cheerfully processed countless (and sometimes complicated) requests for me and even provided suggestions for readings. My thanks to Rachel Churchill of The CS Lewis Company Ltd for special assistance with attaining permission to include the excerpts from William Lindsay Gresham's *Nightmare Alley*. I thank The Estate of William L. Gresham for providing that permission.

I have been fortunate to present portions of the manuscript at invited talks. In particular, I thank the audiences at St Jerome's at the University of Waterloo (2008), Simon Fraser University (2013), the University of Lethbridge (2015), the University of Western Ontario (2015), Lakehead University (2015), the University of Windsor (2016), and the Northern Ontario School of Medicine (2017). Earlier portions and earlier drafts of this work have been published in *The Difference Kids Make: Bringing Children and Childhood into Canadian History and Historiography* and *Histoire Sociale / Social History*. Pookie's story was introduced and analysed using a different framework in an article by Lori Chambers and myself in the *Journal of Canadian Studies*. In working through ideas on paper, I am grateful to Wendy Mitchinson and Christina Burr, who read and commented on earlier drafts. Beth McAuley and Melissa MacAuley helped with an earlier (and densely packed) draft and encouraged me to give ideas some space and "let my ideas breathe."

Acknowledgments

Near the end of this project I happily returned to Waterloo to take a position in the departments of History and Sexuality, Marriage, and Family Studies at St Jerome's University in the University of Waterloo. I thank all of my colleagues for their warm welcome, especially Jim Walker, Geoff Hayes, Lynne Taylor, Scott Kline, Toni Serafini, and Steven Bednarski. I am especially thankful to my close friends and colleagues who provided support and encouragement throughout my research and writing. A special thanks to Wendy Mitchinson, Rex Lingwood, Patricia Jasen, Monica Flegel, Rachel Warburton, David Richards, Ron Turner, Renée Bondy, Tracy Penny Light, Catherine Connolly, Adam Van Tuyl, Vic Smith, Judith Leggatt, Pam Wakewich, and Lori Chambers. Beth Macy commiserated with me about writing freak show history and helped me see the humour in some of the more frustrating experiences. Many years ago, Daniel Bender turned my attention to the freak show and I thank him for pointing me in that direction. David Leeson generously gave me a copy of Gresham's *Nighmare Alley*, which helped me through a difficult period in the project.

Once again, it has been a pleasure to work with Len Husband and the University of Toronto Press. His unflinching support of this project has been incredible. It takes an enormous amount of work to turn a manuscript into a book and I thank him for his steady stewardship in that near magical process. Thanks also to the two anonymous reviewers, who were supportive and generous and provided a careful reading and thoughtful feedback on the manuscript. James Leahy did a beautiful job copy editing the manuscript and I thank him. Many thanks also go to Frances Mundy for carefully guiding the manuscript through the last stages of publication. And I am grateful to Barbara Kamienski for her work on the index and general editing prowess.

Writing can be lonely, and without my family it would have been much more so. Karl and Sebastian and our two pets, Lily and Archibald, make life joyful. I cannot, though, fully explain the ways in which Karl has supported me or how he and Sebastian have showed me the nature of unconditional love, but I know that I couldn't have done any of it without them.

"How'd you like to be shut up in a kid's body that way? With the marks all yawping at you. It's different in our racket. We're up head and shoulders above the marks. We're better'n they are and they know it. But the Major's a freak born."

...

Dust when it was dry. Mud when it was rainy. Swearing, streaming, sweating, scheming, bribing, bellowing, cheating, the carny went its way. It came like a pillar of fire by night, bringing excitement and new things into the drowsy towns – lights and noise and the chance to win an Indian blanket, to ride on the ferris wheel, to see the wild man who fondles those rep-tiles as a mother would fondle her babes. Then it vanishes in the night, leaving the trodden grass of the field and the debris of popcorn boxes and rusting tin ice-cream spoons to show where it had been.

– William Lindsey Gresham, *Nightmare Alley*

Introduction

Pookie's Story

In 1973, the Canadian National Exhibition, Canada's largest and most prominent organization of its kind, ended its long-standing practice of hosting a freak show as part of the midway. It did so in reaction to the limited outcry over the exhibition of a five-year-old girl with intellectual and physical disabilities as "The Monkey Girl." Only ever identified as Pookie, she appeared for one day of the show dressed only in her underwear and reportedly cried on stage. Members of the public reported the exhibition to the police. In the short public debate that followed, participants tended to empathize with the mother and blame the CNE for Pookie's exploitation. Her mother defended her daughter's exhibition, pointing to the difficulties of raising a child with disabilities by herself with very limited government support. Sideshow owner Sam Alexander defended the show, arguing that audience members still wanted freak shows.[1] That year, the midway continued without the freak show and Pookie's story quickly disappeared from newspapers. While I know nothing of what happened to Pookie and her family as a result of her brief exhibition, her one-day "performance" is remarkable in that it led to the announcement of the end of almost a century of freak displays at the CNE.

Pookie's case, while dramatic in its result of closing the freak show at the CNE and ending child performances as freaks, is not a singular story. The freak show was a regularly occurring event in twentieth-century Canada, and in this book I have attempted to understand how and why the live shows continued to operate into the 1970s in Canada as part of the carnival. My argument positions the freak show as part of the modern exhibitionary complex that made bodies spectacles of meaning that were generative and reflective of social relations. In the twentieth century, the exhibitionary complex included a sophisticated carnival business (as part of the outdoor amusement industry) and a consumer culture that reflected and in turn broadcasted important messages about bodily difference and human value. In the crass terms of capitalism, the freak show was a product to be sold. Carnivals and freak shows maintained their presence on the landscape of consumer culture because they continually appealed to new audiences and refreshed their acts. But there was more. The freak show was a popular and accessible means for Canadians to see, understand, and make sense of bodily difference that matched shifting understandings of categories of ability, race, and gender. Scratching at the surface of the carnival reveals a much wider investment than individual audience members and small numbers of savvy showmen. Freak shows, as part of the carnival, became essential to the financial success of government-supported agricultural fairs and appropriated the language of science and medicine to make the shows educational and interesting. The freak show helped to form and reflected cultural ideas of the body and normalcy (defined by ability, race, gender, and age) that remained in almost perpetual contest over the course of the century. To reckon with the history of the freak show is to explore an element in the fashioning and refashioning of the "normal" modern body.

The persistence of the shows also subtly reveals how economic vulnerabilities played themselves out in individual lives. Pookie was exhibited not because she was a freak, but because she was poor and a child with disabilities. However, we should be cautious in concluding that Pookie's life was somehow inevitably tragic, inferior, or unfortunate and cannot conclude that her story is representative of all children or adults exhibited in the freak show. As Rosemarie Garland-Thomson has persuasively argued, disability is not a corporeal "fact" but rather an interlocking set of narratives that define bodies relationally as abled/disabled, fit/unfit, competent/incompetent, and normal/abnormal. These cultural dichotomies produce inequities in social relations.[2] Indeed, Pookie's case is tragic only insofar as it reveals the limits on respect for human dignity resulting from disability, poverty, and age. And all of those categories are not facts of the body itself but rather social judgments layered onto it. That this limit on dignity persisted into the early 1970s in regard to freak shows belies the common progressive discourse of the steady extensions of universal human rights. Humanity, despite the growing post–Second World War declaration of "rights," has been doled out inequitably – not by simple declaration but by complex discourses and structures that render some people more valuable and deserving of everything from life to privacy to meaningful work to dignity to social recognition.[3] The largely silent collective persistence in upholding hierarchical models of difference based in the body cannot be reduced to a few showmen, but rather sits on the shoulders of the thousands more Canadians who attended and paid for the shows, and perhaps unintentionally bore witness to bodily difference rendered as consumer product, as well as the government officials, who in various ways implicitly and explicitly supported the shows because of their profits. The sideshow of the Dionne quintuplets as discussed in chapter 6 is an extraordinary case study of a much wider investment.

The popular narrative of the "fringe" freak show that was separate from "normal" society ignores the government regulations involving the shows, the complicated role of professional medicine in framing and, at times, contesting the shows, and the fact that the shows were part of an organized industry in which thousands of men and women laboured, often in the public eye. Although the freak show has long been situated as a haphazardly organized group of outcasts who found acceptance on the margins of society, the freak show was not in fact marginal to Canadian culture. At various points throughout the twentieth century, concerned citizens protested and called for the end of the shows on the grounds that they were distasteful, but many more kept the shows alive with their nickels and dimes at small and large, urban and rural destinations throughout the country. In order to understand the freak show's place in Canadian culture, the freak show has to be understood as part of a sophisticated carnival business. Chapters 2 and 3 discuss the complex terrain of business, labour, as well as formal and informal regulation by various elements of the state. Although this widens the focus of the book to the entirety of the carnival, it provides essential context for the continuation of shows, revealing how the carnival was interwoven with governments, newspapers, and popular commercial amusements and showing how the freak show was also a site of labour. While the carnival and the sideshow are not neatly synonymous with the freak show, the freak show remained an integral component of the shows and I have used the terms freak show and sideshow interchangeably here, because my interest in the sideshow is focused on the freak. The freak show and sideshow are so enmeshed, however, that one of the challenges in tracing the shows is that, by mid-century, many companies essentially stopped explicitly advertising freak shows as part of the carnival. They had not disappeared; they were just expected.

Other evidence, like photographs and newspaper reports as in Pookie's case, proves their ongoing presence. Indeed, in the early 1970s, sociologists writing on the contemporary carnival noted, "Almost without exceptions, however, the largest show on the carnival midway is the freak show or 'ten-in-one.'"[4] As a whole, placing the freak show at the centre of this study reveals its importance and its connection to business, labour, work, the body, medicine, childhood, poverty, disability, and consumer culture.

As the chapters that follow reveal, however, shows did not remain static. They changed based on both internal and external pressures in an effort to remain solvent and culturally resonant. From the 1920s onwards, carnivals, and the freak shows that formed an important part of them, began catering to children and "cleaning up" their acts (not fleecing consumers outright) to appeal to changing mores and tastes. This was a complicated process involving the social and moral reform movement, changes to the Criminal Code of Canada, initiatives by the showmen themselves, and at least a bit of smoke and mirrors: name changes and good press releases without profound changes in the shows themselves.

Beginning in the 1910s, establishing and maintaining a professional identity as a modern business was important to the successful operation of the carnival. The carnival business as part of the outdoor amusement industry became professionalized as many other entities did: by using narratives of the self-made man who would become the paternalistic figurehead of the business, using practices of paternalism to shape employer/employee relations, and maintaining defined and hierarchical roles for individual workers marked by gender, race, and ability. The shows also evolved to expand their consumer base in the period. By the 1930s, attending the sideshows with friends became a cultural rite of passage, marking a new stage in middle-class children's consumer independence, as child consumers were added to the swathes of adult consumers. The 1930s also brought increasingly impoverished conditions to many families and exacerbated inequities. As discussed in chapter 5, letters from the period reveal families' attempts at caring for children with disabilities by searching out work for them on freak shows. Class and disability divided child consumers from child freak show workers. The 1930s also witnessed the birth of the Dionne quintuplets and the beginning of their exhibition, which dovetailed in interesting ways with the freak show. As discussed in chapter 6, the idea of "cute" structured the Dionnes' display as well as freak exhibits in the period, which garnered for the latter new levels of acceptance and respectability. If the number of freak shows seems to have declined from the 1950s onwards, the freak show never entirely disappeared because they are essential to understanding bodily difference. While live freak shows might have ended at the CNE in 1973, they continued at other venues and significantly were incorporated into other media. The show goes on. Indeed, one can hardly mention that word freak show without someone referencing popular television shows, which have taken up the gauntlet. If television and digital media have become the new freak show, they mostly replace live performances and have shifted the dynamics. While the gloss of education and learning remains, the relationships between consumer viewers and worker performers have changed. Safe within their own homes, consumers need not admit to having such "basic" tastes and need not confront the actual people behind the performances. Live freak shows could at least make viewers uncomfortable – the freak looked back, the freak spoke, and the freak knew you were there.

Disability is at the root of the history of freak shows, although it intersects with other categories of analysis. A triangle of vulnerability (poverty, disability, and childhood), for example, would continue across the decades of the twentieth century, leading to Pookie's exhibition at the CNE in 1973. Focusing on freak performances on the sideshow, then, illuminates not only a lesser-known aspect of Canadian history but also the wider social, cultural, political, and economic forces at work in defining it.[5] The freak show is situated at a critical point for the exploration and the making of the modern able body. My focus on the cultural, however, is not at the exclusion of the social, and as such, the freak show also reveals (although to a lesser extent) issues regarding race relations, poverty, and gender inequality, family strategies of care for children with disabilities, and the limits of tolerance for bodies deemed different or unusual.

The Freak Show and Canadian History

At its most basic level, the freak show is the public exhibition of a person or people deemed to be significantly different from normal. As Susan Stewart argues, freaks are creations of culture, not nature.[6] Freaks were a narrative production that encapsulated the oral, visual, and performative elements of the body.[7] Freaks were usually hidden behind a canvas painted with pictures to garner audience interest. The canvas was both advertisement and barrier as it ensured only paying audiences could go behind it to see the freak. A "barker" or "spieler" paid to broadcast the ballyhoo – a fantastic narrative of what was behind the canvas – built interest in passersby and narrated the show. In "blow-off" exhibits, an extra charge might get audience members a special or more revealing display before the end of the show.

"Freak" is built on the discursive quicksand of "the normal body." As a result, the freak show can tell us much about the production, investment, and policing of "the normal body." The modern idea of "normal" emerged around 1850 and did so in relation to the body. The production of the normal body needed its opposite, which was defined by its limits or what was extraordinary.[8] As feminist scholars have argued, the normal body became synonymous with the masculine, white, universal, liberal, autonomous subject.[9] Defining, policing, and defending "the normal body" took up an enormous amount of professional and popular time. Far from being abstract, the ideal of this normal body had serious consequences for everything from medical intervention to economic prosperity to claiming autonomy and adequate care to life itself. Bodies deemed to be different, deviant, and inadequate were placed under formal and informal scrutiny in medical offices, on the streets, and on the freak shows. If people with extraordinary bodies found themselves vulnerable to staring, poor treatment, and possibly exploitation, such conditions were not natural but rather produced by specific historical developments. In assessing the freak shows of the past, I have tried here to look carefully at both the structures and discourses that produced the conditions of the display of certain people as freaks. Of these, economic need, racism, and a lack of other options for care were prominent. Yet freaks on the sideshow found ways of asserting agency, questioning deeply held norms about the body and ability, and resisting efforts to contain or hide away difference. In total, these histories tell us about the social and cultural failure to recognize and accommodate difference and to eradicate poverty, especially child poverty. The freak show was a product of social and cultural conditions that made certain bodies valuable for their exhibitionary purposes. The freak then is a cultural illusion produced to resonate with hierarchical and dichotomous social categories.

The rise of exhibitionary culture ensured the freak show's place in modern culture. As Keith Walden astutely argued, modern urban culture was a culture of the eye.[10] Exhibitionary culture was never a neutral proposition. Michel Foucault indicated the important place of visuality and surveillance in his work on power and knowledge. Tony Bennett expanded Foucault's framework beyond the prison and the clinic to include exhibitions and public spectacles.[11] As chapter 1 details, the modern freak show is intimately connected to what Bennett described as "the exhibitionary complex," which produced cultural connections between spectacle, power, surveillance, information, and the body, laced together like an intricate spider's web upon which the freak could rest.

While the modern freak show fully emerged in the mid-nineteenth century as a middle-class amusement, by the end of the century it struggled to maintain a gloss of respectability. However, given the wide number of people who attended and the ongoing profits, its loss of cultural status did not neatly equate to a loss of paying audience members. Freak shows first rose to prominence as the modern world moved from rural, agricultural, and home-based production to urban, industrial capitalism. In Canada, as elsewhere, these changes were significant. By the early 1870s, Canada's most urban cities of Montreal and Toronto hosted new industries and factories supported by new transportation technologies, notably the railway. Railroads made transporting both people and goods faster and more efficient. By 1915, Canada's impressive geography was matched by an equally impressive 55,000 kilometres of railway – a transportation system that was widely used by circuses, sideshows, and other travelling shows in addition to roads by the 1960s.[12]

As work became centred in urban areas, the population of cities swelled. By 1921, the Canadian census reported that almost half of all Canadians were urban dwellers, a trend that had begun in the 1870s.[13] Life and work in the city caused no shortage of problems, real and imagined. Poverty and slum conditions were common in major cities like Montreal and Toronto, while many working families found themselves teetering on the brink. Illness, injury, disability, and the death of one member had the potential to imperil the entire family.[14] Families found ways to survive such challenges, including the adopting out (informally) or the taking in of children. Urban industry also reshaped the landscape and ecology. Cities had limited infrastructure to support the swelling population with adequate housing and services, including everything from sewage disposal to outdoor spaces for recreation.[15] The latter were seen as increasingly important for the steady requirement of labour. The need for wholesome, rational amusements – combined with labour activism for safe and reasonable working hours and conditions – made room for leisure time and commercial amusements. Social movements to literally and figuratively clean up the city were primarily the focus of Canada's dominant class: white, Anglo, middle-class Protestants. Reform efforts focused on everything from alcohol consumption and social purity to prostitution and child saving.[16] While perhaps well intended, such efforts tended to be more about instilling the values of the dominant class than attending to the core issues of economic and social dislocation that resulted from a highly stratified society.[17] As a number of scholars have demonstrated, conflicts over leisure and amusement, particularly those directed at young people – especially young women – were undergirded by fears of gender, class, race, religious, and ethnic imbalances in the dominant social order.[18] These were also contests over the more elusive issue of "taste," more particularly what constituted "good" taste.[19] Taste was – and is – a contested category embedded in class relations, and those contests are reflected in the history of the freak show. The freak show and the carnival could be fun and filled with illicit delights on both sides of the canvas. They could also cause anxiety, pity, and outcry. The freak show's peripatetic existence, however, helped to ensure its survival. New audiences were a train ride away, and annual visits meant that sometimes memories faded.

Freak shows also provided an outlet for visualizing and discussing these changes. In the seeming chaos of the modern world, the desire for order and regulation was strong. These changes both literally and figuratively remade the body as modern. Industrial metaphors shaped dominant understandings of the body as a machine as industrialization marked and changed the body in literal ways, producing scars, "deformities," and bodies regulated by the clock and new understandings of the measurability of time.[20] Bodies and the work they did were to be efficient in the new parlance of capitalism. As Garland-Thomson concludes, "if this new body [the modern body] felt alien to the ordinary citizen, the freak's bizarre embodiment could assuage viewers' uneasiness either by functioning as a touchstone of anxious identification or as an assurance of their regularized normalcy."[21] Audience members could also be assuaged seeing a body seemingly more disadvantaged and socially dislocated than their own. Over the course of the twentieth century, with its major upheavals (the First World War, the Great Depression, the Second World War, the atomic age), such anxieties changed in timbre and tone, but remained prevalent. Watching bodies is fascinating, and although freak shows declined in the twentieth century, that they hold on – that vestiges remain – says something profound about the delights of seeing bodies. Staring – intense looking – "is an intense visual exchange that makes meaning."[22] But it is difficult to know as a historian exactly how audience members reacted and saw (literally) freaks. Any number of gazes or modes of looking were possible: the stare, the clinical gaze (detached, distant, and medicalized), the consumer gaze (roving, delighted, and bored), and the carnivalesque gaze (piercing, laughing, sometimes sinister, and always in search of pleasure).[23] As writer Gahan Wilson noted in 1966,

> Much, sometimes all, of the freak's freakishness is determined by the attitude of the freak watcher. A man who observes a Siamese twin clinically, pondering on the complexities of cellular fission, is not going to see the same Siamese twin that a small, open-mouthed boy will see. The small boy will view the Siamese twin through the shimmering, distorting, glorifying mists of myth and superstition ... the small boy will carry away with him the recollection of the strangest, most marvellous Siamese twin who ever walked the face of the Earth. The clinician, lacking awe, confusion, and the love of magic, will only remember a perfectly ordinary Siamese twin.[24]

What is certain is that modernity intensified a particular exhibitionary culture bound with consumerism. For the shows, what audience members thought of the freaks was less important than their dimes and quarters. For freak show performers, being an object to be looked at was the essence of their work, but "starees" could also stare back and their own responses could run the gamut from relish in being seen to anger, shame, and embarrassment. Despite the prevalence of urban culture, freak shows appeared with regularity at rural agricultural fairs held across the country. As such, they crossed the divides of rural and urban, middle and working class, as well as those of gender, race, age, and ethnicity. Such crossings, however, did not imply uniformity among audience members, who witnessed and reacted to the shows in a wide variety of ways. Unfortunately, many of the reactions were left unrecorded – a problem with studying such ephemeral events. Of all the stakeholders here, the audience is the least analysed because of the paucity of evidence.

Bound in with the modern world was the intermixing of science and race. The freak show became institutionalized as part of popular culture in the mid-nineteenth century as many people in the West (both professionally and popularly) sought to understand the origins and hierarchical place of humans and animals (and the line between the two) under the auspices of modern scientific research. In the nineteenth century, and continuing until the mid-twentieth century, debating the hierarchy of humans and animals took on racist tones, and discussing that hierarchy brought colonial and imperial practices into the realm of the freak show. From the "discovery" of new people in distant lands to the ongoing project of the colonization of Indigenous peoples in Canada, exhibits were formed that echoed debates regarding race and humanity. While these exhibits, like many others, had their origins in the nineteenth century, they shaped opportunities for work and structured particular shows well into the 1940s, as chapters 3 and 4 reveal.

Overall, freak shows were not rare events in the twentieth century and they crossed a host of commercial venues including the circus, the carnival, travelling shows, and movie theatres. Movies and fiction, as well as non-fiction articles in various mass-market and specialty magazines and newspapers, augmented live performances. The freak show's place in modern culture was, literally, transitory and transnational. The border between Canada and the United States was, for the most part, permeable, although crossing the border was not always easy. Changes in immigration law and close surveillance of the carnivals sometimes made the border very real. Nonetheless, by the 1920s, Canadians were enmeshed in a North American culture, and freak shows existed as part of that modern dynamic.[25] As a result, on occasion here, I have looked at American performers' experiences, although only for performers who I could confirm also appeared in Canada. Well before "globalization," freak shows relied on world-wide networks of freak hunters (people whose job it was to scour the globe for new attractions), show owners, and audiences. Print culture, especially newspapers that reprinted various articles from other venues, added to the transnational element of the shows. I have, however, kept primarily focused on the lesser-studied Canadian context. Canadian contributions to freak and sideshow histories are substantial and include performers, massive audiences, internationally popular venues like the Canadian National Exhibition in Toronto, and formidable figures like the internationally respected Patty Conklin. The story here focuses on Canada with a recognition of broader transnational patterns and contributions that brought Canadians in touch with the world and the world with Canadians.

Historiography, Theory, and Evidence

This study is situated at the intersection of Canadian cultural history, the history of the body, disability history, consumer history, gender and women's history, and the history of childhood. Of those areas, disability history and the history of childhood remain less well developed but have certainly begun to flourish. Scholar-activists like Tom Shakespeare have tied political and theoretical challenges together in asserting the need to challenge definitions of "normality" and to recognize people with disabilities' self-defined identities.[26] In Canada, historian Geoffrey Reaume eschewed the divide between the personal and the academic in writing a history of the lives of people with disabilities living in a Toronto institution.[27] Post-structuralism's embrace of difference and its dismantling of universal and allegedly coherent categories helped to reframe disability as a multiple, contested, and inconsistent category. Scholars have pointed to how disability is hardly universally understood, applied, or accepted. Garland-Thomson pointed to the blind spot in feminist theory in dealing with disability and gender, while other scholars have called for a more nuanced understanding of gender and disability in relation to differences and hierarchies among permanent and temporary, acquired and congenital.[28] Theoretical work by Tanya Titchkosky and Robert McRuer has challenged scholars to think more broadly about the social and cultural work of disability and how it is often positioned as lesser than or tragic.[29] My perspective on disability (as a category of analysis) is rooted in social and cultural models of disability wherein bodies may have differences but the way in which those differences are socially understood and culturally represented is what gives them meaning. This challenges perspectives that see disability as inherently tragic, problematic, or associated with positions of difference or dependency. Rather, the project is to challenge the assumption that disability is obvious, rooted in biology, and different from normal.

These developments have been important in opening the category of disability to interrogation alongside other categories of analysis like gender, race, and age, but this has not been uncontested. Nadja Durbach, in her work on the British Victorian freak show, argues that the use of disability as an analytical category by historians sometimes borders on being anachronistic. Further, she argues that because freaks worked they were defined as able-bodied.[30] Two points are important to note for the Canadian context. First, the criticism of disability as a category of analysis could apply to others like gender, yet they have proved to be immensely useful to historians. I have generally risked being anachronistic over using other more historically accurate words, which by and large now are deemed to be offensive.[31] That said, readers will find historically accurate language used throughout in both my paraphrasing of and quoting of historical documents. In studying the Canadian context I am using disability as a category of analysis that encompasses any difference or deviation from what was defined as "normal." Second, while freak show performers worked on the twentieth-century Canadian sideshows because of their disabilities, they were often described as working *in spite of* them (whether or not they were actually paid), as discussed in chapters 3 and 4. Further, even though freak show performers laboured on stage, the performative labour was erased in the naturalization of the exhibits during which bodies were allegedly simply "displayed" or "exhibited." It is in regard to labour here that I use the term "performance." Regardless of what actually happened on stages and pits, freaks were an invention of performance and narrative.

By integrating disability alongside other analytical categories, however, I note that I recognize the limits of it. Disability and what constitutes it vary widely, and there are real problems with labelling disability or particular people as disabled. As Robert Bogdan argued in his groundbreaking book on the history of freak shows, "How we view people with disabilities has less to do with what they are physiologically than with who we are culturally. Understanding the 'freak show' can help us not confuse the role a person plays with who that person really is."[32] As such, I am using disability/disabilities here to refer to historical practices of differentiation that figured bodies deemed and performed as different as less than equal or undeserving of a fully realized humanity, or both. Similary, I am using Rosemarie Garland-Thomson's term "extraordinary bodies," but note here that it is an imperfect term. The term does not imply a naturally existing "ordinary" body, but rather references a complicated system of understanding the body framed and produced by binaries. Some of the historical development of this system is discussed in chapter 4.

Age is a similarly complex category, and what we might deem to be standard, discrete biological stages are indeed social and cultural inventions. My use of age as an analytical category in chapters 5 and 6 is a means to highlight the differences between children, adolescents, and adults as performers, workers, and consumers in conjunction with the cultural expectations of work and play, for example, that were to be aligned with those stages. Of course, both disability and age intersected with each other as well as other significant social categories of identity. In all, I have attempted to weave together the categories of gender, race, class, age, and ability to look at the place of the body in a society increasingly driven by consumer culture. The wide and varied nature of the bodies exhibited on the shows compelled such an analysis.

Freak shows have been studied for decades by a range of aficionados and scholars from different disciplines. A host of popular books on the freak show, typically with many photographs, continue to be published either by former circus workers or simply by interested fans. They tend to uncritically and nostalgically examine the freak show.[33] Treading the line between scholarly and popular, some writers have done significant research for publication and have also tried to preserve the ephemeral histories of the shows.[34] In the scholarly literature, prior to the 1980s, freak shows were seen as tawdry, exploitative, and a vestige of Victorian culture best left in the past. A notable exception here is Leslie Fiedler's 1978 book *Freaks*. Using a psychoanalytical reading of a range of freak texts, Fielder argues for seeing the psychic connections between "the freaks" as Others and us.[35] The 1980s were a turning point, as the decade witnessed the rise of the social construction of freaks, which sought to understand freaks not as freaks of nature but as freaks of culture. Essential to this development was the work of above-mentioned American sociologist Robert Bogdan. His book *Freak Show* was influential in looking at the social construction of freaks. It also excavated much of the now-common American freak show history from 1840 to 1940. Beginning in the late 1980s, the influence of post-structuralism, especially in literary circles, led to transdisciplinary readings of the freak show that integrated history, literary studies, visual culture, and other fields. Post-structuralism's attack on Marxism meant that studies of exploitation and class conflict gave way to discourse analysis of the variety of categories that produced freaks – what leading scholar Garland-Thomson termed "enfreakment."[36] The loosening of the "freak," both discursively as a category and methodologically in regard to the multiplicity of "texts" webbed together, produced important insights on the freaks' place in culture and the public imagination. The slide from history to literary analysis was sometimes problematic in that it blurred the line between real people and fictional characters. Accessing the records was also very different, with literature and film more readily available than archival documents.

My argument here builds from the extant international research. In particular, I extend the standard interpretations of the twentieth-century freak show by Bogdan and Garland-Thomson, who place the end of the shows somewhere between 1940 and 1950, in favour of casting a longer view into the early 1970s, if the freak show existed then in only a reduced form.[37] Garland-Thomson, for example, argues that "in the escalating upheaval of modernization between about 1840 through 1940, what we now think of as the freak show flared like a comet and then vanished from view, re-emerging in almost unrecognizable forms in the late twentieth century."[38] Rather than seeing the live freak show literally vanishing, I have traced its continuation to the early 1970s and Pookie's display, which ostensibly formally ended the shows at the internationally regarded CNE. Though it should be noted that even with the end of Pookie's exhibition showman Sam Alexander pointed out that his show would continue in other locations due to audience expectations that carnival and the sideshows would include freak shows; a concern was also noted about Pookie potentially travelling with the show to be exhibited elsewhere in one letter to the editor.[39] Nonetheless, the end of the shows at the CNE marked a significant shift in understanding and the place of the freak show on the Canadian carnival scene.

The interpretations by Bogdan and Garland-Thomson largely argue that medical science ended the shows by replacing cultural myth with scientific facts of the body and that the freak show moved from the realm of the live performance into the world of fiction (both movies and literature). My argument suggests a more complicated narrative that includes ongoing synergies between medicine and freaks shows, especially as the shows adopted medical discourse to frame their exhibitions. This extension complicates our view of the relationship between live shows and their postmodern forms in arts and popular culture. Like Bogdan and Garland-Thomson, Rachel Adams in *Sideshow U.S.A.* argues that the freak show was "evicted from popular culture" but that "their representational currency multiplied, granting them symbolic importance in inverse proportion to their declining status as a profitable mode of live entertainment."[40] Adams contends that American arts and letters absorbed the freak show and it proliferated in fiction and movies. Such an argument is compelling, but as I argue here, it paralleled, as opposed to neatly replaced, live shows. Similarly, Andrea Stulman Dennett has argued that the pseudoanthropological or pseudoethnological exhibits, which also formed an important part of sideshows and freak shows, ended by the early twentieth century. She argues that freak shows faded because medicine "demystified" the body and its differences and because society became more understanding of people with disabilities.[41] While one might take a progressive view of twentieth-century medicine, historical evidence serves to belie the interpretation that people with disabilities found anything but a tokenistic measure of acceptance. The persistence and popularity of eugenics made disability a precarious category that produced multiple vulnerabilities, including poverty, abuse, forced institutionalization, and even death for those who found themselves labelled as disabled.[42] My focus here in the latter chapters has been especially attuned to the child performers, to fill a modest gap in the extant literature. By the early 1970s, a host of social changes in the understanding of childhood, child welfare, and disability challenged the existence of the freak show, which explains Pookie's limited exhibition and the fact that she was one of the few child performers who stirred any public debate at all.

Recently, British historian Nadja Durbach's argument has focused on the interconnections between medicine and freak shows, as well as their place in modern consumer culture. She argues, however, that the shows ended earlier in the 1920s because of changes in disability brought by injured First World War veterans as well as a rising consumer culture that focused persistently on beauty.[43] In Canada, this seems to have been taken up differently. First World War veterans were active in making changes to entitlements for disabled soldiers, but their focus was by and large on men (soldiers) with acquired disabilities.[44] The range of disabilities was thus much narrower than that of the freak show, which included both congenital and acquired disabilities. The highest status for freaks (determined in large part by rarity) was reserved for those with congenital disabilities. Freak shows were not immune to changes in beauty culture and, in fact, in the critical decade of the 1920s, used such a culture to launch new freak performers. One such performer was Mary Ann Bevans, who won a British "beauty" contest to become the Ugliest Woman in the World. Beauty and ugliness (both culturally defined) relied on each other. Consumer culture warned especially women not to be ugly and promoted beauty as its opposite.[45] Beauty and ugliness defined each other in the negative and remained flexible and fluid categories that shaped bodies rather than simply acting as natural or neutral descriptors. Disability was largely assumed to be antithetical to modern beauty standards, and so such standards provided an important point of context rather than conflict for twentieth-century freak shows.

Historian David A. Gerber has cautioned historians that perspectives on the freak show must look critically at social context to assess limits on agency, consent, and choice.[46] In particular, Gerber challenges Bogdan's assessment of the twentieth-century freak show as a business "that created opportunity, status and enhanced power over their lives for the people employed in it."[47] My perspective on the shows aligns more closely with Gerber's than Bogdan's, although certainly some people working in the sideshows found rewards. Those rewards should be understood as emerging from a context of severely circumscribed opportunity for meaningful work for people with disabilities. It also needs to be understood in the context of the complexity of people's lives in the past, especially children's. While we might be tempted to look back at child freak show performers with pity, the history of childhood in Canada reveals complicated and desperate circumstances for many children and their families. Despite the increasing sentimentalization of childhood, many children historically lived grim if not miserable lives by idealized historical and contemporary standards. As such, the carnival could also be a fun, amusing break from monotonous routine, which was certainly the lifestyle espoused by many carnival workers. For both child workers and consumers, an assessment of the freak show reveals a rather mixed bag. A similar conclusion could be drawn for adults as well.

Similarly to Gerber, Ellen Samuels has cautioned scholars, who sometimes also perpetuate the assumption that sideshow performers were complicit in their own exploitation, to be wary of reading resistance and agency.[48] The issues of consent and agency are complicated. We can hardly conclude that infants and small children could understand the performative work they were to undertake, yet they could still express agency, as chapter 5 here reveals. Addressing consent and agency, however, has other complications and can be condescendingly rendered to assume that certain performers because of their disability were unable to understand or consent. People have always made decisions based on their own complicated life histories, and freak performers and workers are no different. My analysis in what follows is more closely aligned with Gerber's call for empathy and the need "to recognize the deeper humanity" of people who worked or were exhibited as freaks.

The evidence for the freak show is scattered in formal and informal archives across the country, both of which have confronted me with issues of access. I am grateful for the access provided by the various archives cited here, however limited in some cases. Much of the history of the carnival either escaped or evaded official record keepers. This, in some ways, simply represents the nature of the peripatetic carnival with its ephemeral performances. Newspapers and trade publications like *Billboard* have proven to be invaluable in filling gaps, but carnivals placed their own copy and advertisements as part of soliciting an audience, so these must be read carefully. Memoirs and published auto/biographies round out the evidence here. The sum of the evidence here has two important limitations. First, readers may notice that many of the sources are from Ontario, and there certainly is a bias here toward that province. Second, by way of example, Pookie's thoughts on her experience, or even her real name, have escaped the historical record. Disability history can also challenge standard historical practice, which places emphasis on the production of textual records in one's own voice. This book contains suggestive and limited evidence in some places, because the alternative of not telling the story did not seem like the best option. Without Pookie's voice or her real name or information of her family, does she have a history? I would argue yes, as limited as the accessible evidence of her experiences as the CNE is. Overall, the evidence is partial and stems largely from dominant record makers like government officials, journalists, and the show owners and managers themselves, who largely controlled the production of promotional materials including pamphlets, photographs, and newspaper articles.

Readers here will notice an absence of oral histories, and I should explain the reasons that this is so. The archives on freak performers tend to contain material produced by show owners and managers, and, as such, ballyhoo biographies are as numerous as photographs. Tracking down even the real names of performers (like Pookie, for example) can be difficult, and many have either passed on or otherwise disappeared from the historical record. Sideshow owners and managers have left rich collections (sometimes including biographies) and I have used those here. I have decided to maintain the focus on textual evidence augmented by photographs in the effort not to further increase the disproportion of evidence in favour of those who (at least historically) had more access to power. Of all of the voices in the debates over the shows, few are from performers and fewer still are from child performers. There are none from children with intellectual disabilities like Pookie. As such, the history of freak performers in the twentieth century is marked by histories of poverty and vulnerability that reappear as historiographical problems for researchers. Finding evidence of people's lives when they did not control the terms of their display or produce their own records is difficult, as many historians have noted.[49] Sideshow acts both produced and obscured performers' autobiographies to meet their own needs; as such, piecing together the "truth" of individual lives is often complicated because of the nature of the available evidence.

Very early on in the archival work, I found myself both fascinated and frustrated by the heaps of visual evidence. Throughout many archival holdings, photographs formed the largest and most complete documentation, which I have used in part to prove that certain workers performed in Canada. I remained frustrated, however, because the photographs were painfully limited in what they could tell me about the experience of shows, the people who ran them, and even the people who performed in them. The latter were also difficult to access through the heaps of promotional and largely fictionalized (ballyhoo) materials produced by the shows about individual performers. In facing similar ethical challenges, Margarit Shildrick has questioned the reproduction of visual evidence of vulnerable subjects asking the question, "What exactly is it that we are looking for?" Ethical questions and more practical issues of copyright led me to limit the visual evidence produced here. As many researchers will attest, gaining access to the visual is much easier than getting permission to reproduce it. Yet, for all of the "problems" with photographs, I have included a selection of them here because they form an important body of evidence, without which the story would be (more) incomplete.

Related to the use of photographs but more generally in exploring this topic, I also took on the risk of reifying the status of "freaks," and in part this project reflects an insertion of myself as a researcher interested in the history of the body and the making of modern culture. As all historians do, I have necessarily intervened in shaping the histories here and have made choices about where to gather evidence and what evidence to highlight, although (in)accessibility shaped some of this, as it does with all stories. There are many more stories to be told of the carnival in Canada, including a more systematic study of individual workers and individual shows as part of the carnival business, as well as how shows interacted with regional officials and audiences among others. Many of the stories could be told in other contexts and as part of other histories. I struggled with completing this project and, at times, wondered what the difference was between historians writing on the past and the showmen themselves. Was I at risk of simply curating my own paper sideshow? At the end, the need to wrestle with a history of the body in Canada that in a small and partial way accounted for disability, that questioned progressive narratives that placed the freak show in an ever-retreating and distancing past, seemed to justify the risk. My goal with this project has been to illuminate the important place of the extraordinary body in modern Canadian society and culture, and to understand how deep-seated assumptions of normalcy and social recognition worked to devalue certain people. My hope is that, at the end of this book, the social structures, discourses, and systems that brought Pookie to the sideshow as a performer are made visible. We may never know exactly who she was or what her thoughts were on being displayed as a freak, but the few brief moments of her life on the public record can help us look carefully at the social and cultural conditions that produce poverty, ideas of disability and ability, and substantive power differentials based on class, race, and gender. If this remains a partial and incomplete history, it is still valuable to have a tiny portion of Pookie's life added to the historical record, as methodologically and historically problematic as that portion is. Leaving the brief story of her exhibition at the CNE untold seems like more of a risk than telling it in piecemeal fashion here. And certainly I should acknowledge that I have included some possibly jarring historical terminology, but that I have also used contemporary language throughout. I am not trying to sanitize the past in doing so or, on the other hand, to offend present-day readers. Faced with a manuscript cluttered with scare quotes, I sought to balance historical accuracy with the need to describe the body in ways that did not reproduce historical judgments about it in my own analysis. No doubt the comprise I have tried to strike here is unsatisfactory. It may just reveal, however, how invested we remain in the ideas of the normal body. The 1970s are part of the very recent past, and even though the freak show may have declined in number, it remained, travelling through the twentieth century spreading sawdust, raising canvas fronts, spieling stories, yelling "Hey, rube," and defining and contesting bodily difference.

Chapter One

Monsters and Freaks: Exhibitionary Culture and the Order of Things

On 19 April 1919 *Billboard* magazine – a key trade publication for show people – published an advertisement for a "Super Sensational Attraction."[1] The attraction was Martin Johnson's show "Captured by Cannibals." In highly dramatic terms, the advertisement described the photographs and films of island "cannibals' (taken "at the risk of life") as including "burying the old people alive, the dance of the savage virgins, reasons for race extinction, and wild women in their wild state." Accompanying the advertisement was a photograph of the alleged cannibals – six Black women, bare-chested in grass loincloths, who look grimly at the camera. Among these women, who were to embody savagery and cannibalism, is one fully clothed white woman grinning at the camera with her arms thrown collegially around the two women standing at each side of her. One might imagine that, if in the company of savage cannibals, one would not delightedly and cheerfully embrace them. Placed in the context of its time, the show and its advertisement were designed to play on popular racist stereotypes of non-Western and negatively racialized women – stereotypes grounded in contemporary science, history, and anthropology – that made them seem savage, uncivilized, and sexualized. The stereotypes present in this 1919 advertisement were not new, and this chapter traces the social and cultural changes from the seventeenth century onwards that formed the context for the modern freak show.

My focus in this chapter is the evolution of the exhibition of freaks and the integration of them into mainstream culture, which occurred with the rise of a complex modern exhibitionary culture. This chapter traces the exhibition of monsters from the Middle Ages to the display of freaks in early twentieth-century film to reveal the origins and development of the modern freak show. Modern exhibitionary culture made visual spectacles available for easy consumption through a host of sites, from museums to exhibitions to movies. Importantly, the shift from monster to freak was reflective of a much more profound cultural shift structured by the search for a scientific order of things. The classification of "things" included the search for racial and gender origins that allegedly divided human beings into sub-categories as well as differentiating them from animals. In the stratification of human beings the freak show became a popular consumer pastime that allowed participants to enter into great debates on race, gender, nation, and natural difference. This chapter seeks to provide the context for which the 1919 advertisement for "Captured by Cannibals" could resonate as popular and educational entertainment.

The Origins of the Freak Show

The freak show is a historically specific phenomenon of the nineteenth and twentieth centuries, but the public exhibition of physical differences in humans and animals extends back to at least the Middle Ages. In a search for the absolute origins of the modern freak show, some have looked to England's Bartholomew Fair, which existed from 1133 to 1855, and has been described as "a sort of mecca for monsters."[2] The focus on Bartholomew Fair, however, barely scratches the surface of the long and shifting history of the reaction and treatment of monsters. People with extraordinary bodies had long been the subject of fascination and were referred to as "monsters." The term "monster" had ancient origins. In Babylon, unusual births were understood to reflect the constellations of stars and Babylonians believed that the stars foretold the future. Variations of this belief were incorporated into ancient Greek and Roman cultures. The Latin word became "monstrum," which incorporated "monstrare" (to show) and "monere" (to warn). Thus, monsters were understood as some sort of warning or demonstration of anger or wonder. Ancients reacted to monstrous births as acts of fate and often resorted to infanticide. Into the Middle Ages, extraordinary births were seen as signs of the supernatural or the divine, but were also attributed to the power of mothers to mark their fetuses in what would become known as "maternal impressions." Christian doctrine during the fifteenth and sixteenth centuries positioned monsters as omens. While various scientific discoveries of this period challenged the more supernatural explanations of so-called monstrous births, stigma was often attached to them. The surgeon Ambroise Paré argued in his 1573 publication *Des monstres et des prodigies* (published in English as *On Monsters and Marvels*) that such births were the result of one of several things: "the glory of God," the punishment of God, the Devil, too much or too little seed, "rotten" or "corrupt" seed, or the smallness of the womb, to name some examples.[3]

During the Renaissance, monsters were deemed to be punishments for sin.[4] Monsters garnered "unprecedented interest" in the sixteenth and seventeenth centuries. By the mid-1600s, child and infant monsters could regularly be seen in England at fairs, in taverns, on the streets, and in homes. Witnesses to such individual displays of the monstrous child body included wide swathes of English society, including members of the nobility, physicians, religious men and women, and ordinary people.[5] Displays of children – the most regular being conjoined twins – sparked debate about theology and morality; such monsters helped to shape debates and ideas about the correct order of the world by divine plan – a plan increasingly thought knowable by natural philosophers.[6]

By the 1700s, the display of monstrous children at fairs, taverns, and coffee houses continued. Children appeared in cities in "raree shows" – essentially peep shows – and at meetings of natural philosophers. For the latter, they offered a chance to study nature's mistakes in order to make sense of nature's order. Individual monstrous children and adults travelled in simple single-person shows to fairs or taverns. Sometimes a manager would accompany them to collect admissions, attract viewers, and make performance arrangements. These partnerships were uneven, and who was in control varied depending on the act.[7] In general these were single acts that had little contact with each other. As earlier, infant and child monsters were also shown in the street, in what amounted to begging. Parents were often involved in the display of children, especially parents of humble means, who required the labour of all children to keep the family secure.[8] Of all of these means of display, exhibiting a child in the street, or door-to-door in what amounted to begging, was the most risky and the most demanding. For infants and those who survived to adulthood, being displayed could be difficult. A.W. Bates has argued that some infants died from "excessive handling," while adults faced intrusive questions and examinations.[9] The demand for such exhibitions also led to stillborn children being displayed either with or without the parent's approval and in one case led to the exhumation of a body.[10] Corpses were also shown, and gentlemen's cabinets of curiosities led to private collections of preserved corpses or pieces of animal and human bodies.[11]

The private collection in cabinets of curiosities would change remarkably from the 1700s to the 1800s. As natural philosophy shifted into modern science, and as modern exhibitionary culture developed, the monster became an important figure in debates about the "order of things."[12] Monstrosities had long been found in "scholarly places."[13] Natural philosophers like Francis Bacon examined monsters for their ability to reveal natural order, while Carl Linnaeus worked up a complicated system of taxonomy that posited such monsters as a distinct species from *Homo sapiens* known as "homo monstrous."[14] The slow rise of modern science, with its search for natural laws and order, evolved to systematic collection and organization in line with empiricism and other disciplinary principles in what would become anthropology and physiology. Private collections, like cabinets of curiosities, passed into the professional realms of the scientist and doctor. By the 1820s, monstrosities were classified according to arrested embryonic development in what was known as teratology. For highly regarded doctors like Rudolf Virchow, teratology was the "doctrine of wonders," but a doctrine whose specimens belonged only to the professional or the advanced medical student. Virchow feared that no others could bear the sight of preserved monstrous corpses.[15] Others disagreed, and from the 1700s onwards there was an impulse to open previously closed collections of art, botany, and bodies to a wider public. Such exhibitions were important in bourgeois self-fashioning – in how to see and be seen, in how to consume and what to consume, in having an educated eye, and in allowing the eye to educate.[16] In the teaching of the "order of things" and the systematic technologies of discipline and power developed as part of the institutions of the modern nation-state, curating bodies became an important element of what Tony Bennett has termed "the exhibitionary complex."[17] In order to understand the wide web of relations at the heart of the freak show, it is necessary to very briefly explore both Foucault's theory of discipline and surveillance and Bennett's subsequent work on the museum.

In *Discipline and Punish*, Foucault asks the reader to consider two contrasting disciplinary regimes through the examples of the tortured body of Damiens the Regicide in 1757 and the condemned body subject to the schedule of the modern prison in the 1830s. In comparing and contrasting these two disciplinary regimes, Foucault argues against seeing the "progressive" model of modern incarceration as more humane. Rather,

Foucault posits that this alleged progress in penal culture is simply part of modern disciplinary power that formed an edge of the power/knowledge matrix. From the late 1700s to mid-1800s, modern institutions like the school, the factory, and the prison introduced new techniques of surveillance, including self-surveillance designed to produce "docile bodies" that were easy to govern.[18]

At the same time, Bennett argues, the exhibitionary complex developed. If, as Foucault argues, modern discipline was removed from the public eye, the modern exhibitionary complex moved objects and bodies in the opposite direction: from the private collection to the public exhibition. Like the modern disciplinary regime that is formed across discourses, institutions, and techniques to form a web of surveillance, discipline, and punishment, the exhibitionary complex was a web of institutions, vehicles of representation, and discourses that shaped meaning, order, and value in a systemized and controlled way. In short, ad hoc displays became well-ordered modern performances rooted in systemized and ordered meaning. As Bennett argues, "The emergence of the art museum was closely related to that of a wider range of institutions – history and natural science museums, dioramas and panoramas, national and later, international exhibitions, arcades and department stores – which served as linked sites for the development and circulation of new disciplines (history, biology, art history, anthropology) and their discursive formations (the past, evolution, aesthetics, man) as well as for the development of new technologies of vision."[19] Exhibitions played a critical role, and freaks did as well, as they were exhibited across the institutions of the museum complex.

During the late 1800s and the early 1900s, exhibitions of freaks became part of the rising cultures of popular amusement and could be found in a variety of venues that brought multiple performers together. Museums, dime museums, pleasure gardens, fairs, and circuses were some of the more popular places where people could see extraordinary bodies. In the late 1800s and early 1900s, these included the Laotian child Krao – exhibited by Canadian showman Bill Hunt (using the pseudonym Farini) – who allegedly represented a link between monkeys and humans, as well as Laloo, a boy from India with an asymmetrical conjoined twin.[20] As such, freaks were part of the impulse towards using bodies to produce "a set of educative and civilizing agencies" in a easily accessible visual form. Freaks provided lessons on modern geography and imperial conquest, on the colonization and hierarchies of race, and on theories of degeneracy, eugenics, and better breeding.

Freak shows, as part of midways and fairs, "constituted an order of things and of peoples."[21]

The understood order of things was defined by white, masculine, bourgeois identities, fashioned at the same time around ideologies of evangelicism and firmly delineated spheres of public and private (at least in theory), marked rigidly by gender.[22] In Britain, a furore of middle-class enthusiasm for freaks in the early 1800s gave way to a period of early Victorian reform. As Heather McHold has recently argued, freak shows weathered the storm of moral reformers who objected to the displays because showmen and women in Britain, influenced by American P.T. Barnum, reframed freaks themselves as having the ability to meet white bourgeois expectations of respectability regarding work and gender.[23] Freak show performers emphasized their own hard work as well as family histories of hard work, while they informed patrons about their appropriately gendered and respectable leisure time. For example, Canadian-born Charles Tripp, billed as an "Armless Wonder," highlighted his father's work as an engineer on the Grand Trunk Railway. Nova Scotia–born giantess Anna Swan loved hosting friends and entertaining.[24] McHold notes that freaks in Victorian Britain were advertised in ways that differed from American "hucksterism" and "sassy defiance" in emphasizing hard work, domestic virtue, gender differences, and consumerism. Yet Barnum's influence was clear in the appropriation of his strategies, like displaying "midget" families in cosy pictures of heterosexual domestic bliss.[25] Barnum, unlike scientists like Linnaeus who saw monsters as an entirely separate species, emphasized the freak's human qualities and connections or asked audience members to question the line between species. Although some historians have celebrated Barnum's ability to stress "the normal character development of people," notably children declared to be monsters, his influence was far from benign.[26]

The origins of the modern North American freak show proper are usually traced back to Barnum in the 1800s, whose skills at exploitation and advertising shaped the modern freak show. Barnum did not invent the display of extraordinary bodies as entertainment, but he did modernize it, exemplifying the exhibitionary complex and entrenching it within the modern freak show. Barnum biographer A.H. Saxon argues that Barnum displayed freaks as more than simple raree shows; rather, Saxon argues, Barnum added structure, order, and decorum – all important for appealing to bourgeois patrons. Barnum added narrative histories, appeals to science and medicine, and an opportunity to interact with freaks by way of questions.[27] Modern freak shows were not simple peep shows, but sophisticated visual spectacles designed to cut to the heart of modern society and all of its anxieties.

Barnum's first real foray into the world of exhibiting freaks was with Joice Heth in 1835. Heth was an elderly Black woman and slave whom Barnum purchased for $1,000 and exhibited as the 161-year-old former nurse of George Washington. At the time of her purchase, Heth was blind, toothless, and paralysed, but could talk and sing for audiences, telling them stories of "dear little George."[28] Heth died less than a year after being purchased by Barnum, although his exhibition of her did not stop then. On 25 February 1836, 1,500 spectators paid to watch her autopsy. As historian Benjamin Reiss argues, the spectacle launched Barnum's career. Heth's body in life and death provided the basis for white Americans to debate racial essentialism and difference.[29] The degrading event came at a confluence of important moments of modernization: the rise of mass media, commercial culture, and modern medical science, as well as the changing and contested meanings of race in America. Barnum, as a former editor and publisher, had a "masterful understanding of the nation's press" and provided newspapers with ready-made advertisements and stories.[30] Modified as a strategy of modern public relations, the placement of ready-made material in newspapers would become essential to the twentieth-century carnival. Heth's display in life and death came at a turning point in American culture, with its increasing focus on commercial amusements and move towards mass culture. Such a context was important for publicly framing debates about contemporary science and racial difference.

In the 1800s, colonialism, imperialism, and racial difference were essential components of the freak show and this would continue into the twentieth century, as chapter 4 documents. After Heth, Barnum exhibited the Feejee Mermaid – a crafted fake made from a stuffed monkey and a fish tail. Barnum's "genius" was in advertising the creature as at the centre of debate among scientists, but one open to the general public and encouraging "social engagement" in investigations into the order of things.[31] As such, freaks shows intersected with other aspects of nineteenth-century popular amusements like ethnological shows, which were shows consisting of non-Western Others and framed by the discourse of anthropology. In fact, although the two are sometimes distinguished with race-defining ethnological shows, and disability freak shows, such divisions are fraught, at best. Lennard Davis argues that racialized displays of exotic Others are intimately connected with disability: "The disabled person is not of this nation, is not a citizen, in the same sense as the able-bodied ... In addition, discussions of disability always slide into discussions of race. The connections we have discovered between non-Western people and disabled people – both in the simple sense of non-Western culture being seen as 'freakish' and in the glib elisions made between microcephalics, non-humans, and the colonized world – show dramatically how similarly race, nation, and physical identity are defined."[32] Disability and race worked synergistically. Barnum showed "Aztec Children," who had been allegedly captured in Central America from a caste that believed in intermarriage.[33] Variations on the show would become a mainstay, with performers being known as "Pinheads." In reality, in the case of both Barnum's original "Aztec Children" and the subsequent copies, the performers were American-born people with microcephaly.[34]

In his classic work on the freak show, American sociologist Robert Bogdan describes two central modes of presentation that encompass both race and ability: the exotic and the aggrandized, the former describing people from "strange" lands and the latter exaggerating descriptions of people who had a "status-enhancing characteristic."[35] Exotic presentations, such as Krao or the "Native Canadian North American Indians" displayed in Victorian Britain, attempted to affirm the superiority of whiteness and were used to reassure diverse audiences' claim to citizenship by promoting feelings of comfort in looking at a body more radically different, exploited, and disenfranchised than their own.[36] Pseudoanthropological displays of racialized Others, such as the Igorots, were often bound to discourses and displays of savagery and primitivism, which in turn worked to solidify the Western powers' claim that the people could not be self-governing.[37] That some performers in the nineteenth and twentieth centuries were shown in zoos further reflects the fact that they were seen more as animals than self-determining people.[38] Even on the sideshow, racialized performances used both wild and domesticated animals as a tactic of misrepresenting race to suggest that negatively racialized peoples were closer to animals than white people were. Linda Frost has described this process as one of "primitivization" and "bestialization."[39] In this way, freaks were used as a means of creating consent and legitimating imperial and colonial conflict. The freak show's liminality also meant that they could be used as a symbolic way of bringing the people of the empire or the country together, while simultaneously reinforcing the hierarchy between them.

One of the most enduringly popular examples of the intersection between ethnological displays and freak shows is of Sarah Bartman (also known as Sartjee Baartman, or the "Hottentot Venus"). Bartman, whose real name is unknown, was a Khoisan woman who, from 1810 until her death in 1816, was displayed by her Afrikaner manager in France and England. After her death, Georges Cuvier, an influential figure in modern biology and anatomy, dissected her body, portions of which were kept in laboratory bottles and displayed in a museum. In fact, until the 1980s, portions of her dissected body were on display in France, and it was not until 2002 that her remains were returned to South Africa for burial. While Bartman's story has received much scholarly attention, as Anne Fausto-Sterling and Bernth Lindfors argue, she was not unique.[40] The practice of bringing "human evidence" of colonial encounters back to European centres can be traced back to at least the sixteenth century. Explorer Jacques Cartier returned to France in the 1530s with Indigenous peoples of what is now Quebec, including Iroquoian chief Donnacona.

There were many other groups and individuals shown, with varying degrees of consent, across Europe, North America, and Australia. In 1880, eight Inuit men, women, and children were brought from Labrador to be exhibited in ethnological shows and zoos in Germany. Less than six months later, all had contracted smallpox and died. Letters from one of the Moravian brothers who facilitated the displays reports his discomfort with the baptized families being exhibited like animals, but notes that they could not "refuse" Adrian Jacobsen, a trader in ethnographic peoples and things, acting on behalf of German zoo owner Carl Hagenbeck.[41] The group of Inuit people included Abraham Ulrikab, who kept a diary of his journey. While Ulrikab's diary clearly reveals that people on display could return the gaze of paying customers, the power inequities were real. On 7 November 1880, he recorded the following in his diary about the experience of one of his fellow Inuit travellers: "Had sorrow again. Our companion, the unmarried Tobias, was beaten with a dog whip by our master, Jacobsen ... If Tobias is frequently as stubborn, he won't get paid, but if he is nice, he will get greatly paid. After this incident, Tobias was very sick."[42] Far from home, separated by culture and language, and treated as less than fully human, people put on exhibition could be vulnerable to physical, mental, or financial abuse.

Inuit peoples were brought and shown at the World's Columbian Exposition in Chicago in 1893, under the direction of renowned

American anthropologist Franz Boas. Boas allegedly encouraged explorer Robert Peary to bring Inuit peoples back to New York as living museum specimens. In 1897, Peary brought six Inuit adults and children to New York, where they were displayed in the basement of the American Museum of Natural History.[43] In short order, four succumbed to illness and another took an opportunity to return home. Minik, who was a child when he left his Arctic community, stayed in New York with a family associated with the museum. He was greatly distressed when, in the early 1900s, he found his father's bones on exhibit at the museum. His tumultuous life included running away to Quebec, and a ship's journey northward in a box, before dying of influenza in 1918 back in America.[44] The unsettling legacies of these transports continue now in the contests over the culturally appropriate burial of remains. In 1993, the Australian Indigenous community reclaimed the remains of Tambo, a young Aborigine boy who had toured the United States with P.T. Barnum.[45]

Modern Science and the Categorization of Difference

Racialized taxonomies were based in nineteenth-century science, which included life sciences as well as social sciences like anthropology and sociology, all of which had empiricism at their core. Every aspect of human life was understood to be structured around universal laws, which the scientist merely discovered. Modern science included widespread practices of measuring, sorting, and categorizing. These practices were often heavily influenced by Western social and cultural assumptions of race, gender, and class, and as such, the categorization, and its empirical basis, were often firmly rooted in the social. If eighteenth-century Enlightenment thinking stressed universal humanity and commonality, by the nineteenth century, this belief had largely been replaced by a focus on difference, categorization, and hierarchy.[46] Theories on degeneracy, criminality, and feeble-mindedness, among other issues, developed as a result.

Emerging at the intersection of commercial culture, medical science, scientific racism, and the rise of the discipline of anthropology, ethnological exhibits were titillating with a gloss of scientific education. As Bennett argues, anthropology was important to the spread of exhibitionary culture and its extension into "entertainment zones" that transformed negatively racialized people "into object lessons of evolutionary theory."[47] Fairs in the late 1800s and early 1900s used racial

Othering to reinforce ideas of a cohesive national public and imperial superiority.[48] They also became central elements to the rising consumer society, where strict ideas of racial hierarchy informed everything from soap advertisements to the display of goods and people at international exhibitions.[49]

Late nineteenth-century debates about evolution and species prompted by Charles Darwin's 1859 *Origin of Species* lead to questions regarding the line between animals and humans. Darwin's evolutionary theory challenged the belief in the uniqueness of humanity and instead posited that humans and animals existed on a continuum. Such debates were deeply racialized, with Indigenous peoples and Blacks thought to be less evolved and more closely connected to animals. The search for "the Missing Link" brought science and popular culture together. This marriage, propelled in part by the discovery of gorillas, lead to a variety of exhibitions including that of Krao, Julia Pastrana, Lionel the Lion-Faced Boy, and What Is It.[50] All of the previously mentioned performers were exhibited as though they tested the boundaries between animal and human. Pastrana, born in an Indigenous tribe in Mexico, was shown in the 1850s and was exhibited under a variety of descriptive titles, including the "Bear Woman," the "Baboon Lady," and the "Ugliest Woman in the World." After being abandoned as a child, she worked in the governor of Sinaloa's home until discovered by an American showman. Pastrana's exhibition at a variety of locations, including Boston's Horticultural Hall in 1855, garnered a lot of popular and professional attention. In 1857, her body had been described in good detail by a physician in the prestigious medical journal *The Lancet*. Under questionable conditions of consent, Pastrana married a second manager and, in 1860, died giving birth to their son, who died within hours of birth.[51] Similarly, Lionel, the Lion-Faced Boy, allegedly tested the limits between animals and humans due to his hypertrichosis. Racialized displays of Black men under the question "What is it?" served to provoke debate on Black men's place in the spectrum of humanity. From the 1860s onwards, Barnum's museum, and later travelling shows, almost always had a "What is it?" show, which consisted of a Black man acting animal-like. Audience members were asked, typically by the man's "keeper," to guess whether he was in fact a lower order of human or a higher form of monkey.[52] It is unsurprising that the advent of the "What is it?" shows coincided with the publication of Darwin's theory of evolution. Such displays were at the heart of colonial and imperial projects, which stressed the necessity of the global spread of white, Christian, middle-class values, as well as the progress brought by white "civilization" in regard to science, technology, and world view, which included medicine, anthropology, and history.

Scientific exploration crossed paths with imperialism and colonization. In addition to discovering new goods and lands, explorers, travellers, and colonizers turned their scientific interest to peoples and animals. Peoples displaced by colonial aggression, either in the name of imperialism or science, found themselves as objects of study at the intersection of education and entertainment in museums and zoos, which were intimately enmeshed with freak shows and managers.[53] As Adams argues, "As freak show scouts traveled to remote areas of the globe in search of unique curiosities, their efforts overlapped with those of natural scientists, explorers, and missionaries. Framed in a pseudoethnographic language by showmen who called themselves 'doctors' and 'professors,' anthropological exhibits at the freak show often provided American audiences with their primary source of information about the non-Western world."[54] In nineteenth-century Europe and North America, consumers were often fascinated by ethnological displays of so-called savages, and freak shows included a regular roster of savages, cannibals, and missing links. As later chapters reveal, such shows would continue to be popular into the mid-twentieth century.

Barnum, the Freak, and Middle-Class Identities

In 1840, Barnum opened the American Museum in New York City. Museums with cabinets of curiosities and live performers were popular in nineteenth-century Britain and North America. Usually originating from scientific collections, museums in American cities by the 1840s were struggling. Museums' collective effort to provide amusement that was rational, scientific, educational, and respectable was faltering. Barnum's American Museum altered the format of the museum and brought renewed success. Shows consisted of a number of different attractions drawn together in the same venue, including arcades with distorting mirrors, "test and trial" amusements, a menagerie, human oddities, paintings, drama and singing performances, and a lecture room where moral dramas and occasionally freaks were seen.[55] It was an affordable and respectable place for middle-class Americans to spend their leisure time, typically costing a dime, which was a substantial reduction when other museums charged fifty cents or more.[56] As much as Barnum excelled at duping the public and often pushing the cultural limits, he was sensitive to the fact that the American Museum had to maintain at least the appearance of respectable entertainment. Barnum deliberately appealed to people who wanted moral and educational amusements. According to historian Andrea Stulman Dennett, "Barnum's museum represented a new concept in chaste entertainment, and it provided women with a safe and easily accessible meeting place for lunch, conversation, and amusement, free of rowdy or drunken men."[57] Female consumers – key participants in the burgeoning culture of consumption – were important not only for their money but also for the veneer of safety and morality they ostensibly brought with them. By the 1870s almost every major American city had a dime museum with varying degrees of success.[58] By the peak in the 1880s and 1890s, dime museums employed a full range of freaks, including fat people, giants, and human skeletons, and even freak hunters – people whose duty it was to find and secure new exhibits.[59]

In Canada, many dime museums copied Barnum's configuration, but like other dime museums in smaller centres, they endured a more precarious existence. In the 1880s, many Canadian dime museums found that they could not support such a venture and quickly closed.[60] Unsurprisingly, the larger, more urban cities like Montreal and Toronto fared better. By the 1880s, commercial culture had pierced Montreal's leisure scene, and included dime museums and variety theatre.[61] In Toronto, dime museums, like the Robinson and Company Dime Museum and the Musee Theatre, balanced permanent exhibits with temporary features such as lectures, dramas, variety acts, and freak shows. Freak shows at dime museums in Toronto drew large crowds and turned some of the freak show performers into stars.[62] Toronto's Musee Theatre was exceptional in its success. Opening in 1890, the Musee followed Barnum's layout and balanced educational material with variety theatre and freak shows. The Musee contained an art museum, a wax display contrasting a family ruined by alcohol and a happy, sober family, a Hungarian band of musicians, and a two-headed boy.[63]

While large museums like Barnum's, which at one point employed about three hundred people, were tied to a particular location, others travelled to survive the increasingly complex commercial amusement scene. Part of the problem faced by the museums was that new attractions were difficult to find and produce. It was far easier to survive economically as a travelling show.[64] Many limited their displays to so-called human oddities, reducing other amusements. By the end of the 1800s, the word "museum" had been replaced with the word "sideshow."[65] As such, part of the entertainment of the dime museum went the way of vaudeville, while other acts, like freaks, hit the road as travelling sideshows.

Victorian Canadians had other domestic opportunities to see freaks. In the late nineteenth century, former members of Barnum's shows would appear at Canadian fairs, including a fat woman, a human skeleton, a bearded lady, a strongman, a mermaid, missing links, and Zulu warriors.[66] Pleasure gardens of the nineteenth century offered a range of entertainments in manicured landscapes that included freaks. By the turn of the twentieth century, they were transitioning into modern amusement parks, like Toronto's Hanlan's Point.[67] Large and small, rural and urban agricultural fairs were one of the most popular venues for seeing freaks. As Nadja Durbach has recently argued in regard to British freak shows, they were "able to draw in a much broader public than many other Victorian commercial entertainments that catered exclusively to metropolitan customers."[68] For example, the Toronto Industrial Exhibition (renamed in 1903 the Canadian National Exhibition), which drew visitors from both urban and rural areas every year, included a variety of sideshows that offered an assortment of attractions including freaks, acrobats, and dancing women.[69]

In addition to dime museums and the ubiquitous fairs, carnivals and travelling sideshows offered freaks of all sorts to communities large and small, as did circuses. While the former were associated with the cheap and tawdry, circuses were allegedly organized shows of talented and skilled people and animals. Both carnivals and circuses were interrelated in that they travelled to consumers, bringing their largely visual and oral messages to consumers who need not be able to read or travel. As such they were part of a wider web of modern culture like movies and department stores.[70] Large and small circuses frequently toured Canada, which included the Ringling Brothers and the Clyde Beatty Circus. Nonetheless, the circus, like the carnival and the travelling show, survived and continued to host freak shows as part of their displays.[71]

At the heart of the Victorian Canadian freak show were wider cultural shifts. Canada was enmeshed in, not apart from, developments in the exhibitionary complex. Gazing at other people was an important part of modern culture as it allowed people to study, attempt to organize, and make sense of the shifting world around them. It is unsurprising that fairs and exhibitions proliferated in this period. Nor is it surprising that other pastimes rooted themselves in practices of people watching.

As Janet Miron has argued in her book on nineteenth-century asylum tourism, such practices "fit very comfortably within this culture of exhibition and spectacle," which had at its root the visual "consumption of human bodies." Miron argues that asylum tourism and freak shows were parallel parts of a modern visual culture that promised "education and self-improvement" as encouragement.[72] Further, prisons and asylums, key parts of modern regimes of discipline and surveillance, were not cleaved off from the general public. In addition to tourists' visits, institutions in cities like Kingston, Ontario, were sometimes host to freak shows put on for staff and inmates.[73]

All in all, freak shows existed as part of a web of modern exhibitionary culture in which people who had the means and time could pay to study, under the guise of leisure and learning, a host of people deemed to be different or unusual.[74] As Keith Walden argues, however, such practices were rooted in particular social identities. By the 1870s, fractures in middle-class identity were apparent. Was middle-class identity furnished by decency, character, and gentility, and based on social responsibility and self-restraint? Or was middle-class identity defined by a sophistication of taste and a "capacity to make discerning cultural judgments"?[75] Such questions were significant when it came to debating commercial amusements like the freak show. Walden argues: "The availability, decoration, and posing of bodies was directly related to established social hierarchies. The white, middle-class gaze was paramount ... The inequities of gazing were no more apparent than when the activity was transposed into commercial ventures. At the fair, this was most obvious in sideshows, where the appeal of many attractions derived from the extraordinary access they provided to the bodies of 'low others' – in this case mainly freaks, exotically presented non-whites, and scantily clad females."[76] Such events were part of the drive for rational amusement, in which exhibitions played an important role in suggesting and defining order in a society rapidly influenced by industrial capitalism and consumerism. Rational amusement combined entertainment with education in ways that were deemed to be productive and purposeful to allay fears of the degradation of existing hierarchies of class, gender, and race. Freak shows, like the prison and the asylum, worked to present a world of neatly classified order – or, at least, the drive towards such order – that could soothe modern anxieties and assist in the production of docile bodies. Order of people, things, and animals was important in making sense not only of the natural world, but also of modern society in the nineteenth century. Such spectacles needed not always happen close by as Victorian Canadians had plenty of opportunities to travel, due largely to a new world of more rapid transportation.

World's Fairs, Exhibitionary Culture, and the Consolidation of the Modern Carnival

World's fairs, begun in London, England, in 1851, added another important layer onto the symbolic meanings of freak shows and provided a further respectable venue for Canadians travelling abroad to witness freak shows. Canadians participated in world's fairs as business owners, presenters, competitors, and consumers. On the Midway Plaisance in Chicago in 1893, Canadians set up displays, competed, showed off their business acumen, and performed. In the latter category, one of the displays included fifty-eight Inuit people as part of Newfoundland's contribution to the fair. Such exhibitions were common, yet it is worth noting here that Indigenous peoples, like other Canadians, were also consumers and spectators.[77] Seeing someone very like you on exhibition, however, changed the dynamics of the midways for people with disabilities, negatively racialized peoples, and others, which speaks to the complexity of the composition of the audiences and the possibility for dominant and non-dominant readings of the spectacle.

The world's fairs played an important role in revitalizing the cultural value of midway shows and represented an important shift in culture, from growing distain in the last quarter of the nineteenth century, with the push for wholesome, rational amusement, to limited acceptance alongside other commercial leisure opportunities after the turn of the twentieth century. The development of the midway was also significant since it continued to legitimize the alleged educational value of studying the wondrous or different body and provided a formula that could be easily copied by smaller sideshow companies that would circulate throughout North America for the next several decades.

At the Centennial Exposition in Philadelphia in 1876, a small number of ethnological shows were included in the fair's roster of events. Outside the official gates, however, scores of showmen set up their own exhibits in what amounted to an unofficial midway, including the Wild Men of Borneo and a 600-pound woman. It became clear to exhibition officials that such attractions were popular and profitable and, more importantly, had a place within the official fairgrounds.[78] At the 1893 World's Columbian Exposition, held in Chicago, a midway appeared as part of the official fair. Moreover, Chicago brought the sideshow into the centre of the fair and named it the Midway Plaisance – the latter being used to refer to both pleasure and pleasantness. The most plentiful displays included pseudoethnological ones, including "natives" and "cannibals" from foreign countries, along with the original Little Egypt Hootchie Cootchie dancer, and sword swallowers and snake charmers.[79] That year the Midway Plaisance took in $4 million and ensured a spot for sideshows at subsequent world's fairs. As Bogdan concludes, "it launched a new form of popular amusement in which the freak show loomed prominently."[80] Freaks thus found their home among a wide variety of acts, which, in total, would become mainstays of the twentieth-century travelling sideshow. Canadian historian Elspeth Heaman argues, in regard to the Midway Plaisance: "It also strengthened the impact of the sideshows, making them a cultural event in their own right, with a certain legitimacy. The midway's obvious popularity forced commentators to come to terms with the scene, and it prompted other exhibitors to follow along. Agricultural exhibitions had already begun to pay for sideshows, but after 1893 they unabashedly set up their own midways." The Toronto Industrial Exhibition got a midway in 1898, no doubt because Toronto officials had long kept an eye on American developments at both major exhibitions and permanent sites like Coney Island.[81]

The permanent place of the midway was a triumph of modern commercial culture. If exhibitions were to be celebrating industrial and agriculture prowess, by the end of the 1800s there was tension between the goals of education and entertainment. As Heaman argues, "Exhibitions had tried to bring popular taste to the level of cultured elites; instead, matters had gone the other way. The exhibition now catered to the masses, and the classes had to accommodate themselves willy-nilly."[82] After Chicago, midways at world's fairs were deemed to be essential. The midways transformed at the end of the nineteenth century from small individual shows to large travelling companies in the outdoor amusement business.[83] Their place at twentieth-century world's fairs, although less central than in Chicago in 1893, gave them some limited continuing purchase on middle-class respectability. They were culturally low and seen to appeal to youthful and working-class tastes, but their existence at great international events, and, better yet, their profitability, certainly helped to keep them in the mainstream. As Stanley Appelbaum argued, regarding the 1893 Chicago's World's Fair, "the Midway meant solvency."[84] The profitable sideshows could not be

1.1 World's fair freaks at the Canadian National Exhibition. Canadian National Exhibition Archives. G. Hollies Photograph.

dismissed, despite their diminishing cultural value. Their message of Otherness soothed social anxieties regarding race, class, and gender, and reinforced dominant messages of the fairs, which tended to celebrate progress and the white liberal order.

In turn, respectability played an important role in keeping the midway going. World's fairs were generally seen as more reputable than smaller travelling circuses and carnivals. Nonetheless, the smaller carnivals and circuses did benefit from other larger displays at world's fairs. Shows developed for the world's fair would sometimes be scaled down and used by other travelling shows. At other times, the shows were simply copied. Increasingly, even the smaller shows would try to emulate the panache and glitter of the world's fairs, if only in keeping shows clean and attempting to run a "Sunday School" show.

Gambling was limited and show managers ensured that the audience was at least entertained and not just taken.[85] If some Canadians were distinctly uncomfortable with the ongoing existence of the sideshows, the historical documents reveal the very real difficulty they had in trying to marginalize a popular nationwide (if not North American–wide) amusement. And while the sideshows of the 1800s and early 1900s experienced a sense of cultural decline, they remained profitable and held on to their popularity (even as they remained contentious) as other working-class "cheap" amusements like movies entered the mainstream and established middle-class audiences.[86]

Conclusion

The raree shows – or individual peep-style shows – of the 1700s gave way in part due to Barnum's influence to well-ordered displays that intersected with contemporary questions regarding science, race, and humanity. The complex consumer scene, with fierce competition for consumers' dimes, meant that some shows needed to travel to survive; from the dime museum we have a reinvigoration of the travelling carnival show. If "monsters" of the 1700s and 1800s had been exhibited either in one-off shows or door-to-door, modern travelling shows of the 1800s and early 1900s were modern Barnum-esque spectacles with slick production and, typically, casts of many.

Travelling shows meant an increased chance of economic survival, especially since showmen and women could set up shows outside of the official grounds of exhibitions and world's fairs. The popularity of such ad hoc midways led to the birth of the modern midway at the centre of the exhibition. Social reform movements would challenge both the central location of the midway – it would eventually move, in the early decades of the 1900s, to the periphery of the grounds – and the freak show itself. The challenge to the latter was resisted due to its profits and popularity. All in all, the modern exhibitionary culture of the freak show was remarkably flexible, due, as later chapters illustrate, to the persistent desire to gaze upon bodies understood as different and unusual.

The extraordinary body played an important role in modern exhibitionary culture as a basis for debates about natural order and wonder. Different or unusual bodies on display provided citizens of newly formed modern nation-states the chance to debate the order of race, disability, and nation. Those bodies were marked as fascinating objects of study for new disciplines in search of knowledge, which was subsequently mobilized as curated bodies on the freak show. As Bennett argues, exhibitionary culture "sought to allow the people, and *en masse* rather than individually, to know rather than be known, to become the subjects rather than the objects of knowledge."[87] That knowledge could become internalized and people would become self-regulating. The freak show's systemized display across the museum complex meant that nineteenth-century Canadians had plenty of opportunities, domestically and abroad, to see well-ordered, well-narrated, and well-structured modern shows and learn what constituted a "normal" modern body.

The lessons of what constituted the normal body and its relation to questions of race and disability among other categories of identity were broadcast with regularity across Canada in the twentieth century. To understand the scope and persistence of the freak's place in Canadian culture, the freak show needs to be understood as part of the carnival business, which carved out an important place on the consumer scene. The next chapter looks at the role of carnivals and circuses in the ongoing development of freak shows as businesses and the continuing legitimization of exhibitionary culture in Canada. Canada, as it would turn out, was an important place for the freak show, attracting American showmen and women to regularly visit or permanently take up residence due to the potential profits.

Chapter Two

The Carnival State: Protests, Moral Regulation, and Profits

In 1919, *Billboard* ran an extensive article refashioning the carnival as "Chautauquaized Carnivals."[1] The timing was auspicious. The Great War had narrowly drawn to a close and wartime sanctions against carnivals, like those in Canada, were being lifted. The need for moral education had long been of interest to reformers, and other efforts to create a healthy, happy (based on white, middle-class standards) society had seen success during the war years. Temperance, prohibition, and female suffrage were some of the key successes of the moral and social reform movement. In the United States from the end of the nineteenth century onward, the Chautauqua offered continuing educational opportunities as well as amusement for adults. Carnivals as fun and popular sites of amusement faced new pressures in the period to reform. The Chautauquaized carnival was one attempt to do so. As author Wm. Judkins Hewitt argued, "Censorship is permissible and welcomed by showmen when justly applied, as, for instance, the one that pertains and is enforced by the city of Toronto, Ont., Can. Sameness and justice are at that place fully dispensed ... The public knows that when amusements are allowed to enter that city that they can patronize them with full impunity, patronage limited only by the contents of their purses. Would that more cities had similar regulations, some do. If more it would not take long to eliminate rank operations."[2] As with many articles in the immediate postwar years, this one was optimistic and bordering on fawning, but it served an important purpose in indicating a period of internal reform. Further, it hinted at the close relationship between showmen and officials whose job it was to regulate the carnival and provide, perhaps, an unofficial stamp of approval of the amusements provided.

This chapter argues that the relationship between carnivals and various Canadian officials was driven at first by profits. Despite the social power of reform movements, profits largely shaped government relations with carnivals, although the number of individuals and state organizations within the expanding government bureaucracy complicated the relationship. This is not to say that there was uniform acceptance of the carnival. As this chapter demonstrates, protests, which peaked in the 1920s, reveal contests over the regulation of taste in Canadian culture. Criticism of the carnivals also prompted at least the appearance of internal reform to "clean up" the shows as government officials occasionally flexed their muscles in regard to licence fees, taxes, and immigration. From the 1920s onwards, however, the carnival faced increasing scrutiny and a sometimes challenging web of government bureaucracy that had them negotiating with, and being tracked by, various municipal, provincial, and federal government bodies. Both internal changes (driven by the carnivals themselves) and external ones, namely professional contracts and state regulations were related to the widening net of moral regulation in the period.[3] Given that freak shows were essential to the carnival for the period under study here, it is important to situate the carnival broadly to understand how it was maintained and supported. As much as the carnival has been seen as a world unto its own – a myth perpetuated by carnivals themselves and often exemplified by the figure of the freak – it was, in reality, enmeshed with "regular" society, governments, and organizations that helped to ensure its ongoing success. In all, this chapter aims to reveal how carnivals operated as sophisticated businesses in the twentieth century in the context of shifting social and cultural ideas of professionalism, morality, taste, and state regulation.

The Carnival in Canada

A carnival was a collection of live shows, rides, and games that travelled to sites for short stays, typically ranging from a day to a week. As John Thurston notes in his work on the carnival in Canada, "by the 1920s [the freak shows] were the big attraction on the midway."[4] Travelling from town to town during the spring, summer, and fall months, shows like the Johnny J. Jones Shows and Conklin, among many others, toured regularly to large and small towns, where they were received with either enthusiasm or ambivalence, and sometimes both simultaneously, albeit from different quarters. Most of the shows, however, travelled extensively if not almost continuously, taking a break over the winter months in warmer locales. For American-based companies this often meant wintering in the southern US, while Canadian companies like Conklin Shows and the Wallace Bros. Shows had winter quarters in southern Ontario.[5] Showmen, however, used the off season to look for acts and secure contracts for the next travelling season.

Despite criticisms to the contrary, the companies, employees, and performers were not exclusively American. Conklin, which operated under various incarnations of the Conklin name from the 1920s onward, would become synonymous with the Canadian carnival and internationally renowned.[6] Smaller, local operations, like Winnipegger E.J. Casey's carnival, operated in Canada from 1935 until 1957.[7] Other Canadian companies working into the 1950s included the Wallace Bros. All-Canadian Shows, which staged shows in Ontario and Western Canada, and the Bill Lynch Shows, which operated on the east coast.[8] Other companies added a superficial Canadian gloss, like the Royal American Shows, which became the Royal Canadian Shows north of the border.

All in all, their collective success was notable. In 1904, there were twenty carnivals touring in North America and, only one year later, that number more than doubled to forty-six.[9] By mid-century, in 1948, one estimate put the number of carnivals touring the United States and Canada at approximately 350.[10] A sociological review published in the early 1970s noted that 1,963 carnivals were listed as touring North America in 1969.[11] It is impossible to measure the accuracy of the numbers. Even insiders describe the numbers as "elusive" since a couple of shows strung together might count as an individual carnival for a few weeks until those shows contracted to and essentially merged with other larger shows.[12] Tracing the shows historically provides an additional challenge. Some companies were well established and had long histories, while others lasted a season or two only to be lost to history, their contributions largely unrecorded.[13] It was also not unusual for one showman to have a number of different shows under different names travelling at the same time. In the 1900s and 1910s, American showmen like Rubin Gruberg, Johnny J. Jones, and Clarence A. Wortham were important for the number of shows they managed. By 1920, Wortham alone had five different shows on the road.[14] The Polack Bros., for example, added a second separate travelling outfit in 1917 and a third in 1918. The latter was called the World at Home Shows.[15] Some of the shows were of a considerable size. Internal documents from the federal Department of Immigration and Colonization, which kept detailed

2.1 Johnny J. Jones Freak Show, CNE Midway, 1913, City of Toronto Archives, fonds 1244, item 0279f.

records of travelling shows, indicate that in 1924 the Johnny J. Jones Show was travelling with 398 people, while the Rubin and Cherry shows had 374.[16]

If accurate numbers of carnivals are unknowable, we can speculate on why the numbers continued to rise until mid-century even as some of the carnivals consolidated into large companies, which dominated the outdoor amusement scene in Canada.[17] The demand for carnival entertainment by fairs and other organizations may have led to the increasing number. In 1949, a *Maclean's* article on "Queen of the Midway" Jean Nanson, who ran her own girl, animal, and freak show that appeared with the Conklin shows that year, described "the nickels, dimes, and quarters [that] rattled into the silver stream which annually becomes a $3 million pool for Canada's showmen."[18] Ten years earlier in 1939,

2.2 Crowd in midway carnival in front of sideshows, 1940, City of Vancouver Archives, PNE Collection, Public Domain.

sideshow owner Lou Dufour (who would later work with the Canadian showman Patty Conklin), of the Dufour and Rogers shows, reported almost $2 million in profit at the New York World's Fair on an estimated $300,000 investment.[19] Accurate sums of the overall takings are difficult to know in the period before the late 1970s, due to the practice of "skimming" (not reporting or sharing profits with host fairs or organizations) and the fact that most of the carnivals kept numbers to themselves. Nonetheless, in the early 1970s the amount of money being taken out of Canada by the Royal American Shows in the Canadian west concerned federal tax officials. In 1974, various members of the Airport Squads of the RCMP witnessed carnival employees leaving Canadian cities with suitcases containing large amounts of cash, between $25,000 and $200,000. This represented a fraction of the money made.[20]

The establishment of a commercial leisure culture and the expectation of entertainment opportunities, even throughout the Depression of the 1930s when entertainment budgets shrank, may have contributed to the carnival's increasing numbers, although throughout the 1900s, sideshows faced strenuous competition from other commercial amusements, especially when movies and later television emerged as more popular forms of entertainment between the 1920s and 1950s.[21] In the early 1900s, carnivals had offered moving-picture shows as part of their attractions.[22] By the 1920s, movies became widely popular and available across the country in local theatres. As a cheap amusement, it competed directly with carnivals. Theatre owners in some parts of the country also organized against carnivals in the 1920s. The rise of movies was significant, and movie houses across the country offered entertainment that appealed to thousands of people across classes and age groups. In 1922, *Billboard* reported that movie-house owners supported legislation in New Brunswick, Nova Scotia, and Prince Edward Island that proposed to ban carnivals. On the other hand, various labour and voluntary locals with the International Longshoremen's Association and the Great War Veterans' Association, who benefited financially from partnerships with carnivals, challenged the push to have them banned. *Billboard*, much in line with the general movement to clean up the shows in the 1920s, pointed out that good-quality carnivals had not been travelling in the area and that more of them were needed to keep agitation at bay.[23] By 1926, it was apparent that movie-theatre owners' opposition to carnivals was not restricted to the Maritimes. It was simply another challenge to the survival of the carnival business.[24]

The carnivals' ongoing appeal to the middle and working classes, especially youth, also may have played a role in increasing the number of travelling shows in large or small, urban or rural communities. Unlike fixed amusements, they could consistently reach new paying audiences by travelling to them. The style of performances also meant that audience members could participate whether or not they spoke English. Unlike other popular amusements, carnivals travelled constantly and revised acts to meet shifting tastes and interests, and could increase or pare down the number of employees seasonally, if not more often. If girl shows came under further scrutiny in the 1920s, Conklin responded by staging an educational exhibit on the human body. In the 1920s, the show included The Naked Truth, which promised and likely delivered lessons in anatomy.[25] In addition, stranded employees and missing payroll were not unknown. Carnivals, then, were flexible organizations that were highly responsive to economic challenges.

Admission prices to carnivals varied but there was usually an entrance fee. In the 1910s and 1920s, a dime was typical. The prices rose modestly throughout the first half of the twentieth century, and by the 1960s adult consumers could expect to pay $1, teens 50 cents, and children under twelve 25 cents. The sliding scale reflected established and emerging categories of age and the expectations of fun and available money related to those categories. Beginning in the 1920s, separate children's pricing began, with some larger exhibitions offering free admission days for children. Once admitted, adult and child consumers found a series of amusements that were either free or required another small fee in order to watch, play, or participate. Carnivals included a range of live shows that were either on small stages or behind canvases in pits. The latter would be known as "pit shows," the place where freaks were commonly displayed. Carnivals included freaks, as did circuses and other small, one-off travelling sideshows. Carnivals of a small scale were also called Gilly shows, and many show owners, like Patty Conklin, started with a Gilly show and expanded.

In some circles, the terms carnival and circus are used almost interchangeably. Strict definitions are difficult as the two have often overlapped in the popular imagination, in practice, and even in the advertising placed by companies themselves. Yet carnival workers seem to have been quite clear on the distinction, and carnival workers often looked down upon circus workers and vice versa. Former circus performers Joanne Wilson and Trudy Strong, whose careers began in the 1950s, recalled that carnival and circus employees did not want to be called by the other's name. Strong stated, "We used to think, no, don't call us carnival people because we're circus people. And they used to say the same thing – 'don't call us circus people, because we're carnival people!'"[26] Circus workers often saw themselves as working in an art form that extended from the theatre, which provided higher status in terms of class and taste. Carnivals were perceived as connected with street culture and other less desirable subcultures, including gambling. Other differences are important to note: circuses are defined as having shows in rings and having a management structure where all employees work for the owner. Rather than rings, carnivals are measured by front footage (the space a front would take up on the midway). The amount of footage was carefully calculated by owners and reflected the shows' expected prestige and profits. Carnivals were run by owners who had a direct relationship to the enterprise, but also by independent operators who held a series of contracts with individuals who formed the show.[27]

Protests and the Question of Taste

Throughout the late 1800s and into the 1930s, shows faced a host of problems, including, but not limited to: complaints about noise and damage to property; illegal acts and gambling games that increased the risk of being closed by local officials; and competition among themselves.[28] In Canada, especially Ontario and in particular Toronto, carnivals faced an active social and moral reform movement, a largely Protestant-driven collection of efforts to clean up society. It grew out of Evangelical Protestant revivals in the nineteenth century with their vision of a pure, healthy, and moral Canada. Reformers focused their attention on a host of issues from clean milk campaigns to prostitution to the prohibition of alcohol. Catholics, wary about the Protestant reform movement, had more tolerant positions on gambling, tobacco, and alcohol, but shared some concerns, including birth control.[29] By the late nineteenth century, a maturing capitalist society with a burgeoning culture of consumerism as the foundation of modern identity led to "tensions in bourgeois morality."[30] The carnival became one area where these tensions played out. These were no small matters. By the 1920s, the commodification of the self existed in a complex web of identity and commodity culture. These were questions of personal and national importance. In particular, carnivals came to the attention of some members of the especially active reform movement in southern Ontario concerned about unwholesome leisure, vice, gambling, and sexually provocative displays. Given their success in pressuring the state on other issues, the protest to regulate or – better yet in the view of reformers – to outlaw the carnival should be seen as a serious challenge. Importantly, freaks themselves make few appearances in the records documenting the protests. Disability rendered freaks so Othered in society that they did not even garner much attention from the social and moral reform movement. These protests are important to understand as they have a significant effect on the modern carnival.

In the 1920s, carnivals faced new pressures to "clean up" their acts and faced public censure for allegedly imperilling the social and moral health of society. As quickly as the midway sideshow was solidified, its claim to middle-class respectability as a form of amusement softened and the shows became targeted by the social reform movement in both the United States and Canada. As sideshow companies, referring to themselves as carnivals, blossomed in the early years of the 1900s, they were quickly challenged. The popularity and financial success of the carnivals like Johnny J. Jones and Conklin was matched by public outcry from some municipalities, politicians, churches, and concerned citizens, who protested their existence and commented on their undesirable effect on audiences, especially allegedly impressionable youth. The push to have the shows banned peaked in the 1920s, even though it had existed in previous decades, and was predominantly but not exclusively driven by the middle class. One exception appeared in in 1913 when the *Globe* included a brief article entitled "Freaks on Midway Objected to by Labor Men," which argued that they had a "demoralizing effect on the minds of spectators."[31] In the 1910s, part of the impulse to create an association of carnival showmen was to internally address issues of gambling and graft on the sideshows. In 1912, showmen and women organized into the Carnival Managers Association of America. Within the year the name was changed to the Showmen's League of America.[32] More than likely, this internal reform was intended to address outside pressures to clean up the shows. It also meant that larger companies, which could survive without fleecing patrons in fixed games of chance and gambling, would continue to have a leg up on upstart or smaller companies.

The peak of protest in the 1920s was due, in part, to the end of wartime regulations under the War Measures Act that had all but banned travelling circuses and sideshows from entering Canada. In 1915, the *Globe* announced that "hereafter all freaks are to be barred from Canada. Whether they are here for exhibition or other purpose makes no difference, the Government has decided that foreign monstrosities must disappear ... hereafter no freak of any nature calculated to hurt the eye of [the] spectator or offend they eye of [the] spectator ... must be allowed to enter Canada." The wording implies that consumers were seen to be in need of protection from unsightly and offensive bodies. This idea mirrored the rationale behind some American jurisdictions' so-called "ugly laws," which sought to protect the public from confronting offensive bodies in the public.[33] Although no such specific legislation seems to have been passed in Canada, the War Measures Act was used to limit the number of freak show performers crossing the border. In 1917, with the more stringent wartime restrictions in place, the PNE in Vancouver noted that "immigration authorities will not allow freaks or monstrosities to come into the country, and refused this year to allow a pair of Siamese twins to cross the border."[34] Bans were short-lived, although they made an impression on at least one American showman who saw them as a sign of Canada's parochialism. One showman recalled the strict regulation of freaks, but seemingly placed the blame on Canadians' conservative and outdated belief in maternal impressions, which he promptly mocked. F. Beverly Kelley, who worked as a publicist for the Ringling Bros. and Combined Barnum and Bailey Circus, recalled: "For years circuses were not permitted to exhibit their human curiosities in Canada, where belief in prenatal influence prevailed. To ridicule this, a sideshow executive of our acquaintance would effect a dourly serious manner and say that, unfortunately, the superstition had been proved for a fact. Then he would tell about the pregnant woman who had been so frightened by an escaped circus polar bear that she had delivered a baby with bare feet."[35] Regulations, laws, and protests may have hampered the carnival, but showmen could still laugh, make jokes, and find ways around them.

In the interwar period, city councils, voluntary associations seeking social reform, and churches formed the backbone of the protest movement to end the shows. Indeed, there was no shortage of ink spilled on calls for the prohibition of sideshows, especially in Ontario, which, as Canada's largest and most populous province in the period, led the way in regard to regulation, as it did with movie censorship. In particular, Toronto's efforts to combat carnivals were noted across the country, while towns like Sarnia and Brantford attempted to sway the federal government through the Department of Immigration to prohibit the shows from even entering the country.[36] Sideshows were, for the most part, depicted by critics as tasteless, cheap, detrimental, offensive, and American. Their popularity with consumers was a concern for community leaders.

The protest over sideshows may also have been influenced by the rising tide of cultural nationalism of the period and the seemingly American origin of the shows in Canada. American companies could see the potential in Canada and made inroads, with some later styling themselves as Canadian. But the timing for a positive reception was not wholly in their favour. The 1920s and 1930s saw the consolidation and Americanization of capital in Canada.[37] Canadians, like their American counterparts, were enmeshed in a North American culture that was exemplified by the cross-border trade of films, magazines, and literature that both concerned and delighted Canadians.[38] Freaks and other sideshow acts were simply another element of this cultural consumption. To some English Canadians, commercial culture and the new popular amusements were associated with the United States and Americanization. The trend towards the Americanization of popular culture had started in the decades before the 1920s. In 1913, Bernard K. Sandwell described English Canadians as "absolutely dependent" on American popular culture.[39] With the end of the First World War and the social and cultural changes it ushered in, the problem garnered more attention. By the 1920s, the concern over American culture received frequent attention in newspapers and magazines and prompted politicians and national elites to discuss and implement solutions.[40]

Further, Canada's contributions in the First World War signalled maturity as a nation, and the postwar period was a time when Canadian intellectuals and the cultural elite consciously sought to cultivate a distinctly Canadian culture. The contrast with the freak show is stark. High culture was meant to be morally enriching and educative and to be enjoyed in a quiet, contemplative way. This ideal was remarkably distant from the raucous live performances of freak shows on crowded fairgrounds. The distinction was most clearly marked out by class and related questions of taste. High culture reflected bourgeois ideals, while the carnival was working-class entertainment. Such distinctions rarely held in social practice and could always be challenged, but the hierarchy of culture was a "social weapon" used to make class-based distinctions among consumers and what they consumed.[41] Certainly some of the conflict over modern culture stemmed from the broad popularity of working-class amusements like films. Carnivals, sideshows, and freak shows had lost their middle-class gloss by the end of the 1800s, but had remained popular as working-class amusements in the early 1900s. As such, they were subject to some of the common middle-class angst and the subsequent surveillance to monitor their value. As carnival historian Joe McKennon describes, carnivals were often called "the Poor Man's Entertainment."[42] Such divisions, however, do not fully capture the range of audience members, including, from the 1920s onwards, children who crossed class boundaries.

For critics and concerned citizens, however, the sideshows fell into the category of depravity. Reform groups, churches, and concerned citizens expressed their distaste for the shows. Sideshows appearing in Winnipeg and Brandon, as in other locations, raised concerns over the impropriety of freaks, the lewdness of girl shows, and the gambling; the latter two in particular seemed to delight local men and boys.[43] Specific shows, like Hootchie Cootchie performances, so-called Half and Half performances of allegedly intersexed performers, and "girlie shows" (strip shows), raised ire. At the turn of the twentieth century, a farming newspaper in Manitoba expressed distaste at the girl shows and the "lewd men" who announced them. In 1906, Brandon fair organizers closed a sideshow that was deemed offensive.[44] In the late 1910s, western Canadian newspapers carried articles and letters to the editor that levelled a variety of criticisms at the midways associated with agricultural fairs. Writers expressed upset at the sideshows' immorality, the hideous nature of the "deformed" performers they exhibited, and the "American" nature of the outfits. Revealing performances were a problem. In 1917, the attorney general of Ontario received a complaint regarding a sideshow performance "in a number of Ontario towns" that included "three voluptuous rather scantily dressed females, posing and dancing. Two of the dances were crude, vulgar and quite suggestive." In 1919, Peterborough lawyer J.G. Guise Bagley wrote his member of provincial parliament in regard to the same show, which he saw as part of a wider problem of gambling and "fake" shows. He wrote, "This goes on right under the noses of the police, who stand around and do nothing, under the pretence that the Provincial Inspector is in charge, the real facts being that the managers of the fairs need the money, are well paid, and the police are chloroformed."[45] The Sault Ste Marie Board of Trade passed a resolution similar to other groups in different Ontario cities and towns that called for the premier, the attorney general, and the Ontario Provincial Police to "take the necessary action to forbid the showing in Ontario of questionable amusement orgies and carnivals of inanity and vice, of which Ontario had a surfeit during the Summer of 1920 and which made for weeks of immense pollutive influence from the United States being focussed upon and intensified in Canadian communities."[46] In 1921, members of the Brantford, Ontario, Chamber of Commerce responded to a referendum on carnivals and included their own comments on them. Respondents wrote that carnivals "are degrading and a worn out class of entertainment," and "a positive danger to our young people."[47] Since the 1880s, leisure time and entertainment had come under scrutiny by social and moral reformers worried about modern youth, the future of civilization, and the various social and moral plagues of urban life. In response, community leaders attempted to provide wholesome amusements as alternatives.[48]

Some Ontario complaints were also laced with antisemitism, as they were in other locales. In 1920, for example, Hamilton chief constable of the OPP, W.R. Whatley, received a letter from Joseph E. Rogers, superintendent of the provincial police, warning him of Witts World Famous Show, which was operating in Ontario without a licence. He described the show as "a strong Jew out-fit who think they can do as they like in this Province."[49]

2.3 Girl performers circa 1920, City of Toronto Archives, fonds 1244, item 0279d.

One of the central complaints from boards of commerce across southern Ontario, however, was that the shows took too much money from local citizens. In similar resolutions adopted in 1920 and 1921 by Belleville, Chatham, Brantford, Galt, Oshawa, and other communities, the local chambers of commerce or other boards objected to travelling shows from the United States because they "take from the province a large amount of money without giving a proper return and thereby have a serious effect on local trade generally, necessitating in many instances through citizens spending their money at these places of questionable amusement, the carrying of a vastly larger amount of credit by merchants."[50] The cheap amusement of the carnival and its alleged appeal to working-class tastes chafed against middle-class leaders' desire for wholesome amusement and prudence. One suggested resolution that was adopted in Galt, Ontario, and Chatham, Ontario, referred to high levels of unemployment and the need for "economy."[51] Similar complaints of money being taken out of a city occurred across Canada in the 1930s and 1940s.[52]

Notwithstanding these outcries, Joseph E. Rogers, superintendent of the OPP, and Edward Bayly, deputy attorney general, did not support the prohibition of travelling shows. Rogers noted that despite the resolutions passed in some communities, "many of the municipalities like to have them." He also noted that municipalities had the right to refuse to provide licences to the shows if they chose to do so. The deputy attorney general noted that prohibiting the shows because "they are vicious or demoralizing" would be a criminal matter for the federal government to decide and that immoral or indecent shows could contravene existing sections the Canadian Criminal Code. He also noted that "a very high license fee could be imposed."[53]

In 1927, the Saskatoon city council followed Ontario's lead. It asked its solicitor for an opinion regarding whether or not the city could prohibit carnivals. In a written opinion, which was later adopted by the council, the solicitor warned that based on the wording of the current bylaw and case law originating in Ontario, banning sideshows was not recommended. He also pointed out that circuses would just set up beyond city limits, "resulting in a loss of the license fees and amusement tax to the City, but not preventing the attendance of the citizens thereat."[54] This jurisdictional dance occurred in Winnipeg into the late 1940s. That city had limited carnivals in an effort to protect the proceeds from their agricultural fair. In 1947, an article in *Billboard* noted that it made "no difference except that the city loses out on taxes they might assess the visiting shows." The article went on to note that the Royal American shows played in the neighbouring municipality of West Kildonan and "practically all the attendance is from Winnipeg." Even Winnipeg local E.J. Casey, who operated the E.J. Casey Shows out of St Vital, had difficulty playing within the city limits and did so once at a church bazaar but only after the passing of a special bylaw.[55]

Despite attempts at legal action, the calls for the end of the sideshows eventually fell silent.[56] Reining in the sideshow would have been difficult through strictly legal measures because what constituted "a freak" was difficult to define. Further, the larger fairs like the PNE and CNE continued to rely on them for their financial success, suggesting the need for a more symbiotic than combative relationship with various levels of government and other powerful public officials. While the First World War led to a brief ban on freaks, it also introduced supposedly "temporary" provincial amusement taxes, which would remain in place long after the conflict in Europe ended.[57] Amusement tax meant money in the public coffers, and as the quote above from Saskatoon in 1927 reveals, the loss of this revenue was an important consideration. Carnivals working in tandem with local operations like exhibitions found a measure of security as well as profits – the latter of which everyone shared in.

Carnivals were also hardly unresponsive to these loud protests. In the 1920s, the businesses took on a more proactive role in cleaning up the shows, at least publicly. In 1922, Toronto hosted the Convention of the International Association of Fairs and Expositions. As *Billboard* reported, "every carnival manager and carnival agent that can spare the time and afford the trip will be on hand."[58] That the convention and debate were held in Toronto was interesting because of the city's reputation for strict morality. As *Billboard* noted, "the fight was on Canadian soil, where conditions are fairly spotless in amusements." Apparently, "Canadian delegates attended in force."[59]

The hot topic of the convention was cleaning up the shows – in particular, eliminating graft (gambling) and the "lewd" girlie shows. In December of that year, *Billboard* announced, "Victory: The Old Order Passes with the Dawning of a New Day." Reportedly with only one dissenting vote, the following resolution passed: "Be it Resolved by the International Association of Fairs and Expositions, That we go on record as favoring clean fairs which maintain the highest possible standards for all attractions and concessions, and that nothing be tolerated on our grounds of a degrading or dishonest nature, to the end that our fairs and expositions render the maximum service in the years to come."⁶⁰ While there was clearly some limited dissent, the "resolution against graft and dirty girl shows" benefited the larger operations like the Ringling Bros., a key force behind the resolution, which could operate and make money without those shows.

In reality, the resolution was a great piece of public relations that did little to actually rid the sideshows of gambling or girl shows. It did, however, provide a public response to the outcry of moral reformers, and it did show that at least some of the operators were featuring more "Sunday School" shows – shows that were clean of nudity and gambling but still included freak shows. In 1929, for example, a *Billboard* article argued that successful exhibitions needed a midway, and that with the transition to cleaner shows in the 1920s, this was further assured. The author wrote, "A visit to Toronto, Dallas, Minneapolis, Syracuse, Indianapolis and others is proof that the midway is nigh an indispensable feature and an asset of value to the well-managed exposition or fair ... the public goes to fairs to be amused and the midway, with its modern shows and riding devices, cannot be replaced with educational features without becoming top heavy."⁶¹

A year later, a Canadian chapter of the Benevolent and Protective Order of Elks wrote to W.R. Motherwell, the federal minister of agriculture, requesting that the exemption offered to agricultural societies under the Criminal Code (a softening of the proscription on gambling) be extended to carnivals working under the auspices of charitable organizations.⁶² In 1925, the Criminal Code's restrictions on gambling included a formal exemption for agricultural fairs. (This exemption would persist into the late 1970s).⁶³ Motherwell may have been sympathetic. Earlier in the 1920s, he had refused to ban sideshows, although this certainly seems to have been an ongoing, if limited, discussion carried on in his department during the decade. In 1923, his private secretary, Isabel Cummings, received a letter from William Chisholm of the James Fisher Company Limited. Chisholm included an article which had appeared in *Printer's Ink*, a trade journal for advertisers. The article discussed, supported, and quoted an editorial from *The Country Gentleman*, which decried the midway as a show whose "performers [are] dirty, sweaty, wildly throbbing, physically tainted," and who are nothing more than "scum of the earth, pandering to low emotions."⁶⁴ Motherwell was unmoved. Carnivals were not banned, but contracts, taxes, licences, and immigration provisions provided communities with a measure of control and a share of the profits.

Carnivals challenged some reform-minded Canadians' ideals about taste and healthy leisure pursuits. In response, the carnival modestly reformed in practice and dramatically reformed on paper; that is, the modern business practices of emphasizing the carnival as a happy paternalistic family and maintaining good public and consumer relations flourished. By the 1930s, the moral and social reform movement had lost much of its steam. Efforts to morally regulate the CNE, for example, were sometimes met with ambivalence.[65] The futility of regulating morality was apparent by the end of the 1920s, as issues of "vice" were slowly transformed into issues of "health."[66] Yet the reluctance to ban the carnival and the freak show by government officials was largely due to the profitability of shows for fairs, cities, and the provinces. Amusement taxes, licences, and revenue sharing made the shows financially interesting. That they were brief, seasonal events and often confined to particular spaces (midways at the fairs, for example) perhaps made it easier for officials to briefly look the other way. To fully understand the complexity of the relationships between carnivals and other organizations, as well as the rationalization and professionalization of the carnival operations, it is important to look at the role circuits, contracts, and partnerships played in both.

Circuits, Contracts, and Partnerships

Supported by grants from the federal Department of Agriculture, fairs were seen as an important element in maintaining rural Canada's place in the country's largely anti-modern vision and for showing the significant benefits of rural work and industry. Fairs were to be morally uplifting, educational, and ideologically orientated towards liberal values, although these ideals sometimes clashed with the carnivalesque atmosphere and the hodgepodge of shows, exhibits, and people who attended.[67] By the 1920s, such lofty goals were increasingly difficult to support financially and the carnival became a necessity. In October of 1928, *Billboard* magazine carried a story by American W.S. Guilford under the headline "Carnivals Are Essential to the Fairs."[68] This is something that large fairs like the CNE already knew. In 1919, for example, the midway receipts alone were estimated to be worth between $69,000 and $81,000 for the Ex.[69] The importance of the midway did not diminish in the 1930s. Indeed, in challenging the discourse of the decline of the carnival, sideshow owner Rubin Gruberg, writing in the trade publication *Billboard* in 1930, declared, "In 13 days, at the Canadian

National Exhibition, Toronto, I grossed $228,000 with my largest show, the Rubin & Cherry Shows. And in playing other fairs in the States and Canada it is nothing unusual to gross from $25,000 to $60,000 on the week. Does this appear as the carnivals are losing public interest? The business as a whole is better stabilized than any time that I can recall."[70] While the numbers may have been inflated and the interest exaggerated, the numbers are not beyond the realm of possibility. In his 1939 *History of Fairs and Expositions*, H.W. Waters noted that midways were essential to the financial success of all fairs in Canada, large and small. He wrote, "Of these attractions the midway or amusement zone is looked upon by some as the necessary evil and, although the revenue from this source often makes the difference between a loss and a profit in the operating account of the Fair, it is not infrequently relegated to some remote corner of the grounds."[71] Waters argued that it was important that the pay attractions be well managed to avoid competition from free attractions and that the grounds be well designed to ensure that the crowds would have to walk through the area twice (he suggested blocking off the end of the road).[72]

Major exhibitions, even though they relied on the midway for revenue, had choices about which company to employ. In 1932, the president of the PNE in Vancouver worried about the quality of its shows. The next year, the PNE's bulletin reported that "the midway or skidroad was excellent, there being no complaints whatsoever from the public."[73] The trend continued into the 1940s and 1950s. At the PNE's "Skid Way" (by the late 1940s called the "Gayway") managers enthusiastically reported when they secured larger midway companies (in 1950 it was the Polack Bros. Circus) and, of course, profits.[74] In 1952, the PNE surveyed fairgoers and reported that over a quarter of attendees indicated that the Polack Bros. Circus was "the attraction in which they had the greatest interest."[75] This success continued throughout the 1950s, even when PNE organizers felt hampered by a lack of space that restricted their ability to put on a top-quality show.

For sideshow companies, Canada was usually divided in half, east and west. By 1911, the west, which sometimes included stops in northwestern Ontario at the Lakehead, was further divided into circuits managed by the Western Fair Association. The development of circuits was convenient for show managers as well as those seeking to contract with them, although it meant that fairs had to coordinate dates and potentially give up preferential dates for their community.[76] Provincial funding was also sometimes used to encourage cooperation in setting dates so that multiple fairs could accommodate travelling shows in an efficient way.[77] In part, the east/west division was created when the Western Fair Association combined local fair organizers into a single body in 1915, and the circuits (ranging in size and prestige from "A" to "E") were officially established in 1918. No such organization seems to have been established in the east, but Ontario, with hundreds of agricultural fairs and exhibitions, organized its own provincial association in 1935, called the Ontario Association of Agricultural Societies. The western circuits were decided in conjunction with the Showmen's League of America, which was officially formed in 1913.[78] The circuits, like other individual stands, were decided by bidding at the Western Association of Exhibitions annual meeting.[79] In a 1949 article Herb Dotten described the bidding for the Canadian circuits as "strictly business." Dotten observed that there was little "partying" and delegates only relaxed after the A circuit was awarded. He noted: "When and how business is to be conducted is set forth clearly. Conditions upon which bids are to be raised are posted. And before delegates begin to hear verbal bids the showmen are called in and briefed on how proceedings are to be conducted. Meanwhile, they have prepared written briefs detailing what they have to offer, the price, etc."[80] Establishing and maintaining a schedule of fairs based on a competitive bidding process was a major step towards the rationalization and formalization of the carnival's business. Carnivals hardly drifted aimlessly, setting up and taking down at will; by the 1920s, routes were decided in advance, transportation planned and booked, and shows organized in tight schedules.

The circuits covered the entire western territory but the levels (A, B, or C) were decided by size and (potential) profits of the fairs. The circuits indicated the routes as well as the type of place the carnival would visit. For example, the A circuit was the most prestigious since it included the larger cities and fairs in western Canada and thus would be more popular. The B circuit would be awarded to a company that was relatively good and was composed of smaller regional (as opposed to interprovincial) fairs, which were of a shorter duration. The largest and best sideshow companies would compete for the A and B circuits, while the smaller companies would have to be satisfied with the C, which tended to be local, one-day affairs in smaller communities, involving more travel and more time setting up and taking down. The C circuit also included the western fairs ranked as D or E.[81] By the 1930s, *Billboard* reported on the winners of the bidding.[82] In 1949, the magazine stated that the "biggest sensation at the annual twin meetings of the Western Class A and B fair circuits here [Winnipeg] this week was the granting of a five-year midway contract to Jimmie Sullivan's Wallace Bros.' Shows." The article described the Canadian company's multi-year contract as "the most startling development."[83] Usually, once granted a circuit, companies whose shows appealed to audiences and kept offences to a minimum found themselves in a more competitive position in subsequent years. For example, for most of the 1920s, the western Canadian A-class circuit was held by the Johnny J. Jones Exposition, and the C-class circuits were awarded to Conklin, who was still in the early days of his career.

In 1925, Conklin was awarded the B circuit[84] and by 1937 had secured the CNE. The Canadian National Exhibition was the premier show for carnivals. In 1919, Johnny J. Jones held the show, which included a huge range of rides, concessions, and live human and animal shows. That year, the freaks included the Midget City, Daisy and Violet Hilton, Princess Ha-Ha the Aztec Wonder, Carl Lauther's circus sideshow, which featured Percilla the hairy girl, Serpentine the girl without bones, and Fat Folks. In 1919, just over a month after the CNE closed, Jones took out an advertisement in *Billboard* that included a photograph of his cheque from the CNE for $153,598.70.[85] The lucrative nature of some of the larger fairs like the Canadian National Exhibition meant that they could negotiate with the companies directly on an annual basis. Eventually, large fairs like the CNE and the PNE would enter into more permanent contracts with specific sideshow companies, which in turn would allow for greater investments, innovations, and developments by the carnival company.

Just because a company was not on the circuit did not mean that it would be unable to bring its acts to Canadian audiences. Often companies acted independently of fairs and exhibitions, although they generally endured a more precarious existence. They travelled across the country without the guaranteed security of a circuit or a lucrative contract like the CNE's. For example, although the Polack Bros. ran the World at Home Shows midways for the CNE from 1915 to 1917 before losing the contract to a bigger show, they continued to visit Toronto. In 1919, they reported that their midway attractions at Toronto's Dufferin Park were a success even though they opened just two weeks before the CNE.[86] Competition among various businesses was serious and the Polack Bros.' 1919 show in advance of the CNE was certainly meant to cut into the latter's profits. Carnivals were not once-a-summer events in larger urban areas. Major operators like the Ringling Bros. and Barnum and Bailey Circus, which was so powerful that it could tour on its own, did not need to play fairs in order to make ends meet. They booked and maintained their own schedules.[87]

Despite all of the advance planning, hard times could hit a carnival. Outdoor amusements were dependent on good weather. Rain caused more than one sideshow owner to lament the poor takings on cold, wet days. In 1922, a *Billboard* headline read "Rain Cuts Attendance at Ottawa Exhibition," formally known as the Central Canada Exhibition. Three days of rain meant five thousand fewer admissions than years earlier, but apparently the World of Mirth midway still did "a splendid business."[88] In 1937, eight days of rain threatened the season opening of Conklin's shows in Hamilton, Ontario. The lot was described as a "huge mud pie." Patty and Frank Conklin attempted to mediate the problem by laying "80,000 feet of plank," making a makeshift boardwalk in front of concessions and show fronts.[89] That same year, "cyclonic winds" interrupted the Royal American Shows midway at the Saskatoon Exhibition.[90] Poor weather conditions in 1942 could not be remedied and Conklin reportedly grossed less than ten dollars at the Calgary Stampede.[91]

The contracts between the carnival companies and the exhibitions or fairs attempted to ensure mutual social and economic benefit. In 1917, Vancouver's PNE defended itself against criticism that its unique venue called Skid Way (sometimes "skidway" or "skidroad"), which was contracted to the Great Wortham Shows, included freaks. In their annual bulletin of that year, the chair of the attractions argued: "Some criticism has been levelled at these shows, most of which we think, is not warranted. It has been stated publicly that there were a lot of freaks. We know of no freaks having been on the lot, as we understand the term. We hardly consider a big steer, or fat girl, as such."[92] Clearly there was no agreement as to what constituted a freak or a show in bad taste. Nonetheless, contracting out the carnival ensured that associations could defer controversy and share blame for offensive shows.

The carnivals themselves offered fairs and exhibitions ready-made, convenient amusements. By 1917, these businesses had come to be relied on by a host of fair organizers who wanted a dependable company to stage their shows. For example, organizers of the Pacific National Exhibition in Vancouver in 1917 reported:

> One of the most difficult features of the fair is the securing of a satisfactory carnival company. In the first places all the good companies can be

counted on the fingers of one's hand. Next it requires a continuance of close shipping points to enable a carnival company to travel. In order to make this condition possible a number of fairs must combine and arrange their dates so that there is no lost time or dead weeks between events; also they must run in sequence as to distance, so that there will be no long jumps. In order to arrange all these details the managers of various fairs in one locality get together and induce some company to "play" their circuit. They must offer sufficient "weeks" to make it an object for the company to work in their direction.[93]

A good deal of power lay with the amusement company, which promised to bring a certain number, style, and quality of events in bidding for contracts. While competition existed among the carnivals themselves, fairs needed to compete to attract the best and most entertaining. Carnivals needed to be able to deliver on their promises or risk losing the contract in subsequent years.

What contracts made clear was that the burden of matching public opinion in regard to the sideshows lay with the company and not with the local organizers. Respectability was made the purview of the carnival company, although this often had less to do with freaks than performances of dancing women and games involving gambling. The weight of this burden was not lost on the sideshow operators. The issue came to a head in the 1920s, when some showmen argued that the contracts simply ensured that local operators would not bear the brunt of controversy over popular attractions and games. In 1922, *Billboard* included an article entitled "Fair Managers, Local Politicians and Local Fixers Are to Blame." The anonymous author gave credit to shows for cleaning up their acts and limiting gambling and girl shows. The author then went on to quote from a letter of a sideshow operator: "Why do they [fair association secretaries] condemn the entire profession when it is the fault of themselves alone for selling privileges to an independent operator ... Who is the 'fall guy'? The operator? No! The owner of the show or amusement playing the engagement." The letter went on to point out the hypocrisy of fair associations that denounced the shows (with all of their questionable practices) and then took huge portions of the profits.[94]

By 1928, the contracts were detailed, reflecting a new level of professionalism. The contract between the Vancouver Exhibition Association and the British Columbia Amusements Company included "permission to furnish for the year 1928, Skid Road attractions in connection

2.4 Skid Road Attractions, with Hastings Park racetrack in the background, 1919, City of Vancouver Archives, PNE Collection, public domain.

with the Annual Exhibition." The carnival company, which not only needed to make its substantial investment back and cover its internal costs including labour and travel, would also provide a set percentage of profits back to the association. The contract also detailed the amusements the carnival promised to provide.[95] Contracts made it clear that the owners, not the fair associations, accepted the risk associated with the individual shows. For example, in July of 1940, the Vancouver Exhibition Association (which hosted the PNE) entered into a contract with the Browning Amusement Company Inc. of Salem, Oregon. The contract stated that the Amusement Company was "to provide for the Association for the Exhibition period in the year 1940, not less than five riding devices of first class character, quality and equipment and not less than four shows acceptable to the Association, all of the foregoing to be of merit and unobjectionable of which the Association shall be the sole judge and agree to the furnishing, management and operation of the same to abide by the rules and regulations and orders of the Association at all times during the said Exhibition period." The contract further stipulated that the Amusement Company "will not suffer or permit anything to be done of an objectionable nature or contrary to law, and will forthwith upon the request of the Association, close out and eliminate any such objectionable feature from the said area and will co-operate with the Association to the fullest possible extent in keeping everything in, about and upon the said premises of a fit and proper character."

In return for the sum to bring the company to Vancouver, the company was to pay the Vancouver Exhibition Association "25% of its gross receipts in respect of its shows and 30% of its gross receipts in respect to all riding devices after deduction of Amusement Tax." The contract also stipulated that the Amusement Company had to pay for its own electricity, but that "the ticket takers were employed by the association and under their management."[96] Given that the tickets would be the evidence for the percentage payments indicated above, this clause was intended to ensure the Association received its cut. As a later investigation in Alberta would reveal, however, the clause was not foolproof.[97] Yet the contracts seem to suggest that the amusements companies carried any legal burden of questionable shows or practices. That said, the 1949 PNE program noted the "rigid contract" for the midway and stated, "Visitors to the Gayway have a host of amusements to choose from and enjoy. Their welfare and enjoyment is assured at the Pacific National Exhibition."[98] The balance was a delicate one, as the need for profits and amusements that would attract paying customers remained strong.

One way to mediate the risk was to subcontract the freak show to another organization. This sort of cascade in risk and responsibility can be seen with the CNE. In 1937, the CNE reported that Patty Conklin would be directing the organization of the midway as part of his extraordinary multi-year contract with the CNE. In 1936, Conklin submitted a bid to provide the midway for the CNE. He was awarded the contract, and his long history with the CNE started in 1937. According to one 1941 article, in negotiating with Elwood Hughes of the CNE, Conklin attempted to secure the display of the Dionne quintuplets. With $25,000 in cash he spoke with Senator F.P. O'Connor at the King Edward Hotel in Toronto, who promised to speak with the prime minister and

Ontario's minister of public welfare, David Croll. Apparently the latter quashed any idea of the quints being displayed at the CNE. Yet, Conklin's much-lauded moxie and determination impressed Hughes and got Conklin the 1937 CNE contract.[99] In the mid-1940s, annual contracts began to give way to longer five-year contracts for the Conklin Shows. In 1944, they announced a "five-year pact" with the Eastern Townships Agricultural Association. One year later, they announced similar deals with four Ontario fairs in Leamington, Belleville, Lindsay, and Kingston as well as a five-year deal with the Lions Club in Winnipeg for a fair held in West Kildonan.[100] These fairs were in addition to the rides Conklin operated at Belmont Park in Montreal, Sunnyside in Toronto, and Crystal Beach in Fort Erie.[101] In 1946, CNE general manager Elwood Hughes offered Conklin an unprecedented ten-year contract for the midway, and ten-year contracts were announced between Conklin and seven other fairs based in Ontario and Quebec.[102] At the same time, the carnival was changing. Live shows had started to give way to mechanical rides. While mechanical rides had first appeared in the late 1800s, they were novelties that existed as part of the midway. By the late 1930s, freak shows were some of the only live shows that continued to make a profit.[103]

Rather than bringing in a travelling show, Conklin brought in independent acts in order to provide the best and freshest show. The CNE's Elwood Hughes stated, "Altho [sic] we have had probably the finest midway of any fair, we have felt the need for new, novel and outstanding attractions that are beyond the scope of the traveling carnivals."[104] Conklin organized press-release handbooks through his press representative Walter Hale. In one from the 1940s, the front cover declared that "this year the Exhibition will have its OWN Midway and not an organized carnival company making another stop on its tour from the United States."[105] In practice, the midway was simply contracted out to an independent sideshow operator who cobbled together the shows. Like other showmen in the 1940s, Conklin began to contract out the freak show to showmen such as Pete Kortes, Jack Halligan, Harry Lewiston, Ward Hall, Lou Dufour, and Sam Alexander. The latter four, among others, worked primarily as freak show operators, who put together shows to display independently or to contract to larger carnival organizations. In 1942 *Billboard* reported that "Jack Halligan, sideshow impresario, has again booked his World's Fair Freaks with Conklin shows, making his fourth season there."[106] One year later, Conklin engaged "Pete Kortes's No. 1 Side Show unit, Look at Life" for the Western Canada Class A

Circuit. The freak performers included Albino twins, an elephant girl, Eko and Iko [the Muse brothers], an armless wonder, Jolly Dolly fat girl, a frog boy, and an ossified girl.[107] In 1947 and 1948, Conklin contracted the sideshows for the CNE to Ray Marsh Brydon, who, in April of 1948, noted that he had the following freak show performers under contract: "Richard Miller, armless-legless five-year-old; Lionella, billed as the lion-faced girl; Laurello, styled the man with the revolving head, and Royal Midgets, to appear in his side show units."[108] In September that year, after the shows had closed, Conklin reported that the top-grossing shows were the girl show followed by the side show. Conklin also reported that Brydon had added Charles Lucas's Darkest Africa and a fat show.[109]

The relationship between a carnival owner and a freak show subcontractor was mutually beneficial. In his frank autobiography, Harry Lewiston described teaming up with Conklin in the late 1930s at the CNE. Conklin was by then the president of the Showmen's League and was credited by Lewiston for ensuring the survival of the League during the Depression. On his own, Lewiston fared moderately, landing the Quebec Exposition Provencale whose program announced a midway with "jeunes prodiges de Lewiston."[110] Now working in conjunction with Conklin, he wrote: "I decided I would be better off with Patty. Besides his personality and abilities, there was the fact that his show was scheduled to play the great Canadian National Exposition [sic]. Earlier, as a barker manager with the Ruben and Cherry Shows, I had played this stand, so knew that, if nothing else, there was a good chance that I could make a full season's profits right at that one stand."[111]

According to Lewiston, widespread fears of a polio outbreak kept numbers down, which suggests that he is writing about 1937, when a polio epidemic had city officials warning families to keep their children home from the CNE. Although the CNE refused to cancel Children's Day that year, attendance that day was reduced by 78,000 and the CNE's overall admissions were lower by 300,000. Lewiston noted, however, that he still managed to break even.[112] His freak show seems to have been popular. That year, a newspaper reporter for the *Globe and Mail* noted the throngs of fans on the midway with its "freaks, girls and trained animals." The article, "A Midway by Any Other Name Still Gets Its Quota of Fans," noted that "the Midway, for which many a citizen constitutes the main attraction at the Canadian National Exhibition, continues to exert the old appeal."[113] Ward Hall, another freak show owner who worked in Canada with Sam Alexander, noted the success of working Canadian destinations like Montreal, Hamilton, and London in the 1950s and 1960s, but also stated that by far the best and most profitable site was the CNE.[114] The quest for new and novel sideshow acts led to some enthusiastic reporting. In 1954 *Billboard* announced that Conklin, on the eve of his European cruise, had landed the exclusive rights to the Ripley's Believe It or Not exhibitions.[115] The next year the Conklin Shows placed a want ad in *Billboard* with the notice that they had a "special proposition for good side show."[116]

Many sideshows retained partnerships with various local organizations, aside from and in addition to the essential fair associations, well into the 1940s. Sometimes they were hosted by local groups, such as local battalions, the Red Cross, or the Shriners, to raise money for charities as they did in the 1920s for disabled veterans.[117] Such partnerships originated in the late 1800s in Chicago with the Elks, a popular fraternal association. According to one carnival historian, the Elks found street festival and fair midway fundraisers so successful that "several prominent Elks organized their own midway/carnival groups and took them on the road."[118] The style was copied north of the border. In 1908, a Toronto newspaper reported on the fun happening in Hamilton: "Hamilton's celebration is modelled upon the familiar Elk carnival lines of over the border towns and summer resorts. The committee encouraged all sorts of midway, freak, and side show organizations. The managers of these traveling troupes and devices sized up the carnival as a good thing for people in that line, and the entire business heart of the town is a gigantic midway plaisance."[119]

As fundraisers, the sideshows received a boost in the immediate years following the First World War because of their ability to make money. The Canadian Victory Shows was a small Canadian carnival company initially organized in 1918 by Victor J. Neiss. In 1919, it opened its season in Welland, Ontario, reportedly "under the auspices of the Great War Veterans."[120] In 1920, H. Carrington of the Ottawa chapter of the Army and Navy Veterans in Canada wrote to the chief of the OPP asking for a reference for the Canadian Victory Shows. Carrington noted that the shows had agreed to pay the provincial licence and turn over 15 per cent of the concessions takings. In exchange the veterans association was to "secure the grounds." Show owner Victor Neiss had provided Carrington with the letter of reference from the OPP but Carrington wanted to verify that the show was "reliable." Similar letters were received from similar organizations in Woodstock and Toronto. In each instance, Rogers wrote back stating that they had treated the veterans fairly and had received no complaints.[121] By 1922, the carnival was offering a range of attractions including Princess Corita and her midget ballet, "Canada's Fattest Boy," Col. Hope's "Freaks of Nature," wild animals, Oriental Dancing Dolls, diving girls, four riding devices, and a pony and monkey circus.[122] The show seems to have had a short lifespan of about four seasons. Its range of questionable entertainments (dancing girls "recruited from the redlight district in Montreal," in particular) may have led to its demise.[123] It was also competing against many well-established shows in southern and central Ontario and failed to gain any significant ground with any of the major fairs.

The shows' continuing popularity, despite their less-than-wholesome reputations, meant that such charitable profit-sharing understandings were mutually beneficial, although the relationships sometimes did not always work out as planned. In 1926, the Far Quhr Shriner's Club of Stratford, Ontario, contracted with the Bob Morton Circus to benefit the General Hospital in Stratford. They ended up losing money, and the Shriners requested a refund from the province for the tax and licence. It was denied.[124] Yet, the ideal was that shows would get a modest boost in respectability, and charities and hospitals would benefit financially. In Ontario, they also got a tax exemption, which increased profits for both parties. In 1927, the amusement tax in Ontario was further revised to exempt anyone under the age of twenty-five, which coincided with shows' efforts to build child and youth audiences.[125]

State Regulation

Taxation was a tool the state invoked as means of surveillance and raising revenues. Carnival operators kept close watch on any changes in taxation, some of which were reported in *Billboard*. For example, the new 1941 customs tax added "$100 per month for each ride, $50 for each show, and $25 for each concession."[126] Enforcement was an ongoing challenge. By the mid-1950s, the Ontario Treasury Department was concerned that some carnivals were failing to collect appropriate taxes or pass them on to the province. In 1955, James Healy, chief inspector, Hospitals Tax Branch, wrote directly to the district superintendent of immigration requesting information on shows crossing the border so that the chief inspector could ensure they were properly licensed and accompanied for the duration of their stay in Ontario. Independent operators seemed to be giving the government the slip. As Healy noted, "We have no way of knowing when these shows enter Ontario, but we do from time to time catch up with them."[127] Despite an evolving set of regulations and requirements for carnivals, enforcing them when the shows travelled constantly (and between jurisdictions) remained an ongoing problem throughout the twentieth century.

Protests over sideshows led to increasing provincial government intervention, and one of the more popular and profitable means of accomplishing this was through the issuance of licences. Although sideshows could not be entirely prohibited on legal grounds, cities and provinces could regulate the attractions by requiring sometimes expensive licences in addition to an amusement tax. The efforts to regulate the sideshows began in earnest in the 1910s, when municipal governments revised regulations and increased fees. Between 1910 and 1950, for example, the city of Saskatoon required shows to pay a fee of either $300 or $500 per day (the price fluctuated in the late 1910s before settling at $500), in addition to the provincial amusement tax. The penalties were serious if the show went on without a licence. In Saskatoon, the fine was $50 in addition to the licence fee and a potential prison sentence of six months. In 1929, the bylaw was amended to ensure that all applications required approval from city council.[128]

Legislation on travelling shows, including carnivals, was also enacted in a number of provinces. In Alberta, the 1914 legislation was revised to introduce a sliding scale for circuses that depended on the number of train cars the shows pulled into town with. The number of cars that shows travelled with varied considerably. By 1903, the Ringling Bros. owned sixty-five train cars. In 1913, the Johnny J. Jones Show owned twenty train cars that transported everything from the animals, workers, concessions, and games, to Jones himself in a "deluxe private car." In 1918, the Polack Bros. World at Home Show travelled with nine cars.[129] While the sliding scale and the unit of measurement were not unique, the proposed revision would have substantially reduced the fees smaller shows paid. Under the 1914 provincial rules in Alberta, each "circus, menagerie or wild west show and not more than one sideshow" was required to pay $250 per city, or $50 per town or village, with additional sideshows being charged $10 each. In 1922, only shows travelling with thirty or more cars were charged $250 (city) and $100 (town/village). New Brunswick's 1923 legislation contained similar provisions and, by late 1920s, allowed the provincial Board of Censors "to permit or to prohibit" public amusements for which fees were charged.[130] The revision in New Brunswick suggests that legislators had to balance the need for regulation with the desire for revenue. Federal tariffs also added costs to operations. It was with relief that *Billboard* reported a change in tariffs on American carnivals playing at Canadian agricultural exhibitions. The article noted, "This year [Dominion government tariffs] will be levied on a 30-day basis instead of a calendar month basis."[131]

Bylaws were updated to protect local exhibitions from competition. For instance, between 1914 and 1952, the city of Saskatoon wrestled with the best way to ensure the city's exhibition was protected. In the 1920s the city ended up prohibiting shows during the months of July and August, when The Ex was on, and slowly changed the bylaws so the officials of the exhibition board could make exceptions. This measure was taken in order to preserve their own exhibition's revenues and to limit competition. Other shows that were granted licences were required to hold off any advertising before the last day of the Saskatoon Exhibition, which had its own midway.[132]

Licences and taxes required sideshow employees to plan routes well in advance so that letters requesting permission and licensing fees could be paid. More informal fees of either cash or gifts were also part of the business operations. Typically, shows had an employee, known as a "legal adjuster," "fixer," or "patch," travel in advance of the performers to meet informally with local police. Unofficial payments to local men in power were part of the publicly unacknowledged costs of doing business. Everything from cash payments to free goods or tickets to shows were used as bribes to ensure that potentially offensive performances could be staged. Maintaining a good relationship with authorities meant that the shows could function year after year.

Although there are few official records from the period under study here, show owners and managers recollect that such meetings often involved cash payments and assurances that police would ignore shows that tested local moral and legal limits. In 1905, three Ontario police constables reported to the Ontario Fairs Convention regarding the gambling that was rampant at midways, and told attendees: "On reaching the place where the exhibition is to be held, local police are first seen and, if necessary, bribed."[133] In 1920, the Greater Sheesley Shows, which played in Ontario and then won the Western B circuit for 1921, provided the chief of the Ontario Provincial Police with a pair of claws after asking if he preferred to have them mounted himself, or mounted before they were mailed. William Hicks, the superintendent of the Sheesley Shows, promised that, either way, they would cover all the expenses.[134] In 1922, the OPP chief returned a payment he had received from a showman, indicating that it should be redirected to the local police officer. Other shows requested that particular officers travel with them throughout the province because they had established a good working relationship. Larger shows like the CNE in Toronto wrote to the chief of the OPP to ask for "the names of the members of your Dept." who might want a season's pass. From 1917 to 1921, the records indicate that the passes went to members of the OPP, the chief, as well as his wife and daughter.[135] While this evidence is anecdotal and suggestive, it does hint at the possibility of payments or in-kind gifts to local officers or their superiors.

Some show owners felt the relationship to be a burden. In his 1935 memoir, Al G. Barnes described "queer laws" in Canada. He described "playing a little town in Canada" with a "clean" dance on the sideshows that chief of police threatened to stop until he paid him ten dollars.[136] In the 1940s, another carnival operator stated that "no matter how clean a show you've got you'll once in a while meet up with cops that have their hand out, just because you're carnie."[137] There were few guarantees that advance fixing would pay off. In 1947, an article on the Conklin Shows in Quebec City noted: "The back-end was slowed down to a walk, the censors here being unusually active and stern."[138]

Decades later, in June of 1978, the *Report of a Public Inquiry into Royal American Shows Inc. and Its Activities in Alberta* included discussion on "black books" and "gift sheets," which included significant payments – large and small, cash and in-kind – to officials and police officers across North America.[139] In regard to members of the Calgary police force who admitted to accepting gifts from approximately $50 to $500, Justice Laycraft noted:

> Each of the Calgary police officers involved in these money gifts was vehement in his statement that no favour was asked for, or given, in return for the money. The circumstances of the gifts bear this out. When money is given to a patrol officer on the last day of the Fair, there could be no assurance that the same officer would appear in succeeding years on patrol at the Fair grounds. In many cases, they did not. For the individual officer there was no sense of being compromised, though there can be no doubt R.A.S. [Royal American Shows] hoped to build within the Force an atmosphere of friendship which would have future value. The *payments were a custom of long-standing*, but a custom most definitely opposed to police practice.[140]

Laycraft's view is generous in presuming officers would not talk to each other or otherwise have knowledge of the "long-standing" custom in advance of working the shows. Clearly, however, having a good fixer was important to make certain that the customary relationship worked smoothly. Showman Harry Lewiston was interested in working with Conklin in Canada because he was a good fixer, and Lewiston's freak and girl shows, the latter of which he admitted bordered on the illegal, drew large crowds and sums in Hamilton and London, Ontario, in the late 1930s. Police reports from the period, however, seem only interested in ensuring that gambling was not happening on the midway.[141]

The combination of official and unofficial fees could be prohibitive to smaller shows and some did request leniency. Despite the protests and concerns, governments seemed willing to accommodate carnivals and travelling shows. In 1917, Fred A. Meigan, the general agent for the James Patterson's Trained Animal Shows combined with the Gollmar Bros. Circus, requested that the city of Saskatoon substantially reduce the required licence fee to $150 per day or the show would have to bypass the city altogether. To make the appeal more persuasive, Meigan wrote that the show was "always clean, moral and very high class," and that it had travelled through the northwestern American states. Meigan argued, "You can easily judge from that, the charachter [sic] of our shows as those cities would not keep welcoming us if we were not strictly high-class and giving first class performances." City council agreed to reduce the fee to $300 and the exhibition board did not object to the circus performing in July.[142] In other instances, it was the local partners who requested ostensibly on behalf of the show for a return of a portion of the licensing fee. In 1930, the Order of Elks requested that Saskatoon's city council refund the Conklin and Garret shows 50 per cent of the licensing fee. On 9 June 1930, the standing committee recommended that the request be granted, although council made no recommendation on the matter two months later.[143]

The Immigration Act became an important piece of legislation used to regulate the shows at a national level during the First World War, but with the lifting of wartime restrictions, it lost some of its power. In 1921, the minister of immigration and colonization wrote a letter of response to the Reverend J.H. Edmison, general secretary of the board of Home Missions for the Presbyterian Church of Canada, responding to its call to prohibit shows from entering Canada. The minister pointed out how the end of wartime regulations and the more limited reach of the Immigration Act had loosened restrictions, and noted as well that travelling shows continued to receive widespread support from soldiers' and veterans' organizations and the management of Canadian fairs and exhibitions. He noted that there was no agreement on whether or not the shows should be allowed in Canada. Yet, the minister concluded: "The Officers of my Department are doing their best to prevent the entry of the mentally, morally and physically unfit. They have turned back many of the human freaks and others, whose connection with a show merely excites the morbid curiosity of people, beyond this, we are not empowered to go at present, and while the problem will always be watched with the greatest possible care, I can see no present hope of shutting out the travelling carnival shows."[144] Regulation was piecemeal, inconsistent, and incredibly complex given the sheer number of shows and the thousands of circus and carnival employees travelling the country at any given time.

For all employees of American-based travelling shows coming into Canada, changes to the American Immigration Act made entering Canada after 1 July 1924 more difficult. The Immigration Act of 1924 lowered the American quotas for immigrants in a xenophobic effort to control "undesirable" immigration. For travelling acts, this meant that employees leaving the United States, even for a short period, would not be allowed to return unless they could prove their American citizenship or landed-immigrant status. Prior to this change, the manifests declaring the citizenship of all people entering Canada were usually enough evidence to ensure employees' return. After 1924, this was not the case. The Canadian federal government kept a close eye on who came into the country, when, and with how many employees. On 18 July 1924, the division commissioner of immigration in Winnipeg reported to Ottawa that three circuses were currently operating in the west: Johnny J. Jones, with 398 employees; the Rubin and Cherry Shows, with 374; and the Levitt-Brown-Huggins Shows with 189.[145] Carnival operators were required to provide a manifest listing employees, a cash bond "to indemnify the Department [of Citizenship and Immigration] against any expenses which might result of the failure of any members of the carnival to abide by the conditions of their entry or leave Canada."[146] For show operators, filling out the manifests to get into Canada was seen as a complicated and onerous task.[147]

The Canadian Department of Immigration and Colonization expressed a special concern regarding the American legislation and sideshow performers, who crossed the border frequently and were seen almost uniformly as undesirable, although certainly there was variation in the level of undesirability. Singled out by various members of the Department of Immigration and Colonization were Japanese and Chinese Americans, as well as African Americans, although they did not fall under the American legislation as many would have been natural-born citizens. Before the American law took effect, discussions between Canadian and American immigration departments laid out the seriousness of the changes, especially for circuses and carnivals, and the message was quickly relayed to officials across the country. In August 1924, a circular to all immigration inspectors-in-charge was released, stating, "It is now necessary that the greatest of care be exercised in the admission of circus employees."[148]

Any employees left behind for any reason (because of illness, hospitalization, or arrest) were carefully tracked until they either left the country on their own or were deported. Organizations were responsible for the costs accrued by employees who stayed behind and were required upon entering the country to put up a bond from which such costs could be deducted. Managers and owners assured various government officials that hospitalized employees had their bills covered and that they would travel back to the United States promptly upon discharge. On one occasion, a nineteen-year-old African American citizen left the circus in Vancouver and applied to stay in Canada. After a brief hearing on 20 September 1922, his request was denied and he was deported. A charge of $4.25 was requested of Ringling Bros. under their agreement to pay the costs of returning any employee to the United States who joined the circus there. In October, Ringling Bros. sent the money to the Department of Immigration.[149]

For officials, tracking individual carnival employees could be tricky. In 1917, Crown Prosecutor Robert M. Matheson of Brandon, Manitoba, wrote to the chief of the OPP to inform him that an employee of a carnival had been recently convicted of assault causing grievous bodily harm against another employee. Matheson wrote that the employee was given a suspended sentence after "all parties" agreed that he "was to *leave Canada at once.*" Matheson was concerned that he went to the US briefly before joining the World at Home Shows in Winnipeg, which was on its way back to Toronto. He described the employee as "an undesirable" and "a tricky individual" who was "very meek when before the Police Magistrate here, and impressed the authorities that he would get out of Canada at once and stay out." Matheson advised: "I would respectfully suggest that you take no excuse from him or his associates."[150] In response, Matheson was told that they could not find the man in Toronto but had "learned he was here for a few hours but left and will join the Shows as soon as they arrive back in the United States."[151] Despite the efforts of multiple (if uncoordinated) arms of the state, carnivals' transient work and workers still could prove frustrating.

Sometimes, though, government departments had long memories. In advance of their work at the Central Canada Exhibition in 1966, immigration officials wrote to the Amusements of America and noted that new procedures were being put into place for this show due to past problems. Officials explained:

> Problems have arisen with relation to the entry and departure of personnel of your organization largely due to the fact that they do not arrive and depart in a group but travel separately and cross international boundaries at different ports. Oftentimes, copies of the Manifest are not available at these ports resulting in delays and numerous telephone calls to Ottawa where the Master Manifest is held. The most serious problem occurs with respect to refunding the Bond which cannot be returned until we are satisfied that all members of the show have left Canada. As you know, your people often leave Canada after midnight and their departure is reported to members of services other than Canadian Immigration who are not familiar with our procedure and correction – concerning the show and verification of their departure is overlooked.

As a result, the department initiated six new procedures for this carnival to follow, which included providing individual numbers and two copies of a letter of identification. The first copy was to be surrendered upon entry and the latter upon departing Canada. Once the government had received all the letters from departing employees and crossed checked the names with the manifest, the $2,000 cash bond would be released.[152]

Despite these efforts to restrict the midways and track employees, the carnival continued. Some events, like the CNE, fared better than others, even despite Toronto's reputation as being more conservative and needing only "respectable" shows. And, despite the severe economic crisis of the 1930s, which closed some of the smaller carnivals, travelling shows continued to perform and make money. In their book on the Brandon Agricultural Exhibition, Kenneth Coates and Fred McGuiness conclude that in the 1930s "the midway attracted much attention and most of the money."[153] The potential profits were not unknown to showmen themselves. The carnival was profitable not just for operators but also for those who benefited from the collection of the amusement tax and licensing fees. If moral regulations swelled in the first four decades of the twentieth century, the carnival was at least a wedge in the wheels of the bureaucracy developed for moral policing. Those wheels could jump into motion and shut down shows or grind to a halt, revealing moral enforcement to be a complicated issue involving differences in taste and morality, especially with significant sums of money at stake.

Conclusion

Freak shows, whatever delights they offered audiences, were questionable at best to social reformers, who encouraged government officials to regulate or criminalize the shows. Despite protests calling for the end of sideshows, they persisted. The cries against commercial culture petered out in the 1920s, as consumerism flourished and youths, as well as other Canadians, embraced it with their nickels, dimes, and attention.

Travelling carnivals were complex businesses requiring a lot of time and energy. Travelling hundreds of kilometres every season, with potentially large numbers of employees, they negotiated contracts, venues, employees' work and living conditions, and transportation. Every year they played to thousands of Canadians in large and small cities and towns across the country. They negotiated with multiple levels of government, and travelled almost consistently between May and October, while frequently crossing the Canada–US border. Owners and managers had to negotiate the levels of bureaucracy required for their shows to perform legally. The carnival business was gruelling, and while some upheld at least the illusion of being a family, they must be seen first and foremost as businesses. Some employees found acceptance in being a carny, but family is always rife with tensions and differences. The carnival was no different. Freak show labour as a freak was also work, although that work traversed multiple poles of experience from exploitative to appreciative. The next chapter looks at these issues as the carnival business reformed in response to protests and regulations to become a sophisticated operation with complex relationships.

Chapter Three

The Carnival Business in Canada: Paternalism, Belonging, and Freak Show Labour

In his memoir showman Lou Dufour made a plea for seeing the carnival as a business that offered amusement to everyone. As Dufour recalled,

> It took tireless energy and lots of guts to carry on, but showmen learned some fundamental and realistic facts about outdoor show business, a business that not only survived but went on to unprecedented successes. In times of national sorrow, the outdoor showmen, at fairs, carnivals, circuses and amusement parks, have helped the great masses of citizens to put aside their sorrows and enjoy themselves. It always has been bargain-basement fun that everyone can afford, on both sides of the U.S.–Canada border, and I hope that national leaders recognize that fact.[1]

The phrase "bargain-basement fun" is an appropriate one, referring to sales of often-imperfect goods in department stores. Freak shows were a good parallel as a cheap and imperfect amusement, but also as a modern business. Although the carnival is sometimes seen as a fly-by-night fringe organization of social misfits, I argue here that the business of the carnivals reveals a different perspective, one that is more closely aligned with common twentieth-century business practices that fit within capitalism's efficiency framework, including rationalization and professionalization. The modern carnival combined paternalism with public relations, consumer relations, and other modern business practices. Overall, from their motley origins, carnivals evolved to attain professional identities. In part this simply reflected how businesses needed and were expected to efficiently operate in the twentieth century but the promotion and maintenance of an identity of professionalization helped the carnival and the freak show to continue. This chapter focuses on the business of the carnival, looking at how carnivals were organized around a self-made man who embodied the ethos of the carnival: hard work, grit, and moxie. Further, this chapter examines how this ethos structured the very operation of the carnival, and finally, it looks at the experience of working on the carnival and the freak show.

The Self-Made Man and the Business of the Carnival

An overarching if informal ideology of the carnival glorified nonconformity, hard work, independence, freedom, and the self-made man. The myth of the self-made man hardened in the mid-nineteenth century. Self-made men were not physically stronger or intellectually smarter than their counterparts, but worked harder to attain financial and social success. The myth of democratic opportunity premised only on hard work persisted well into the twentieth century and continues today. In the twentieth century, self-made men were autonomous achievers who constantly strove for success, never settled, and, much like the carnival itself, "required perpetual motion."[2] As Jackson Lears notes, "the career of the self-made man embodied the dynamism inherent in all capitalist development."[3] The biographies of show owners reveal this ideology, telling success stories of the "American Dream" in which impoverished individuals "pulled themselves up by their bootstraps" to achieve success single-handedly. For example, the biography of Johnny Jenkins Jones exemplifies the "rags to riches" stories of carnival owners. Jones was born in 1874 in Pennsylvania, and by the age of ten was working in the coal mines. Eventually, he started selling newspapers and then candy on the streets. By 1895, he was selling goods at fairs. His entrée into the carnival business came when he built his own Ferris wheel and in 1904 opened the Johnny J. Jones Carnival Company. After a series of short-lived partnerships, Jones went into business on his own with a fat man named Jolly Joe in 1906.[4] Jones's company continued to grow and expand, and by the mid-1920s, he employed about four hundred people. By 1920, he often secured the prestigious midway at the CNE and the largest fairs in the Canadian west.[5] Before his death in 1930, Jones also allegedly quit drinking and converted to Christianity. As biographer Bob Goldsack puts it, "determined to turn his life around, the man short of stature, but gifted with a big heart, was baptised a Christian."[6] Even death did not stop the show or the legend of its founder. In 1931, the company was called the Johnny J. Jones Exposition and advertising included the slogan "Mighty Monarch of All Tented Shows."[7]

The narrative of success and the "American Dream" in the Canadian carnival circuits is exemplified in the biography of Patty Conklin. If Johnny J. Jones was the "Mighty Monarch" in the 1930s, he was dethroned by Conklin, who was often referred to as the King of the Carnival. American by birth, Conklin ended up dominating and defining the carnival in the twentieth century both in Canada and internationally. Conklin was born Joe Renker in Brooklyn, New York, in 1892. Little is known about his childhood other than that he was poor and left home in 1900. After a brief stay with foster parents, Conklin ended up selling peanuts in New York City at the age of twelve. Shortly after, he worked at Coney Island until his late teens, where he sharpened his skills and learned about the carnival.[8] At some point, Conklin reunited with his brother Frank and both ended up working with Jim Conklin, a carnival owner who ran the Clark and Conklin shows. Joe Renker became James Wesley Conklin, although he was known as Patty Conklin.[9] In 1921, the Conklins headed north to western Canada for the "easy money."[10] By 1937, Conklin had secured the CNE, which was an important career move that came, according to Conklin's son Jim, as a result of Conklin's charisma and hustle.[11] He was popular and well-respected among showmen internationally, and was elected president of the Showmen's League of America in 1935.[12] By his death in 1970, Conklin was a financial and professional success as Canada's carnival leader.

The narrative of the self-made man created lofty images of father figures who garnered much respect. Every member of the carnival was to be defined by their hard work, and owners were to embody this work ethic for all employees. The 1931 Johnny J. Jones advertisement that referred to him as a monarch also highlighted his business ideals: "This great outdoor amusement organization was founded on the IDEALS of its organizer, Johnny J. Jones, 28 years ago. This gigantic institution is paramount, operated on high-class principles of business ethics, which has been solely responsible for its long and successful career. It was founded on Honor."[13] American author William Lindsay Gresham described The World of Mirth owner Frank Bergen (who frequently brought his shows to Ottawa) as a simple, hard-working carny who shunned the established hierarchy among show owners and employees, making him seem down to earth and caring. According to Gresham, Bergen embodied the qualities of a successful carnie: "a rugged physique, a wide variety of skills and a knowledge of human nature ... a warm heart and a fatalistic trust in Providence."[14] Gresham's description of Bergen reflects idealized notions of modern masculinity popular among middle-class business men: physically strong, intellectually sharp, and congenial. In many ways the entire carnival as masculine enterprise reflected the ideals of modern manliness in the form of freedom, independence, hard work, grit, and generosity. Yet, like many masculine endeavours, the carnival was personified as feminine. One often-quoted description from carnival historian Joe McKennon styled the carnival in colourful terms as "a lusty busty bawdy bitch ... she has kicked up her frolicsome heels and masqueraded under many guises and names."[15] If the carnival had an uncontrollable feminine persona, she was disciplined and controlled by the self-made man's modern business practices.

The carnival ideology was steeped in class-crossing masculine ideals. Success stories of modern men in business are, in other contexts, often stories of becoming middle-class. In the context of the carnival this is more ambiguous, with owners maintaining values of common sense, valuing practical aspects of life, and maintaining an ongoing identification with social inequality and marginality.[16] Carnivals depicted themselves as fringe communities built on values of universal acceptance and often provided orphans and newsboys special days or free admission as part of this identification. Yet, carnivals like Conklin's were serious businesses with the trappings of middle-class professionalism. Showmen organized professionally, held annual conventions beginning in 1912, and published professional journals and publications like *White Tops* and *Amusement Business*. The carnival's outsider status obscured their connections with various levels of government and with the agricultural fairs. The success stories of the self-made man also provided a compelling persona for the businesses that operated under these men. As Donica Belisle argues in regard to large Canadian department stores, paternalistic practices with father-like figures and "family" atmospheres were enmeshed with modern business practices like public relations.[17] While the peripatetic carnival with its social misfits and freaks and sawdust-covered lots might seem like the antithesis to the locally rooted, well-ordered, pristine, and middle-class department stores, business practices were a shared ground.

Carnivals often reported business practices in trade publications, but more widely appealed to notions of a family run, almost without exception, by a self-made man styled as the show's father. Treading the line between respectable, hard-working employees and close-knit family the carnival contradicted the appearance of a corporation. Newspapers told stories of the carnival that identified the businesses as families. In 1952 the *Winnipeg Free Press* included a story comparing a Royal American

Show to a city. Reporter Monty Pilling wrote: "Behind the gaudy glitter of the 'world's largest midway,' 1,200 people live and work in a miniature city on wheels." The article discussed the huge number of technical staff, the costumes, signs, and largely unseen labour needed to operate the shows.[18] Three years later an article in the same paper described the world "Behind the Glittering Tinsel": "The family is big on the six-month road circuit. In the 1200 are electricians and railroad men, roughnecks and bally workers, musicians and animal-trainers, concession operators and cooks."[19] The appearance of family shaped relations between the owner and individual employees. Frank Bergen, who ran the World of Mirth carnival, which regularly held the contract for the Central Canada Exhibition in Ottawa in the 1940s, 1950s, and 1960s, described the feelings of family that shows promoted:

> You see, in this business what is a freak to the customers is just one of the boys or girls to us. It's all in the family. We don't have no upper crust and no underworld. Everybody's equal. You take the girls in the girl show – most of the girls are married, some of 'em to boys they met on the show, canvas men and so on. We had one this season – little girl who works on one of the games and a boy who's on the rides. Whenever I see a boy and girl always going around together and it looks like it's getting serious I try to speak to the boy and find out just how he feels about this girl. If they are really in love then I tell him I'll get the license for 'em and give the bride away; I'm a great hand at giving away brides. And that way they can travel together and stay out of trouble.[20]

Bergen's paternalism is obvious as he quickly transitions from owner to father of the bride. Employees like the freaks and the girl performers (children and adults) seem to have been just one of his boys or girls. The use of the words "boys" and "girls" itself reveals the subtle workings of paternalism in everyday employee/employer relationships. Overall, however, the ruse of family was important to the operation of the carnival business. A happy family coming to town for a visit was a substantially different image than a good-sized corporation coming to take money from local consumers before heading on their way down the railway tracks with suitcases of cash.

The early 1930s saw a number of lengthy articles on the future of the modern carnival published in *Billboard*. In part, operators were reacting to the pressure of the social purity movements and the expanding reach of the modern state, which sought to shape morality and make good citizens. In part, the changes also reflected much more widespread shifts towards rationalization and professionalization. The carnival was not alone in undergoing this process from the 1910s to the 1940s: the rodeo (often connected, like the carnival, with agricultural exhibitions) underwent a similar transformation.[21] For carnivals, building modern businesses meant courting a diverse audience that included women and children as well as building relationships with local papers and advertisers. In the case of the former, carnivals advertised that their shows were "suitable for the GREAT AMERICAN FAMILY of the UNITED STATES AND CANADA."[22] Businessmen also indicated a need to professionalize operations by keeping shows running on time, ensuring employees were clean and professional, and maintaining overall efficiency. They had the parlance of modern business practices down pat. As F.H. Bee Jr put it, "Carnivals can hardly become as well organized as chain stores, but they can change their methods to keep up with the times."[23] As they became subjected to a variety of laws and regulations developed to forge moral and modern citizens, carnivals needed to maintain professional relations and organize themselves as modern businesses. Like the retail giants of the period, carnivals continued nineteenth-century paternalistic management structures by adopting modern business practices like public relations and customer service.[24]

The idea of family reflected paternalistic practices and was used as an important aspect of public relations. Public relations (through the placing of newspaper articles and advertisements) built up goodwill, made the often large (and sometimes shady) carnival business seem like a big, happy family, and revealed some of the positive "welfare work" carnivals undertook, notably free admission for newsboys and orphans (discussed in chapter 4). Good publicity worked to change the public face of the carnival, making it "clean," familiar, and even "child-friendly."

A narrative of hard work defined the carnival from the economic ascension of show owners to the roustabouts who hustled hard for long hours. This hard work, which transformed landscapes into temporary sites of amusement, often became an informal part of the show itself. Watching the carnival arrive in town and set up was part of the unofficial spectacle. Recalling his boyhood in Saskatoon in the early 1930s, Robert Thompson wrote:

> The Royal American 'Show Train' arrived in the city on Sunday evening, having travelled all day from its previous engagement. Hundreds of

spectators would go out to watch the long train unload. Elephants pulled huge wagons down from the flatcars on the railway siding, working in the light of flares. Unloading was usually finished sometime between 11 p.m. and midnight, and then you drifted onto the fairgrounds to watch the roustabouts set up the midway with its rides, sideshows, gambling booths, souvenir stands, and eating concessions. By early morning the bald prairies had been changed into a youngster's wonderland.[25]

Producing the carnival and working on the freak shows involved a substantial amount of labour, which, as Thompson's recollection reveals, became part of the shows themselves. Carnivals boasted about long train jumps, partnerships with important exhibitions, their business meetings, their earnings, their investments in the socially progressive agricultural exhibitions, and more. Being recognized as businesses helped normalize and legitimate the carnival. It also gave the carnival, like the circus, the appearance of a "totalizing aura of perpetual industry."[26]

In the early 1940s Conklin, in what seems to be a placed publicity article, noted that when "as usual" little boys appeared and "gaped in wonderment" at the carnival being set up, Conklin "management" "asked police to let the swelling crowd" into the park. The article noted that that act "did away with the usual peering through knot-holes, climbing over fences, sneaking past cops, etc." While the little boys watched in wonderment from the inside of the carnival grounds, the company also hired "an estimated 70 local men." The press release made good on two fronts: entertaining local children for free and supporting the local economy through employment.[27] A different press release placed in a local paper quoted Frank Conklin as saying that with a staff of four hundred the carnival left "many hundreds of dollars behind" in local communities, supporting everything from butchers to local beauty shops.[28] The carnival needed to fight against the lingering criticism that they were American companies swooping into Canadian communities, taking money, and leaving with nary a dime spent locally. In this regard, professionalization led to some very practical initiatives. Throughout the 1940s Conklin invested in paving midways. Sawdust and dirt caused no end of problems for operators, especially when it rained and the midway turned to almost impassable mud. As Patty Conklin noted in a 1948 article he wrote on midway design, paving the midway also had "psychological" benefits in mitigating some of the "transitory" reputation of carnival companies. Conklin argued: "A permanent midway also

3.1 Photograph of carnival workers. Galt Museum and Archives, Lethbridge and District Exhibition, July 1953.

serves to discount the theory so prevalent among the general public that a show company takes all the money out of town."[29] It was an obvious sign of the carnival's local investment.

In times of crisis good PR was essential but in relation to the freak show had become increasingly subtle. Importantly, by the 1930s the freak show and the individual acts that composed it no longer figured prominently in advertisements – they were simply expected as a key part of the carnival – but they were included in a variety of newspaper articles. In 1938, for example, Conklin shows played in Hamilton under the sponsorship of the local Lions Club, and an advertisement included the words "Circus Side Shows." A photograph and article in the *Hamilton Spectator* revealed that the shows included "a four-foot-high African bushman, who is 104 years old" and "African pinheads."[30] By the early 1940s carnivals had a host of strategies including placing traditional advertisements and placing pre-written articles that were virtually indistinguishable from other print copy in local papers. Newspaper articles could provide longer and more alluring descriptions than advertisements. Placed articles written by the show employees also ensured that the advance and current press was positive. For readers, the difference between placed articles and those written by local reporters would have been very difficult to distinguish, lending a sense of local approval to the shows.

During the Second World War, Conklin made carnival amusement seem essential for supporting the war effort. As James G. Gardiner, minister of agriculture, explained in a special article in *Billboard*, war meant changes for exhibitions and carnivals. The need to mobilize for the war meant that the buildings and grounds of exhibitions were requisitioned for accommodation and training. Federal operating grants for the exhibitions were also reduced.[31] In 1939, with the start of the Second World War, the CNE grounds were used by the Department of National Defence. The CNE continued to operate until the spring of 1942, when the grounds were used year-round as a military camp. After the end of the war in 1945, the grounds were used as a demobilization site. The CNE started up again in 1947.[32] Conklin hosted the Fair for Britain in Riverdale Park instead, which included Jack Halligan's Side Show.[33] In an advertisement that appeared in the *Brantford Expositor* on 10 June 1944, the carnival's publicity machine went into overdrive:

> We must back them up as the battle intensifies and, as each day is a day nearer to victory, it is our job to back to the limit our men and women who are giving their all on far-flung battle stations. Whatever our job, in industry, on the farm, in an office, wherever it may be, we must give our best every day. We must buy and hold War Savings Certificates, Victory Bonds and support the Red Cross and the many other necessary appeals. And to do a bigger and better job we must have recreation and entertainment. It is important that in these strained times we all have sufficient recreation and entertainment. Again this year, we are pleased to be able to play to thousands of service men and women, war workers and people in all walks of life, giving them good clean entertainment and contributing in a small way to their recreation and enjoyment in leisure hours."[34]

Amusement and consumerism for a good cause made having fun seem like patriotism.

Placed newspaper articles could also reveal companies' philanthropic efforts. In 1941, a standard copy placed by Conklin in local newspapers declared "Carnival Performers Help War Charities" and promised that 25 per cent of proceeds from the midnight show would go to The Evening Telegram British War Victims' Fund.[35] Ensuring that the customer had a good experience and would return again next year was the foundation of consumer relations for large carnivals. In his 1939 book *History of Fairs and Expositions*, H.W. Waters reminded readers of the importance of the midway in building future audiences. Targeting youthful fair-goers interested in the midway, he argued, "plays a great part in building up the 'Fair-going habit.'" Adult nostalgia for the delights of the midway could be cashed in by future fair organizers.[36] Conklin worked hard to cultivate audiences including children and seniors.[37] Strategies publicly shifted from fleecing rubes to providing service to customers, although in practice this shift was incomplete and probably more theoretical than actual. Nonetheless, good PR and good customer service went hand in hand. In 1942, a newspaper article in the *Regina Leader Post* made extensive mention of Conklin employee identification cards that reveal the carnival's mix of paternalistic and modern business practices. The paper reported that the cards had "Patty Conklin's code" printed on the reverse. The code went:

> Never show your temper. Indulge in no sarcasm. Permit other people to have views. Never contradict an irritated person. Keep unpleasant opinions to yourself. Be considerate of the rights and feelings of others. Always use pleasant words. Take time to be polite. Never order people about. Be gracious and accommodating. Always grant a reasonable favor. Don't try to fool your caller – he may be a smart man. AND MAKE SURE YOUR WAY IS BEST BEFORE INSISTING UPON IT.[38]

It is unlikely the identification cards actually characterized the behaviour of workers on the carnival, but the code was important in setting standards for customer relations and reveals how paternalistic practices extended from the mythic personas of the self-made man that defined each individual carnival to the individual pockets of workers on the carnival.

Like all modern businesses, carnivals were defined by a mix of twentieth-century ideas of consumer relations and nineteenth-century paternalistic practices. Some of these developments caused concerns for local citizens, who, especially in Ontario in the 1920s, saw the carnival as a sign of moral depravity and of the Americanization of Canadian culture. As businesses, carnivals negotiated a complicated system of regulation involving all levels of government. Professionalization was reflected in the need to keep to a strict and well-planned schedule. Rationalization structured the twentieth-century carnival.

Travel and Transportation

The self-made man provided inspiring tales of the American dream and cozy narratives of the carnival as a family. These narratives obscured what was in reality a hierarchical structure of owners, managers, and workers, the latter of whom were defined by the tasks they performed to keep the show on the road. The carnival's modern business practices were rationalized for efficiency, and nowhere was this more obvious than in their routes. Moving hundreds of employees across the continent was no easy task. It required coordination of transportation (trains and barges), planned schedules well in advance, and routes that moved logically from one community to the next. PNE officials noted this issue (as discussed in chapter 2) as well as the need to coordinate circuits to attract good carnivals.

For all members of a show, the travel was constant. Shows made money only if rides were operating, booths had people playing, and performers were on stage. The Canadian carnival season was typically between May and October. The winter season was busy for organizers attempting to secure lucrative contracts for larger exhibitions and the best of the western circuits. Other shorter dates for individual stands would fill in the schedules that frequently took companies across larger portions of Canada. While developments in the railway made travel much easier in the twentieth century, there was still a need for significant organization in advance.[39] The schedules were often very tight, and the days of setting up, performing, and taking down were long. Days off from exhibiting meant days of expenditures with no revenue, so owners attempted to book dates one after another. Such planning and gruelling schedules could mean the difference between solvency and bankruptcy.

Small circuses like the Coop and Lent Circus (also known as Coop and Lent's New United Monster Shows) tended to play short stays, which required frequent set-ups and take-downs. Coop and Lent's toured for about three years from 1916 to 1918 with about twenty railway cars. The sideshow included snakes, a tattooed man, a fat woman,

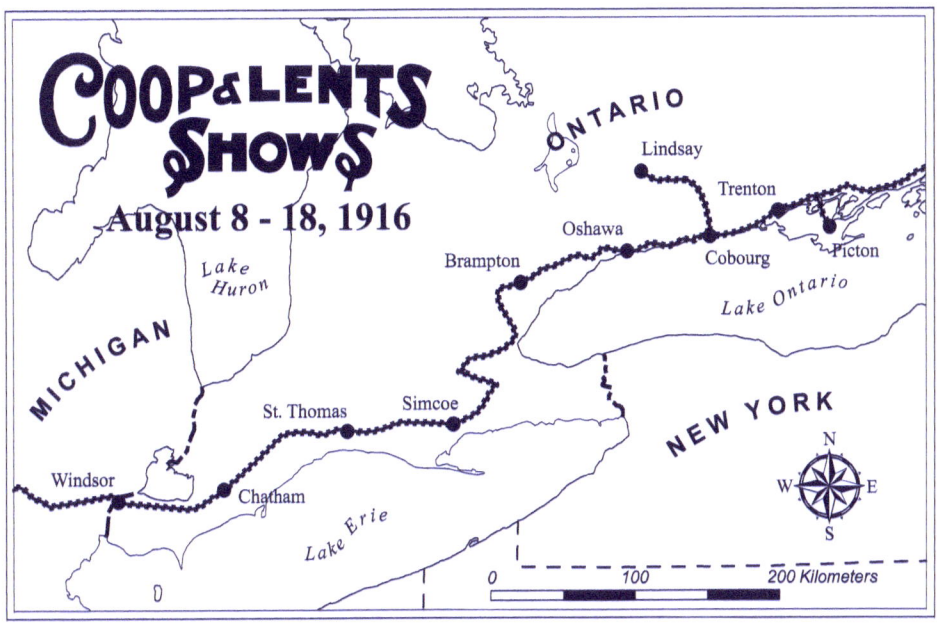

3.2 Map of Coop and Lent Circus's route for 1916.

cooch dancers, and other shows.[40] In 1916, the Coop and Lent Circus's schedule included ten dates in ten different cities and towns in southern Ontario in the month of August alone.

Coop and Lent's Circus travelled by rail. For example, in southern Ontario, they travelled on the Canadian National Railway or the Grand Trunk. The Lord's Day Act prevented shows from occurring on Sundays. Coop and Lent struggled financially; in 1918, they declared bankruptcy and had their wares, including animals, auctioned off.[41]

Often the distance between shows meant more days off, and in this regard, the Canadian geography was a challenge. Conklin bragged of the distance his carnival covered in 1927 in an article submitted to *Billboard* magazine: "The railroad jumps in the territory we traverse is an item that takes a stout heart to face. Our longest jump is 1,000 miles. The total mileage traveled on the season is 7,000 miles." That year, the show was scheduled to play at nineteen fairs in twenty-four weeks.[42] In 1937 and 1942, Conklin reported other sizeable "jumps in venue" to *Billboard*. The first was from Prince Albert, Saskatchewan, to Brantford,

Ontario, and the second was from Brantford to Brandon, Manitoba. Distance travelled could be a source of pride, but also expensive.[43] In 1931, Conklin wrote on the "Carnival Problems in Western Canada" for *Billboard*. In the article he noted the stiff haulage fees, the "widely scattered" cities, and the big "jumps" in territory cobbled together by rail and water transportation.[44] The Canadian west posed particular challenges to efficient travel, given the vast land and small and dispersed population. As Conklin noted, this created challenges with everything from advertising to planning. Advertising was important. Advance press agents (and fixers) would travel ahead of the carnival and paper the towns and cities with posters, newspaper advertisements, and carefully placed newspaper stories. He continued, lamenting that, "In all four provinces where we've been showing there are only about 15 cities of more than 5,000 population. That means, speaking generally, the customers in our territory are very widely scattered. And that means we have to put up a lot of paper and do a lot of long-distance chasing around the country before we can tell ourselves that the show has been thoroly [sic] advertised. That costs money and constitutes yet another peculiarly Western Canadian problem." The benefits, however, seem to have outweighed the significant issues Conklin detailed at length since the western circuits were actively pursued by a number of shows and showmen in the period.

Other shows travelling and performing in western Canada experienced challenges with travelling and scheduling. The James Patterson Trained Wild Animal Show, along with Gollmar Bros. Circus, performed in thirteen locations for one day at each location in Saskatchewan over a two-week period in 1917.[45]

For larger, more established shows that held contracts for local fairs and exhibitions, the stays in communities were longer. For example, in 1920, the Polack Bros.' "Twenty Big Shows" held the contracts for exhibitions in Fort William and Ottawa. Their stays in other communities in Ontario were also longer, typically stretching over a five-day period. For example from 5 July to 18 September, they performed in six communities stretching from Fort Frances to Ottawa.[46]

Travelling carnivals crossed the Canada–US border regularly, and one carnival historian has referred to the North American nature of carnivals as "midways sans frontières."[47] Although border crossings were subject to scrutiny, show circuits tended to develop along a north–south rather than an east–west axis, choosing to cross the border multiple times to play in towns on either side of the border as they moved east

3.3 Map of the James Patterson Trained Wild Animal Show and the Gollmar Bros. Circus, 1917.

to west. In the summer of 1922, for example, the Ringling Bros. and Barnum and Bailey Combined Shows, travelling by train with almost 1,200 employees, had a route that included three full months on the road with interspersed Canadian and American dates. Travelling from Bangor, Maine, to Spokane, Washington, the shows crossed the border into Canada twice to play dates in Quebec and Ontario and then Manitoba, Saskatchewan, Alberta, and British Columbia.[48]

From Edmonton, the company wrote an enthusiastic article for *Billboard* about its first year playing dates in Western Canada. In particular, "the management expresses itself as delighted with the railway services thru this country and says it has been given faster runs and better all-round service than in any part of the United States."[49] The infrastructure and management of the railway lines were important to the daily operation of carnivals.

In 1954, the Canadian E.J. Casey Shows travelled extensively in western Canada and northwestern Ontario. Casey's shows, which

3.4 Map of Polack Bros.' "Twenty Big Shows" route, 1920.

originated in 1935, funded by his military pension, carved out a special niche in northern communities in addition to the western B and C circuits. The 1954 season reveals the extensive travel and wide reach of the carnival, which began on 8 May in St Boniface, Manitoba, travelled around Manitoba and northern Ontario, and closed the season in Timmins, Ontario, on 22 September. Casey's shows included rural remote communities in Manitoba and Ontario such as Shoal Lake, Rainy River, Emo, and Kapuskasing as well as other small locations where all the equipment was brought in by barge.[50]

As shows carried on throughout the twentieth century, technology changed and other challenges appeared. In 1934, Conklin announced the purchase of steel railway cars to replace its wooden ones.[51] One year earlier, the wooden cars had carried Conklin's carnival throughout its season from 6 May to 6 October. Over those months, the carnival had engagements in thirty communities in Ontario, Manitoba, and Saskatchewan, travelling east to west and then returning east again.[52] Despite the Depression, the carnival carried on and continued to place

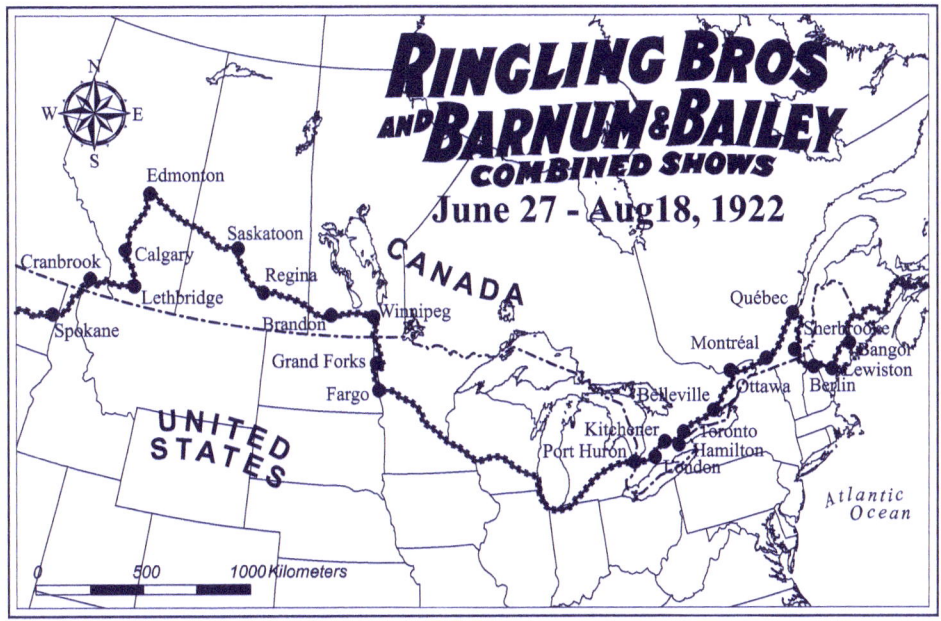

3.5 Map of the Ringling Bros. and Barnum and Bailey Combined Shows route, 1922.

want ads for workers in *Billboard* magazine. In 1937, Conklin's Shows advertised for "talkers for the front of shows" and a lecturer for a crime show for dates in Ontario and Canada, including Guelph from 10 to 15 May and Windsor from 17 to 22 May.[53] The years of the Second World War provided their own challenges in regard to transportation. In 1943, with the ongoing war effort and domestic restrictions, the Canadian government declared Conklin's train travel through western Canada to be "non-essential." Western fair organizers lobbied the federal government to loosen this restriction and achieved moderate success. Until 1945, Conklin's show went on, but reduced in size.[54] That same year, the E.J. Casey shows cancelled their dates on the western C circuits to focus on the western B circuits. As one of the first carnivals to travel exclusively by road, the Casey show had to convert to rail because of wartime restrictions on gasoline.[55] In 1950, Casey opened a permanent amusement park called Rendezvous Park in Winnipeg because of the strain of constant travelling. In 1957, he sold his travelling shows to an American showman.[56]

Most carnivals continued to travel by rail until the end of the Second World War, when trucking became a less expensive option due to the establishment of an improved road infrastructure. The desire to travel by rail continued in the postwar period, and in 1963 George Barnum of the P.T. Barnum Circus wrote Donald Gordon, president of the Canadian National Railway, with a detailed proposal to have circuses return to the railways. Barnum claimed to be representing other American circuses and showmen.[57]

Life on the Road

Travelling conditions varied depending on the workers' place within the hierarchy of the organization. Owners frequently had their own private cars, while managers or other professional staff shared well-appointed cars with separate sleeping and living quarters. By 1941, the Conklin Shows carried 45 cars, designed to carry 700 people, and included a private, five-room, air-conditioned coach for its owner.[58] Such luxuries reflected the hierarchical nature of the organizations. Freak show performers found travel benefits to be more modest. Extraordinary contracts with big shows, like Krao's 1916 contract with the Ringling Bros., offered the perk of a larger trunk.[59] Given the constant travel and the fees associated with it, being able to travel with more goods or travel in more comfortable, less crowded conditions spoke to a person's status. Labourers on the shows lived in gender-segregated units, and the living conditions were spartan.[60] In the 1950s, Marcel Horne, working as a roustabout with a carnival, described his sleeping conditions on the train in stark terms: "I slept in a car with about thirty other carnies who never washed and stank like hell – hoboes, roughies, and idiots."[61] Soon after, he was promoted to assistant electrician, and his living conditions improved. Horne's career spanned the transition from railways to trucks. When travelling by truck, he noted, he always "lived comfortable on the road sleeping in a trailer," even if it was "always cold."[62]

Life on the road meant that work was nearly constant as shows played for a full day, took down, moved, and set up in another town, often within a day or two. Horne described the difficult conditions. He wrote: "We played each town for two or three days. Every time we finished, all the equipment was torn down, loaded in trucks and we drove all night to the next town, anywhere from a hundred to five hundred miles. No sleep – and as we arrived we set it all up and operated as soon as it was done – no sleep – Christly tired."[63] As Davis notes in her history of the American railway circus, "roustabout labor – for humans and animals – was gruelling."[64] Conklin's train was described as including bunks for sleeping but they were "never made up because most of the passengers are pretty busy and sleep when they get the chance."[65] Such conditions, along with the highly transient workforce, set serious challenges for any workers who wanted to organize.

Living on the road and constantly travelling included practical challenges. Hazel Elves, who was born in West Vancouver in 1926 to a "carnival family" (her father, Frank Hall, was a long-time carnival worker), operated various sideshows for the Wagner Carnival from the 1920s to the 1960s. The Wagner Carnival played at large and small sites across Ontario and western Canada, with the biggest show happening at the PNE, where they played in 1960.[66] In her early teens she began travelling with her father in the Canadian M.F. Wagner Shows, and noted that washing was difficult. In her autobiography she recalled: "Washing and keeping clean were quite a chore when we played two towns a week. If one was fortunate enough to find a dry cleaning store the second the train stopped, one was lucky if the cleaning was ready before the show left town again." Too shy to bathe with the show girls "unabashedly in their quarters," Elves had the financial means to purchase twenty-seven shirts to rotate and occasionally splurged on hotel rooms twice a week to keep clean.[67]

Throughout the period from 1900 to the 1960s, general labourers or roustabouts were a constant source of transient cheap labour who helped keep the shows on the road and in the black. Hazel Elves recalled that into the 1940s "carnies were still pretty shady. They had to be to earn a decent living as the set wage was a pittance." Elves also noted carnies were bound by a tradition of hard work taken on "without a whimper."[68] Wartime labour shortages made the situation more acute, a sharp change from the Depression years when well-educated men sought work on the carnival.[69] The Canadian E.J. Casey Shows, which toured the northern rural towns in Ontario and the prairies from the mid-1930s to the 1950s, lost six male employees in one day during the early days of the Second World War. For those who remained the labour could be intense. In 1944, Ward Hall, who later became a successful show owner and manager, first joined the Cole Bros. Circus at the age of fourteen in Denver, Colorado, but he found the work too strenuous and quit.[70]

Employees embodied the ethos of hard work, sometimes for no pay. In 1964, after a few bouts in jail and a few more stints operating sideshows, Marcel Horne was back working as a general labourer on the Canadian carnival circuit. Employed by Roy Cooper, who had a sideshow based out of Peterborough, Ontario, Horne describes "working hard as hell from early morning to late at night – pulling nails, building, painting, fixing the equipment. I got no pay but it didn't matter because I wanted none – meals and tobacco were my wages. I learned more and more about side shows as the days went by. This was my home. At last I felt a part of something. Strong relationships grew between me and the owners of the carnival."[71] Free room and board was a significant benefit, but the manly discourses of working hard and proving oneself were equally powerful. For general labourers working behind the scenes a measure of anonymity and the ability to disappear, if need be, at any time were other benefits. Working conditions, however, were often challenging and sometimes dangerous. In 1947, Harry Lewiston reportedly lost fifteen teeth "when walloped by [a] snake."[72] Accidents caused financial hardship for the E.J. Casey shows in both 1946 and 1948, when road accidents damaged equipment and caused delays.[73] In 1946 Casey reported a litany of issues by August alone. These included: accidents with cargo and a passenger bus; a "mild" cyclone; and injured workers (due to a snake bite and an accident with a bed-of-nails act).[74] As Christopher Dummitt argues, taking and managing risk was a modern masculine work endeavour. Elves described two routes for carnies: work hard without complaining or leave.[75] Some managers also complained that days of rain caused them to lose employees such as workers in charge of set-up and take-down.[76]

Carnies often described themselves as social outsiders bonded against "normal" members of society. Certainly some employees found a sense of acceptance and belonging in what might resemble a familial relationship. The carnival world has been described as difficult to pierce for journalists and researchers given the unwritten codes and insider language of the carnie but those insider codes provided a basis for identification.[77] For Marcel Horne it was the freak show in particular that provided a sense of belonging. He wrote, "The side show people became my idols – I felt close to these people considered outcasts and freaks. Our eyes locked when we met, and even though I was not disfigured, I knew inside I was really one of them. I hung around the side show, digging these strange people who were content in their own world – not putting people down but getting put down by others."[78] Horne, who grew up in Leamington, Ontario, recalled a childhood of poverty and social isolation. He described "getting pushed around and laughed at by other kids who threw stones because we were different, poor, wearing hand-me-downs. Here come the Horne kids – stay away from them, they're different. Not like us. Being poor is a sin."[79] If not a literal "freak" (he worked behind the scenes initially and then later as a fire breather), Horne and many others saw the freak show as representing the ethos of difference yet acceptance in the carnival.

This sense of solidarity sometimes led to a contemptuous and violent relationship between travelling carnival workers and locals.[80] In 1920, the superintendent of the OPP described a fight between carnies with the Sheesley Shows and locals in Belleville, Ontario: "A bunch of local toughs ... undertook to beat up some employees of the show. The management immediately took care of the people who were visiting the shows and drove the toughs away. There is no doubt that blows were struck and the police were called and everything was quiet. For the balance of their stay in Belleville the Show paid for two policemen to do duty on the ground while the show was running."[81] Hazel Elves recalls frequent violence and harassment by local youths and adults to which carnies from across North America had developed the alert "Hey Rube." If a carnival worker yelled "Hey Rube," others would come running, ready for whatever altercation might arise. As Elves described it: "That is the call which arouses the carnies, armed with crowbars, wrenches and any handy tool to rush to the defence of the carny kingdom. It is usually preceded by a riotous hassle between a carny and a local."[82]

The sense of belonging on the carnival was, as in other areas of Canadian society, influenced by race, ethnicity, and gender. Horne's feeling of acceptance did not mediate his views of First Nations' sideshow visitors in northern BC communities, which he described as "wild, poor towns with only Indians on welfare."[83] Elves described the polyethnic community of workers in more cheerful terms, but used common ethnic and regional stereotypes, revealing the persistence of differences among the carnival family. She described "'Newfies' from Newfoundland [as] big rough hard working fellows who usually worked on the rides; hunkies from North Bay, Ontario, good-looking, uncouth and loyal; transplanted Scots, American slickers, wild Irishmen, Ashkenazi Jews and many French Canadians all fitting into their respective stations and getting along like one big scrappy family." Gender mattered, too. Elves describes "corn fed" farm girls picked up through the prairies who worked briefly on the girl shows before returning home "in disgrace" or going "haywire over some idiot who treated them outrageously."[84]

Elves's description of some female employees hints at a more nefarious side of the carnivals' paternalistic practices. For female workers, sexual vulnerability and violence were additional factors. In their memoirs a few showmen recalled sexual favours being demanded and expected from potential female employees. Harry Lewiston recalled setting up his own girl show at the request of Max Linderman, who had contracts with fairs in eastern Canada in the 1920s. Lewiston describes asking the women to strip for him as part of their "interview" and having sex with one woman. In the case of the latter he writes: "I knew at this point that I wasn't going to leave that room without having some of this. Even if it meant rape." Having started up his own sideshow in the mid-1960s, Horne recalled, "I wouldn't hire a girl unless I knew she would go to bed with me." In one instance, he had hired a woman he only ever refers to as a "Hindu," but when Horne discovered her past work as a sex worker, he abandoned her without paying her last day's wages.[85] Sexual vulnerability could be deepened by negative racialization. These stories of rape and sexual coercion, however, did not pierce the organizations' carefully crafted public image of carnivals.

The sideshow community was a fractured one; under the surface carnival families ran the gamut from loving and caring to dysfunctional and abusive. The Ontario Provincial Police dealt with a range of cases in the 1920s alone, including stranded employees, a fight among workers, and a letter from a disgruntled employee alerting the police to illegal activities.[86] In her memoir, Elves describes a hair-raising scene of domestic violence in the 1960s, where a female employee and her two small children took shelter in Elves's room to escape a drunk and violent boyfriend who was chasing them with a switchblade.[87] Sometimes the violence among employees drew attention from government officials. One example illustrates the divisions as well as the surveillance and attempts at regulation by the federal Department of Manpower and Immigration. In the early hours of 1969 police in Fort William, Ontario, broke up a "confrontation" involving about twenty-five employees of the South Dakota–based Thomas Shows, who were playing the local Canadian Lakehead Exhibition. It seems that one employee drew a hunting knife in order to "protect himself against others who were coming at him with tire irons and chains." Later that day, Harry Hill appeared in court and was sentenced to a fine of $35 plus costs or five days in jail. The incident was reported to the Director of Immigration Operations, Ontario Region, in a memo from the officer in charge in Fort William. The officer described the employees as being "of the lowest category" and went on to state that "our local police force were not impressed with the calibre of many of those making up the balance of the show and feel that prostitution and other criminal elements were present." Immigration officials had further concerns. In a memo from the Regional Admission Consultant, Prairie Region to his Ontario counterpart, J.E. Fleming noted that the bond for the Thomas Shows had increased annually from $500 to $2,000 per year in 1965 because of personnel issues. In 1962, in Regina, the carnival had covered the costs for the "lengthy illness" of an employee. One year later in 1963 only $858.11 was returned to the company as the remainder was used to cover the detention costs of two employees. Officials noted that the carnival was uncooperative, that "for some unknown reason" they were paying less than the requested $2,500 per annum bond when crossing the border into Canada despite a recommendation passed in 1961, and had a reputation for firing or stranding employees while they were still in Canada. As a result, the bond required from the show for crossing the border was increased to $5,000.[88] If such events had the potential to reaffirm stereotypes of the carnivals' rough and rowdy reputation, they also reveal the cracks in the narrative of peaceful, loving, and caring family relations.

Whether it was for the work or the feeling of belonging or a combination of both, running away to join the carnival still appealed to young people. In spite of the hierarchies of difference at the carnivals, diverse youngsters made their way to the show trains. For some the carnival was an escape. Scholar Steve Koptie recalls that his "grandfather escaped a residential school ... and ran off with a travelling carnival in the 1930s."[89] Koptie's grandfather was not alone in running away to join the carnival. Other boys and girls seem to have taken the initiative. In 1932, Jean Nanson disobeyed her father to attend a carnival in Edmonton and never returned home. She ended up running her own successful girl and wild animal shows.[90] Decades earlier, in a police report from 1914, officer A.B. Boyd, travelling with the Ringling Brothers throughout southern Ontario, noted that he had turned three boys, who had followed the show from Toronto to Kingston, over to the local police.[91] In the flurry of criticism over the sideshows in Ontario in the 1920s, the Brantford city council reported that two young women had left town to follow the show throughout southern Ontario. A few distressed parents contacted authorities to track down a son or daughter who had joined a sideshow. In 1920, Mrs G. Brown, "A Lonely Mother" from Midland, Ontario, wrote the chief of police in Toronto requesting information about the whereabouts of the Brown and Dyer shows, as her seventeen-year-old son had run away to be with them. She wrote: "I don't want him with a show and he won't answer my letters. I am a Widow depending on my family he was such a good boy till he got in with the show."[92] A week later, the superintendent of the provincial police wrote to Brown and informed her that he had met her son in Windsor, Ontario, and that the son was planning on getting work "on a boat sailing on the lakes."[93]

A similar letter came from Frank Whit, whose sixteen-year-old brother had taken temporary work with the World's Famous Shows in southern Ontario in 1920. Although Whit and his sister had recently moved to Billings, Montana, and the World's Famous Shows were back in the United States, Whit requested assistance from the Ontario Provincial Police. He wrote: "We do not wish our kid brother to get away with that rough show. Would be glad if you would try and locate him for us. We were told that you are the proper person to whom to apply." The superintendent informed Whit that the show had left Ontario and that there was nothing further he could do to help.[94] In the documented cases there seems to have been little that authorities could do or were willing to do given how frequently the shows travelled and crossed municipal, provincial, state, and federal jurisdictions.

For children and youth who ran away to be in the circus there is little explicit evidence of the reasons why they defied their families and joined the shows. Evidence from the wider literature on family history in the period provides some context for speculation.[95] For Indigenous children forcibly removed from their families, residential schools used horrific tactics to pursue a policy of what the recent Truth and Reconciliation Commission of Canada (TRC) has described as "cultural genocide."[96] Although very risky, running away to the carnivals could be an act of resistance and survival for these youngsters.[97] For non-Indigenous children, it should not be surprising that parents and siblings turned to the police to try to find family members who had run away with the carnival. Girls and boys deserted their families for a host of reasons, although the problem of desertion was seen as more grave for girls, who bore the brunt of social penalties for "deviant" behaviour, especially when related to sexuality.[98] Many adults assumed that children left home because of a combination of flawed parenting and the lure of modern commercial culture. Children ran away from home typically because of physical and sexual abuse, conflict over dating practices, household responsibilities, and conflict over expectations of obedience and behaviour. The widow Mrs Brown (quoted earlier) seemed to lament the loss of her boy as well as his financial support. For working-class boys and girls, expectations about work and turning over money to parents caused conflict, as did expectations for unpaid domestic labour.[99] Running away with the carnival was an opportunity to escape difficult if not abusive homes, to travel, to work, and perhaps, to find acceptance.

Short-term and seasonal workers sometimes fractured the carnivals' sense of community. By the 1950s and continuing into the 1970s there were sharp divisions between employees who were "carnies" – expected to work lifelong for the carnival – and more temporary seasonal or local workers. In 1956, the *Winnipeg Free Press* included an article entitled "Co-Eds Carnival Stars," which detailed how white, female university students from the US worked as performers to pay their tuition. One woman described her co-workers in ways that clearly distinguished her from them. She told the reporter: "The people in a carnival are a combination of show business and gypsy with a bit of conscience thrown in for flavor – they train their dogs beautifully but often neglect their children. They may rob kids blind on the midway, but they will donate time and money to charity. Friendly and natural, they can be as narrow and discriminate as any in a small town."[100] In turn, carnies themselves often disparaged these types of employees, describing them as a "first of May" – a name that reflected a limited stint with the carnival. These distinctions were important to a sense of carnival identity. Carnival work was often defined by a sense of individualism and freedom from the boring lives led by the "marks" (suckers/consumers), whose routine work in factories and offices was hampered by rules, repetition, and a permanent sense of place. As fire eater Josephine Brenner told one unnamed reporter, she was bored with the dull repetition ("eat, work, sleep") of life, wanted to travel, and was uninterested in industrial work.[101] The perceived freedom and "rugged individualism" that marked lifelong carnival work provided some carnies with feelings of superiority over members of "normal society."[102] Yet, by the 1970s, carnies lamented the professionalization and mainstreaming of their world as few "old-time" committed carnies were left working the circuits. In 1977, Dottie Marco, described affectionately as the Godmother of the Midway, lamented the standardized hourly wages and punch cards. She described the Conklin show she worked for as "a big corporation. It's run like a downtown office building. All shows are getting to be the same."[103] Even the carnie went corporate in the 1970s.

Carnival Labour and the Freak Show

Part of the carnival's allure was the narrative of family and acceptance exemplified by the image of the freak. The freak show was also a site of labour and a deeply fractured one. The carnival was performative labour and consisted of both seen and unseen work. The exhibitionary complex required that certain bodies perform in public to edify a particular social order. For the most part, however, the performers' labour was erased in the process. The point of the shows was simply to reveal either the shape of the world's natural order or the flaws in that system. The gloss of the show meant that freaks were simply to "be themselves" on stage or to dance and sing in such a basic, silly way as to be ridiculous. Yet, this was an illusion that ignored the theatrics of the freak show as well as the toll it could take on the body of the worker (performer). Further, the widespread belief that disability compromised workers' bodies or excluded them from work altogether diminished the perception that freak shows were labour. Work, autonomy, self-determination, and moral virtue were bound up with working identities and liberal notions of personhood and dignity. The body's perfectability and machine-like efficiency were fragile in the face of bodily difference. Historically, extraordinary bodies were classified into disparate categories: cripple, idiot, moron, and so forth. All these categories were differentiated based on ideas of which part or parts of the body had failed to achieve the threshold of normal. Although the technical, historical definitions appealed to science, the categories remained at best fuzzy around the edges precisely because they reflected not something in particular but an absence, or what Garland-Thomson has described as "*any* departure from an unstated physical and functional norm."[104] Those departures often rendered bodies as unproductive and as economic drains on society that required long-term care in institutions. The notion of disabled bodies as unproductive ignored the poorly paid but often essential labour of inmates.[105]

In the freak shows performative labour was rendered invisible and the humanity of the performers questioned. For example, in 1930 C. Hailock wrote to the editor of the *Globe* admitting to being haunted by a freak show he witnessed in Toronto: "To think of such a show being allowed in a decent city like Toronto is something awful. Poor creatures (half human, half animal) put upon a stage for everyone to stare at is a most degrading sight to say the least ... Such monstrosities should be hidden away in some asylum, away from curious eyes, and kindly treated. Surely they must have come from foreign parts, then why are they allowed in Canada?"[106] This short letter speaks to two important points. First, it reveals how disability and race were conflated in the exclusion of certain people from full claims to citizenship, as Lennard Davis has observed in other contexts.[107] Eugenics theory shaped Canadian immigration law in the early part of the twentieth century, which banned entrance to Canada by those deemed "feeble-minded," a category that worked to restrict the immigration of people with disabilities as well as those of "undesirable" ethnicities.[108] Hailock's reference to "foreign parts" and the questioning of freaks being "allowed in Canada" speaks to a widespread policing of the nation's imaginary cultural borders. Freak bodies did not fit the image of strong, hardy, and healthy Canadian bodies; messages of animality in the shows were clearly convincing to Hailock. Problematic bodies, like those of the less-than-satisfactory recruits of the First World War, were to be found and "fixed" to preserve the health of the entire nation, but different species or "creatures" clearly could not be "corrected."

Second, to observe the freak show as the display of monstrosities to "be hidden away" speaks to "progressive" agendas of care that sought to institutionalize different bodies in order to protect society. Often the freak show was pitted as an alternative to institutionalization (the latter historically seen as a measure of progress and care) or, later, the "dependency" of the welfare state. The work versus welfare dichotomy is based on the assumption that bodies with disabilities cannot be productive bodies. Yet, midways operated long hours and performances needed to run almost continuously to maintain the flow of cash. For example, in 1934 the CNE midway was open from 9 a.m. until 10 p.m., the catalogue promising "continual performance" of Rubin and Cherry's "new and greater Midway."[109] Through long hours on stage, performers would repeatedly hear similar stories told about their bodies, perform similar routines, and act in particular ways over the course of a day in what could amount to an exhausting and monotonous routine. Teasing audience members, refusing to perform properly, or shouting back at unruly spectators were ways workers could express agency and/or deal with boredom.

Throughout the twentieth century, the freak show has been defended as a safe place for people who would otherwise experience pain, ridicule, and mistreatment. Writers defending the freak show as a site of inclusivity sometimes blamed embarrassed families, who were ashamed at a disabled family member, but were still willing to accept the financial rewards that went with sideshow exhibition. In the early 1950s, American writer William Lindsay Gresham, who travelled with the World of Mirth Shows, explained:

> Some side-show proprietor hears of a local child who is fantastically different from his neighbors, seeks him out and tactfully presents the advantages of working in show business. For many this comes as a welcome release from an intolerable home situation in which the parents are cruel or for some twisted reason "ashamed" of their offspring. But even with loving parents, the desire to be self-supporting in a world where he is accepted on his basic value as a human being is often enough to cause the oddly formed person to take the plunge. Many an individual, mercilessly beaten and imprisoned by his parents, has come to be the support of those parents in later years and often of a raft of shiftless brothers and sisters, all perfectly normal.[110]

Similarly, when showman Ward Hall described working with Betty Lou Williams, who performed as "the Double Bodied Girl" with her asymmetrical conjoined twin, he noted her generosity and the fact that she "contributed heavily to the well-being and progress of her family."[111] Sideshow owners and employees repeatedly defended their exhibits and way of life as being more humane for those labelled "freaks." As Elves explained,

> Many people who do not fit into everyday life find their way into the carnival grounds: people with physical disabilities or those condemned by nature to be different from the so called norm. Freaks you call them, side show entertainers we call them; human beings with feelings and desires as all people have. They fit in, on the carnival, as most carnies see people for what they are. They are able to work with each other performing the many hazards which constitute carnival life. Here they are all safe and if people wish to stare at least they must pay for the privilege, affording these special people a chance to work and maintain themselves.[112]

Feelings of acceptance were legitimate for some performers. Fat Lady Celesta Geyer recalled the limited but still important power she had in being able to speak back to audience members or at least make them pay for the privilege of staring.[113] This experience was not universal. It was, however, part of a discourse of legitimation that positioned the carnival as an accepting alternative to mainstream society.

In 1934, the *Toronto Daily Star* condensed and reprinted an article from the *Reader's Digest* by way of the *New Yorker*. It began: "The biographies of circus freaks are sometimes success stories of the most inspiring kind. They tell how, for example, an obscure village idiot rose to be an internationally celebrated Pinhead." The article went on to tell the story of a boy who became a "mental case," "suffering under the inspection of inquisitive eyes," who had broken out of institutions three times before. "As a freak among freaks he found life endurable and his professional spirit soon developed to render him insensitive to the shuddering curiosity of spectators."[114] The perspective that the freak show was better than other forms of dependency was vigorously defended in the late 1960s when some southern American states, which remained popular and profitable venues for freak shows, threatened to ban them.[115] Show people pointed to the troubled histories of welfare and institutionalization. The stigma of government assistance was almost universal in the twentieth century, and beginning in the 1940s and 1950s, Canadians expressed concerns over the institutionalization of children and people with "mental retardation."[116] By the 1960s, de-institutionalization had gathered a momentum that would continue to usher in changes from the 1970s onwards. Owners and managers told alternative stories of fame, independence, and joy that worked to defend their place in the exhibitionary complex. If Victorian British freaks withstood reformers' efforts because they could fulfill white, bourgeois notions of work, gender, and domesticity, twentieth-century freaks did so by pointing to the opportunities of work and more humane treatment outside the locked doors of an institution. This had the effect of briefly turning middle-class notions of progress and care on its head.

Owners and managers sought out people to work as freaks for exhibition and were aware that good freaks required staging and narrative. In a 1933 statement, Clyde Ingalls of the Ringling Bros. and Barnum and Bailey Combined Circus revealed the cultural production of freaks. He stated: "Aside from such unusual attractions as the famous three-legged man and the Siamese twins combinations, freaks are what you make them. Take any peculiar looking person, whose familiarity to those around him makes for acceptance, play up that peculiarity and add a good spiel and you have a great attraction."[117] *Billboard* magazine regularly carried "want ads" by show owners and managers searching for freaks from the early 1900s to the 1960s. In the early 1900s, for example, it carried word of extraordinary births under the standing heading "Freaks to Order." The column announced everything from "remarkable roosters" to the exhibition of the Ormsby quadruplets, who had been born in Chicago in 1901 and were displayed at dime museums in Chicago until a child welfare agency shut the exhibit in 1908.[118] Details varied in the descriptions, but the 1 February 1902 column carried a more fulsome announcement than usual: "A two-bodied baby, with one head and two faces, was born at Omaha, Neb., Jan. 18. One face is in the natural position, the other at the back of the head. The bodies are joined together from the neck to the hips. The child died in a few hours. The body will be exhibited. It is the only case of the kind on record."[119]

In 1914, one want ad for a company in Montreal stated, "Freaks – Wanted – Freaks All Kinds of Living Freaks, for Finest Arcade in Canada." Two other ads appearing in the same issue in 1919 spoke of the benefits of Canadian stands. The Canada Carnival Company was looking for shows and concessions for the Cartier Centenary Celebration, while Hugh E. Jay of Strathroy, Ontario, was looking for "clean shows" for Old Home Week that year.[120] In 1959 Sam Alexander's want ad for his show at Belmont Park in Montreal read: "Freaks – Working Acts Bally Runts and Bally Acts WANTED." The advertisement promised the "best of treatment and working conditions."[121]

Sideshow owners and managers competed over securing contracts with parents of different or unusual infants. Some of them were frank in their near-global searches for freak acts. Clyde Ingalls, who recruited for the Ringling Bros. Barnum and Bailey Combined Circus and the British Bertram Mills shows, reportedly toured the world annually in search of legitimate (not faked) acts. An article in the British *Sunday Chronicle* reported: "He finds them in all sorts of odd places – some in circuses, some dragging out a miserable existence trying to earn an ordinary living in spite of their disabilities." Ingalls was quoted as saying, "We often come across freaks by chance. My agent once spotted one in a circus audience. He was the tallest man he had ever seen. He was then a clerk. His salary now is that of a successful businessman." Ingalls noted, though, that searching for freaks could be frustrating. He stated that "searching the world for freaks is a difficult and tiresome business. Wild goose chases are frequent. I once travelled a thousand miles to see a 'freak,' only to be disappointed and find that, as a commercial proposition, he was 'no go.'"[122]

In the early 1940s, freak show managers "discovered" Dolly Reagan in Saskatoon, where she was working at a local fair selling tickets.

When she joined the sideshow she worked as "The Ossified Lady" until her death in 1991. According to one showman, having been "born with a rare bone disease causing a calcifying of the bones, she became an ossified woman, her head, right arm, and hand can move, while she is otherwise totally rigid."[123] Later in life, Reagan recalled, "My parents were always worried about me because they didn't want to see me put into an institution or become a burden to my brother after they died, and yet what could I do to earn a living?" When a showman offered her fifty dollars a week to join the freak show, she did, describing the wages as "a regular fortune!"[124] In 1942, Jack Halligan's World's Fair Freaks for Conklin's Frolexland wanted freaks "for long season and sure pay."[125] Individual performers also advertised their services. That year, one "Singing, Dancing Fat Girl" advertised for work with the following description: "460 pounds actual weight, desires to join beef-trust revue, museum, park or carnival."[126]

Some sideshow freak performers were able to negotiate contracts for shows on an annual basis, allowing them the flexibility to search out more lucrative contracts or better living conditions. Beginning in the 1930s, sideshow performer Celesta Geyer worked for a number of different shows and then contracted herself out to them as an independent player. After her first season working for another fat performer, Jolly Pearl, in the late 1920s, Geyer discovered *Billboard* magazine and its slew of "Fat Lady" want ads. For her second season, Geyer's husband "narrowed the deals down to two or three" before they decided to join S.W. Brundage's "Congress of Fat People."[127] In subsequent seasons, Geyer contracted out to shows that made her the best offer. Similarly, in the 1940s, Celia Raucci, who performed as "Fat Woman" Winsome Winnie, worked at the Palace of Wonder, World's Fair, Chicago, and the Barnum and Bailey Combined Shows before joining Conklin. Raucci was described as "580 pounds of cheerful personality ... who loves every minute of her work with Conklin's Shows ... despite the fact that people look upon her as a freak."[128] Performers like Geyer and Raucii could be more difficult to manage because of their ability to negotiate their own contracts and make their own demands, although these expressions of agency were not always appreciated. Elves recalled that her father described the fat show as one of the most difficult to manage, as the performers were constantly fighting among themselves and being "stubborn and demanding" and "very temperamental."[129]

In addition to paid weekly wages (if any) and room and board, freaks also sold *cartes de visites*, postcards, pamphlets, and Bibles to augment their earnings. These sales could significantly add to a performer's earnings. Celesta Geyer, who joined a sideshow as a fat lady in 1927, recalled in her autobiography that fellow fat performer Jolly Pearl told her, "There's really money in these pictures ... They cost so little and sometimes we sell over a thousand a week. A lot of folks will give us more than a dime. I've gotten as much as five dollars for ones of these ... We'll make some nice ones of you too, and you'll be surprised to see how many people will want a picture of such a pretty fat girl."[130] These souvenirs acted as future advertisements for performers, boosted performers' incomes with their sales, and allowed visitors to take a tangible piece of the freak show home. That said, not all freak show performers got the profits from selling Bibles. Harry Lewiston sold cheaply acquired Bibles at his freak show and kept the profits for himself.[131]

By the 1950s, sideshow employees charged with finding new freak acts lamented wider social changes that were making their task more difficult. American show woman Helen Alter complained to *Time* magazine in 1958, "You can't get good freaks any more. Seems like they're all dying off." Her husband, Lew Alter, concluded, "They take 'em and put 'em in an institution now ... They don't want 'em exposed. Now I ain't going to mention any names, but I know an insane asylum where there's three good pinheads right now. But you can't get 'em out."[132] Others recalled that the freak show was more than a venue for work and described it as a site of care and social acceptance. Paternalistic and maternalistic ideas of care for acts were common in framing sideshows as a site of warm, even familial labour relations and acceptance. As sideshow manager Elves recalled of her father, "Dad was a champion among many of these people who were dependent on the carnival for survival of mind and body. He protected many and came to their assistance whenever called upon."[133] What this protection and assistance amounted to is unclear and certainly varied between shows, which seem to have been primarily concerned with finding new acts and increasing profits.

When real freaks were unavailable, sideshow owners and independent contractors made their own. In sideshow terminology, faked freaks were called "gaffed freaks." Owners also collected the remains of "deformed" fetuses. On 14 March 1914, an advertisement appeared in *Billboard* that read, "Freak Infants Like Siamese Twins, for sale. Lifeless. Weight 14 pounds. Front connection. Address 2032, Portland, Oregon."[134] Lou Dufour, who contracted freak shows to Conklin into the early 1970s, is credited with inventing the "pickled punk" shows –

exhibiting fetuses and infant bodies in jars – in the late 1920s.[135] These shows of medical-like specimens were sometimes faked or gaffed using modified toy dolls; according to one showman, such displays remained profitable well into the 1970s.[136] In a *Maclean's* article in 1950, Toronto-based Archie Johnston recalled making mermaids, an octopus for the Johnny J. Jones show (from one that died in Johnston's hotel bathtub), and a two-headed baby (referred to as a monster) for the Victory Shows. Sideshow operators worked their spiel and ballyhoo to convince audiences of the authenticity and rarity of their attractions. In regard to the preserved gaffed two-headed baby described above, the *Maclean's* article noted that "the operator threw in a scientific lecture by one of the carnival girls who was rigged up in a nurse's uniform."[137] How convincing these attractions were to audiences is unclear. Perhaps some were fooled while others relished seeing through the elaborate facade. Others still may have felt cheated or duped out of their money.

The range of work and salaries varied considerably on the freak show, as did the reasons for performing as a freak. Differences in gender and race could be considerable, with women making less than their male counterparts and negatively racialized peoples making less than whites. Black off-stage workers were sometimes employed to act as "Zulus." Initially, the Boer War made actual Zulus fascinating for British and North American audiences. Farini capitalized on the conflict in South Africa by bringing men, women, and children to British and later American audiences. He began in 1879 with an unnamed boy exhibited as "Zulu Kaffir Boy" and an infant known as "Umgame, the Baby Zulu" before exhibiting adult women and men. Although Farini invented a fantastical tale of his "adventure" in Africa procuring the "savages," the reality was likely far more tame and domestic.[138] For show owners and managers, however, the authenticity of the display was not an issue.

Savagery was an invention of performance. By the early 1900s, the word "Zulu" had lost any sense of specificity in the world of circuses and carnivals and came to signify, as it was used in *White Tops*, "negroes who participated in spec. [spectacle]."[139] More often than not, managers gaffed or faked such displays by hiring poor African Americans to perform as "savage" Zulus. More than likely, black labourers took on these roles because of the bump in their pay packet or simply as an employment opportunity. In 1937, Torontonian James Gibson was employed on the CNE's sideshows in one of these types of displays. As a young black man in Toronto during the Depression he would have found his

3.6 Possibly James Gibson at the Canadian National Exhibition, 1930s. Canadian National Exhibition Archives.

opportunities for work limited by race-based hiring practices that kept black men segregated in particular jobs and sectors, as well as by the overall economic contraction and stagnation that marked the period. Yet, his recollection of working on the freak show reveals two important points: first, that performers were sometimes "in" on the invention and found audience reactions to be ignorant and laughable; second, that for some youthful employees the perks of employment went beyond simply wages. Gibson recalled, "I think I was 12, 12 or 13, or somethin' like that. And I actually had to do a little dance; I invented a little dance to do. And all the people were '... this African' [laughs] ... Course, I liked it 'cause ... on the Midway, I could go into any place I wanted to go. I had a free pass. I can go behind the scenes and watch how they do things. It was great for me. Then I had to wiz back for my act, right?"[140] Gibson's understanding of his work serves as a reminder that employees could shape their own experiences in meaningful ways in spite of wider structures and discourses that framed the work of the freak show and the staging of the freak in very particular ways.

Nonetheless, opportunities to work on the sideshow were shaped by race in three ways. First, black working men had fewer options for employment on the sideshows beyond the role of labourer or waiter, which were poorly paid positions. Second, since Zulu and other primitive performances supported racist ideology, the performances reaffirmed local racial hierarchies. As Bernth Lindfors argues, "It may have served British colonial interests to portray subjects in Africa as freaks and savages, but these negative oversimplifications and distortions also served the vested interests of those in the New World who sought to deny basic human rights to black people."[141] Third, the better-paid performances did not cause conflict with other employees invested in maintaining a racial hierarchy within the travelling show itself, since the boost in pay was related to the extra work of performing.[142]

Negatively racialized workers found themselves to be vulnerable in other ways. For example, poor American blacks travelling with shows were vulnerable because of their poverty and their racialization by the Department of Immigration, which made border crossings more precarious. In the 1920s, increasingly strict immigration laws in the United States and Canada also created or exacerbated problems for Asian workers and disabled workers, for whom xenophobia and discrimination meant that they had much more difficulty crossing the border.[143] In some Canadian towns, negatively racialized workers were targets of violence by locals. Violence among employees also brought out local prejudices.[144]

For many workers who laboured as performers, the conditions of their work and their treatment also varied, depending on their perceived levels of autonomy and agency. Child performers and those with intellectual disabilities had little control over the means of their display and were sometimes bought and sold as commodities or traded through informal adoption. For children, their ability to negotiate and exercise agency in regard to their employment was circumscribed by age and ability. How much of their pay they controlled could be limited as well. Some performers were not paid. In his book *Monster Midway*, William Lindsay Gresham notes that "'Pinhead' Julius Graubart's pay was sent to his family."[145]

Harry Lewiston, a barker and owner who frequently toured in Canada in the period, briefly described the treatment of two white American microcephalic performers referred to only as Kiki and Bobo. They were billed as albino African pygmies and, as with other shows, called Pinheads. As Lewiston writes, "You can't tell people, 'Now, we've got these idiots here; take a good look at them.'"[146] In preparing shows for Conklin, Lewiston found four related black children with microcephaly in Mississippi. He allegedly promised the family one hundred dollars a week, plus food and transportation. By his own recollection the travel conditions would be rough because "this carnival doesn't have berths or accommodations for colored people." The family would have to travel in the coach car and sleep sitting up. For Lewiston this arrangement was preferable to having to rehire other workers he had exhibited as part of his Darkest Africa exhibit earlier in the 1930s. He could barely stomach working with Doc Drewer, the "owner" of two men with microcephaly whom he treated like animals to keep them performing.[147] Although the evidence is merely suggestive of broader trends, it seems that the most vulnerable employees – who tended to be poor, young, negatively racialized, or intellectually disabled – sometimes laboured on stage without wages or access to their pay. They also travelled in rougher conditions (even by carnival standards) and could be abused.[148] If parents collected money in exchange for allowing showpeople to take their children on exhibition, it is unclear if any of the money ever trickled down to the performing child, either in childhood or when they grew up.[149]

Even for performers who may have consented to or chosen to work on the freak show, wider social, economic, and cultural limitations due to discrimination and stigma played a role in limiting options. At least two twentieth-century female sideshow performers, Mary Ann Bevans and Grace McDaniels, made their living by performing and being known as "ugly." On 23 August 1924, the *Globe* ran the article "Ugliest Woman upon Earth Possesses Beautiful Soul." Five years earlier, Mary Ann Bevans had won one thousand pounds in a beauty contest run by the *London Daily Mail* for being the "ugliest woman in the world." By the 1920s, beauty contests were popular in modernizing societies like Canada, Britain, and the United States. They were the perfect, if still contentious, spectacles to reveal the widespread assumption that equated health with beauty. In 1924, Bevans was in Toronto performing at the Canadian National Exhibition (CNE) with the Johnny J. Jones show – the company awarded the CNE's lucrative midway contract that year. Bevans had been born into a large working-class family and had been widowed with four children in 1914.[150] Bevans told the *Globe* reporter, "Yes, I don't mind being ugly if it will help my children to get along in the world."[151]

Grace McDaniels's story was similar, although her discomfort with performing as a freak is notable. McDaniels appeared at the CNE with the World of Mirth Shows in the 1940s. In *Life* magazine, her performance was described as follows: "Heavily veiled, Mrs. McDaniels mounts the platform inside, Jean Frazier introduces her and then the mule-faced woman removes her veil. The crowd stares, some of them turn their faces away. For what they see is a face so disfigured by an enormous wine birthmark that the nose and upper lip hang down in a great purple mass, the chin sags upon the chest. The good-looking young man at the ticket box outside is Grace McDaniels' son. She has supported herself and raised her boy by her work in sideshows."[152] The owner of the show described McDaniels as "a grand trouper" and noted that she made a good living, lived among friends, and had the respect of her colleagues.[153] According to another showman, however, McDaniels's freak performances caused some personal discomfort when she began to perform in the 1930s. Initially, she did not want to be referred to as a freak, wore cosmetics during the performances, and would cover her ears during the spiel. The barker was uncomfortable with this arrangement, but was told by the sideshow owner to continue because she was costing a great deal.[154]

Bevans and McDaniels were not alone in their economic needs, which should not be surprising given their status as single mothers in a society that privileged and expected a male breadwinner. Single women with children were and are a group disproportionally represented among the poor, and many relief schemes in North America were reserved for men.[155] Overwhelmingly, the sideshows defended themselves as organizations where people with disabilities could find paid work.[156] This was an argument that was difficult to criticize, and even American judges in the 1960s who struck down legislation banning the freak show, found the argument compelling.[157] In 1973 the trade publication *Bandwagon* included a lengthy article on freak shows. Author Andrew J. Bakner made a lengthy argument for the continuation of the freak show as employment. He wrote, "Freaks are not ashamed of the 'abnormality' so why should potential patrons be ashamed of walking under the banner that has the words 'Side Show" painted on it? After all, if nobody came into the tent there would be no Annex of Wonders and all the strange and curious people inside would have to live off unemployment checks."[158] The dichotomy on which that argument was based, however, worked only if there was already deeply seated social exclusion in regard to disability and work.

Conclusion

Carnival businesses fashioned professional identities with figureheads of hard-working, self-made men. They used modern business practices of public relations and used paternalism to promote and shape their organizations. If carnivals perpetuated the myth of a band of hard-working outsiders led by successful self-made man, that told only part of the story of the carnival in Canada. The level of organization and planning required to keep the shows on the rails and roads was impressive. The ability to make a profit, and the contractual obligation to share the profits, helped to keep the shows alive. In reality, the carnival was monitored by different governmental departments at the federal, provincial, and municipal levels as it criss-crossed the country in search of fresh audiences. As an essential part of the carnival, the freak show received subtle but important support from many different individuals and organizations. Yet, freak show labour was often not seen as labour, although showmen defended the opportunities for work it provided in the face of criticism. They argued that it was better than welfare or institutionalization. That the established options of freak show versus welfare "dependency" were so firmly established as to provide the basis for such an argument needs to be understood in the context of the rigid policing of the normal body. The primary erasure of the actual labour, like the idea that dependency was the only other option, was rooted in the idea that disabled bodies could not be productive bodies because they were "abnormal." The next chapter looks more closely at disability on the freak show as it intersected with medical discourse, ideas of normality, and race.

Chapter Four

The Twentieth-Century Freak Show: Medical Discourse, Normality, and Race

In 1924, the *Globe* published an article about the off-stage lives of sideshow workers toiling late into the night. Beyond the difficult labour in keeping the shows running, the article revealed something far more important to the operation of the freak show – fundamental differences based in the body:

> Occasionally a very late visitor, slipping through the half-light of the gates will see a tiny man, a foot or two high, and a huge giantess of seven feet or so, walking up the road together. The late visitor rubs his eyes and wonders. Or perhaps it will be a very fat man and a tiny little Japanese girl; or a couple of midgets on their way home. For after midnight the freaks are freaks no longer; and one thinks they gaze wistfully at the hot-dog stands, the games of chance or the intriguing buildings, and wish they, too, could join the jostling crowds from whom they must be forever separated by the painted show front.[1]

The conflicting sentiments of not being freaks and yet forever being perpetual outsiders show how deeply connected their performances were to social and cultural understandings of the body. Freaks might have been a product of narration and staging, but those performances were rooted in the idea that there was such a thing as a "normal body." Neither the freak nor the normal body was natural or absolute, and sociocultural factors played a significant role in creating conditions for their existence. These factors also changed over time. Twentieth-century exhibitionary culture continued to interweave science, medicine, and ideas of normality.

An important aspect that contributed to the continued existence of the sideshows was the definition of "disability" and the solidification of the "normal body." Both required ideological redefinition related to medicine's understanding of the body. And, as this chapter will argue, there were close and ongoing connections between medicine and the sideshow, not the least of which was the appropriation of medical discourse to shape the narrative inventions of freak performers. Such narratives worked to legitimate the shows as well as the audiences' interest in them, making the shows seem more educational and less like simple gawking. Throughout the 1900s, sideshow operators remained responsive to popular issues in medical science and adapted displays accordingly. By the 1930s, sideshows came to focus on their ostensible connection to medicine and on their performers' remarkable abilities despite their apparent disabilities. Such strategies appealed to medicine's power to both interpret and explain the body, as well as the profession's social cachet. Focusing on ability made the normal seem wondrous and added another element to the shows that explicitly worked to evoke pity or censure, although audience members' reactions were unpredictable. Freak show operators were attuned to changes in medical discourse and its influence in popular understandings of the body and reshaped shows because of it, but some shows continued untouched by these changes. The scientific racism of the nineteenth century and the racial taxonomies developed from it persisted in pseudo-ethnological shows in almost unchanged form. If the appropriation of medical discourse modified displays in relation to disability, scientific racism was so deeply entrenched as to remain unchanged.

Fundamentally, the shifts in the display of the sideshow in the 1900s that did occur were based on wider shifts in the understanding of the normal body. The project of normalizing the body presumed that the normal body could be defined, policed, and regulated on an individual as well as a national level. Normal bodies were presumed to be useful and productive. As Wendy Mitchinson and Mona Gleason have argued in regard to women's and children's bodies, medicine absorbed social and cultural ideas of gender, sexuality, and age into the paradigm of medical science, which in turn enforced and shaped ideas of the body.[2] The normal body was white, male, and adult. This formulation of a normal body was not a conspiratorial project but more simply a reflection of the fact that doctors and medical health professionals were also human beings working in the context of particular times and places.

Nonetheless, physicians and medical discourse were powerful and persuasive in shaping social order. All of this matters to the sideshows because they, too, were embedded in a much wider world than the carnival themselves. Whatever they invented by way of fictionalized characters representing freak identities, both the discursive tricks and the people they represented had their basis in so-called normal society. Managers, owners, and operators borrowed from popular medical and scientific theories as they worked from popular understandings of disability and race. As such, sideshows were intimately enmeshed with "normal society," especially in regard to medicine and its culturally dominant understanding of the body.

According to Bogdan, sideshows developed two dominant strategies for presenting (or, more accurately, inventing) freaks. Sideshow owners fabricated the life histories and biographies of freaks by stretching the truth through exaggeration, half-truths, or outright lying.[3] Bodgan argues that freak presentation can be understood to fall within one of two modes: the exotic, which "cast the exhibit as a strange creature from a little-known part of the world," and the aggrandized, which "endowed the freak with status-enhancing characteristics."[4] As Bogdan concludes, however, such modes are best seen to characterize nineteenth-century freak shows, as the wider social understanding of disability shifted at the end of the nineteenth century to provide a different interpretative framework. He writes, "By the early twentieth century the audience was learning to view freaks as people who were sick – who had various genetic and endocrine disorders – and exotic hype lost its appeal. The razzle-dazzle died down, to be replaced by a more staid presentation."[5] This is partially true. The exotic mode continued well into the twentieth century in Canada, where the freak show continued racist spectacles of blackness and indigenity, as discussed in the last section of this chapter. Nineteenth-century scientific racism had a long history and continued to base understandings of alleged racial difference in biological theories.

Twentieth-century freak shows, like their nineteenth-century precursors, were largely fictionalized performances that revealed simmering tensions regarding disability and race in dominant society. In the twentieth century, however, the fantastical tales of performers largely disappeared in favour of more "factual" displays. This shift reflected wider cultural changes in the understanding of disability, gender, race, and class as part of the prevailing medicalized understanding of the body. As Durbach has recently argued, historians need to be sensitive to the "popular and professional cultures of the body that we often erroneously think of as separate and discrete."[6] Durbach points out that nineteenth-century British freak shows "were self-consciously engaging in a dialogue with the medical profession."[7] The "sickness" of disability, which relied on the medicalized notion of the normal body, became another mode of presentation. Overall, within a powerful framework of modern exhibitionary culture, twentieth-century freak shows provided a popular outlet for dominant and subversive messages of the normal body and ability. Freak shows provided an accessible means to consume visual images and messages about what constituted normality.

Medical Definitions: The Normal Body and the Monster Body, 1850s–1900s

By the 1900s, the dominant, but not exclusive, interpretation of the body rested with professional medicine. Wider social and cultural changes from the philosophical understanding of the soul to the supremacy of liberal individuality to the slow rise of modernity and the professions gave medicine extraordinary interpretive powers in determining and treating the body.[8] Throughout the 1700s and 1800s, in North America and Europe, physicians had worked to consolidate power, competing with other religious and secular groups and struggling to determine the medical management of everything from birth to death. By the early 1900s, medicine and medical science had become powerful social and cultural forces in Canada, the United States, and Britain; the entire medical profession had rapidly changed in the mid- to late nineteenth century, simultaneously consolidating its power and fracturing into specialities. The regular profession had shored up enough significant power to dominate the interpretation of the body and its illnesses or differences, and doctors found that their reach was well beyond the simple treatment of individual bodies. In short, medicine was not confined to clinical rooms or to individual patients. By the early decades of the 1900s, physicians had come to be regarded as public experts.[9] Medical knowledge was woven into popular culture by way of advertisements for everything from cosmetics to cleaners.[10] As the experts in treating and interpreting the body, physicians played an important role in defining and treating disability for the wider public. Yet the hold of medicine as the dominant power over the body was never absolute. Alternative medicine and belief systems continued to be available, and people could accept, dismiss, ignore, or challenge dominant medical science, depending on their own beliefs and what worked for them and their families. As the literature on twentieth-century efforts to produce scientific motherhood reveal, physicians continued to compete both with other groups, religious and secular, and among themselves.[11]

Physicians' desire to gain access to and examine the extraordinary body was the result of the belief in the normal, ordinary, or average body, and the seemingly pressing need to define and measure it using modern, scientific metrics. Medical practitioners struggled to make sense of the variations in the human body, while modernity itself was informed by the belief in progress and the perfectibility of the body. By the mid-1800s, standards or norms had created an ideal "normal" body, but achieving it and maintaining it throughout the life course seemed difficult. For physicians, the problems of the human body were many and required intervention and treatment to cure and correct if the body was to run as smoothly as a machine.[12] Industrialization, combined with processes of normalization, linked discourses and practices that Lennard J. Davis has described as "the social process of disabling."[13] Solidifying a measurable and thus socially enforceable concept of the normal, able body required various other social changes, including the science of measuring and surveying (e.g., phrenology), and the development of statistics, which gained rapid influence in the 1830s.

In 1842, a Belgian statistician named Adolphe Quetelet came up with the concept of "the average man," setting the stage for an allegedly precise and scientific formulation of what was to be considered normal. Using the new social science of statistics, Quetelet defined the normal body based on supposedly universal human laws just being discovered through modern science.[14] Quetelet provided average heights for boys and men from five months of age until maturity in their twenties. A decade earlier in 1832, he had developed the Quetelet index, which was renamed in 1972 as the body mass index.[15] Throughout his career, Quetelet refined his work, setting the stage for the emergence of statistics to classify the normal body. Defining "the average man" created rigid boundaries that, when crossed, created scientific anomalies like midgets, giants, and fat people – all subjects that drew Quetelet's attention. (Deviancy was also extended to the mind, giving rise to the concepts of the criminal mind and tendencies towards criminality.) Quetelet argued:

> It may be imagined ... how much importance I attach to the consideration of *limits*, which seem to me of two kinds, *ordinary* or natural, and

extraordinary or beyond the natural ... When the deviations become greater, they constitute the extraordinary class, having itself its limits, on the outer verge of which are things preternatural, or monstrosities. Thus, the men who fall, in respect of height, outside of the ordinary limits, are giants or dwarfs; and if the excess or the deficiency of height surpasses the extraordinary limits, they may be regarded as monstrosities.[16]

The average man, however much it was claimed to be universal, was a discursive construct that policed normalcy as much as it played a part in its invention. The now-common definition of "normal" emerged in European languages around 1840. (Before this time, "normal" meant perpendicular.) Other derivative words were redefined in the same period: "normality" appears in 1849, "norm" appears about 1855, and "normalcy" in 1857.[17] These concepts were developed in relation to the body. Before the 1840s, there were ideals to be envied or looked upon for beauty's sake. The middle decades of the 1800s saw normalcy as a universal concept that could be measured, policed, and enforced. It is unsurprising that the term "freak" – as a term related to unusual anatomy – emerged around the same time, in 1847.[18] As part of a widely solidifying scientific discourse, Quetelet and his contemporaries, including Isidore Saint-Hilaire, defined the dominant paradigm for seeing the extraordinary body in rational and scientific terms rather than in wondrous and superstitious ones.[19] The perceived defect was a problem to be solved.

The concept of the average man proved to be immensely popular in North America as it did in Britain and other countries.[20] In 1893, Harvard anthropologist Dudley Sargeant displayed sculptures of the average American male and female at the Chicago World's Columbian Exposition. Sargeant had a sculptor make these figures based on measurements he had taken of thousands of students at Harvard and other colleges in the United States. The anthropometric figures in the Anthropology Building at the exposition could have been juxtaposed nicely with the freaks on the midway.[21]

In 1896, physicians George M. Gould and Walter L. Pyle published a hefty encyclopedia entitled *Anomalies and Curiosities of Medicine*. In their introduction, the authors offered justification for their focus on the unusual:

> The strange and exceptional is of absorbing interest, and it is often through the extraordinary that the philosopher gets the most searching glimpses

into the heart of the mystery of the ordinary. Truly it has been said, facts are stranger than fiction. In monstrosities and dermoid cysts, for example, we seem to catch forbidden sight of the secret work-room of Nature, and drag out into the light the evidences of her clumsiness, and proofs of her lapses of skill, – evidence and proofs, moreover, that tell us much of the methods and means used by the vital artisan of Life, – the loom, and even the silent weaver at work upon the mysterious garment of corporeality.[22]

Gould and Pyle's rather elegant description reveals the close connection between normality and abnormality. Throughout the text, they offer samples from freak shows as evidence of various conditions and abnormalities. Famous nineteenth-century freak show performers, like conjoined twins Chang and Eng and Little Person Tom Thumb, alongside other less famous exhibits like conjoined twins Rosa and Josepha Blazek, appear as evidence throughout the book. The encyclopedia includes a variety of "major" and "minor" "terata" and makes frequent reference to monsters and cases of monstrosity. As Gould and Pyle suggest, abnormality was a window onto normality. Rather than being two separate enterprises or processes, abnormality and normality were twinned and interdependent.

By the end of the 1800s, when Gould and Pyle were compiling their work, teratology – literally, the study of monsters – had established itself as a medical speciality. Scientific study of abnormal births became a subfield that Saint-Hilaire coined teratology, from the Greek *teras*, or monster,[23] the study of severely malformed fetuses and infants. Discoveries in genetics, embryology, and obstetrics helped to solidify the field. For example, animal experiments, in embryology sought to discover the source of monstrous births by intentionally creating them.[24] For much of the 1800s and 1900s, medical professionals referred to children born with various anatomical "defects" or "anomalies" as monsters. As chapter 1 revealed, monsters had long held an important social and cultural place in pre-modern and early modern societies. Although "freak" was a product of the mid-1800s, it coexisted with "monster," rather than neatly replacing it. The expansion of the discourses on "the body" in the 1800s created a much more complicated terrain.[25] As much as the elaboration and explanation of "the body" were rooted in scientific discourse, the results were far from precise or clear. "Freak" emerged as a concept in both popular and professional discussions and "monster" remained an important medical term into the middle decades of the 1900s. In 1964 the *Journal of the American Medical Association* received a letter from Dr H.E. Thelander criticizing the use of the term monster in relation to disabled children. He wrote, "Parents of a deformed child have enough difficulties without the additional implication of having produced a 'monster.' Is it not, therefore, rather monstrous for physicians to call infants, no matter how greatly deformed, 'monster'?"[26]

Like other areas of medicine, teratology also absorbed the popular discourse of eugenics. Eugenics, a theory first espoused by Francis Galton, posited that carefully controlled breeding could produce a stronger and better race of people. Charles Darwin himself believed monstrosities to be "some considerable deviation of structure, generally injurious, or not useful to the species."[27] Social Darwinism was laced with white, middle-class values and held those ideals as universally good. One of the key principles of social Darwinism was that hereditary traits from the biological to the sociological were determined by germplasm. As R.J. Bean reported in "The Etiology of Embryonic Deformities" in the *Canadian Medical Association Journal* in 1926, the deformities resulted from "defective fertilization," "defective maternal environment," or "defective germ cells."[28]

In Canada, physicians and progressive reformers took up the challenge of eugenics, and disabilities from intellectual delays to physical differences were often seen in moral terms and as *naturally* undesirable. In 1924, the *Canadian Medical Association Journal* ran an article on a recent lecture on anomalies at the Hall of the Royal College of Surgeons in Edinburgh. The unidentified author declared:

> At the present time we can do very little for these cases, either in the way of cure or of prevention, but whatever may be attempted in the coming years in the way of devising therapeutic measures applicable to such deformities, prevention is surely better than cure, and happily the progress of modern knowledge in the field of teratology seems to afford some grounds for entertaining the humane anticipation that the day will come when such unfortunate sufferers will not even enter upon their miserable existence. This is an ideal, and may never be fully realized; nevertheless it is our duty to strive to approximate thereto as closely as may be.[29]

Identifying, studying, and containing the monstrous body were important roles for physicians in the treatment and perfecting of the individual and national body. The individual health of citizens became increasingly important as indictors of the health of the nation. If Canada was to achieve its natural destiny as a northern nation of strong, heathly, Anglo-Saxon individuals, the health of citizens and of those trying to immigrate needed to be carefully monitored. Doctors were compelled to take on this work for a number of reasons, ranging from their own prestige in treating and caring for the body to pressure from their patients.

In the early decades of the twentieth century, other specialties continued to develop as professional medicine began to focus on the small bodies of infants, children, and adolescents.[30] As Mona Gleason has argued, "the main rationale for the development of pediatric specialization was the understanding that child and infant bodies were markedly different from adult bodies and that those differences could prove pathological. Merely being small and young, in other words, required medical attention."[31] Over the course of the 1900s, pediatrics grew as a speciality of its own, although it had first emerged in the early nineteenth century.[32] In Canada, pediatrics was institutionalized with separate wings for child patients in hospitals, beginning in Montreal in 1822 and, later, separate hospitals like Toronto's Hospital for Sick Children in 1875. Beginning in the late 1800s, medical education reflected the growing presence of pediatrics with the development of separate courses in medical education, as well as specifically dedicated faculty; by 1935, the University of Toronto's Faculty of Medicine established the first separate department.[33] The development of pediatrics was premised on the uniqueness of the child body, childhood illnesses, and treatments for children.

If all children were potentially vulnerable simply because they were children, children with disabilities were seen as a special category both medically and culturally. Falling outside the realm of "normal" meant that these children would never mature into "normal" adulthood, and dominant medical discourse argued for early identification, intervention, and containment of "the disabled child."[34] In cultural terms, disability compromised the dominant discourse of the protected child. If many other children by the 1920s were seen in largely sentimental terms, disability rendered this almost impossible. As Nic Clarke shows, disability framed childhood in older economic terms, especially in regard to usefulness, where children's value was seen in their ability to productively contribute to the family economy.[35] Many professionals perceived children with disabilities as problems to be contained and, if possible, cured and solved so as not to "drain" family or government resources, although individual families did not always see their children in these terms.

Disability was equated with an assumed natural (as opposed to socially produced) disadvantage, but not all disabilities were the same. "Monstrosity" was most frequently used to describe cases of congenital defect or deformation (or something made apparent in very early childhood) as opposed to acquired disabilities from accidents or disease. General practitioners called to attend to families and birthing mothers were often the first physicians to become aware of a specific case. In the Canadian medical literature, they tended to be the ones reporting on monstrosities. Children born with unusual anatomy, for example, were interesting enough to be reported to the wider medical community through various high-profile medical journals on a fairly regular basis. As the professional medical journals reveal, this was also an important moment for seeing, accessing, defining, and reporting on the monstrous body. Physicians reported on cases of monstrous births that they attended at a difficult labour, or on cases that appeared in hospitals where parents were looking for care for a related or unrelated condition. For example, in 1931, Dr P.W. Head of Birtle, Manitoba, reported a case of "a monstrosity in the form of Siamese twins (thoracopagus)" (joined at the throat) from a mother who presented at the hospital after three days in labour.[36]

Cases of so-called monstrosities, those newborn or recently born bodies that exceeded "normal disability" as defined in regard to teratology, made frequent appearances in major Western medical journals like *The Lancet*, the *British Medical Association Journal*, the *Journal of the American Medical Association*, and the *Canadian Medical Association Journal*. Like the pamphlets and cards sold at sideshows, many medical reports included photographs of the body accompanied by a narrative. Rather than allegedly first-person accounts, however, medical reports rarely, if ever, included the patients' voices and were written in a detailed and "objective" manner from the doctor's point of view. The difference between medical and freak show texts was one of degree, not kind. Importantly, however, freak show texts allowed freaks to speak and included their voice, even if the narratives available to them in such a text were limited. Medical reports often convey a sense of excitement at the chance to investigate and report on unusual anatomy. H. Beattie reported "A Case of Anencephalous Monster" in *The Lancet* in 1904 by beginning, "The case described below, of which a photograph is reproduced, may prove of some interest."[37] The boundary between education and entertainment has long been tested in medical reports on patients and in medical museums that preserved "specimens."[38]

Physicians' interest in the extraordinary body was primarily to categorize and treat, with the hope of eradication of the illness, disease, or deformity. As such, medical journals saw their role as one of education and eradication, while sideshows saw their goal as one of education and entertainment.

Despite the developments in experimental embryology, teratology, obstetrics, and public health, the reasons for monstrous births baffled the medical profession, members of which sought to both assign and mitigate parental blame. In the assignment of blame to parents, physicians identified any range of biological or social defects using the pseudoscience of eugenics. Cases of monstrous births were typically prefaced with descriptions of parents' subnormal biology, often including intelligence. Descriptions included the elastic category of "feeble-minded." In attempting to explain the birth of a monster, physicians influenced by eugenics provided details on the perceived health – medical and social – of parents or other family members. For example, in 1933, J.E. Josephson of the Department of Physiology at Queen's University and Dr K.B. Wallers of Rockwood, Ontario, reported on the birth of anencephalic identical twins. They described the father as a labourer, the brother of the mother as having a club foot, the twins' fifteen-year-old twin brothers as having criminal records and being institutionalized in the Ontario Hospital for the Feeble Minded, a sister as having a speech impediment, and an "exceedingly pugnacious" brother. A detailed report of the autopsy was concluded with the following statement: "The occurrence of the condition in both babies, born of a family with low mental development, supports the theory that the condition is an expression of inherited tendencies rather than an antenatal accident."[39]

In other cases, physicians sought to temper any parental blame for the monstrous birth by pointing to evidence of "successfully breeding" in the parents or other offspring. In the 1920s, Dr Clifford Hugh Smylie, a physician in Port Loring, Ontario, recalled a winter in the mid-1920s when he was called to deliver a baby. Upon examining the mother, he felt "a soft mass surrounded with what felt like a circle of sharp teeth." With time before the delivery, he left to consult books "to find out what I had to cope with." Upon his return, he wrote, the mother gave birth "of a child with no skull. We call it an anancephalic [sic] monster. The fact that the parents were intelligent people who already had two healthy children, made it easier to explain that no blame could be attached to anyone or anything for this malformed child. It is a freak of nature that happens rarely and so far is unexplainable."[40]

Other physicians and parents held on to older beliefs in trying to explain the birth of different children. In the twentieth century, physicians continued to debate maternal impressions, the mind–body connection, and its potential impact on a fetus. Maternal impressions were experiences and thoughts of pregnant women that physically or mentally marked their unborn children. While in the 1800s the influence of maternal impressions in teratology was typically described in fairly detailed cases, beginning in the 1880s more critical essays attempted to completely debunk the connection to maternal impressions.[41] From 1900 to 1920, the medical belief in maternal impressions declined but did not entirely cease, and the topic was debated publicly by physicians.[42] A Dr Cawas Homi wrote to *The Lancet* in 1920 to describe a phocomelus (armless) monster born in London, England, that year. Homi described how the mother had witnessed "a discharged soldier in a fit which lasted over half an hour." He attributed the "deformity" to "the strong maternal impression, which led to the arrest of the ontogenesis in the embryonic and neofoetal stage of existence of this child."[43] Homi's conclusion reveals how science and superstition could wed in explaining a monstrous birth. Even well into the century, belief in maternal impressions linked children with extraordinary bodies to discourses of monstrosity, sin, and corporeal warnings. As Wendy Mitchinson has argued, maternal impressions revealed both women's agency in determining their own bodies and a sense of how women and their families understood and bore responsibility for different children.[44]

Sideshow promoters sometimes used maternal impressions to explain the extraordinary body of a particular act. Beyond the medical office, maternal impressions retained currency in pop culture explanations for corporeal differences. For example, Lionel, the Lion-Faced Boy performed into the 1920s with the Ringling Bros. and Barnum and Bailey's Circus's Congress of Freaks. Lionel was born in Poland with hypertrichosis, a condition that causes excess hair to grow on the face and body. He was reportedly born looking like a lion because his mother, while pregnant, had witnessed her husband being mauled to death by a lion.[45] In another example, a pamphlet entitled "The Life History of Howard the Lobster Boy" explained the life of Howard, who performed during the first half of the twentieth century, who was born with hands and feet described as resembling lobster claws. The pamphlet explained that this was the result of his fisherman father who had startled his pregnant mother with an unusually large lobster.[46] The pamphlet, as with all others, was sold as a souvenir.

Monsters, Medicine, and the Freak Show

Monsters were of interest to physicians for a variety of reasons, but their intersecting significance in regard to the sideshow was twofold: first, physicians played key roles in defining normality and its boundaries, as well as disability; and second, freaks were defined by rarity. It is unclear how closely show operators worked with physicians in the twentieth century, if ever, but the overwhelming power of physicians to interpret and define the body meant that biomedical discourse was the key interpretive framework for the body. A 1908 edition of *Scientific American* reprinted an article from the *New York Medical Journal* about "circus and museum freaks," saying that "these humble and unfortunate individuals whose sole means of livelihood is the exhibition of their physical infirmities to a gaping and unsympathetic crowd, are pathological rarities worthy of more serious study than they usually receive."[47] The difference in "study" was certainly one of degree and not kind. Interest in the rare and unusual created shared ground among physicians, sideshows, and audiences, although certainly the reaction varied among these groups.

The relationship between sideshows and medical professionals had been close in the mid- to late 1800s. At the time, physicians still had difficulty in gaining access to "unusual specimens" while, as discussed in chapter 3, sideshow operators had their own means of procuring acts for their shows. Because of this, physicians and sideshow managers entered into mutually beneficial relationships. The doctors could gain access to unusual bodies for examination (with the potential for publication), and in exchange, the show manager would get a blurb for advertisements attesting to the freak's authenticity or rarity.[48]

While more rigorous professional standards led to the end of these types of arrangements, the relationship between physicians and freaks persisted in various ways. Most prominently, sideshow managers simply co-opted medical discourse to give their shows a gloss of scientific knowledge and thus educative amusement. For example, asymmetrical conjoined twins Jean and Jacques Libbera (1884–1936) were featured as an act in the Barnum and Bailey Shows. Jean Libbera had a fully formed adult body with a portion of another lower body coming out of his chest, which was named Jacques. Libbera's pamphlet included the following description:

> The scientific explanation is the fusion of two living germs in the one ovum. Jean Libbera has been examined by the leading Medical and

surgical Experts of both Europe and America. In Paris, Professor Ponier presented him to the Surgical Society and he was pronounced to be the greatest anomaly of nature ever known. In Cologne, Prof. Berdenheimer made a very thorough and complete examination, using the X-ray, and in his report declares there is imbedded in the normal body a formation that resembles a rudimentary head; this he claims has a circumference of about 15 centimeters. Recently Prof. Van Dayse of the University of Gand, Belgium, has given to this phenomena the term of EPIGASTRIC PARASITE.[49]

The medical term "epigastric parasite" referred to Jacques, the partially formed lower body attached to Jean's chest. The emphasis on the term indicates the educational aspects being promoted and gives the freak display a sense of authenticity and even a gloss of respectability. The medical discourse provided a sense of wonder, rarity, and unusualness within the confines of scientific study, framing the freak show not as a spectacle for gawking but more like a scientific study.

The relationship between medicine and the sideshow was complex and reflected the differences among physicians. In the medical literature, the sideshow appeared in a variety of ways. In 1912, an unnamed doctor stated that various conjoined monsters made their living by "trading in on their weird deformity."[50] Another physician saw potential advances in surgery to separate conjoined twins that would have the social benefit of ensuring children would not end up exhibited as freaks. In a 1928 report on parasitic twins, Sir John Bland-Sutton reported on several cases of asymmetrically conjoined twins, including Laloo, who was a popular nineteenth-century sideshow performer. Bland-Sutton used the cases to argue that surgical separation should be attempted. He argued, "The facts of this case are worth reporting not only from the intrinsic interest, but also for the stimulus it gives to surgeons to separate conjoined twins and spare the autosite not only a dreadful life of bondage, but the disgust and ignominy of being exhibited for gain in public shows."[51] The argument that surgery could "rescue" the freak from a grim life had both historical antecedents and future implications, especially in regard to the separation of conjoined twins as an attempt to make the body normal.[52]

If some physicians like Bland-Sutton negatively judged the shows, others were willing to engage with them professionally. On 18 January 1935, the Princess Beatrice Hospital in London, England, held a clinical meeting where freaks and human oddities working for Bertram Mills's circus were displayed to physicians in a "hall packed to capacity."

The show included the Giraffe Woman, the Leopard Woman, and the Human Ostrich in addition to other acts. Notably, the circus employed a little person billed as "the world's smallest woman." The hospital arranged to have two patients shown at the same time by Dr Buckley Sharp. In the write-up that appeared in the *British Medical Association Journal*, two child patients were described as "one a type of coeliac infantilism in a child aged 2, and weighing 17 lb.; the other a type of renal dwarfism in a child of 10 with the size and weight of a child of 5."[53] In putting on a sideshow under medical pretences, the hospital revealed how closely clinical study could resemble a freak show.

Some sideshow officials, however, had little praise for advances in medicine or public health. By the mid-1900s, owners and managers began to express open criticism of medical science and especially public health campaigns that aimed to "cure" or "protect" extraordinary bodies. Fred Smythe, manager of the Ringling Bros. and Barnum and Bailey Combined Shows, lamented during the Second World War that the great strides in public health had reduced the number of potential freak performers and was promoting the idea of placing them in institutions. He ranted, "This country isn't producing freaks so much anymore. These sanitary codes and health laws have a lot to do with it. Improve the public health and they beget fewer monsters. You get sanitary codes and you don't get many three-legged and two-bodied people." Smythe also expressed consternation that one of his employees who was hospitalized with illness had been treated for pituitary dysfunction, which had caused him to grow: "He didn't grow big enough to be a man, but he grows big enough to where he isn't a very good midget. You would think a doctor, a fellow with a college education, would have more sense."[54] Nate Eagle, who worked with the Ringling Bros. and Barnum and Bailey Combined Shows, repeated a similar story in 1964. Eagle pointed out that wider changes – ranging from surgical interventions for conjoined twins and hydrocephalus infants to new health regulations regarding tattooing – reduced the number of genuine freaks. He noted, however, that some of his best "customers" over the years were physicians, who were "interested rather than just curious" in the "clinic of sorts" that was the freak show.[55]

The Relationship between Freaks and Physicians

It is unclear from the historical record what might be considered the "average" or "normal" relationship between individual sideshow performers and physicians in the twentieth century. Few performers have left any records that speak to their experiences. Far more abundant are medical journals in which patients are described for their pedagogical value. The power imbalance here is one which historians seeking vulnerable subjects frequently bump up against. The few records in this section are intended not to illustrate any single experience of freak performers in regard to the medical profession as representative, but to speak to a range of possibilities.

In the late 1910s, Miss Gabriel, known as "The Only Half-Lady by Birth," due to the fact that she was born without a lower body or legs, noted in her life history pamphlet that medical professionals were excited at her birth and "flocked to see the phenomenal creature." Professional medical interest could be a point of pride for performers like Miss Gabriel, who used it to interest audience members and convince them of the authenticity of her extraordinary body. She mentions no concern over this attention, and her pamphlet was written in a decidedly chipper in tone, meant to be sold to audiences.[56]

In other performers' experiences, physicians were feared for their invasive examinations and invasive photographs. This is well illustrated in conjoined twins Daisy and Violet Hilton's careers. Born in Brighton, England, to a working-class mother named Kate Skinner (described in one piece as "an unmarried barmaid"),[57] the twins were sold to the midwife (sometimes referred to as a nurse) who delivered them and were almost immediately put on exhibit in the back of a bar.[58] A newspaper clipping from 1926, most certainly a press release issued by their managers that made its way onto the entertainment pages, tells a much different personal history: "Their mother died immediately after their birth, and the father was killed in an accident a few months later. They were brought to this country in their infancy by an aunt and uncle, Mr. and Mrs. Myers, of San Antonio."[59] Daisy and Violet's autobiography reveals another version of their childhood with more insidious details of their treatment at the hands of their "adopted" parents as well as physicians. In explaining their childhood with "Auntie," the midwife who initially adopted them, the twins recalled: "She never petted or kissed us, or even smiled. She just talked: 'Your mother gave you to me. You are not my children. Your mother gave you to me.' The speech grew longer as we grew older: 'I'm not your mother. Your mother was afraid when you were born and gave you to me when you were two weeks old. You must always do just as I say.'" Daisy and Violet also describe "Auntie's" belt and frequent whippings and beatings: "'She'll never hit your faces, girls,' Auntie's third husband Sir Green, whispered to us one day. 'The public will not be so glad to pay to look at little Siamese twins with scarred faces.'" When Auntie died, the girls were willed to her daughter Edith and Edith's husband, Myer Meyers (Rothbaum), who exhibited the girls throughout Australia, the United States, and Canada in the early decades of the twentieth century. A chance encounter with a lawyer willing to take on their case allowed them to sue for their independence and earnings. In early 1931, newspapers and trade magazines reported that the twins had taken the couple to court, and in June 1931, *White Tops* succinctly reported: "Siamese Twins Win Legal Tilt."[60]

From the time of their birth, the medical profession was excited about Violet and Daisy's birth – a rare, living set of pygopagi twins.[61] In 1911, Dr James A. Rooth reported in the *British Medical Association Journal*: "The case of the Brighton twins has excited a good deal of popular interest, and is, I think, of no less interest to the medical profession, as cases of pygopagi who have survived more than a few weeks are extremely rare."[62] From the time they were infants, they had been exhibited at various shows, and suffered physical, emotional, and financial abuse at the hands of their guardians and managers. But, as they suggested in their memoir, their abusive care was preferable to the thought of being turned over to doctors, with whom Daisy and Violet had multiple visits and violations, including being photographed. They wrote,

> How we loathed the sight of a hospital and the very bedside tone of a medical man's voice! We were punched and pinched and probed until we were almost crazy – and we always screamed and scratched and kicked. When the doctors and scientists left, Auntie would often whip us with the belt and call us ungrateful brats. Then we came to wonder – what if Auntie were offered some fabulous price by the doctors and scientists? Would she stop showing us on the stages and let the doctors have us – to punch and pinch and take pictures of us always?[63]

Although the girls were given to the midwife who delivered them, and then willed to their daughter only to sue in 1931 for their emancipation, medical examination was a key point of concern.[64]

American giant Robert Wadlow was also uncomfortable around the medical profession.[65] Individual physicians could be persistent in their desire to investigate people with extraordinary bodies, for whom this invasion of privacy was unwelcome. Those who had the personal and family resources could fight back against all the attention and what they felt were inaccuracies in their description. One such extraordinary case happened in the United States in the mid-1930s and it is of importance here in revealing the contested nature of medical representations. Wadlow was born in Alton, Illinois, in 1918 and grew to be 8 feet, 11 inches tall. On 2 June 1936, American physician Dr Charles Humberd called at Wadlow's house. Wadlow refused much of the attention his extraordinary height garnered, including most of the advances by circuses and carnivals offering to employ him as a freak performer. The few times he consented to performing, he did so only on strict terms that refused any of the usual staging of freaks.[66] His biography reveals that his parents refused all offers on the grounds that they wanted him "to lead as normal a life as possible." His parents agreed that until he came of age and could decide on his own, he would never appear in a sideshow. And he never did – his limited appearances in circuses in New York and Boston were in the main ring.

Physicians and curious citizens routinely visited his parents' home just to see him, although neither he nor his parents allowed many to enter. Humberd was one exception. Wadlow refused both a detailed examination and the doctor's offer of five dollars for an examination at another time. Although Humberd persisted and made other attempts to examine him, Wadlow refused to consent to anything more than a simple measurement of his height.[67] In 1937, Humberd published an article on Wadlow in the *Journal of the American Medical Association*. In the article, Humberd described Wadlow's body and medical history in intimate detail, including personal, non-scientific judgments of Wadlow's character: "His expression is surly and indifferent, and he is definitely inattentive, apathetic and disinterested, unfriendly and antagonistic ... He is introverted and morose." The physician also commented: "His motor coordination is not good, or else he is unduly sloppy by nature. He is careless in dress. His handwriting is untidy and poorly legible."[68] Wadlow was offended by the personal nature of the descriptions and sued both the doctor and the journal. Agreeing with the defence, the court initially ruled that the "article was to be considered only as a one-day case history" and not a general representation of Wadlow's character. The suit against the journal was dismissed after Wadlow's death in 1940, at the age of twenty-two.[69] Robert Wadlow's case is unique in that he successfully resisted being examined and was able to maintain control over his eventual limited performance. No doubt, this was a result of his more privileged position of being white, middle-class, and in the care of parents who were invested in giving him a "normal" life and "normal" childhood.

Wadlow's case is dramatically different from that of the Hiltons, whose mother by all accounts was working-class and possibly unmarried, leaving her in a precarious economic and social position. She did not actively participate in the exhibition of her children. Physicians' ability to access the extraordinary body seemed to be connected to power inequities that made vulnerable people, like those who primarily came to be exhibited on the sideshows, more ready targets. It is also significant that the cases here involved performers who could speak and write and create their own records. All of this is not to say that children did not find treatment or medical care beneficial. Ernie Defort, discussed in chapter 5, seems to have accepted the surgery that separated him from his conjoined twin. It is difficult, however, to ignore the power of the discourse of "the normal body" and medicine's role as its interpreter.

Understanding how medicine and sideshows intersect provides important context for understanding the show's continuation in the 1900s. While references to the "monstrous" persisted, the medical profession's understanding of the origins of such births became increasingly sophisticated. The scientific term that was coming into vogue was "birth defect."[70] The ideological implications of "defect" are clear. As the quote cited earlier from the *Canadian Medical Association Journal* indicates, many physicians saw these children and adults as pitiful and unfortunate, a sentiment often shared by institutional directors, educational experts, and teachers. In 1907, nurse Menia Tye reported on an infant born with spina bifida: "Fortunately the child died."[71] Similarly, in a letter to the New York's World's Fair directors in 1938 for the purposes of offering a child for exhibition at the freak show, New Jersey–based physician Marc Wallace expressed regret that a child had survived, but saw the freak show as option to mitigate the situation. He wrote, "The child, a girl, was born October 2, without any single arms or legs, and unfortunately for all concerned, is healthy and likely to live for some time."[72] Yet parents did not always share these sentiments. As Nic Clarke's research reveals, parents of institutionalized children continued to have contact with them through letters. Care and concern remained.[73]

"Nature's Mistake": Medical Discourse Reshapes the Sideshow

From the 1980s onwards, theorists and historians have grappled with the rise of visual culture and how to explain the complexity of competing

4.1 "Nature's Mistakes." Performers in a midway carnival ten-in-one sideshow, 1940. City of Vancouver Archives, PNE Collection, Public Domain.

gazes, means of looking, the role of spectacle, and engagement by ordinary citizens with visual media. The freak show was firmly embedded in visual culture – a spectacle dependent on the consumer gaze. As Garland-Thomson argues, the consumer gaze "often entails not the intense, focused scrutiny of staring but rather the casual visual cruising of window-shopping or Web surfing."[74] The consumer gaze can be contrasted with the serious, focused empirical observation of what Foucault termed "the clinical gaze." Freak shows combined consumer stares with the clinical gaze so that consumers could take on a sort of personal medical study in their own observations. As Alice Domurat Dreger has argued, the medical gaze, even in the twentieth century, was not distant from the gaze compelled by the freak show. Patients, like freaks, were constructed as "the unauthoritative, needy 'other,'" based on the power of medical professionals.[75] The medical gaze gave the medical profession authority to access and interpret the body. Physicians' observations became more important than patient experience, something to be shared in professional journals. Medical technologies such as the stethoscope and the camera opened the body up to further observations.[76] While Canadian historians have shown patients' ability to assert agency, the construction of "the patient," like "the freak," was based on power imbalances.[77] In attracting consumers and deflecting any unfavourable moral associations, show owners encouraged consumers to see freaks in medical terms. The compelling power of medical science also provided the gloss of legitimacy that sideshow operators used to highlight the educational aspects of their displays. The medical gaze could thus be incorporated into popular spectacles like the freak show. If audience members were hesitant to spend a dime simply to gawk, the respectability of medicine could help overcome any reticence. This popular interpretation of a quasi-clinical gaze, combined with a powerful belief in the normal body, helped reframe the shows to focus on difference *and* ability. The shows could highlight how disabled bodies could still do ordinary actions. Such a frame reaffirmed difference as strange and unusual while making it acceptable to perform in and witness the exhibitions.

By the 1930s, sideshows were becoming less about the fantastic tales that epitomized nineteenth-century shows and more about simply gawking and staring at unusual bodies. Freakishness was removed from the realm of the wondrous and naturalized as corporeal abnormality. Scientific and medical authority had consolidated enough power that twentieth-century displays needed to change. Freak shows did not, however, simply disappear into the medical theatre or the institution. Medicine and medical authority provided a new context for the display of freaks, which focused on their medical rarity, on the facts of their extraordinariness, and on their ability to overcome the limitations of their unusual anatomy. Such a narrative trick worked to reaffirm the person as disabled, but put a positive spin on it by focusing on the individual's *ability*, encouraging audiences to wonder at their skills, which may have diminished feelings of pity or made them sublime. By the 1930s, this had become a popular mode of presentation, and a few examples highlight this shift.

Johnny Eck could do what any "normal body" could in spite of his anatomy. Eck was born in 1911 in Baltimore, Maryland, without the lower part of a body from his ribs down. As a young adult performer, he was billed as "The Only Living Half Boy" and "Nature's Greatest

Mistake," travelling with the Johnny J. Jones shows in the 1930s. His 1935 pamphlet noted he had "traveled quite extensively all over the United States and Canada, having played in a number of large traveling shows ... His accomplishments today are unlimited. Look at the list on the next page and compare it with any boy you know that has all the advantages of a normal body."[78] Eck was hired to appear in Tod Browning's 1932 film *Freaks* – he was scouted for the role while performing in Montreal[79] – and was one of the named performers in the Canadian National Exhibition's official catalogue for 1938.[80]

Ability in spite of differences was highlighted in other displays. Frieda Pushnik was born in Pennsylvania in 1923 without arms or legs, and worked in the 1940s and early 1950s with the Ringling Bros., which toured in Canada in 1950.[81] Pushnik, like most other freak show performers, sold *cartes de visite*. The cards or pamphlets included biographical details of performers along with pictures or photographs. They were usually commissioned, bought, and sold by performers to supplement their income. Performers would offer to sell these "takeaways" to audience members as souvenirs. Pusknik's undated *carte de visite* noted her twelve years of public education and her many hobbies and pastimes. Her pamphlet also noted that she could do "most everything as a normal person. I need no assistance at mealtime (can handle silverware, glasses, cups, etc.), apply my own make up, brush my own teeth, do all my own letter writing, can type, and have won several penmanship awards."[82] Nonetheless, focusing on ability was one angle, but encouraging pity was part of showmen's roster of tricks. As freak show operator Harry Lewiston notes, these tricks ran the gamut of "quips, comedy, and tear-jerking sympathy where it was necessary." Lewiston found such tricks necessary with Pushnik in the late 1930s. He recalled, "I would milk the sympathy angle for all it was worth. 'Would you give a million dollars not to be like this?' I would ask. Then I would point out that Frieda had her mother to take care of her now, but who knew how long this state of affairs would last." Lewiston would then offer to sell Bibles with the profits promised to fund Frieda's lifelong comfort. It was a scam and he pocketed the money, although Lewiston privately argued that he paid Frieda well at seventy-five dollars a week, plus room and board for her mother and sister.[83] As such, the ballyhoo narratives of performers with physical disabilities were far less about the fantastical nature of their extraordinary bodies and far more about their abilities, but undergirded by the assumption that disability was a tragedy. As a newspaper release for the Conklin shows in Regina in 1942 stated:

"When you see a person who has overcome tremendous handicaps to succeed, it makes you feel pretty small when you remember how you can 'beef' about petty annoyances."[84] That year, Jack Halligan's freak show as part of the Conklin shows featured Dolly Reagan (referred to as Dolly Sharzner) as a freak performer. Halligan noted, "Dolly has worked hard since the age of eight to overcome her handicap."[85] In the 1930s and 1940s, stories about people who lifted themselves beyond their "tragic' lives were a heart-warming narrative that fit well with liberal notions of independence and autonomy and, more importantly, opened the wallets of audience members, who suddenly felt thankful for their own state of being. Similar strategies would be used by fund-raising campaigns and telethons from mid-century onward.[86]

The presentation of Ernie-Len (Ernie Defort) reveals how medical discourse was appropriated in the staging of his exhibit. Ernie Defort was born in Winnipeg in the early 1930s and had a parasitic twin, which consisted of a lower body joined at his abdomen. In the exhibition as well as in the pamphlets, the doctor and nurses present at his birth were named, the statistical rarity of his birth was mentioned, he was described as the talk of the medical profession, and audience members were compelled to "ask their doctors."[87] Presumably, audience members could ask doctors to confirm the legitimacy (it was not a fake) and rarity of what they witnessed in Ernie-Len's body and that they had heard of the case. In other press releases that were published in Canadian newspapers under the headline "Even Nature Makes Mistakes; See Them at Conklin Shows," it was reported that "the greatest medical men in the world have been consternated by the amazing humans who appear in the exhibition and Zandu the quarter boy, in particular, has amazed the medical profession by going through twenty-nine years of his life without an inch of intestines."[88]

Other displays were even more explicit. Lou Dufour bought a "medical specimen" in the form of a two-headed baby stored in a jar of formaldehyde from a physician to start one of his first shows in the 1930s. It was displayed at the Chicago Century of Progress Exposition along with a woman dressed in a nurse's uniform and included a long and detailed medical description. Racism framed the exhibition as the baby was declared to have "Negroid characteristics," and the baby's death from improper feeding was blamed on the "ignorant mother," revealing an unsubtle connection to scientific parenting, with its own racial parameters.[89] The show was incorporated into Dufour's LIFE exhibition, which included hundreds of such fetuses and infant bodies on display in what was commonly (and crassly) known on the sideshow circuits as "pickled punks." In the mid-1960s, Dufour permanently staged his LIFE exhibition in Niagara Falls, Ontario. Dufour saw the permanent exhibit as a means to survive financially as well as to educate the public. He declared, "My little pickled specimens are doing just nicely ... People see the progressive stages of prenatal development ... Older folks, romantics, newlyweds, and school groups – everyone visits, and learns."[90]

Other performers provided explicit "lessons." Al and Jeanie Tomaini, for example, performed as Giant and Half-Girl. Their pamphlet from the late 1930s promised the "Life Story of Mr. and Mrs. Al Tomaini, World's Strangest Married Couple, Giant and Half Girl," but also "A Lesson in Glands."[91] The lesson in glands was most likely a reference to the pituitary, which produces the growth hormone. Presumably, audience members learned by witnessing the couple's differences and listening to what spiels were drafted to explain their sizes. Staid presentations such as this, to use Bogdan's terminology, fit within this new medicalized mode. They also drew on older concepts that positioned opposites (the fat lady and the thin man) together to further highlight difference.

Staging was an important part of the medical mode, and this included other performers dressed as doctors and nurses, which was especially useful for displays of freak infants and children. Nurses were typically women from the girl shows performing double duty on the freak show. Banners strung in front of the shows, an essential element for luring audiences once on the fairgrounds, sometimes included images or other references to medical professionals. A 1936 show with the Beckman and Gerety Carnival was described simply as a "Two-Headed Baby." The canvas included two paintings of the child with nurses and doctors bathing and examining it. It further described the child as "Nature's Only Terata-Anditima" – a puzzling reference to monsters. The canvas noted that the child had been "born to normal parents."[92]

Disability resulting from industrial accidents also provided for moments of "overcoming disability." In 1942, Conklin's show touring western Canada included Andrew Gawley, described in a Regina newspaper as a feature of the freak show "who has overcome a great handicap. Gawley lost his hands in an industrial accident. He made a pair of hands out of steel and after determined practice can write, sew and handle table utensils flawlessly. During the winter, he operates a bicycle repair shop at Meaford, Ont. While on tour, he rides a bicycle to and from the fairgrounds."[93] Another newspaper report stated that Gawley had lost his hands working at a northern lumber camp and that he now "manufactures steel hands for other men similarly disabled."[94]

Sideshow pamphlets noted "nature's mistakes" but often focused on their ability to perform simple, everyday tasks that subtly revealed their independence as well as their ability to participate in common leisure activities. In 1951, the *Globe and Mail* noted the "Carnival Hobbies" of sideshow workers, including Betty Lou Williams, who was born with what was then called a parasitic twin. Williams, like other child performers, began her performances with the Ripley's Believe It or Not! Odditorum in the mid-1930s. After working the sideshows, she landed with the Royal American Shows and died in 1954 at the age of twenty-two from an asthma attack.[95] Shortly after her death, sideshow operator Dick Best with the Royal American Shows described her as one of the best freaks ever.[96] In Shaw's report, Williams's hobbies, which included knitting, sewing, playing the piano, and cooking, were highlighted.[97]

A few years later, in 1957, "Armless Wonder" Jose de Leon toured with the Royal American Show to Fort William, Ontario. A newspaper reported that while he was "billed as a 'freak' on the Royal American Midway, Jose de Leon is more often referred to as a genius." De Leon's performance was a classic one for an Armless Wonder. He did everyday, ordinary things like shave, pick up dimes, write, and light a cigarette. The report concluded, "Jose de Leon is a youth who was determined to take his place in the world independently without pity. That is why people say that this hard-luck lad from Mexico City is a genius and not a 'freak.'"[98]

In the 1960s, some of the "mistakes" continued to be shown with direct reference to medicine. One dramatic exhibition ostensibly provided ordinary people the opportunity to see national news stories in person. In 1966, the "Frog Girl Side Show" was included as part of the Bernard and Barry Shows of Canada, an Ontario-based carnival which toured Ontario and Quebec until 1978, when Conklin purchased it as part of their expansion.[99] The Frog Girl's banner described her as a "thrilling" and "shocking" "freak," and asked, "Was it thalidomide?"[100] Four years earlier, thalidomide, a sedative developed in the 1950s and prescribed to pregnant women with morning sickness, was restricted in Canada. The drug caused "birth defects" in 125 Canadian children, who would not receive compensation until 1992.[101]

Medical discourse and eugenics profoundly shaped the freak show from the early 1900s up to the 1960s. If the freak had become a medical specimen, that hardly stopped show owners from exhibiting extraordinary bodies. Rather, it simply provided another means for framing their shows – one with significant amounts of legitimacy and permission for the audience to stare and assess. For performers, medicine may have undercut their claim to be wondrous and fantastic, but it also provided a means to focus on their abilities. This was not insignificant since, well into the 1960s, Canadians were not shy about expressing bigotry towards people with disabilities.[102] We might cautiously celebrate these performers' agency and resistance, which came at the cost of the persistent and dominant view that saw the body as disabled and thus fundamentally flawed and expected people with disabilities to cheerfully meet normative beliefs about how the body was expected to function. The freak show's remarkable persistence throughout the twentieth century speaks both to the power of the category of the normal body, and to the flexibility of the staging and narration of the freak body, which could incorporate and reshape presentations to absorb medical discourse. The normal body also reflected racial hierarchies that were supported by modern science and continued, almost without change, from nineteenth-century displays of evolutionary theory, colonial conquest, and scientific racism.

Race, the Body, and the Sideshow

Racial taxonomies have shaped the display of colonized or negatively racialized peoples into the middle decades of the twentieth century as part of a host of projects designed to regulate and normalize racialized bodies.[103] As such, the carnival's sideshows dovetailed with other projects designed to spread messages of the biopolitics of white supremacy, which positioned the normal body as the white body. Away from the sideshow, for example, H.A. Tanser, superintendent of schools in Chatham, Ontario, wrote an influential book in 1939 that noted a "positive correlation between intelligence and White blood." As Barrington Walker argues Tanser was part of an influential group who believed in the hereditary model of intelligence. Although the framework (notably IQ tests that ignore social differences) was persuasively disputed in the 1960s, Tanser's book continued to be cited into the twenty-first century.[104] Ideas of intelligence and race would continue to be part of the sideshow. The bodies of Indigenous children forced into residential schools across the country were brutally made to fit white ideals.[105] Importantly, the treatment of Indigenous children was a significant element to Canadian nation-building as these practices helped sustain and mobilize ideas of the healthy and modern Canadian body.

By the early twentieth century, racism and disability had been conflated to the point that freak shows worked to forge ideas of defective individuals and defective races. People with intellectual disabilities, as well as those who were negatively racialized, were labelled as primitive, uncivilized, incurable, and unsuited for education. Further, women and immigrants were also seen as inherently disabled by their biology (gender or ethnicity, or both), justifying further inequities, from withholding the vote to barring legal immigration.[106] If fantastical tales had any salience in the twentieth century, it was when race and disability intersected. In the early 1940s, Conklin's freak show included pinheads from the Belgian Congo. Another press release echoed late nineteenth-century imperial fantasies in emphasizing the "freak hunter" who found the "Congo 'Pin-Heads.'" The release described them as "'pin-headed' pygmies from the Belgian Congo, brought to North America in 1930 by Frank 'Bring 'Em Back Alive' Buck." As with other pinheads, the performers had their heads shaved, leaving only small knots of hair on top. The hairstyle created the distinctive look of the pinhead's skull. Their costumes included wild animal skins for men and grass skirts for the women. To further emphasize their animality, the press release described them as "strange semi-savages [who] have little intelligence and resemble the Simian in both face and figure." In contrast to the alleged backwardness of the people on display, the midway, which was called "Frolic-Land," was described as "ultra-modern."[107] Negatively racialized and colonized peoples found themselves enfreaked in fictionalized performances that reassured racial and colonial hierarchies. For people with disabilities who were also negatively racialized, the fictional and fantastical narratives that shaped nineteenth-century performances extended well into the twentieth century. Eugenics undoubtedly played a role in ensuring their freakery marked them as less than human.

In 1932 the CNE included "Ubangi Savages" who were described as "Belles from the French Congo with lower lips of dinner-plate size. First time any of these natives have been seen in Canada. Midway, North End."[108] The canvas declared that they were "Half Human Half Monkey" and that this was their "First Time in Captivity."[109] Three years earlier, however, *White Tops* magazine announced that "Disc-Lipped Savages" would be "featured with the Ringling Bros. and Barnum & Bailey Circus." The short article noted that they were a "group of real

African savages, with disc-mouthed women."[110] To demonstrate savagery the performance at the CNE in Toronto in 1937 was staged to trade in on popular racist myths about an allegedly pan-African culture. As with Zulu, other quasi-ethnological shows were stripped of any cultural specificity. A Toronto newspaper reporter created a fantastical scene of his visit to the late-night performance. He noted that the Ubangis danced in and through fire to throbbing drums and a quickening rhythm. One of the women handed the reporter "the shrunken heads of a blonde woman and a red-headed man."[111] The reporter noted he quickly left. The whole report had the air of sideshow ballyhoo, using savagery to draw in curious audience members looking for a thrill. A year later as part of the Western Fair, the so-called 'firewalkers" were allegedly from the Belgian Congo.[112]

Lou Dufor's shows, paired with Conklin's in the 1940s, included similar racialized spectacles. One photograph reveals a "firewalker" running semi-nude through a fire pit lined with human skulls.[113] In 1961, *White Tops*, which had always focused on preserving circus history, carried an article on some of the historical sideshow acts. In regard to the Ubangis the article revealed that the name Ubangi was given to the performers by a press agent. If the savageness of the show was tempered by this revelation, it was maintained in the description of the people. The article continued: "They did not bathe, smelled and acted like animals, and were exhibited in the menagerie."[114] While some performers found themselves on the sideshow platform proper, others were exhibited at zoos, aquariums, and museums. At the intersection of invention and deception, "Ubangi" and other negatively racialized performers were dehumanized as strange and savage animals.

In 1937, a newspaper article announced that "the Circus side show" at the CNE included "the savage pygmies, the Four Abyssinians, Madame Zondia, mind reader, Stella, the Tattooed Lady, the magician sword swallower, fat lady, armless and legless wonder." Of the "Abyssinian Pigmies" [sic] the piece included a bolded special section describing them: "Abyssinia's renowned Four Pigmies, wild savages of the hinterlands of the deposed Emperor Haile Selassie's kingdom, still can't accustom themselves to civilization. Beds are queer gagdets [sic] of the 'Evil One" so far as they are concerned ... They shun the society of whites, and only beam happily when in the neighborhood of the lions' cages ... The white man is beyond their comprehension. The pigmies are a star feature of Conklin's Shows."[115] The inaccurate description of the "star feature" did not merely describe the Abyssinian Pigmies

4.2 Ubangi savages at the Canadian National Exhibition. Canadian National Exhibition Archives. Photography by G. Hollies.

but invented them.[116] Such performances relied on a particular mix of exoticism and eroticism. African and "Oriental" performances such as the Abyssinian Pigmies were formulated at the intersection of race and sexuality. Negatively racialized performers found themselves represented as less than human and, as such, often performed in little clothing. Nudity, along with their presentation as savage and animal-like, ensured that the performances were shot-through with sexual tension. In the wake of eugenics, this tension was both alluring and concerning. Both could be successful strategies to draw in paying customers.

A small number of Inuit men and women continued to find themselves on display in Canada in the 1930s as part of the shows at the CNE. In 1937, the front of the Inuit show called "Eskimoland" referenced former fur trader Philip Godsell, who wrote popular magazine articles and books on the north and also organized exhibitions of Indigenous performers at the Red River Pageant in honour of the Hudson's Bay Company's 250th anniversary in 1920.[117] The reference

4.3 Eskimoland at the Canadian National Exhibition. Canadian National Exhibition Archives. Photography by G. Hollies.

to Godsell added at least a gloss of expertise and legitimacy to the exhibition in 1937. The display captured headlines when one of the women allegedly purchased an electric refrigerator. Newspaper articles excitedly reported that she bought it because it quickly made ice for eating, although the accompanying photograph simply showed her putting in a tray of artichokes, which were clearly a prop to make her look more "exotic." According to one article, the Toronto salesman "produced his white-man's magic" in ensuring the sale.[118] The purchase of the refrigerator was almost certainly a part of the performance designed to garner headlines and increase interest in the display. Before the sale, a newspaper headline declared that the "sweltering days of August [are] getting CNE Eskimos down," and reported that the Inuit "would have little difficulty in making their wants known if a refrigerator salesman dropped around."[119] The refrigerator was simply a prop used to highlight what were deemed to be the essential differences of the Inuit and their unfamiliarity with dominant white culture and its modern conveniences – even if those products remained beyond the means of many Canadian families in the 1930s. By 1941, only one in five Canadian families had a refrigerator.[120] The Inuit supposedly needed the fridge because of their desire for ice, although one article also reported that the dog musher would use it to store the husky puppies when they got too hot.[121] The dogs were not alone in being unaccustomed to the climate. Like other displays that relied on negative racialization, the argument that those on display could not acclimatize to the local weather was a subtle appeal to biological understandings of race.[122] The alternative use of the machine to cool the dogs also pointed to the disjuncture between Inuit peoples and modern goods, where the Inuit were depicted as simple in their use of the technology.

The timing was important as well. Peter Geller argues that between 1920 and 1945 the Canadian government initiated and supported particular types of image-making of the "North" and the Inuit for southern audiences as a means of integrating the land and its people into the national framework. It was a process of visual colonization, exemplified by the still-shown film *Nanook of the North* (1922). The Hudson's Bay Company (HBC) also used a variety of visually based strategies to show their support of, and role in, Inuit welfare. The HBC distributed material that attempted to persuade southern audiences that their role in the north was benevolent. In particular, federal authorities, companies, and individuals conceived of the Inuit as childlike, primitive, and in need of paternal authority.[123] The sideshows brought such messages to live audiences, making the Inuit seem at once strange and familiar. As such, the display involving the fridge and the dogs worked in conjunction with other wider representations to show the Inuit's alleged distance from modern consumer culture and its attendant luxuries, as well as their close proximity to nature and the dogs. As with other displays of negatively racialized peoples, animals were used to indicate a lesser humanity.

In 1931, the CNE included the "Village of Seminoles, Picturesque Nomads of Florida Everglades" in what was an excellent example of colonial fabrication. The Seminoles were described as follows: "The population of the American continent of a much earlier day, for they are almost purely Mongol. They live in the mystic, gloomy, labyrinth in swamp and hills and channels of the Everglades of Florida, a water-sodden land of alligators and snakes and mystery, romance and adventure."[124] Romance and adventure were part of a narrative strategy used to obscure the forcible removal of the Seminoles to Oklahoma and the other bloody battles they fought against colonizing forces. The fact was that by the early 1930s there were few Seminoles living in Florida, and by some accounts those who did gravitated to the Everglades to avoid colonial conflict – a situation that would be partially acknowledged in the 1940s as part of a successful land claim. Further, the Everglades was symbolically understood as one of the last truly wild areas of the United States and sometimes compared to Africa, affirming the perceived savagery and wildness of the people who lived there.[125] As the CNE catalogue announced, their village on display at The Ex included rattlesnakes, dogs, monkeys, and alligators, "all typical of the land of half-light which has protected them through centuries and which is recognized as their impregnable last home."[126] As part of the show, the Seminoles caught live alligators in performances that highlighted the supposed risk taking and savagery of Indigenous masculinity. As Patsy West argues, the performances of the Seminoles may have commodified Seminole culture but they also provided much-needed income for families. The shows also helped ensure a cultural legacy.[127]

The display of Indigenous people was also used to highlight the colonizer's claims to progress and modernity by emphasizing and often distorting their traditional way of life. Performances were frequently not authentic in their presentation of a pan-Indigenous culture, but that mattered little to audiences wishing to be entertained. In one such spectacle at the CNE in 1937 Indigenous actors (men, women, and children) found themselves on display effectively for most of the day and in the evenings. Significantly, the actors performed and worked in an area separate from the midway, called Frolexland, heightening the educational aspect. Newspapers described the "Indian encampment" as "true" and featuring "Ojibway Braves from Northern Ontario." According to one newspaper report, one evening "1,000 spectators waited 75 minutes for the show to start."[128] The display of wigwams, "traditional" clothing, and Indigenous people simply living in the encampment revealed the deeply ingrained colonialism in Canadian society. Indigenous people were rendered as Others with "primitive" ways that subtly affirmed aggressive acts of colonization by displacing them from modern, urban life. Making "living" a spectacle affirmed Aboriginal peoples as subjects to be looked at and surveilled. The types of displays had changed little since earlier ones at the Toronto Industrial Exhibition, the precursor to the CNE.[129] Indigenous life was depicted as flat, stagnant, and homogeneous, and little attention was paid to regional, linguistic, ethnic, or cultural divisions. Perhaps the only thing that stayed the same was how the white imagination perceived Indigenous peoples.

Yet, as a number of scholars have shown in relation to royal visits, independent exhibits at fairs, and other performances, Indigenous people found ways to negotiate and shape their participation.[130] While amendments to the Indian Act in 1895 banned "savage" performances, an important exemption was made for agricultural exhibitions. As with the easing of Criminal Code provisions on gambling, an agricultural exhibition exemption meant that carnivals could continue to operate games and shows not otherwise available.[131] We might presume that such exemptions also helped to attract consumers. The banning of performances, however, meant that being able to stage them provided the opportunity for Indigenous peoples to practise, stage, and pass along traditional culture as well as demonstrate "political defiance and cultural persistence."[132] As Michael David McNally argues in regard to the staging of Song of Hiawatha pageants, performance represented "both a possibility and a limit" for Indigenous communities "under siege." Performance provided an opportunity to engage and publicly show Indigenous culture otherwise heavily circumscribed.[133]

By the 1930s, Indigenous actors on the sideshows were also performing some ceremonies that were almost entirely white inventions. Yet, even within these racist scripts, Indigenous men and women exerted agency. For example, in 1937 at The Ex, two performers (Grace Kagong and John Wahbunosa) in the "Indian encampment" married. Newspapers speciously reported that it was to be the "first Indian wedding in Toronto in 126 years."[134] One newspaper detailed that both had been to Anglican residential schools and were married in an Anglican church, although this seems to have happened only after there was some doubt as to whether a minister from Sault Ste Marie could officiate the ceremony in Toronto.[135] While the small Anglican marriage ceremony in Toronto was common, Kadong and Wahbunosa's much more public reception, which was allegedly based in traditional Ojibway customs, marks them as foreign and different. The bride, however, found subtle ways of undermining the dominant script of difference. She noted that the "Indian wedding reception" held at the CNE in front of three hundred spectators was not her or her husband's idea. The newspaper reported: "Mr. and Mrs. Kay were informed yesterday afternoon, they said, that pale-faces felt there should be more fuss about it all when an Indian couple at the C.N.E. were wed. 'So we told them to go ahead with anything they liked,' Mrs. Kay said in perfect English and a shrug of her shoulders."[136] At the "Indian wedding reception," Kadong revealed that they held the reception to please the audiences and that the "Indian garb" she was wearing was "too darn hot." Further, she told the reporter, "We'll sure be glad to get back to the Soo and change back into real clothes – just like you people are wearing."[137] Kadong's disclosure to the reporter undermined the alleged authenticity of the entire display by revealing her role in what amounted to a stage production with costuming that was neither authentic nor part of her real life. She was not alone in disrupting the performance. Other subtle acts of rebellion that performers had at their disposal included talking back to the audience, refusing to act in the way that they were expected to, and, more generally, not performing.

Conclusion

Sideshows of the twentieth century continued to intersect with the medical profession and, from the 1930s to the 1960s, effectively used medical discourses and the clinical gaze to reframe shows for popular audiences. As such, freak shows remained important points of intersection with normal society, trading on shifting notions of disability, medicine, race, treatment, and care. Freak shows were instrumental in the process that Lennard Davis has described as enforcing the normal body.[138] While the ideal of the normal body became rooted in science and medicine, individual families and people bore the burden of the enforcement of the ideal. As Davis also notes, race was essential to the structuring of the category of disability. If "national images and identities are tied to notions of the body," shows of Otherness marked by disability and race subtly excluded some bodies from making claims to the nation so as to avoid subverting ideals of national integrity and unity.[139] Freak shows worked to help naturalize white supremacy in presenting popular displays with messages of primitivism, savagery, and biological backwardness. Age mattered, too. The next chapter focuses specifically on children, looking at their performances on the sideshows and how they can be seen as avenues for work and care as well as expressions of agency.

Chapter Five

Not Just Child's Play: Child Freak Show Consumers and Workers

In a 1929 article on "The Psychology of Conjoined Twins," British physician Bland-Sutton argued that it was "a curious problem; such couples, as well as individuals so unfortunate as to be hampered with a parasitic twin, should be objects of pity. Most of them are born to parents in poor circumstances, and when they survive their birth are apt to fall into the hands of crafty showmen who exhibit them for gain."[1] There was some truth to Bland-Sutton's assertion, although as this chapter demonstrates parents also sought out showmen to employ or show their children. As both performers and consumers, children were important to the ongoing success and popularity of sideshows in Canada. From special children's days with reduced prices to free admission for special groups of children to rides, games, and prizes targeted to youngsters, children and youth were vital to the carnival's ongoing success. For children in pits behind the canvas, social exclusions resulting from poverty and disability made the freak show a potential site for the expression of familial agency. Although Bland-Sutton thought the children "should be objects of pity," others saw the freak show as an opportunity. This chapter looks closely at the experiences of children who worked as freaks on the sideshows within the context of twentieth-century constructions of disability, childhood, and consumerism. The latter part of the chapter focuses on the Canadian case of Ernie Defort.

The history of child freak performers includes some of the most famous from the height of the shows' popularity in the mid- to late nineteenth century. For example, Charles Sherwood Stratton performed as General Tom Thumb (discussed further in chapter 6) from the age of five, although Barnum advertised him as being eleven to make his small stature appear more dramatic.[2] Evidence from the many freak performances of the twentieth century suggests that many performers started their careers as children, including Krao Farini, Emmitt Bejano, Percilla Lauther, Daisy and Violet Hilton, Yvonne and Yvette Jones, and Frieda Pushnik. The historiography on freak performers, however, has yet to fully consider the age of the performers or the participation of children as performers. Children working on the sideshows are historically significant for three reasons. First, they highlight significant cracks in the dominant ideologies of childhood. Poverty and disability put certain children at risk of not having a childhood. Certainly not all poor and disabled children ended up working as freaks, but for those who did, that combination was almost universal. While work as a freak was often a genuine economic opportunity (whether or not it turned out to be lucrative), it was performative labour defined by the restrictions of other avenues open to children. Second, these performances – unwittingly or not – perpetuated and legitimized differences of ability that functioned to delineate the category of "normal" as discussed in chapter 4. Third, beginning in the 1920s, sideshow operators began to appeal more directly to children as consumers, as part of a wider trend in the development of modern youth culture, with commercial culture as its base. As such, the sideshow became an important place to explore child and youth consumerism. Reinforcing the other two points, an account of consumer culture also sheds light on the varied expectations and experiences of childhood, with many children having fun in the audience and a few performing and working on the stage.

My purpose in this chapter is to explore the presence of children on the sideshow set within the wider context of the intensification of white, middle-class ideals of "the child" and childhood, along with the growing and changing presence of institutions designed to shape children and maintain particular ideologies of childhood. When progressive reformers announced that the twentieth century was "the century of the child," rights, health, and education became public focal points that put small bodies under special scrutiny. For children with disabilities, the shift from seeing children in economic terms to sentimental ones remained, at best, incomplete. Children with disabilities remained more vulnerable, especially to eugenically informed discourses, measures, and reforms.

Although child freak performers were rendered abnormal because of a range of disabilities, they did share the experience of largely unregulated and unseen performative labour with the normal and beautiful child stars like Baby Peggy and Shirley Temple. As sideshows reformulated and restructured in the early twentieth century, reacting to wider cultural and social changes that challenged their existence, they organized as part of the burgeoning professional entertainment industry. Illustrative of this fact are the ubiquitous references to the carnival as part of the outdoor amusement business. These discursive moves to align with an upwardly mobile industry whose products were increasingly appealing to middle-class tastes and consumers revealed the professional nature of the associations. For all performers, it gave them greater cachet. As with child movie stars who became idealized and popular visions of childhood itself beginning in the 1920s, child freak performers had performance-based work that separated them from other children and other workers.[3]

Excavating the histories of children who performed as freaks has been a frustrating experience. Children's histories and the history of childhood have developed significantly in recent years, and the methodologies for uncovering the complicated histories to address the significant issues in the primary evidence have grown increasingly sophisticated. As many historians of children and childhood have noted, the available evidence is usually made by and for adults.[4] I am working largely from representations of children in newspapers, archival documents, and photographs. The voices of actual children, especially children on the sideshow whose lives and careers were often bound by fictionalized biographies, are incredibly difficult to access, but records of the sideshows and of other places where children were exhibited do exist, albeit in scattered form. As such, this chapter is very much about representations of childhood, and although I am discussing "real" children, they are only present in very limited ways in the historical records that I have used. They neither manufactured nor controlled the representations of their lives or bodies and still do not here. I have tried to piece together the information of their lives while being sensitive to wider processes that brought their lives into the realms of sideshow history.

The Child Consumer

In 1900, Swede Ellen Kay declared the twentieth century to be the "Century of the Child." Her declaration was taken up in many countries, including Canada. Historians Comacchio, Golden, and Weisz argue that "this historic designation became the rallying cry of reformers who looked with tremendous enthusiasm and optimism toward

5.1 Freak performers. Note the children in the audience.
CNE midway freak show, City of Toronto Archives, fonds 1244, item 2515.

a world in which the lives of children everywhere would be significantly improved."[5] But the child referenced by Kay and taken up by other advocates was narrowly defined and largely excluded children with disabilities; as such, it is not terribly surprising that reformers and advocates rarely, if ever, seemed to have focused their attention on sideshow performers, which is why Pookie's case in the 1970s is so extraordinary. To understand how and why this happened, it is necessary to look at the modern construction of childhood.

That the twentieth century could be declared one for "the child" was based on wider changes in the conception of childhood. Significant shifts in the construction of "the child" and modern childhood in the West began in the seventeenth century. By the end of the nineteenth century, childhood had been transformed and, according to Viviana Zelizer, sentimentalized.[6] Rather than seeing children largely in economic terms, childhood had come to be seen as a distinct life stage in need of protection and segregation. Children were defined by their innocence, irrationality, and impulsiveness. As such, childhood was seen as a life stage that was radically different from adulthood. Sentimentalized children were seen to need protection and special care and spawned what was known throughout the West as "child saving." Children were seen to be in need of care and protection from neglect and abuse, but also in need of control and punishment for perceived transgressions.[7] At its root was a dialectical view of childhood that focused on the endangered child and the dangerous child. The goal was to make childhood "safe" and to produce good, moral, and obedient citizens.[8] Play and leisure time became important, although types of commercial amusements varied in their acceptability and caused seemingly endless debates. Nonetheless, as Comacchio points out, by the 1920s social scientists advocated positive social outcomes of well-spent leisure time.[9] Within this framework the carnival held an ambivalent place. Yet modern leisure time was intimately connected to commercial culture and youth – with increasing amounts of time and money at their disposal, young people helped to reshape modern popular culture.

Modern consumer culture in Canada emerged in the late 1800s as a result of wider changes in urbanization, technology, and mass production. Never equitable in any sense of the word, consumer culture promised at least a democratic impulse. Changes in production made goods cheaper and more widely available, but structural inequities meant that democratization was not realized. Participation in the culture of consumption varied widely depending on a host of factors including class, race, gender, and age. Longer periods of leisure time made possible by changes to labour meant that an increasing number of people had more time to spend on commercial amusements in addition to goods. Wholesome leisure was seen as positive in regards to work as it was seen as refreshing and recharging for workers. These labour changes, along with the increasing accessibility of public schools and for longer mandatory periods, produced changes in the culture of childhood and youth. By the 1920s, youth culture was firmly embedded in commercial culture, and older youths (those in double digits and up) were recognized for their increasing spending and cultural power. The perception of their power led to increased attention, if not pressure, by commercial leisure places and advertisers. For the children and youth themselves, however, there were still very real material and familial limits to the spending of their money and leisure time. Familial conflicts were not uncommon.[10]

For much of the first half of the twentieth century, exhibitions, fairs, and circuses represented childhood fun and freedom from the regular strictures of social propriety and the daily grind of life, work, community, and church for both rural and urban populations. Travelling in and out of towns for short periods of time during warm months, the shows represented a life of freedom and escape. In the 1920s, thirteen-year-old Merle Jones enjoyed "nearly all the sideshows" with her friend Mabel at the fair held in Brandon, Manitoba.[11] Robert Thompson grew up in Saskatoon in the 1930s and recalled: "Exhibition week rivalled Christmas for the excitement it created in kids' minds."[12] Small children had to be accompanied by their parents or another chaperone, but Thompson recalled that once they had reached the age of ten or eleven, girls and boys could go with friends and attend every day. According to Thompson, "the sideshows were always fascinating." He remembered the fat lady, the Thin Man, and the Alligator Man.[13] In 1950, Grant MacEwan nostalgically looked back on his youthful experiences: "There were sideshows, and if the farm boy had to choose between a two-headed calf and a two-legged girl show, his agricultural interests were easily restrained. If the decision was not an easy one, it was because the girl show cost fifteen cents while the calf monstrosities could be seen for ten."[14] In *Growing Up*, his book on the history of childhood in Canada, Neil Sutherland quotes Grant Buddy: "Fairs should be seen 'from the perspective of a nine-year old. As a child, the Pacific National Exhibition [in Vancouver] ranks with the cardinal events of the year: Halloween, Christmas, Easter, your birthday. At nine, the fair is magic. It means rides, music, faces, *freaks*, the hot sweet scent of candy apples, seagulls swarming spilled popcorn, three-day tattoos and having your fortune told by a mouse." From his own research, Sutherland continues: "Youngsters felt they had taken a major step towards maturing when they were permitted to tour the midway and, eventually, go to the fair on their own."[15] If some youth looked to exhibitions, fairs, circuses, and sideshows as a fantasy world of fun, it was because of wider changes to the culture of childhood that made this so.

Sideshows billed themselves as places of fun for adults and children, and with the rising dominance of youth culture – itself firmly embedded in commercial culture – show promoters began to appeal more directly to children from the 1920s onwards.[16] The combination of showpeople's need to build paying audiences and children's increasing consumer power was a potent match. Special children's days and special pricing for admissions, or sometimes even free admission to the show along with reduced rates for rides, were common. In August 1924, a *Globe* article announced, "New Record Reached as 203,000 Children Throng Great Fair." The article noted: "The amusements of the Exhibition, and they are so many that for the average visitor one day seems but a moment, suffered a similar fate. Fat people and midgets, clowns and ponies, freaks and houses of mystery – for them was a gala day indeed. But the entire Exhibition lent a free hand and Young Canada underwent no restrictions. Free admission came from the officials of the Exhibition, while from the Midway people the sum of five cents admitted even to the most costly of the main attractions."[17]

In 1927, the West Algoma Agricultural Association's Fair attracted an estimated 9,000 children from the twin cities of Port Arthur and Fort William, Ontario, on "Kiddies Day." The newspaper described the children as a "juvenile army" and noted that the midway was "the great attraction."[18] It was not just about fun, however. In 1935, a manager of the Krause Great Shows argued in *Billboard* that "another important step is the education of the child. The world moves forward on the feet of little children."[19] In 1938, the Polack Bros. Circus offered reduced admission prices for children in Vancouver at a carnival sponsored by the Gizeh Temple Patrol. Children's tickets sold for 25 cents, while adult tickets cost 40 cents.[20] The World of Mirth shows, which played in Canada, notably at the Central Canada Exhibition in Ottawa, used "shrewd psychology."[21] Conklin seems to have done the same. In the early 1940s, a press release quoted him as having told the Exhibition Board (which one was not specified) that "pleasing the public is the showman's duty – not garnering every last dollar. With this in mind, I am creating, just for example, a special fun division for the children where they will be entertained while under the watchful eyes of trained attendants … all parental worries will be eliminated."[22] Whether or not parents trusted Conklin with the temporary care of their children is unclear, but he certainly made the attempt to create child-friendly zones at the shows.[23] Writing in the late 1940s and early 1950s for a variety of American periodicals, William Lindsay Gresham described the use of space designed to appeal to children. He wrote, "On each side of the entrance are booths selling toys and novelties, while directly in front of the customer as he enters is the frozen-custard wagon. Children find it hard to pass any of these."[24] Games with prizes of toys, special treats like candy apples, and other items appealed to children's tastes. The heavy appeal to children and their pennies, however, was not always met with full agreement by children themselves. In August 1939, the *Globe and Mail* reported on children using a facsimile machine at the fair. One of the boy's self-authored headlines was "Master Ted Talhot Declares Too Many Freaks on Midway."[25] Children could and did have tastes of their own.

Of all the children who attended, sideshow promoters seemed especially interested in newsboys, working-class children engaged in low-paying often late-night work, and orphans. In 1926, seventy-five newsboys in Fort William, Ontario, were guests of Johnny J. Jones at the carnival. A newspaper article reported that the boys were delighted and that the "assemblage of fat folks had smiles wreathed across the faces of the kids in no time and here an unusually fine time was enjoyed."[26] One year later, the *Vancouver Sun* announced that the Elks were planning on taking "a party of orphans and pupils of the school for the deaf and blind, 300 in all" to the Al G. Barnes circus. The circus included a sideshow with "Mr. Sky High," "Fat Rosie," Liu Yu-Ching, an allegedly nine-foot-tall Chinese giant, and other freaks.[27] That year the *Vancouver Sun* announced that forty newspaper boys in Nanaimo accepted an invitation to see the Conklin and Garrett carnival.[28] In 1941, the Shriners and the Canadian National Exhibition teamed up to bring two thousand orphans to The Ex. According to a newspaper account and accompanying photograph, the children were entertained by Conklin's sideshow and its performers.[29] Appealing to newsboys and orphans functioned to stake a claim to working- and middle-class respectability by illustrating a sense of care for local hardworking or vulnerable children. In the shifting context of the construction of child welfare, such an appeal was politically, culturally, and commercially savvy. Johnny J. Jones's company went further in 1922. Jones reportedly had his son donate "$25 toward the fund for The Winnipeg Tribune orphans' picnic."[30] The donation was especially smart given that shows relied on newspapers for promotion. For children who did not live the ideal childhood – working boys in paid labour and orphans – the fairgrounds were a place to reclaim the sense of fun, abandon, and wonder of "normal" childhood. Yet the photographic evidence is telling in its juxtaposition. Children at play on the midway stood outside the canvas banners advertising children working as freaks.

Child Freak Show Workers

Working-class newsboys and orphans, along with the other children who attended, got a break at the fair, but for other children, sideshows were not entertainment but work. Importantly, child freak performers experienced fairs and sideshows differently than the children who were courted and came as audience members. The cultural narrative of children's freedom at the fair needs to be tempered with the experience of child performers in order to open up more nuanced discussions on the nature and experiences of childhood for those who were excluded from white, middle-class, able-bodied ideals of the child by virtue of disability and poverty. Either on or off stage (and almost regardless of economic need), work on the sideshows was beyond the reality of either respectable work or dominant visions of childhood. Sideshow families, born and made, were transient and children lived well beyond the ideal of white, middle-class domesticity. Work on the sideshows, however, was often referred to as "the family business." In *It's All Done with Mirrors*, Canadian carnival worker and owner Hazel Elves describes her brothers' work as performers on the Canadian sideshow circuits from the ages of four and five. While it is unclear from her autobiography how old she was when she joined the family business, it is clear that when she did she remained firmly under her father's authority. Her autobiography also describes adolescent interests in addition to her work experiences on the sideshows.[31]

Over a century after Kay's declaration, work by Canadian historians has shown that for all the achievements of the 1900s, the declaration "Century of the Child" rang hollow for many children.[32] Nineteenth-century "child-saving" movements and twentieth-century attempts at child welfare have received significant criticism from historians, who have seen the measures as means of social control or moral regulation aimed particularly at the working classes – a product of wider social conditions and power imbalances.[33] As much as these reforms may have been intended to be universal, they were, in fact, largely defined by white, Anglo, middle-class ideology. Even as the discourse on the protected child was solidifying, industrializing countries like Britain and Canada relied on the labour of children. In the nineteenth century, few working-class and rural families could afford to give up the income and labour children provided. Only by the end of the century, in the 1890s, did paid child labour begin to decline as a result of the rise of working-class purchasing power. Yet, during that decade an investigation undertaken in Halifax, Quebec City, Montreal, Ottawa, Toronto, and Hamilton found scores of children working over sixty hours a week at home in the needle trades.[34] Boys and girls performed important paid and unpaid work, with that work divided along gender lines – girls were expected to mind children and do household chores, and boys were engaged in more formal paid work outside the home, such as delivering newspapers.[35] As a result, while ideas of childhood changed, many Canadian children's lives were defined by exploitative conditions and harsh treatment. Understanding the ideal of sentimental childhood tells us about the ideologies of the time rather than the actual experience of children across the spectrum of class, gender, and ability. The need for some children to work, combined with the lack of protection for children with disabilities, publicly advertised as freaks, helps to explain how the carnival sideshows continued to function without state intervention.

Undergirding the sorting, treatment, and care of disabled children was the concept of the "normal" child. In the 1920s efforts to define normal childhood and normal families intensified. Constructing categories of "normal" and "childhood" created a hierarchy of classifications for children and their families.[36] By the 1930s, discourses structuring normalcy and child welfare solidified to the point where provincial governments – led by Ontario – developed complex systems of regulation and intervention for families who fell beyond the norm, but this rarely, if ever, pierced the sideshow world.[37] As Veronica Strong-Boag argues, "children designated as handicapped roused little enthusiasm from state or private authorities."[38] Work as a sideshow performer was still work and could be valuable income for a family, something state officials may have been hesitant to interfere with. It is difficult if not impossible to tell from the extant sources whether disabled children sparked less sympathy, their work was deemed too necessary to families, or tracking the children in the transient sideshow world was too difficult.

Children with disabilities were also seen as less desirable for adoption and foster care. Provincial institutions by the 1920s were overwhelmed with less "desirable" children. By the end of the decade – before the massive economic crisis of the Depression – one staff member of the Canadian Council on Child Welfare described the different types of "disabled" and "undesirable" children already in institutions: "Children with bow legs, cross eyes, ugly brick red hair, jug-handled ears, near-sighted children, half-caste children, the child who stutters, the child with the frowning countenance, the bad complexion, the birth mark or those whose hair stands straight on end, the child who, through physical weakness or lack of training, has not acquired clean personal habits and, perhaps most pitiful of all, the child with the bad heritage."[39] As Strong-Boag concludes, "Abnormality stigmatized countless children and helped ensure that they would be hard put to find supporters or function with confidence."[40]

By the 1940s, children with disabilities received more public attention as people with specialized needs, and children were used to raise funds for specific diseases, disabilities, or conditions.[41] Beginning in the 1950s and 1960s, more specialized community and institutional care emerged with a focus on children with special needs. These changes signalled a slow change in public attitude, but for working-class and middle-class families, finding adequate care and support proved difficult.[42] During an address of the dinner meeting of the Cerebral Palsy Section of the Canadian Council for Crippled Children and Adults in Winnipeg in April 1960, William F. Macklaier recounted the recent "discovery" of a child with cerebral palsy "born to a family of northern 'colons' in a remote part of New Quebec." According to Macklaier, the "ignorant" parents had cared for the child by keeping him in a baby carriage for his fourteen or fifteen years, leading to further psychological and physiological problems.[43] Despite the increasingly sophisticated welfare system, children with disabilities and their families often found few good options.

So how did some children end up on the freak show? The history of the sideshow reveals the ongoing exchange of children in the nineteenth and twentieth centuries. Freak show operators contacted parents, offering them contracts and money for the display of their children. At other times parents contacted shows and offered them for exhibition. Some of these children's lives have been recorded in thin archival files or, as I primarily rely on here, extraordinary letters to the New York World's Fair by Canadians and Americans. In large part the letters written to officials in New York were initiated because of the one-million-dollar offer to exhibit the Dionne quintuplets. As the next chapter details, the Dionne family was contacted by at least two showmen immediately after the girls' birth. The context of the Depression is significant here, too, as many families faced a deepening crisis with few social and financial supports. Other official records are nearly impossible to find, so the evidence here is suggestive and incomplete. The fact that so many of the records stop abruptly or cannot be traced speaks to the wider issues raised in Karen Balcom's book on the trafficking of babies between jurisdictions in Canada and the United States from the 1930s to the early 1970s. Gaps in jurisdiction, child welfare policies, immigration policies, and laws created a situation ripe for trade that was difficult to trace.[44]

Child freak show performers existed in the nineteenth century. Some of the earlier cases on record begin with African American conjoined twins Millie-Christine McKoy. Born in the United States in 1851, they were bought, sold, and kidnapped repeatedly – even after the Emancipation Proclamation. According to one source, they were briefly in the hands of Farini.[45] Other popular sideshow child performers Hiram and Barney Davis (known as Waino and Plutano) were either sold, informally adopted, or given to showman Hanford Warner sometime in the 1850s. Reportedly, the death record of the twins recorded their parentage and birth place as unknown. Newspaper reports allege that the twins were either American or born to white missionaries.[46]

The difficulty in finding and tracing records is apparent in Canadian cases as well. In 1887, Indian officers at Rat Portage, Ontario, undertook the difficult task of tracking down a showman based in London, England, who had "borrowed" an armless child from a nearby reserve, based on a contract with the father, for the purposes of exhibiting the child. The contract was drawn up by a member of the Hudson's Bay Company, with Indian agent R.J.N. Pither's knowledge. While searching for the child, Pither wrote to his superior that he had "advised his father at the time not to let his son go." When the promised money of fifty dollars per month (to be equally divided between the boy and his father) was not forthcoming, the father enlisted Pither's help to track down the boy. As of May 1887, the father had allegedly received only one payment of twenty-five dollars and had no contact from his son or the showman for two years. In 1885, the showman wrote to the father telling him that there were "lots of men and women born without arms on the streets of New York and other cities in the States." He had decided to take the boy to England where he named him "Borett, the son of Big Bear Chief of the Cree Indians," rationalizing that it was better than "the son of a common Indian."[47] According to a letter from the showman to the father, he was having trouble making money because the boy's condition was rather less extraordinary in large cities, where there were many street beggars with disabilities. The records end abruptly and other records if they exist eluded my searches.

Other children were allegedly adopted by showmen, who ostensibly became both parent and manager. Children like Emmitt Bejano, known as the "Alligator-Skinned Boy" (and later, the "Alligator-Skinned Man"), was, according to one source, "adopted" by Johnny Bejano. Bejano was a showman who put him on the sideshow circuits. Showman Ward Hall recalled, "When Emmett [sic] Bejano, the Alligator Skin Man, was a child, he was adopted by the dean of the sideshow men of the nineteen twenties and thirties, Johnny Bejano. It was common practice in those days for sideshow owners to adopt children who were considered human oddities, from parents who either did not want them, or who realized the advantages they would receive in such circumstances."[48] In 1938, Emmitt married Percilla Lauther – the "adopted" daughter of showman Carl Lauther – who was exhibited as a child as "Little Hairy Girl," and later "Monkey Girl."[49] The surrender of children to sideshow promoters, however it was negotiated, would have been a complex process. More than likely, these were not legal adoptions, but invoking the word "adoption" gave the exhibitors legitimacy and implied a sort of legal sanctioning on the part of birth parents and the state. Such arrangements were not uncommon, even by the mid-1900s. Poverty, lack of childcare, and single parenting (either from widowhood, desertion, or illegitimacy) put families as risk when little, inadequate, or no social welfare was forthcoming.[50] The complicated histories of domestic relations in Canada reveal that children were placed with kin or strangers in private exchanges, "especially in disadvantaged groups haunted by death, disease, and disability."[51]

Historically, children had also been formally or informally "adopted" into families for work, as in the case of Canadian home children.[52] Adoption itself was a contested and shifting concept, and even at mid-century there were questions about infants whom authorities had lost track of, as well as the North America–wide "traffic in babies."[53] The exchange of a child between adults was not that rare, especially for work, but what was unusual about the sideshow "adoptions" was that they involved disabled or extraordinary children for the purposes of public exhibition. The word "adoption" glossed over the messiness of procuring a child for financial benefit. For a variety of reasons, however, parents gave, sold, and lent their children, but also exhibited them.

Sideshows defended their use of children as freaks by pointing to the inadequate and inhuman treatment of children with disabilities in "regular" society. That perspective and its critique at the time obscured the real issues of poverty and stigma. Parents of children with disabilities found only very limited support available from their local governments or state welfare, despite widespread need. Such vulnerability is apparent in the offers to and from the New York World's Fair in 1939 and 1940. In both years, organizers attempted to secure the Dionne quintuplets as an exhibit. While their attempts failed, news of the offer caused North American parents, along with at least one teacher, one newspaper editor, and one doctor, among others, to write to the fair offering their children for exhibition. The letters were directed to and received by various officials associated with the fair, although the midway had been contracted out to Dufour and Rogers.

These letters represent an exceptional archive of negotiations otherwise unrecorded or not archived. More importantly, the letters shed light on why and how some children may have been lent or adopted to work as child freak show performers. In this section, I document several of these extraordinary letters from parents and other adults who provide a wide range of reasons for offering their children as freaks. I have included letters from both American and Canadian writers in the hope of illuminating some of the decision making that went into exhibiting children. I include letters from American families because this archive is so unique in documenting exchanges that eluded official record keepers. Importantly, they show that what brought children to the sideshows as paid performers was not just the result of sideshow operators "hunting" for freaks. What becomes clear in most of the letters is that families of all sorts were driven by economic necessity to write to the fair.

A Mrs Orbeck from Lloydminster, Alberta, for example, offered her two albino sons aged eighteen and nine: "The government wanted to take them but I would not agree to that. People have come from far to see these boys, nobody has ever seen any body [sic] like them. Everybody says that I should put them in a side show. Everybody seen in the paper about taking the Dionne Quintriplets [sic]. They say why not haves [sic] my sons there too as they are just as odd as them."[54] Mrs Orbeck seems to have successfully resisted efforts to remove her children. The fact that she thought the sideshow was preferable to government care for her children is important in revealing the significance of permanent parental care and the possibilities for family members to resist state intervention. Her pride in her sons being "odd" is also suggested. Other parents wrote to the fair without shame, noting that while their children had disabilities, they were also extraordinary, bright, and talented.[55]

Some parents of infants were clearly coming to terms with the lack of options available to them and saw the sideshow as a legitimate, if not preferable, choice for their children. One letter spoke to a mix of economic desperation, disappointment, and embarrassment in having an extraordinary child, but also care and concern. The letter by an American father went:

> Just a few words. I am sorry to write to you about my baby boy, that is so deformed, at birth, May 6, 1939.
>
> He has no arms, and has but one leg. But his is a normal baby from what the doctors say, and there is not cure for him. We tried so not to bring him home, but they said that they couldn't place the baby in an institution, because it was to[o] young.
>
> We are poor people and are on Home Relie[f] and me and the [Mrs] thought that we would like to put the baby on exhibition at the World's Fair, so that other people can see that every baby can't be normal. We have another baby girl 3 years old, which is alright, and very bright. This baby is going to be a burden on us if it lives the rest of our lives. The doctor at the Hospital said that he had never seen or heard of anything like this before as long as he has been a doctor, and the people I speak to say the same. They never seen anything like it before if you can not put it on exhibition a[t] the World's Fair, please write me and tell me what to do. Maybe there is a place to send him to. You see it isn't so bad now. But when it grows up it will be an awful burden as is. So please do what you can for us, every body else turns us down.[56]

Letters like this one reveal families' attempts at other means of assistance, referencing the fact that institutions would not take infants and that other strategies, like surrendering their children, were unsatisfactory or impossible. In Canada, this letter resonated with long-established family strategies of using public institutional care for adults and children.[57] For desperate families, requests for placement were a means of survival. Since care of dependents typically fell to women, whose supposed natural caretaking abilities defined their roles in the family and society, the burden of care could be great. Mother, father, siblings, and other household members, however, would have simultaneously felt varying degrees of grief and relief at the prospect of care. For patients, as Geoffrey Reaume notes, the possibility of institutional care could bring on feelings of fear or relief depending on past experiences and the need for the basic necessities for life.[58]

With the lack of other options, some parents saw a paid exhibit as a way to earn much-needed money. A letter from 1939 reveals one family's efforts to give their child and family "a fair start":

> I am writing to you for a little information, and hope you will give it a little consideration. Almost two years ago I had a boy born into my family of 6 who was born with a great misfortune. He is as smart as a child of 3 or 4 years old and here is his troubles he was born without either legs or arm he has one arm his right but it is webbed together (his hand) and is of [no] use to him now I am on the WPA[59] [making] $24.00 every 2 weeks, but I am in debt. I have a loan on my household goods and am afraid I am going to lose everything I have as I cant possibl[y] pay off this debt. And my baby needs a chance in life and I really cant see any possible chance here, my baby is known as far as your wonderful city I can refer you to the Voice of Experience, Box 100 Grand Central Station. He can tell you of my baby. Now to get down to why I am writing you. I wanted to know if there was some way in which I could give him a chance at the Fair. I hardly know how to explain what I mean, but I am willing to do any thing you suggest. I want my baby to have a start in life. He is going to have to have artificial limbs, his education and a home, and if I cant get something besides this job I have I am going to lose that. So Mr Whalen please (if you are interested) let me know what you can do for my baby at your Fair. I don't care as long as it wont hurt his name in the future. If you will write me I will send you a picture of him then you can see for yourself how he is crippled and why I am asking you if there is someway you could work him in at the Fair to get him a fair start.[60]

The expression of concern over the impact of the child's name speaks to the care and concern of a parent worried that being exhibited as a freak would mark her child permanently.

It was not always parents who wrote to the fair; as noted above, teachers, doctors, newspaper editors, and other people whose relationship with the birth family was unclear also wrote looking for a place on the sideshow for children. The editor of the *Grand Forks Gazette* in Grand Forks, British Columbia, wrote in a typed letter:

A female child oddity was born here on June 11. It has ... a natural tail about five inches long. Otherwise the child is normal and apparently healthy. Both parents are Canadian-born, but their parents *Doukhobors* [written in pen] were both born in Russia. Mother, 22, speaks Russian only, but father, 27, speaks good English. They have another child about 1½ years apparently normal.

Would you be interested in production of the child at your Fair? If so what suggestions have you to offer?

Parents are interested in removal of the tail but preliminary medical advice is that such should not be considered for a year at least.

Would be glad to hear from you in the matter.[61]

While it is unclear from the letter if the editor was writing on behalf of the parents or even with their knowledge, it is clear that seeking out the fair was a temporary measure before "surgical correction." Given the expenses associated with the surgery, displaying the child may have been seen as a way to deal with those costs.

Another letter by an American physician to the New York's World Fair about a child with missing limbs expressed regret that the disabled child might live, although he did note that he had both an X-ray and a coloured movie of the child.[62] As research in American history reveals, the birth of a child with disabilities in the period sometimes led to passive or active euthanizing.[63] From the perspective of many doctors, institutionalization was a good strategy. Yet the decision was complicated by a host of factors, including economic means, location, and levels of care. While physicians might have expressed regret at a child's life or recommended institutionalization, parents did not always share those ideas.[64]

Economic necessity, while very significant, was not the only compelling reason for parents to write letters. Some parents took pride in their children's differences and talents, some were deeply embarrassed, and some saw the child's existence as pitiful and unfortunate but as having special value in teaching others that not all children were "normal." With the exception of people who were not writing about their own children, all the letters shared a concern for the care of the child. All of the people who wrote to the fair offering their children were referred to the company that had been contracted to host the sideshow. Most were standard replies with simple directions to write to the carnival company. The poor couple who wrote that they could not institutionalize their son received a more unusual and heartfelt reply from one of the fair directors: "The Fair is sponsoring no exhibit in which your unfortunate child could be included ... I sincerely hope that you are successful in your negotiations with this concessionaire."[65] The freak show ran the gamut from last resort to opportunity.

Some parents stayed involved and travelled with their children, while others negotiated a more permanent agreement akin to adoption. Sometimes parents or guardians remained involved as their children were exhibited and, in rare cases, children had their own managers who handled the contracts. In 1910, an advertisement in *Billboard* announced the availability of four-year-old "Handsome Johnny Webb," who allegedly weighed 147 pounds and was "the ladies' favorite." The advertisement was notable for its size and use of a photograph, but also because few acts engaged in this type of solicitation. Webb's manager was listed as the contact and he was interested in hearing from "first-class Carnival Cos., Parks and Fairs." Unlike other child performers, Webb's seemingly professional management (he stayed working on the sideshows until he died suddenly in 1938) was different.[66] Most families negotiated adoptions or contracts directly with show folk themselves. One such case, which is reasonably well documented, is that of Ernie Defort. The documentation of the case reveals some of the complexities and nuances of children's work as freaks on the sideshows in Canada.

The Case of Ernie Defort

Ernie Defort was born in Winnipeg in 1931 to parents Emma and Frank Defort, identified in one newspaper article as Polish immigrants. As described in chapter 4, Ernie was born with an asymmetrical conjoined twin, frequently referred to as a parasitic twin, whom he reportedly called Lester.[67] The twin (publicly known as Len in the Ernie-Len exhibits) had a fully formed lower body (including pelvis, liver, and kidneys, although the latter were removed in an operation when Ernie was two years old) and arms and hands.[68] After entertaining a number of offers from sideshows, the Deforts placed Ernie with the Conklin shows run by Patty Conklin. Reportedly, his mother travelled with him, although all promotional materials include only references to medical professionals present at his birth. Ernie-Len appeared as a baby and child on the sideshow circuits, travelling across the country as Conklin's feature attraction in the 1930s and early 1940s, until he had "corrective" surgery to remove the twin. On the sideshow, Ernie was billed as "The World's Strangest Living Boy" and as "Two Living Brothers with Only One Head."[69] One of the custom-made show fronts declared, "Rarer Than the Dionne

5.2 "Ernie and Len: Two Living Brothers with One Head,"
CNE midway sideshow, 1937. Canadian National Exhibition Archives.
G. Hollies Photography.

Quintuplets."[70] The parents had received a number of offers from sideshows (as had the Dionnes), but trusted Conklin, even though he could offer less money.[71] By the 1930s, Conklin had become a significant commercial force in the travelling carnival business, securing the premier carnival circuits in western Canada and, by 1937, the permanent, annual contract for the lucrative Canadian National Exhibition in Toronto.[72]

While sideshow performances were not often seen as respectable work, they continued to draw people and money, as is clearly evident in Defort's case. Even in the heart of the Depression, sideshows continued to make money, and the persistence of the smaller companies certainly speaks to their popularity if not their ability to turn a profit. Children's labour had long been an important resource for Canadian families, especially among the working class, but during the Depression, even middle-class children were expected to contribute in both formal and informal ways to the family economy.[73] In the 1930s children's paid employment took on deeper significance for family survival, and children, sometimes willingly and sometimes begrudgingly, helped their families survive by leaving school for paid work, balancing school and paid labour, taking on unwaged work in the home or on the farm, or through informal, illegal activities like stealing. Children's labour was often about survival, so breaking the law, working at night, leaving school, and turning over portions or all of pay packets were about need and often resulted from parental unemployment.[74] For many families, an alternative like "relief," a limited welfare strategy, was difficult to attain, wrapped in shame, and inadequate.[75] As unemployment rates soared, a few seriously desperate families resorted to murder and suicide. Three years after Ernie Defort was born in Winnipeg, a mother drowned her toddler son, strangled her five-year-old daughter, and then committed suicide out of simple economic desperation.[76] The point has to be carefully made, and I'm not suggesting the alternative to the freak show was death, but I describe this tragedy as a way of framing economic need and the reality of the material comforts brought by work on the sideshow. And while sideshows may have lost cultural status, they continued to be a good draw of people and money. Ernie-Len was reported to have made $14,000 in the seven years he worked only summer circuits – a figure that is almost certainly exaggerated. (Reportedly, once school-aged, he only worked during the summer.)[77] His mother recalled, perhaps trying to justify her decision, "My husband was out of work then and I thought the travelling would build up my boy's health."[78] As with many biographies of sideshow child performers, however, the actual negotiations that brought Ernie-Len to the sideshow remained largely undocumented. The wider context on the care of children with disabilities may be illuminating. In Depression-era Winnipeg, a child with a so-called parasitic twin who may have needed substantial medical attention could have been seen as a social and economic burden to the family. Work as a spectacle on the sideshow might have been rationalized as offsetting potentially expensive medical care and treatment or decreasing dependency on other family members, or both. In 1937, Ernie and his parents travelled to Europe to consult with doctors on the possibility of separating the twins. They were told it would lead to death.[79] The possibility of medical care and of making a living might have made freak work appealing. Unlike some other sideshow child performers, Ernie was not fully removed from his parents' care by means of an informal adoption.[80] Nonetheless, Ernie's work as a freak provided the chance for some semblance of "normal" childhood during the off-season when he was not performing and seems to have ultimately provided the financial means for his decision in the early 1940s to undergo surgery to remove Lester.

Sideshow owners and promoters like Conklin were not immune to shifts in child welfare discourses, which were rooted in wider social and cultural shifts. Beginning in the 1920s, the billing of freak performers changed to tap into both medical discourses and expanding standards of care and education. Pamphlets and *cartes de visite* sold at the show, along with other promotional material, reveal these changes, as owners appealed to audiences' sense of charity or duty by emphasizing that profits would go to the education of the child.[81] In the presentation of the extraordinariness of Ernie-Len's body, Conklin appealed to ideals of "normal" middle-class experiences like schooling, the celebration of birthdays, and interest in particular hobbies. In 1943, the *Fort William Daily Times Journal* reported:

> Questioned regarding Ernie Defort, the two-bodied boy from Winnipeg, who was with him for seven years, Mr. Conklin stated that the boy's operation performed at Rochester [the Mayo Clinic] on October 17, 1943, was a success and Ernie is coming along fine, although he still has to have another operation. He said that it is Ernie's ambition to become a music composer. "Ernie is musically inclined and while in Winnipeg last week I purchased him a violin so he could study music," said Mr. Conklin. He added that he plans to send him to Rochester this summer to undergo his final operation.[82]

Conklin's statement reveals the benevolence of a sideshow owner and could have reassured audience members that their gawking had succeeded in contributing to the norming of an "abnormal" child.

Off the sideshow and fully dressed, Ernie looked like an "ordinary" boy, and studio shots of him fully dressed are unremarkable. Nude photographs, like the popular *cartes de visite* produced of him as an infant and child, revealed Len (Lester) and it is likely that he was exhibited in the nude or near nude. Children's bodies did not carry the same taboo as adult nudes (in large part due to children's disempowered status and so-called "primitiveness"). This idea was invoked in one letter the New York World's Fair in regard to the exhibition of a baby. In early 1940, a J.B. Goyer, on letterhead from the J.B. Goyer, Ltd., Coal and Coke Company of Montreal, wrote to the manager of the New York State Fair offering a "perfect hermaphrodite" for display, arguing that "it would not be immoral, as the baby is only ten days old just now."[83] The ideal of childhood itself provided some gloss of respectability to displays in that children's bodies were to exude innocence, although reactions by the audience need not have met this ideal. As with the Dionne quintuplets, described in the next chapter, Defort's increasing age shifted the alleged innocence and morality of gazing upon him, changing how his body could be viewed and exhibited. Clearly for Defort, his difference, although not as "cute" as the Dionnes were, meant that his body became solely idealized, a child freak in spectacle and display that may have been seen by critics as tawdry and cheap but not sexualized. Although it is impossible to know how Ernie-Len's exhibition may have changed as he grew older, nude adolescent and adult bodies on the sideshow had to be much more carefully regulated and controlled to avoid public outcry.[84]

Defort's case also reveals the absence of public child welfare–based critiques. Similarly, Valverde has noted the absence of child welfare discourse in the framing of the Dionne quints. Indeed, there is little to suggest that freak workers were of serious interest to child welfare authorities. In 1920, J.J. Kelso, superintendent of the Office of Neglected and Dependent Children, reported to the chief of the OPP on the living quarters of two girls travelling with the Johnny J. Jones show. He noted that their living environment was "scrupulously clean," that the children were "well dressed" with "nice manners, well educated for their age." He concluded: "I am satisfied they are not allowed to mingle with the other show people."[85] Clearly, child performers on the sideshows were not hidden from authorities because they were discussed and advertised in newspapers, and, as in the case of Ernie, nude pictures of them freely circulated. Performance as a freak was paid work, and thus it is not surprising that child welfare authorities would not intervene. Ernie was still in school, travelling with his mother, and otherwise taken care of. Given the stretched budgets and overburdened schedules of child welfare authorities in the period, his case would have been unlikely to garner much attention in the largely fallow years of child welfare in the 1930s and 1940s. Further, sideshows had aligned themselves with the rising entertainment industry with its many child performers. Child welfare authorities also struggled to meet the demands as offices across the country remained isolated from each other, poorly staffed with high turnover rates, and at best, modestly funded.

In the early 1940s, Ernie made the decision to undergo surgery to remove the twin at the Mayo Clinic in Rochester and, as with the Dionne quintuplets, his performances ended as he entered adolescence. As early as 1937, his parents had travelled with Ernie to Germany to see if surgeons would operate, but they declined. After the successful surgery in Rochester, Dr Henry W. Meyerding reported that the twin "had sapped much of the strength of the boy [Ernie] before its removal."[86] William Good, a reporter for the *Winnipeg Tribune*, apparently encouraged Ernie to speak with him after surgery. After Ernie expressed concerns about being teased at school, Good suggested that for "other children born with physical defect ... his experience might inspire them to undergo a similar operation, and ultimately find a place in the world as normal men and women."[87] In the interview Ernie provided a fascinatingly oblique response to the question, "Why did you decide to have this operation?" Ernie is quoted as having said, "I made up my mind to have it done and that was all there was to it. I didn't want to keep on the way I was, and an operation was the only answer."[88] It is unclear from the documentary record whether Ernie was referring to living with the conjoined twin or working as a sideshow performer. In newspaper reports, Dr Meyerding suggested that "Ernie was depressed at the thought of losing the twin body."[89] The surgery was heralded a success and widely reported in newspapers across North America for making Ernie a "normal" boy. Although Conklin continued to discuss Ernie-Len in interviews and press releases, Ernie did not return to the sideshows as a performer after the surgery.[90] In the celebratory articles on the surgery, reporters, physicians, and other commentators on Ernie's body repeatedly highlighted the norming of his body through surgery. A few mentioned the sense of grief and loss Ernie experienced in being separated from his brother, but the overall consensus was that Ernie had been saved from abnormality.[91]

The story of Ernie-Len is an example of how commercial spectacles could erase the privilege of childhood. The exhibits reinforced the stigma associated with disabled peoples and reaffirmed the culturally produced line between normality and abnormality. However, the sideshows were not simply exploitative. Given the options and strategies available to parents at the time, engaging the sideshows was a means to assert agency, to be economically productive, and, if possible, to access medical treatment to "norm" the body. Ernie's exhibition allowed him to gain medical treatment and in that way he was able to exercise some agency. Ernie's case, however, was in some ways unique given his surgery. It was another child performer decades after him that brought in significant changes at some Canadian sideshows, and that was Pookie decades later.

Conclusion

For children who performed as freaks in sideshows, their experiences ranged widely. For some it was a short stint, while others found longer careers. Pay packets and related economic opportunities varied as did levels of agency, shame, and pride in their work. By and large, however, it seems that the children who ended up working as freaks did so for two main reasons: first, disability made it difficult for parents or other caregivers to keep them or find other adequate care; second, poverty made the economic enticement of sideshows too great to decline. For the vast majority of children who worked as freaks, it was the combination of both those reasons that led to their display and performance. Many of them began their careers as infants or young children and, as such, issues of choice and consent remain entirely or heavily circumscribed by the nature of their relationships to documentary-producing bodies. Sideshow life may have provided some measure of economic security among a host of other limited choices given prejudices against disability and difference, but it was not a bulwark against a cruel world – it was part of it. If never able to find a place within the category of childhood (and the protection that children received), child freak performers could perhaps find comfort in the fact that they had carved out some place of significance with a measure of material security. One of the sideshow canvases for Ernie-Len described him as "Canada's Problem Boy"; the persistent problem seems to be our collective inability to challenge the structures that produce child poverty and to challenge the (not unrelated) cultural assumption of a singular, normal, able body.

Overall, the continued existence of freak shows and their popularity certainly reflects a massive social and cultural failure to address small bodies in meaningful, humane ways. In part, the social construction of the category of childhood put child freak performers like Ernie Defort in harm's way. Child freak performers were seen almost exclusively as different – and that difference was irreconcilable with the category of childhood that would have given them a certain type of protection and care. The shame resides in the fact that finding a place meant perpetuating the idea of absolute difference and freakery, but that shame is a social and cultural one, not an individual one.

Only by the 1960s and 1970s did public attitudes toward abuse, neglect, and aspects of disability begin to shift.[92] After early twentieth-century discussions on abuse and neglect, widespread public discussion and concern went fallow until the 1960s, when American physician

C. Henry Kempe's seminal work on "battered child syndrome" was released.[93] Although Canadians' reactions were varied, significant legislation resulted.[94] In regard to disability, the fights over publicly funded medical care originating in Saskatchewan in 1947 emerged as a nationally funded program in 1966. Increased national funding in the 1950s led to more assistance, programs, and treatment, although much attention was focused on disabling diseases like polio. By 1960, optimism was apparent in the annual report of the Canadian Council for Crippled Children and Adults, which reported that federal funds, along with partnerships with provincial organizations in all Canadian provinces, allowed for "the basic crippled children's services." Further, they celebrated how "medical and surgical treatment, special educational facilities, treatment centres, summer camping, rehabilitation programs, are now the right of every Canadian child."[95]

While some Canadians were working towards reckoning with aspects of physical disability, other disabilities remained a challenge. In 1962, "A Working Paper on Mental Retardation" noted, "There is professional interest and also intense pressure from lay groups for the evolvement of programs of adequate care, treatment and training of the mentally retarded of all ages. Throughout our country residential centres for the retarded are overcrowded and the waiting lists are heavy. Community facilities are developing slowly but are still far from adequate to meet the varying needs of the retarded. There is also a tragic lack of personnel trained and qualified to work in the field."[96] In the 1980s and 1990s, Canadians debated the issue of the right to life for some children with disabilities through cases like the 1983 Dawson case in British Columbia and the 1993 case of Tracy Latimer.[97] The persistence of child poverty, the continuing exploitation, neglect, and abuse of Canada's First Nations, the regional variables in accessing treatment, and the ongoing struggle for gender, racial, and class parity in work and at home have led to continuing problems. For all the gains and progress made over the course of the twentieth century, children with disabilities, especially those born into poor or otherwise marginalized families, found themselves in precarious positions. It was these circumstances that show owners exploited and that some families worked to mitigate in displaying children as freaks on the sideshows.

Chapter Six

The Spectacularization of Small and Cute: Midget Shows and the Dionne Quintuplets

From the mid-1930s to the early 1940s, one Canadian family held the attention of North American audiences. Born in northeastern Ontario in 1934, Annette, Cecile, Yvonne, Marie, and Emilie, better known as the Dionne quintuplets, became an international sensation. In 1934, the Ontario government passed legislation making the girls wards of the state. Part of the impetus for the government's taking of the children was their father Oliva Dionne's contract with a Chicago-based promoter that would have put the girls on exhibition in Chicago at the Century of Progress Exposition in 1933. Although in their autobiography, *We Were Five*, the quints recalled how pleasant life was at the custom-built hospital where they were displayed in Ontario, they described the widespread commercialization of their lives as a "Coney Island, a World's Fair and Madison Square Garden rolled into one, so we gather, and we were the sole exhibit."[1]

As the Dionne case reveals, by the 1930s, the "exhibitionary complex" included "the cute child."[2] In the early twentieth century, commercial culture embraced spectacles of sentimental childhood, and the state was involved in those exhibitions, especially when they intersected with progressive ideas of science and medicine. The Dionne case is significant as it reveals the investment in displays of childhood and how people worked to distance themselves from the culturally low freak show, even when the displays were strikingly similar. Indeed, with the Dionne case the Ontario government went from regulating and profiting from the shows into operating one itself. The aptly named Quintland speaks directly to the parallel with modern commercial culture, especially amusement theme parks. Here, however, the government commercially exploited "cuteness" as opposed to disability.

While the freak shows had not disappeared, they were nimble enough to respond to and incorporate cultural shifts. The freak show's cute presentations of both children and little people offered audiences opportunities to see displays that were charming and adorable rather than challenging and jarring. This chapter explores the relationship between sideshow displays and the concept of cute, focusing in particular on the Dionne quintuplets and shows featuring little people. While the latter were usually adult performers in the period under study here, their culturally constructed association with cuteness and smallness created further strong associations with children.[3] The survival of the shows was based not solely on catering to the outskirts of dominant society's tastes but also on harnessing other profitable trends that would appeal to a wide swathe of consumers. Cute shows that ran the gamut from babies to little people performers added the beautiful, the feminine, the innocent, and the glamorous to the reality of the commercialized sideshow.

This chapter begins by analysing the development and operation of the modern concept of "cute" in relation to both child and childlike performances. As Mona Gleason has recently argued, body historians need to take size and its meanings into account.[4] The discussion here focuses specifically on the intersection of consumer culture and childhood and how the cute and the miniature were used to frame the display of little people. Historically, people with small stature on the sideshows were called "midgets." I recognize its offensiveness today and, as such, also use more appropriate terms like "little people" or "people of small stature." I have avoided the term dwarfism, despite its current medical usage, since historically the term was often used to differentiate between proportionate and disproportionate peoples of small stature and the cultural meanings tied to dwarfism were very different.[5] Finally, this chapter provides a close analysis of the display of children of multiple births with a focus on the Dionne quints. By the 1930s, with the extraordinary display of the Dionne quintuplets, elements of the sideshow dovetailed with aspects of modern consumer culture, including baby contests. Although the Dionne quints have been studied as an important case in the development of modern consumer culture and modern scientific parenting, there were both direct and indirect links to the sideshow that illuminate how the freak show persisted into the middle decades of the twentieth century.[6] In sum, this chapter reveals how emerging cultural categories like cute worked in tandem with consumer culture to spectacularize certain bodies and how these were incorporated as part of the freak show.

Cuteness, Childhood, and Consumerism

Originally derived from "acute," meaning shrewd, clever, and devious, cute came to mean "charming, adorable, and often diminutive."[7] The shift from acute to cute began in the late nineteenth century with animals and later children, both of whom had rising status in terms of care and protection. Both animals and children were culturally refigured to evoke feelings of innocence, wonder, and desire. Fundamentally nonthreatening, cuteness provided the pleasure associated with purity. As Lori Merish argues, "The cute child, unlike the Victorian sacred child, is pure spectacle, pure display. What is lost in this idealization of the cute is sexuality and the dangers of its powers."[8] If dominant and nondominant sexualities formed an important and explicit part of other freak performances, cute had the gloss of innocence. In regard to the wildly popular nineteenth-century Tom Thumb wedding, Merish argues that it "delighted viewers because it *looked like children imitating adults*, thus assimilating the 'freak' into the familial and familiar structure of domination and hierarchy."[9] Cute was then also linked to stature, and small size was associated with reduced status. In sum, cute was associated with non-dominant identities and things, which could be consumed, petted, and enjoyed through display.[10] Non-dominant did not mean negatively racialized. Whiteness was an essential ingredient in the fabric of cuteness. Cute children and cute midgets were predominantly white.[11]

By the early decades of the twentieth century, cute had become a commodity aesthetic – something that could be visually consumed and enjoyed – that intertwined the impulse to purchase with the impulse of the sentimental reform of childhood.[12] Cute had a specific look (wide-eyed, joyful, and perhaps a bit impish) that was transferred to modern dolls and other representations of children, especially those used in modern advertising.[13] Cute sold goods by provoking feelings of wonder and innocence supposedly natural in the protected child raised according to the best and most scientific standards of mothering. As Gary Cross argues, adults could experience a vicarious pleasure by consuming for their children based on advertisements that encouraged them to see specific products and goods as giving children pure joy. He argues, "It was surely a morally acceptable materialism within the confines of innocence."[14]

It was also a feminized consumerism. The modern construction of "cute" came in the late 1800s and dovetailed with the rise of sentimental childhood, urban consumer culture, and the redefinition of gender relations. The burgeoning consumer culture of this period not only reshaped public, urban spaces but also provided outlets for testing Victorian gender relations. For middle-class women, shopping provided entry into public spaces and an outlet for potential activism.[15] Such changes were premised on wider shifts in industrialization and urbanization, which introduced more mechanized work for both men and women and brought more people to the cities. Of particular concern from the 1880s to the 1920s were young, single women who seemed to both embody modern life and fit too easily with its new focus on leisure and pleasure. Concerns over what were perceived as changes endemic to modernity manifested themselves in particularly gendered ways as Canadians debated the feminization of cities, the decline of white, middle-class manhood, and the need to fortify "the race."[16] With women's perceived increasing political, economic, and purchasing power, modern men seemed to be at risk. Modernity itself was thought to be harmful to white, middle-class masculinity, and inherent in the artistic and cultural movement of anti-modernism was a desire to provide an antidote to the alleged soft and feminized modern society that seemed anathema to vigorous, robust, and healthy masculinity.[17] From muscular Christianity to manliness aligned biologically with soldiering, the idealized and dominant version of masculinity that emerged was tough, strong, capable, ready for war, and powerful, as well as dominated by a decisive, controlled, and skilled mind.[18] Hegemonic manliness was not cute.[19] Rather, cute became a commercialized value associated with female maternal desire (longing) and a feminized sense of empathy. As such, by the 1920s and 1930s, cute worked well to attract implicitly female consumers looking for non-challenging and sentimental displays that would soothe and entertain. Cute displays, regardless of the gender of those on exhibition or those in the audience, were associated with the feminine. In turn, as with other commercial entertainment, women's – but especially white, middle-class women's – visual or literal presence made the spaces and commodities seem safe and respectable. While sideshows were sometimes seen as tawdry and in bad taste, baby and midget shows appealed to different sensibilities through their use of cute, and the freak show could capitalize on both.

Midget Shows, the Miniature, and the Cute

Midget shows were informed by the use of "cute" as a commodity aesthetic, and for people of small stature, their work on the sideshows was different from that of other freak performers, even those of small stature who were identified as dwarfs. Midget shows were about the perfection of a small body, and what made them cute was their childlike size. Dwarfs were deemed to be imperfect and grotesque. As Susan Stewart noted in her historically based discussion on the place of the miniature, "The dwarf is assigned to the domain of the grotesque and the underworld, the midget to the world of the fairy – a world of the natural, not in nature's gigantic aspects, but in its attention to the perfection of detail."[20] The distinction resonated with performers in the 1930s and continued into the 1940s. In a 1933 publication from the United States Eugenics Record Office, it was noted that in sideshow attractions like the miniature midget cities the performers were passionate about the difference they saw between dwarfs and midgets. The latter, they felt, were simply "normal" people of a smaller scale, while dwarfism implied deformity.[21] Performers were regularly described with terms like "perfectly formed."[22] As such, more than body size connected midget shows with children. Their alleged innocence and perfection resonated with contemporary ideals about "the child." If widespread ideas of childhood were popularly dichotomized as "the protected child" and "the dangerous child," midgets and dwarfs were slotted into those existing categories.

Well before the 1930s, however, little people were important to the development of the freak show. The little people shows, as midget shows, emerged and became popular in the late nineteenth century, most notoriously with Barnum's exhibition of Charles Sherwood Stratton, or Tom Thumb, and later his wife Lavinia Warren. Although they performed in the 1800s, their lives are important to discuss since they set the precedent for one important means of exhibiting little people that would continue into the twentieth century. Stratton was one of Barnum's first freaks after his start with Joice Heth. Almost five years old when he first came under Barnum's management in the early 1840s, Thumb became an international sensation. Barnum changed his age to eleven, his birthplace from Bridgeport, Connecticut, to London, England, and his name to General Tom Thumb. The whole effect was to create an aggrandized image.[23] The changes to Stratton's biography elevated his status and emphasized his smaller size. Barnum described Stratton as "a bright-eyed little fellow, with light hair and ruddy cheeks, was perfectly healthy, and as symmetrical as an Apollo."[24] Stratton's "perfect man in miniature" appeal was refined through fine clothing and aristocratic postures and presentations.

As General Tom Thumb, Stratton toured widely in Europe and North America, achieving fame and material security. He even bailed out Barnum when Barnum lost his fortune.[25] In 1865, Stratton married Mercy Lavinia Warren Bump (who performed as Lavinia Warren) in a spectacle that held the attention of the United States, despite the Civil War and the recently announced Emancipation Proclamation. The happy couple used a baby in performances after their marriage to complete a family picture and boost audience interest. The baby was in reality multiple babies. Stratton and Warren would collect a local baby from an orphanage for their shows and then drop it back off.[26] After a while, the ruse lost its shine and newspapers announced the child had died. Grief over a deceased child made the couple that much more real as they shared an experience common to many nineteenth-century families. Stratton died in 1883 and, two years later, Warren married Count Primo Magri, another sideshow performer. Together they performed at Coney Island's "Midget City." Warren died in 1919 with only a modest portion of the fortune that she and Stratton had amassed.[27] Stratton's and Bump's careers spawned many others and the style of their aggrandized exhibition remained popular throughout the first half of the twentieth century.

The nexus of cute, childlike, and innocent in the midget shows worked to produce a level of respectability not afforded to others. These shows were especially important after the "cleaning up" of freak shows that happened in the 1920s. Although sex and graft were still part of some of the carnivals and sideshows, tension within the outdoor amusement business remained, with some operators, host venues, and performers wanting more "tasteful," less controversial reputations as part of the modern entertainment industry. Midget shows could satisfy the demand for difference while not risking offence or sanctions. A key part of the shows was also the whiteness of performers. By the 1920s, most midget shows included exclusively or predominantly white people.

The rise of youth culture played a big role in shaping midget shows. As the previous chapter revealed, the rising youth culture of the period also positioned children as important audience members and consumers. All of this affected the presentation of midgets as performers on the sideshow. Gary Cross argues that leisure and the crowd itself were transformed in the 1920s and 1930s to focus on child consumers, and this changed the display of freaks. He writes: "The freak was cutesified. It is no accident that the 1920s children's ride, the Pleasure Beach Express in Blackpool, used dwarfs as conductors. Over time, 'little people' were taken from the world of the bizarre to the realm of the innocent. Snow White had her cute seven dwarfs in Disney's first feature length cartoon of 1937."[28]

Such changes influenced sideshows in Canada as well. Johnny J. Jones travelled with and showed at least two different midget "families": the Les Marechal Midgets and the Leo Singer's Midgets. In 1920, the company reported in *Billboard* magazine that they were also showing the Johnny J. Jones midgets and that their permanent home was the Midget Castle in Orlando, Florida. The unidentified writer also noted that "Mr. Jones' European agent has just cabled that he has secured for him two more wonderful midgets."[29] As with many other sideshow acts, these performers contracted to particular shows for the season, and the choice to travel with a particular show depended on job opportunities, financial reward, and sometimes just luck.

In the 1920s, for example, the Conklin operation was small but grew fairly consistently and included midget performers from at least 1930.[30] In 1938, Conklin advertised under the headline "Hey, Kiddies!" with a photograph of his midget show, The Tiny Town Revue Midgets. The ad noted "these tiny folks are very personable – you'll enjoy meeting them. They'll be glad to talk with the children and shake hands as they pass out the free Tilt-a-Whirl ride tickets." The same ad advised parents: "Yes, every one of them is over 25 years of age but your three-year-old child will actually tower over them."[31] In the late 1930s and early 1940s, Conklin also offered midget shows, including "Midget Village" and "Weeny Teeny Tiny Town," which included glamorously styled performers identified as Jack Pearl and the Duke of Tiny Town, who, advertisements declared, had been in *The Wizard of Oz*.[32] Not presented as "Munchkins," they performed in tuxedos along with at least one female performer identified as "Lillie," who wore fine dress and fur.

By the 1920s, such "cute" displays had been translated into cinema featuring children.[33] Hollywood, however, continued to hold a limited place for little people in movies such as *The Wizard of Oz* (1939), which held a particular claim to fame among certain sideshow acts. As much as the entertainment industry became a prominent employer for little people, the desire to have them on screen did not lessen the discrimination they faced in regard to both the roles they played and their place within the profession.[34] Nonetheless, the power of Hollywood's stylized images of heteronormative mid-century beauty shaped midget shows in the mid-1900s, which appropriated not only the high, glamorous

6.1 "Midget City," Canadian National Exhibition.
Canadian National Exhibition Archives. G. Hollies Photography.

style in regard to dress and appearance but also the staging of singing and dancing shows.[35]

Small stature was grounds for discrimination in employment, although importantly it was the presumption of adult size and the related built environment that produced social elements of "disability." While there is no hard evidence in Canada, research from the United States suggests that in the 1930s work in entertainment sectors was one of the more viable options for some performers like little people.[36] In his 1944 *Maclean's* article "Midget Mystery," writer Robert Marks noted: "Most midgets have been compelled to earn their living in the carnival field or in show business, but many have special talents which if they were several feet taller would equip them for business or professions."[37] The article noted many of the frustrations, including finding adequate employment as well as appropriate clothes and shoes. Rather than looking at these frustrations as a result of discrimination, Marks concluded that "these contribute to making him [a little person] tense, irritable and temperamental."[38] The paradox here seems obvious – discriminatory beliefs made finding work very difficult, making work as a midget performer a reasonable option, yet performances reinforced many negative assumptions about people of small stature, while also allowing them to show off their many skills.

Midget shows continued and grew in the early decades of the twentieth century, but the relationship to familiar white, bourgeois structures remained. Large families of little people were exhibited in the 1920s and in the late 1940s. In many cases, families were constructed out of a number of different and unrelated performers. The narrative of family, however, worked to create a cute quality: tiny mothers and fathers with tiny children made a cute miniature heterosexual family. As with Stratton's performances of the late 1800s, the appeal to European aristocracy remained. Men and women dressed in fine clothing, some had titles of the European aristocracy, and most were shown as families. The Les Marechal Midgets were allegedly of European royalty and consisted of Prince Dennison of France and his sisters, Princess Marguerite and Lady Little. They were shown with supposed members of the Belgium royal family, Duchess Leona and Baroness Simone. The troupe often included Baron Raymond as well. A 1926 newspaper article reported, "The little folk, whose average weight is 29 pounds, carried themselves in a regal manner, befitting the clothes they had made in their native France."[39] The Singer Midgets performed from 1910 into the 1940s and were so named after their manager, Leo Singer.[40] The naming of performers was always significant and, with the Midget Shows, paternalism was clearly a factor. The troupes were named not after the performers, but rather after their managers.

Their association with cuteness as a commodity aesthetic combined with their ownership by managers marked them as childlike possessions. Nate Eagle, a "normal-sized" white man, was described as "the world's leading authority on midgets," who had "made a fortune by virtually monopolizing the supply of little people." According to Eagle, part of his ambition was to "lift the little people from the level of freak." He did this through careful management and by training performers to have talents ranging from music to acrobatics.[41] The paternalism apparent in Eagle's proud description of his role reveals a sense of acceptance of authority by the purportedly childlike performers.

Midget shows bridged cute and middle-class domesticity. Family strongly implied the latter, and midget shows often included sets of household rooms where performers would live and perform. At the CNE, one midget show included the World's Smallest Home and included singing and dancing performers, including a midget hula dancer.[42] The rooms, like the larger midget cities, were built to scale. In 1924, a *Globe* reporter visiting the CNE noted small spaces and clothes in terms that revealed the connections between cute, family, and domesticity. Such connections were embedded in material goods, especially dolls, to which midget performers were frequently compared. The unnamed reporter described how "fairylike slippers of soft kid, high heeled and boasting of silver buckles, stood under a tiny brass bed. Diminutive chairs and dressing tables stood against the wall. It might have been a doll's apartment but for the row of life-size tooth brushes hanging by the towel rack. Even the most hygienic of dolls does not use a tooth brush."[43] Unlike actual children, however, they could never grow into independence as sideshow performers.

The association of cuteness and little people, along with the means of their exhibition on sideshows, led to people of small stature being literally confused with children. In his 1944 article, Marks noted, "Often midgets are mistaken for children. Sometimes they are plagued by children as they walk along the street. These facts are responsible for a number of defensive attitudes."[44] Decades earlier, in 1927, the *Toronto Daily Star* reported that a midget performing on the CNE's sideshow (who gave his manager the slip and left the grounds) was refused service at local liquor stores because they did not sell to children.[45]

Most of the popular midget shows deliberately mimicked middle-class or upper-class consumer and family patterns. As such, they were not threatening to audience members or authorities invested in ensuring white, middle-class values. The miniature was simply a scaled-down version of "normal." Yet the sideshow manager or owner also reinforced the childlike state of the cute bodies, feminizing the spectacles and reaffirming claims to male middle-class managerial authority – a white, middle-class man with significant benevolent authority surrounded by his happy, childlike workers who clearly thought of themselves as family. In 1959, the World of Mirth included Bob Hermine's Midgets. They were described as "successful not only because they are midgets gifted with extraordinary talents" but also because of Hermine's hard work and lucky streak.[46] Audience members could consume messages of paternal authority that resonated with wider messages of the need to reaffirm the white, middle-class family, especially the anchor of hegemonic masculinity that was at its root. Its respectable message, presentation of paternal father figures, and childlike bodies easily sold to more conservative audiences.

Perhaps of all the standard sideshow performances, midget shows were the least challenging for audiences to witness. Unlike contortionists, sword swallowers, or fire eaters, there was no sense of risk involved in the displays, unless a little person decided to perform one of those talents separately. Girl shows relied on sex to sell, as did so-called Half and Half shows. Other performers like Fat Ladies, Elephant-Skinned Men, and the like appeared in states of undress. Their differences were billed to consumers as both alluring and revolting. In contrast, the midget performances were glamorous, cute, and charming. Glamour, beauty, and talent defined the happy performances. They were orderly, simple, and entertaining. Their managers did not provoke them on-stage to make outrageous, disturbing, or angry sounds.[47]

As Stewart argues, "What is, in fact, lost in this idealized miniaturization of the body is sexuality and hence the danger of power. The body becomes an image, and all manifestations of will are transferred to the position of the observer, the voyeur. The body exists not in the domain of lived reality but in the domain of commodity relations."[48] When sex was hinted at in the text of the midget shows, it was heterosexual and married sex. This was captured best in the 1955 World of Mirth magazine that included a long and celebratory section on Nate Eagle's Midgets. It included a short section on midget women having babies and included a quote from Eagle, who noted: "They settle down and make good husbands and wives. Their intimate relations, too, are perfectly natural."[49]

Cute Children on Display

As Gleason has compellingly argued, "medical and educational professionals contributed scientific legitimacy to the discursive construction of children as innocent, vulnerable, incompetent, and unpredictable."[50] While eugenics and the discourse of defectiveness framed the births and treatment of many children with disabilities, other unusual births gave rise to medical and popular interest. Cute was both profitable and, under the guise of twentieth-century medicine, measurable. As such, everything from multiple births to modern baby contests intersected with commercialism, sentimental childhood, and the emerging concept of cute. Exploring aspects of this intertwined history provides a wider context in which to see both the Dionnes and the use of cute in sideshow displays, which have largely been seen as forums for the display of the "ugly," "imperfect," and "disabled."

Beginning in the 1920s, baby contests were a popular part of exhibitions like the CNE. Parents, typically mothers, would enter their children into the contest to be judged by doctors and nurses. The spectacle was important for individuals but also became a measure of national health. For spectators, it provided the ability to witness cute children gathered together in unusually large numbers. Together, the components of the exhibitions worked to define categories like cute and normal with their juxtaposed displays of cute babies in contests with children on the freak shows.

If children with disabilities were viewed as undesirable and defective, multiple births were often seen as fantastical and wondrous. As one writer for the circus magazine *White Tops* put it, "Most people regard the birth of twins as a beautiful manifestation of nature and love and cherish them. All the more do triplets and quadruplets excite admiration and affection from the public at large. When the Dionne quintuplets survived they attracted world attention, and if exhibited, would be an ace drawing card."[51] Yet, eugenics and the desire for "better breeding" were not entirely absent. Anglo-Canadian Protestant "progressive" reformers interested in eugenics expressed concern over large French Canadian Catholic families, not unlike the Dionnes. Reportedly, shortly after the quints were born, Elzire Dionne responded to her husband's query of what people would think by stating, "They will think we are pigs."[52] On the other side, however, was the surveillance of a wide swathe of children through baby contests and the upholding of specific ideals of cuteness and health through preventive medicine and categorization.

The display of children from multiple births had been included in sideshows and other commercial displays since the early decades of the 1900s.[53] The unsubstantiated rumour of a $1 million offer to the Dionne quintuplets by the 1939 New York World's Fair certainly helped motivate other families interested in commercializing themselves through sideshow displays. The three-and-a-half-month-old Badgett quadruplets from Galveston, Texas, reportedly had a "tentative offer from the San Francisco Fair" when their business manager, T.W. Youngblood, wrote (on stationary including their photographs) to New York officials to test their interest. A Major Roullett from Flin Flon, Manitoba, also wrote a conspiratorial and distinctly odd letter offering to broker a deal with a hidden set of multiples. The negotiations would need to be "kept secret so that the Government would not take control of them as they did with the Dionne quints." A rumoured report of one-month-old septuplets available for exhibition was also received as was a letter from a school teacher about eight-year-old quadruplets who were described as poor but talented. The teacher thought that performing on the sideshow might give them "a boost."[54] The display of large families was also offered to the New York Fair organizers. Two large French-Canadian families – the Masse family of Exeter, Ontario, and the Bourassa family of St Barnabe, Quebec – offered themselves for exhibition at the 1939 World's Fair in New York City based solely on their size. The Masse family billed its twenty-one children as "Healthy, Happy, Normal Children" in a professional-looking pamphlet included with their letter, while the ten Bourassa children and parents described themselves as a family, but "a lovely one and poor."[55]

The intensification of the concern over children, especially their health, led to a number of culturally orientated events designed to promote scientific ideals and the display of perfect (or at least apparently well-formed) child bodies. Baby shows were perhaps the most dramatic, popular, and positive example of this movement. Although freak shows ran parallel displays of extraordinariness, both were informed by a context that upheld ideals of perfectly normal, cute child bodies. These ideals and their mobilization in competitive baby contests first surfaced in the nineteenth century. American historian Susan J. Pearson argues that American baby shows of the mid- to late 1800s, while remaining slightly controversial, achieved widespread support because they "introduced a new form of exhibition: the objectification of normal human beings and of normalcy, coded as domesticity itself."[56] Cute helped to code domesticity with its association of malleable identities to be visually consumed.

By the early 1900s, baby shows, variations of which were held under titles of "baby contests" or "better baby contests," had taken hold across North America and were often held as part of exhibitions, fairs, and adult beauty contests, like the Miss America pageant held in Atlantic City.[57] The powerful combination of keen public interest in paying to gaze upon beautiful babies, along with the reform-based impulse that shaped professional medical practice, made baby shows and contests popular and powerful. There were some significant variations, and my focus here is largely on contests that sought to measure and judge the health of children, rather than contests like "Toronto's Baby Peggy" contest, held by the Pantages Theatre in 1924. Unlike the health-seeking contest, the Baby Peggy contest more closely resembled adult beauty contests and was a publicity stunt associated with the release of *The Darling of New York*, starring Peggy-Jean Montgomery, a silent-film child star less than two years of age.[58] The increased popularity of these shows in the 1920s was tied to an increasingly powerful discourse of maternalism born out of the wake of the First World War, of Canada's alarmingly high rates of maternal and infant mortality, and of modern women's shifting roles as workers, consumers, and public figures. By the 1920s, advice for mothers flowed from the federal Division of Child Welfare, the Canadian Council on Child Welfare, the Red Cross, the Victorian Order of Nurses, and a variety of national, provincial, and local newspapers and magazines.[59]

Baby contests also reveal the intersection of aesthetics, health, and ability. If science as the objective study of the natural world meant, in part, to provide the best and most progressive practices and ideas, it necessarily wove its way into targeted audiences through popular culture. The contests, for all their fun, excitement, and prizes, served two significant purposes: they allowed doctors and nurses who ran them to check up on the care and development of hundreds of infants, and allowed them to broadcast important messages on the correct standards for infant bodies and, most especially, correct standards for modern care. The contests were often broken down into various categories based on age and sometimes gender. Sometimes there was a separate category for twins. Typically babies were measured (sometimes literally) in the judging process against set medical standards, which at the 1920 CNE included "healthy appearance; method of feeding; absence of physical defects; cleanliness; neatness of attire and proportion as to height, weight and circumference of head, chest and abdomen."[60] Solidifying standards like these were influential in the display and treatment of quints as perfectly cute examples of modern, scientific child rearing. Yet, these criteria were far from neutral. Alexandra Minna Stern argues that such criteria, which were common across North America, codified aesthetic judgments and made them seem scientific. Height-weight charts that were tailored to specific ages quantified newer aesthetic qualities of symmetry, proportionality, and perfectability. The charts themselves were also developed using white, middle-class children, introducing racial and class biases that would be perpetuated for decades.[61]

The contests were often held in conjunction with exhibitions that, by the 1920s, ended up having contests for everything from women and babies to livestock and preserves. The travelling show owners and local organizers were well aware of the power of baby shows to attract female patrons. In 1919, an article in *Billboard* magazine declared, "A baby show is a great attraction for women. Whether the baby is theirs or not, they come to see the show and they then see what the park is like. We get them coming." Timing was key and the author noted that having the show at the end of the season was best as it allowed for the women whose babies did not win to have the off-season to release their resentment before returning again the next year.[62] Working from assumptions of women's maternalism, consumerism, and competitiveness, the article covered the basis of female stereotypes in the period. It also intersected with the key developments in the emergence of cute as a commodity for female consumption.

At the CNE, baby contests in the 1920s proved to be exceptionally popular, and their counterparts at the PNE existed into the 1950s.[63] In Toronto, by 1927, the *Evening Telegram* reported that there were over six hundred entries at the Labour Day event, a vast increase on the eighty-five who participated in the first year in 1907, while on the same day in Hamilton, Ontario, a separate baby contest attracted two hundred entries.[64] Winners sometimes had their pictures printed in major newspapers or won prizes donated by stores like Eaton's. While it is impossible to know with certainty every entry, the winners at the CNE baby shows were very likely exclusively white. That triangulation of whiteness, cuteness, and healthiness is important if unsurprising. Negatively racialized children were often excluded from the category of cute and deemed to be of lesser value than white babies, who were seen as a symbol of racial and national preservation and success.[65] Baby contests across the country helped to form and promote ideals of white, middle-class, Anglo normalcy, while mothers who entered their babies had the potential to get positive reassurance for their child and their care. Concerns over child health dovetailed with concerns over eugenics and the social order.[66] Here it is important to note that participants self-selected, hoping or knowing their child fell within the limits of normal. For those who did not, reassurance of any form was difficult in a world with a goal of achieving normalcy if not perfection in "the race."

The intersection of whiteness, health, and beauty did not mean that the baby contest was exclusive to white, urban communities. In 1926, the Indian agent for the Blackfoot recommended twice-yearly baby contests with cash prizes to be held in order to build support for monthly baby clinics designed to encourage particular types of care and reduce infant and child mortality.[67] The Indian agent declared the contest a success with twenty-two entries judged by married former nurses, who declared "that the babies compared very favourably in every respect with white babies, which they had assisted in judging elsewhere."[68] These modern standards were based on white, Anglo, Protestant, middle-class values and were used as a means of morally regulating mothers, who bore the brunt of expert advice and blame if there were perceived "failures."[69] For negatively racialized women, including Indigenous and immigrant women, disadvantage and prejudice could be particularly acute. Potentially isolated, poor, and under intense formal and informal scrutiny from neighbours, social workers, and provincial and federal government agencies, these women were often seen as innately suspicious or backward with respect to mothering.[70] For Indigenous mothers in particular, colonization had a devastating impact on their health and that of their children. Yet the inability to see or recognize the health impact furthered the crisis by neglecting structural causes of poor health, and instead reducing structural inequities to issues of personal care.

Baby contests were perhaps the most popular example of how the display of healthy infants intersected with the sideshow. The potent mixture of education and entertainment at fairs and sideshows produced fertile ground for such exhibitions. Another example included the display of living premature infants in incubators. At the forefront of these displays held across the United States were those sponsored by Martin Couney, whose exhibits were held at the 1933 Chicago Century of Progress Exposition, the 1939 New York World's Fair, and a permanent sideshow at Coney Island that lasted from the early 1900s until 1943.[71] These displays provided an opportunity for parents, the general public, and, importantly, physicians to become acquainted with incubator technology and how it was used to save the lives of premature babies. Couney's displays began in Britain and Europe at the end of the nineteenth century, and some sideshows, notably Barnum and Bailey's, formed their own spin-offs. Some British physicians were displeased with these attractions and a *Lancet* editorial queried the connection between life-saving techniques and regular sideshow attractions. Nonetheless, Couney persisted. In the United States, he formed a strong connection with physician and professor of pediatrics at Washington University Dr John Zahorsky, as well as with noted neonatal expert Dr Julian Hess, who remained at odds with much of the medical profession. Zahorsky's strong association with sideshows seemed more like quackery than modern scientific medicine.[72] When an epidemic of diarrhea coincided with the St Louis shows in 1904, "the exposition became a symbol of infant exploitation."[73] Shows continued until the 1940s, proving that extraordinary "normal" and cute, if very small, bodies could be both profitable and educational, although clearly most members of the medical profession remained distinctly uneasy with relationships to the midway.[74]

The Dionne Quintuplets Sideshow

Baby contests and freak shows intersected to produce the perfect platform for one of the greatest displays of childhood in Canadian history – the Dionne quintuplets. It should not be surprising, then, that when Annette, Cecile, Yvonne, Marie, and Emilie were born, sideshow recruiters would be interested in displaying them. The financial promises in the midst of the Depression were significant. The Dionnes were a French Canadian working-class Catholic family living in Callander, just outside of North Bay, Ontario, a province defined by Anglo, middle-class, Protestant hegemony. There were already five children in the family when the quintuplets were born, and surviving as a family was already a struggle. After a less-than-excited initial response to their birth, the Dionne quintuplets soon faded from public and press interest in Canada, but gained traction south of the border. As word of the extraordinary births was publicized in the United States, Chicago-based showman Ivan Spear caught wind of the event and contacted Mr Dionne, as did many others. But Spear was the one who had success in initial negotiations with the family.[75]

When initially contacted by the showmen, Oliva Dionne consulted with his parish priest and with Dr Dafoe, and both had consented to the deal, provided the girls were well enough to travel. Dafoe was a country doctor who had assisted the local midwives with the birth of the girls but quickly became the public paternal face representing the modern, scientific practices meant to ensure their health and welfare. In the early days of their lives, no one believed they could or would survive, except perhaps the showman who allegedly included in the contract a stipulation that Dionne would get $100 a week until the girls were exhibited and then $200 a week plus a percentage of the receipts once they were on display. The contract between Spear and Dionne included a 7 per cent cut for the priest.[76] When it became clear that the girls would survive, the contract was broken and the government and the media publicly painted the parents, along with the showmen, as sinister and greedy. The parents were deemed to be provincial and gullible, while the showmen were degraded as "American," which translated into commercial, cheap, and tawdry. To showman Lou Dufour, however, Spear had erred in not having the mother sign the contract, which Dufour chalked up to Spear's youth and inexperience.[77]

Decades later, the quints themselves had unanswered questions about the contract with Spear. In their autobiography they wrote, "After nearly thirty years, as this is written, the past has not lost its power to hurt. What were the real feelings in Dad's heart when he put his name to the contract? Did he act only for money, with his eyes closed to all other considerations, or was there a glimmering of love for us? Was the day's work done with regret for its necessity or with relief that there was money in his pocket at last? If he believed that we should die, how much did he care?"[78] These are important questions in regard to the display of all children in sideshows, speaking most eloquently to the issue of poverty that made such displays irresistible or at least palatable. Material concerns almost never fully trumped care and love, but they did restrict choices and open up avenues seemingly unthinkable in other circumstances.

Spear's interest in the quints was not a secret and had been reported in Canadian newspapers. The reporting on the Dionnes, however, changed dramatically in a matter of weeks. In a rather bland article on 1 June 1934, the *Globe* reported on negotiations for the display of the quintuplets taking place in Orillia, Ontario, between Oliva Dionne, Father Daniel Routhier (the parish priest), a J. Green, and two Chicago-based promoters. About six weeks later, on 27 July 1934, the *Globe* ran a front-page article that denounced the attempt to exhibit the babies: "An exploitation scheme 'which meant certain death to one or more of the quintuplets' was circumvented by the Ontario Attorney-General's Department when it broke the contract for exhibiting the Dionne babies at the Chicago Century of Progress Exposition, it was announced last night by Hon. Arthur W. Roebuck."[79] The paper described the recent decision of the Ontario government to step in. It is the only instance for which I was able to find evidence of the government intervening in the procurement of a child or children for the sideshows.

By early 1935, the Ontario government determined the babies needed better guardianship and passed a bill through the provincial legislature to make the girls wards of the Crown.[80] The spectre of sideshows and abusive commercial culture was given as the reason in the public debates. Oliva and Elzire Dionne had been briefly working vaudeville circuits that year as the parents of the now-famous girls, and the original showmen who had contracted the family to be exhibited in Chicago were now threatening a $1 million lawsuit for breach of contract. In 1935, *Billboard* reported that "Ma and Pa Dionne joined the ranks of curiosities at the Canadian National Exhibition when they opened a booth with the famous parents in full view." The crush of the audience the first day led to changes in subsequent days to ensure that people had the opportunity to buy a picture of the girls and see the parents live.[81]

In response to the threat of legal action and as a criticism of the parents' vaudeville performances, Premier Mitchell Hepburn was quoted in the *Border Cities Star* in Windsor, Ontario, as stating,

> If there is any action that the Ontario Legislature can take to protect these babes from profit-seeking promoters, that action will be taken. Any action that can protect them against these chiselers will be taken. And I deprecate to the fullest extent the degrading spectacle of the parents going on the vaudeville stage. It is a disgrace and it's cheap. The parents are of no value as anything but parents. We are going to try to save the children from such exploitation if at all possible ... It is revolting, disgusting and cheap and it reflects on the people of Canada as a whole. But regardless of this, we are going to protect the children.

The article continued: "Mr. Hepburn did not attempt to hide his anger about the situation. He contended that the Dionne parents haven't any accomplishments which would fit them for the stage and that it was just an exploitation of the freak of nature which had sent them five babes at one time ... And they are not because of their previous environment, of the type who protect themselves from the exploiting promoters."[82] About one month later, the minister of public welfare David Croll was quoted in the *Globe* as saying, "We are trying to treat the children as human beings and not as freaks. We want them to be home under the care of their mother and father, rather than exhibited between a sword-swallower and a bearded woman on a Chicago midway."[83] The act that was passed to take control of the children, because they were of "special interest" to the people of Canada, revealed the tension between protecting the girls and profiting from them. Yet, the initial 1934 legislation lasted for only two years. It named four male guardians, the most important being Dr Allan Dafoe. After the initial judicial order that took the girls from their parents' custody in 1934, they were moved from the family home and placed in a new, custom-built hospital. The hospital was named after Dr Dafoe.

Newspapers anxiously reported on the infant quints' health. It was a legitimate concern that the newborn girls were so small. The *Montreal Gazette* reported the daily weights of each of the quints, carefully noting each gain or loss to the ¼ ounce. Hospitals like Toronto's Sick Children's Hospital and Montreal's Royal Victoria Maternity Hospital arranged to have human milk transported to Dr Dafoe in order to feed the girls.[84] Yet, by March 1935, when the second guardianship bill was passed, the health crisis of ensuring that all five survived infancy had passed, and the girls were well enough to be returned home. The 1935 revision to the guardianship, however, extended the girls' wardship from two years to eighteen years. The stage was set for long-term commercial gain by the government.

In English-language newspapers, the government was depicted as benevolent in taking control of the girls and building their own hospital replete with viewing grounds for tourists. Although the girls did not travel, the government-sanctioned exhibition clearly paralleled a sideshow. Cynthia Wright has argued that the lack of admission or parking fees kept the display of the quints separate from "the American freak show model."[85] The resonances with a freak show were deeper than the price of admission, which freak shows themselves sometimes waved for special events. In 1934, the girls began to live their lives "on display." They were shown twice a day in a facility designed for their exhibition to mass audiences – the parking lot at the hospital, for example, had one thousand spots. On 22 July 1935, the *Montreal Gazette* reported, "Today 4,000 persons came in more than 1,000 motor cars to see the famous youngsters perform ... All five are good show girls. They know they are appearing before admirers and react like real troopers."[86] As Mariana Valverde reports, "by 1936, Quintland equalled Niagara Falls as Canada's leading tourist attraction."[87] Visitors were amused by the ordinariness of the quints, who were viewed through one-way glass but who noted later in their lives that they were aware of being watched.[88] As with any sideshow, exhibitors used ordinary, everyday settings to highlight the extraordinariness of their unusual displays.[89] In the case of the quints, viewers on the observation deck would watch them play. In the well-designed rustic northern Ontario scene, the combination of modern hospital and domestic play highlighted cute girls

| EMILIE | MARIE | ANNETTE | YVONNE | CECILE |

6.2 Postcard featuring the Quints with their stuffed dogs, age three, 1937. North Bay Public Library, City of North Bay, Quints Digital Collection. Public domain.

made extraordinary only by their multiplicity. As with freak show performers, souvenirs were also sold.

Unlike nineteenth-century baby shows, however, the Dionnes' was far more in line with twentieth-century baby contests, which were not "prideful, subjective, and sentimental" but rather meant to be "objective, scientific, and educative."[90] This gloss of modern expert authority helped to remove the stigma of their display as mere entertainment. What was missing, however, were the parents. Whereas the contract with Spear included the parents in the show, the government was careful to keep them out of the picture. As Pearson notes, including the mother's body in sentimental displays risked accusations of simply showcasing an effective breeder. The reference is particularly apt given the criticisms faced by the French Catholic Dionnes that their fecundity was menacing or obscene.[91] Unlike the freak-like exhibit at Chicago, the Dafoe hospital created literal and representative distance from the parents. Instead, the toddlers were cared for by nurses and nannies, and they enacted their childhood in a carefully controlled clinical setting where they could be seen in any number of staged performances of normal childhood set apart from the "messiness" of procreative parents or degraded, unscientific domesticity.

The popularity of the girls' exhibition was clear. By 1937, Keith Munro had been named a full-time business manager and the name and image of the girls was under a federal trademark. In almost three years, the girls' trust fund held about a half-million dollars. The girls' pictures appeared on all sorts of commercial products and they made appearances on radio and film (in two Hollywood movies, no less), and had dolls in their likeness made and sold. The right of certain corn syrup companies to proclaim that their product had fed the girls sparked remarkable political and legal battles.[92] Other companies paid to use the girls' likeness in advertising for a wide range of products. Although hundreds of thousands of visitors saw the girls live, many more shared in the girls' exhibition through the purchasing of goods in the heart of the Depression. Later in life, the girls recalled receiving a letter from a young housewife who wrote about the joy the Dionne paper dolls had brought her, despite the hardships her family was facing. Years later, the quints still meant something special in the woman's memory and the quints expressed their own happiness at this remembrance, despite the personal costs to themselves.[93] The exhibition of the girls by the government encouraged tourism and associated commercial developments in the northeastern region of Ontario.[94] The exhibition also played an important role in the development and broadcasting of modern, scientific ideals of child rearing. Only much later did the costs to their childhoods become public knowledge. Although the girls described their years in the nursery as the "happiest, least complicated years of our lives," this might say more about the long-term strain that the spectacle, marked by separation from their parents and professional debates over their care, had on the rest of it.[95] The tension between the girls as a great study in child development and a great capitalist venture shaped both criticism of the girls' display as well as the spectacle itself.

Criticism of the spectre of the sideshow haunted the girls' exhibition and some of those in charge of it. On 28 September 1937, in one of her many letters home to her mother in Sweden, Louise de Kiriline, who nursed the Dionne girls through their first year, wrote, "Dr Dafoe has lost all his prestige among medical men in Toronto. He is called the showman, which is not very flattering."[96] One year later, when the New York World's Fair reportedly offered $1 million to exhibit the girls in a specially built exact replica of the Dafoe hospital, Canadians and Dafoe were incredulous. As one *New York Times* reporter in Ottawa noted, Canadians were more interested in the Dionnes' participation in the fair than they were in the development of the Second World War.[97] The contradictory public response from Dr Dafoe was telling, however, in how it crossed the lines of spectacle, freak show, profits, and health. At the time, Dafoe was in New York for a radio interview and reporters implied that this might have been an opportunity to work out the deal with the fair. The *Globe* quoted him as saying, "'Why, we have our own World's Fair right in Callander,' he beamed proudly. 'Don't you think that the kiddies are a fair in themselves? ... Suppose you were their father. Would you want them on perpetual exhibition as dolls in a store window? The health of the children is paramount, and I feel that the continual exploitation would retard their normal development. They are not freaks.'"[98] At play here was a convoluted mix of medical concern and commercialism. It was also somewhat surprising that Dafoe appealed to the Dionnes' father's circumscribed paternal authority, given the tense relationship that had developed since the parents lost custody of their children. Dafoe also appears to be ambivalent about the display of the girls and what it was meant to achieve. One certainty, however, was the girls' commercial value. The quints were a significant tourist draw and everyone from local businesses to the provincial government had a stake in their ongoing exhibition at the hospital in the town of Callander. In August of 1939, the *Globe and Mail* reported, "Callander is reconciled to their commercial exploitation as a necessary evil, but resents having them considered mere freaks in a circus sideshow."[99] Yet, despite Dafoe's then recently accepted honorary degree of "Doctor of Litters" bestowed in New York by the Circus Saints and Sinners Club in 1939, which he accepted in person, the participation in an actual fair with a real sideshow seemed to trouble him, the press, politicians, and some members of the public.[100] By this time, as well, Dafoe's credibility was being questioned – as was his spending – and by December of 1939, he had been removed from the board in charge of the girls' care, although he remained as a medical adviser. Dafoe's removal from the board was a direct result of legal action by Oliva Dionne. Yet what seems to have troubled the press and politicians at the time was the immediate proximity to traditional sideshow freaks at the world's fair and the potential loss of Canadian tourist dollars if the girls performed

6.3 Dr. Dafoe accepting his honorary degree of "Doctor of Litters" from the Circus Saints and Sinners Club in New York in 1939. William Ready Division of Archives and Research Collections, McMaster University, Dafoe Collection, box 1, file 16.

in New York. They never did. While the girls were never displayed in a true travelling freak show, their actual display in the Dafoe hospital was not free from the criticism that it was its own sideshow.

In 1941, at the age of seven, the girls were returned to their parents, although they wouldn't live together for another two years.[101] Their parents had never accepted the removal of the girls from their custody, and the return of the quints to their care was a result of the parents' cumulative efforts as well as pressure from the Catholic Church and the francophone community in Ontario and Quebec. As Denyse Baillargeon argues, "The famous premature quintuplets, celebrated all over French Canada as evidence of francophone fertility, had been the focus of an ethnic conflict that French Canadians had finally won."[102] Yet perhaps the most potent reasons for dismantling their display were "the girls' loss of baby cuteness," their media overexposure, which meant diminishing media and tourist interest (and a related decline in revenue), and a need to modernize the growing girls' appearance.[103] In short, by the early 1940s, the quints were rapidly losing commercial value, and a return to their parents quelled some of the rising debate over the government's custody.[104]

Their increasing age was another underlying factor. The appropriate display of children for middle-class audiences in the 1930s used "cuteness" – a category, as discussed earlier, that was also shaped by race and class – to compel a maternal response. Gazing upon five beautiful babies or small children had sentimental value for audience members and could be deemed to be wholesome. The purity and innocence associated with the tender years was something that audiences could share. Gazing upon older children heading into adolescence was another matter. Adolescence was deemed to be a time of rapid physiological change – staring at five young women smacked of licentiousness.[105]

Two conclusions in relation to the freak show can be drawn: that the girls were and remained commercially viable and profitable to everyone but themselves, and that with the government stepping in and ostensibly setting up their own sideshow, the parents and the girls themselves lost autonomy in managing their display. If the deal with Spear had proceeded, the parents would have been able to negotiate their contracts and the terms of the girls' display, and they would have had direct access to their portion of the money earned. As discussed in chapter 4, when nineteen-year-old Robert Wadlow appeared as a giant in the Ringling Bros. Shows in New York City and Boston in 1937, he did so after negotiating a precise contract. He and his father's transportation and hotel were paid for, his introduction to the audience was to be dignified, and he was not to be shown as part of the sideshow. His appearances were feature attractions with no other performers. They happened twice a day for three minutes each. He wore normal clothing and did not perform.[106] Unlike the Dionnes, Robert and his parents had autonomy in the performances. While this particular case was exceptional, and while it is important to note that not all freak performers had such negotiating power, the quints and their parents lost even the potential to negotiate the terms of their display. In the crosshairs of cuteness, health, and spectacle, the Dionnes' display revealed the growing acceptance of the commercialization of child bodies for consumption. In that way, they shared the stage with other "cute" children like baby contestants and even child movie stars of the decade like Shirley Temple. It is striking to note, too, that Temple came to prominence as a child movie star in 1934, the same year the Dionnes were born.[107] Temple was also part of Hollywood's mid-century rise of glamour that midget shows so readily tapped into. Cuteness as freak performance connected certain child and adult performers, who could be seen in similar terms of sentimentality, morality, and female consumer desire.

Conclusion

By the 1930s, the freak show resonated with wider patterns in consumer culture, especially in relation to the mobilization of "cute." Significantly, the popular and profitable display of the Dionne quintuplets relied on their cuteness in addition to their multiplicity. While there were literal connections between the Dionnes and sideshows, the spectacularization of the quints in commercial displays reveals the importance of the image of the sentimental child in consumer culture. The sentimental child was implicitly racialized, and the privileging of whiteness emerged as a pattern across displays of babies and children, from the Dionnes and earlier displays of multiples to baby contests. Although limited by the Depression, consumer culture continued to take hold, and at its heart was a female consumer. Displays of babies and small children were intended to harness such female shoppers. It is significant, given the general lack of reaction to other children on display as freaks, that the Dionnes would garner a protective response from the Ontario government. In the midst of the Dionnes' very successful display at the Dafoe hospital, Ernie-Len, discussed in chapter 5, was on exhibition at the CNE. The confluence of ethnicity, cuteness, ability, and potential profit seem to have been factors in the attempts at intervention. Given the wider history of children with disabilities on display as freaks, it cannot be the contract with Spear alone that pushed government authorities into action.

Cuteness was also something sideshows harnessed to attract respectable patrons, as with the ubiquitous midget shows. If other elements of the sideshow offered attractions that were allegedly "ugly" and "disabled," midget shows revealed perfection, glamour, and beauty in miniature. Performers were depicted in positive terms but certainly would have felt the weight of attitudes that situated them as perpetual children in need of protection and direction. Although Nadja Durbach argues that consumer culture, with its emphasis on beauty, helped to finish off the shows, in Canada the relationship was more complex.[108] Consumer culture defined beauty relationally and thus needed the ugly and different to define its margins. Beauty and ugliness are dialectical, not dichotomous. Further, ideas of beauty or ugliness are invested with and defined by specific sets of cultural values. Consumer culture also spectacularized the body in ways that were reminiscent of the freak show, and freakery was not always about ugliness. It also harnessed differences in modes of display that relied on the "cute" with children and little people.

Epilogue

"I guess it really is all over" – The End Which Is Not One

In 1977, *Globe and Mail* reporter Jim Christy published a lament for the CNE's midway, and especially the freak show, entitled "Chalk One for the Bland and Boring." Christy chatted with Conklin employee Dottie Marco, referring to her as "Godmother of the Midway." She described the show's modern bureaucratization, singling out the hourly wages paid to young student workers tracked by a time clock. Christy wondered, "I thought of myself as a kid running away to see the carnival and I rather doubted I would have done it if I had to punch a time clock. I wondered whether the India Rubber Man would punch a time clock, or the sword swallower, or the half-man, half-woman. I thought of Tod Browning's classic movie, *Freaks*, and wondered how they would work the clock into the remake." Marco continued to describe the carnival as big business. She reportedly stated, "This outfit is a big corporation. It's run like a downtown office building. All the shows are getting to be the same. The ones that don't change, die. Yeah, just like a downtown office building."[1] The piece concluded with Christy's friend and former sideshow operator saying, "I guess it really is all over."[2]

But what was over? The carnival from the 1910s had begun to professionalize, with modern business practices being touted in the 1920s as the carnival modernized. Rationalization, paternalism, expanded government bureaucracy, and new strategies of public relations and consumer relations defined the twentieth-century carnival. The profitability of the carnival through the 1920s to the early1970s meant that government officials needed to balance regulations with potential profits. By the 1970s these modern business practices had intensified as Marco's comments reveal. Yet, by that time the department store and the carnival had already shared ground in regard to business practices for decades. Nonetheless, the intensification of changes in the 1970s were profound. Carnival profits were no longer informally counted and shared. In 1978 a public inquiry into the practices of the Royal American Shows led to permanent changes and increased government oversight. That year, however, five years after the CNE's ban resulting from Pookie's exhibition, the midway hosted a nostalgic freak show identified in archival records as "Conklin's Antique Carnival," with exclusively adult performers, including a fat show.[3] The carnival had gone corporate, but the freak show survived, even in diminished form.

Pookie's exhibition, as brief as it was, represents a distinct turning point in the Canadian history of the freak show. Officials were willing to respond, to make a bold public declaration, and to follow up on it. No more children would be on display as freaks. By the early 1970s it was no longer socially palatable to have a child with disabilities on exhibit. The recently declared war on poverty, the flourishing recognition of children's rights, and calls for the rights of people with disabilities converged to make Pookie a sympathetic victim of circumstance as opposed to a freak. Her exhibition as "The Monkey Girl" might have reflected still-held atavistic beliefs, but it was more likely that her exhibition, when she cried on stage in her diaper, simply seemed pathetic or heart wrenching. For Pookie, such a new frame for her exhibition could still prove to be a problem in rendering her "pathetic," but in the early 1970s such changes were often seen as progressive. The announcement of end of the freak show at the CNE was significant, even if it was not truly the end of the freak show.

Over the course of this research, I have had countless conversations with friends, acquaintances, colleagues, and strangers who recalled their own experiences visiting freak shows in the 1970s and 1980s. In the 1990s, postmodernism would revive nostalgic, if equally troubling, versions for those discontented people searching for something real and authentic in the world of screen and simulacra. And then, of course, postmodern art revived the freak show and popular culture followed suit with a host of televisions shows ("reality" and fictional) that offered new perspectives (but not necessarily new shows or ideas) on the freak. There is something so culturally compelling about the freak show that we cannot seem to shake it. But the heyday of the live carnival freak is over. As I have argued here, it extended well into the 1950s, diminishing in the 1960s and then declared over in the early 1970s. This longer trajectory is important even if the freak show was past its peak. We cannot sigh and be grateful it is behind us, evidence only of people's short-sightedness and poor taste in the past. It is still with us, extending into recent memory.

My argument here has pointed to the flexibility of shows as businesses, their relationships with governments, as well as the persistent category of normal, which positions almost all bodily difference as disability and abnormality. As a critical part of consumer culture in the twentieth century, freak show were attended by a large number of Canadians across the country. The freak show's flexibility in being able to absorb and react to shifting social and cultural trends was one of the key factors in its survival throughout the turbulent twentieth century. Shows ran the gamut of ugly to cute, although neither of those categories was "innocent" or more accepting. The freak show's near-constant ability to make money for itself, as well as for other organizations like agricultural fairs and exhibitions, was another factor in its longevity. In the 1960s, Lou Dufour expressed criticism of world's fairs organizers who thought people had changed and no longer needed the "amusement" of the freak show.[4] At the same time, countercultural social movements in the 1960s and 1970s embraced freakery in new ways.[5] Was not everyone a freak? Did the freak not have value as a critical symbol of human difference that we covered over with the false consciousness of conformity? In the 1960s, freaks were embraced by the growing counterculture as a nostalgic antidote to the repression of the postwar years. In the early 1960s, Canadian audiences were introduced to Tod Browning's 1932 horror film *Freaks* for the first time. A cult classic, it garnered a modest amount of positive attention.[6] The identification with difference would continue, as consumers of the postmodern freak show came to identify with the freak. By 1973, however, the live freak show had changed from its earlier incarnation, which relied on fantastical tales, to be more reflective of changing discourses of difference, ability, medicine, and cuteness. The Monkey Girl reflected a failure of the state to protect her from a greedy mother, to stop her exploitation by one of its own funded exhibitions, or to support single mothers and their children at a time of rapid increases in food costs and the stagnation of wages and support.

It would be easy to conclude that there was something deep-seated about the need to gawk at and wrestle with difference as a defining characteristic of human nature. But for all its seeming permanence on the landscape of twentieth-century culture, the freak show is neither fundamental nor necessary. Capitalist consumer culture and the exhibitionary complex provide the cultural and economic foundation for the freak show. The hardening of the ideology of "the normal body," the medicalization of that body, the relentlessness of able-bodiedness, the persistence of poverty and social dislocation, and racism and sexism undergird the freak show and its place in modern Canadian culture. As the chapters here reveal, the freak show was not some minor footnote in twentieth-century Canadian culture. The history of the freak show in Canada in the twentieth century intersects with business history, social and moral reform, ideas about disability, social disadvantage, and child poverty, among others. The freak show is about culture, society, politics, and economics. The freak show is about the denial that disability is the normative position.[7]

In the study of the freak show many people have looked at Tod Browning's now-classic 1932 film *Freaks*.[8] In one scene the carnival freaks take revenge on the beautiful but morally corrupt strong man and acrobat, who have plotted to take money from the little person, Hans. The circus acrobat, Cleopatra, pretends to fall in love with Hans, but is revolted at their wedding dinner in having to share a meal with his friends and co-workers, the freaks. As an act of revenge for cruelly using Hans and breaking his heart, the freaks disfigure Cleopatra and, off screen, seemingly castrate the strong man. While they take this action, they chant "one of us." It is interesting that a statement that reads as one of inclusion is often cited as one that embodies the horror in the film. What does it mean to be "one of us"? The chilling horror of the chant "one of us" reveals why the freak show persists.

Notes

Introduction: Pookie's Story

1 Linda McQuaig, "Retarded Girl, 5, Taken from CNE Freak Display," *Globe and Mail*, 17 August 1973, 1; Linda McQuaig, "CNE Bans Freak Show after Girl, 5, Is Taken from Display," *Globe and Mail*, 18 August 1973, 5; editorial, "Protection for a Child," *Globe and Mail*, 18 August 1973, 6; Linda McQuaig, "Tricks Replace Freaks Show Uses Headlines as New Drawing Card," *Globe and Mail*, 20 August 1973, 5; H.H. Dymond, letter to the editor, "CAS Calls Sideshow Editorial Vindictive," 22 August 1973, 7; Marjorie McCoubrey, letter to the editor, "Pension Urged for Mentally and Physically Handicapped Child," *Globe and Mail*, 24 August 1973, 7; C. Morrison, letter to the editor, "Can Girl Be in Another Freak Show?" *Globe and Mail*, 23 August 1973, 7; Margaret M. Buchanan, letter to the editor, "Freak Show," *Globe and Mail*, 27 August 1973, 6; Betty Quiggin, letter to the editor, "Child Welfare," *Globe and Mail*, 30 August 1973, 6.
2 Rosemarie Garland-Thomson, *Extraordinary Bodies: Figuring Physical Disability in American Culture and Literature* (New York: Columbia University Press, 1997), 6–7.
3 Dominque Clément, *Canada's Rights Revolution: Social Movements and Social Change, 1937–82* (Vancouver: University of British Columbia Press, 2008). On social recognition see Judith Butler, *Undoing Gender* (New York and London: Routledge, 2004). For social recognition, embodiment, and disability see Tanya Titchkosky, *Reading and Writing Disability Differently: The Textured Life of Embodiment* (Toronto: University of Toronto Press, 2007), 6–7.
4 P.C. Easto and M. Truzzi, "Towards an Ethnography of the Carnival Social system," *Journal of Popular Culture* 6, no. 3 (Spring 1973): 552.

5 Work on the freak show in Canada is limited but can be found in Gerald Lenton-Young, "Variety Theatre," in *Early Stages: Theatre in Ontario, 1800–1914*, ed. Ann Saddlemyer (Toronto: University of Toronto Press, 1990), 166–213; Tina Loo and Carolyn Strange, "The Travelling Show Menace: Contested Regulation in Turn-of-the-Century Ontario," *Law and Society Review* 29, no. 4 (1995): 639–67; David Gardner, "Variety," in *Later Stages: Essays in Ontario Theatre from the First World War to the 1970s*, ed. Ann Saddlemyer and Richard Plant (Toronto: University of Toronto Press, 1997), 121–223; Keith Walden, *Becoming Modern in Toronto: The Industrial Exhibition and the Shaping of a Late Victorian Culture* (Toronto: University of Toronto Press, 1997); Elsbeth Heaman, *The Inglorious Arts of Peace: Exhibitions in Canadian Society during the Nineteenth Century* (Toronto: University of Toronto Press, 1999); Fiona Angus, "Midway to Respectability: Carnivals at the Calgary Stampede," in *Icon, Brand, Myth: The Calgary Exhibition and Stampede*, ed. Max Foran (Edmonton: Athabasca University Press, 2008), 111–46; A.W. Stencell, *Circus and Carnival Ballyhoo: Sideshow Freaks, Jabbers, and Blade Box Queens* (Toronto: ECW Press, 2010); and Donald G. Wetherell, with Irene Kmet, *Useful Pleasures: The Shaping of Leisure in Alberta, 1896–1945* (Regina: Canadian Plains Research Center, 1991). The literature on agricultural fairs is also important. See Grant MacEwan, *Agriculture on Parade: The Story of the Fairs and Exhibitions of Western Canada* (Toronto: Thomas Nelson and Sons, 1950); David C. Jones, *Midways, Judges, and Smooth-Tongued Fakirs: The Illustrated Story of Country Fairs in the Prairie West* (Saskatoon: Western Producer Prairie Books, 1983); Kenneth Coates and Fred McGuiness, *Pride of the Land: An Affectionate History of Brandon's Agricultural Exhibitions* (Winnipeg: Peguis, 1985); Guy Scott, *A Fair Share: A History of Agricultural Societies and Fairs in Ontario, 1792–1992* (Peterborough: Ontario Association of Agricultural Societies, 1992); and Guy Scott, *Country Fairs in Canada* (Toronto: Fitzhenry and Whiteside, 2005.)
6 Susan Stewart, *On Longing: Narratives of the Miniature, the Gigantic, the Souvenir, the Collection* (Baltimore: Johns Hopkins University Press, 1984), 109.
7 Rosemarie Garland-Thomson, "Introduction," in *Freakery: Cultural Spectacles of the Extraordinary Body*, ed. Rosemarie Garland-Thomson (New York: New York University Press, 1996), 7.
8 Lennard Davis, *Enforcing Normalcy: Disability, Deafness, and the Body* (London: Verso, 1995).
9 Elizabeth Grosz, *Volatile Bodies: Toward a Corporeal Feminism* (Indianapolis: Indiana University Press, 1994); and Margarit Shildrick, *Embodying the Monster: Encounters with the Vulnerable Self* (Thousand Oaks, CA: Sage, 2002).

10 Walden, *Becoming Modern in Toronto*, 119.
11 Michel Foucault, *Discipline and Punish: The Birth of the Prison* (New York: Vintage, 1977); Michel Foucault, *The Birth of the Clinic* (London: Tavistock Publications, 1973); and Tony Bennett, "The Exhibitionary Complex," *new formations* (Spring 1988): 73–100.
12 Margaret Conrad and Alvin Finkel, *History of the Canadian Peoples*, vol. 2: *1867 to the Present* (Toronto: Pearson, 2002), 86.
13 John Herd Thompson with Allen Seager, *Canada, 1922–1939: Decades of Discord* (Toronto: McClelland and Stewart, 1986), 1–5.
14 Classic works on urban poverty are Terry Copp, *The Anatomy of Poverty: The Condition of the Working Class in Montreal, 1897–1929* (Toronto: McClelland and Stewart, 1974); and Michael Piva, *The Conditions of the Working Class in Toronto, 1900–1921* (Ottawa: University of Ottawa Press, 1979). On survival strategies, see Bettina Bradbury, "The Fragmented Family: Family Strategies in the Face of Death, Illness, and Poverty, Montreal, 1860–1885," in *Childhood and Family in Canadian History*, ed. Joy Parr (Toronto: McClelland and Stewart, 1982), 109–28. On adoptions and also fostering, see Joy Parr, *Labouring Children: British Immigrant Apprentices to Canada, 1869–1924* (Montreal: McGill-Queen's University Press, 1980); Veronica Strong-Boag, *Finding Families, Finding Ourselves: English Canada Encounters Adoption from the Nineteenth Century to the 1990s* (Toronto: Oxford University Press, 2006); and Veronica Strong-Boag, *Fostering Nation? Canada Confronts Its History of Childhood Disadvantage* (Waterloo, ON: Wilfrid Laurier University Press, 2011).
15 Walden, *Becoming Modern in Toronto*, 224–5.
16 Conrad and Finkel, *History of the Canadian Peoples*, 132–7; Walden, *Becoming Modern in Toronto*, 225–6; Suzanne Morton, *Ideal Surroundings: Domestic Life in a Working-Class Suburb in the 1920s* (Toronto: University of Toronto Press, 1995); Mariana Valverde, *The Age of Light, Soap and Water: Moral Reform in English-Canada, 1885–1925* (Toronto: McClelland and Stewart, 1991); and Xiaobei Chen, *Tending the Gardens of Citizenship: Child Saving in Toronto, 1880s–1920s* (Toronto: University of Toronto Press, 2005).
17 Valverde, *The Age of Light, Soap and Water*.
18 Carolyn Strange, *Toronto's Girl Problem: The Perils and Pleasures of the City, 1800–1930* (Toronto: University of Toronto Press, 1995); Joan Sangster, *Regulating Girls and Women: Sexuality, Family, and the Law in Ontario, 1920–1960* (Toronto: Oxford University Press, 2001); Tamara Myers, *Caught: Montreal's Modern Girls and the Law, 1869–1945* (Toronto: University of Toronto Press, 2006); Cynthia Comacchio, *The Dominion of Youth: Adolescence and the Making of Modern Canada, 1920–1950* (Waterloo,

ON: Wilfrid Laurier University Press, 2006); Donica Belisle, *Retail Nation: Department Stores and the Making of Modern Canada* (Vancouver: University of British Columbia Press, 2011); and Jane Nicholas, *The Modern Girl: Feminine Modernities, The Body, and Commodities in the 1920s* (Toronto: University of Toronto Press, 2015).

19 Pierre Bourdieau, *Distinction: A Social Critique of the Judgment of Taste* (Cambridge, MA: Harvard University Press, 1987).

20 Cynthia Comacchio, "Mechanomorphosis: Science, Management, and 'Human Machinery' in Industrial Canada, 1900–45," *Labour/Le travail* 41 (Spring 1998): 38–9. See also Erin O'Connor, *Raw Material: Producing Pathology in Victorian Culture* (Durham, NC: Duke University Press, 2000).

21 Garland-Thomson, "Introduction," 11.

22 Rosemarie Garland-Thomson, *Staring: How We Look* (Oxford: Oxford University Press, 2009), 9.

23 These types of looking/gazes are well explained in Garland-Thomson, *Staring*. To her excellent overview of the dense literature on gazing/looking, I have included here the carnivalesque, which is connected to exoticism. See Lucian Gomall, "The Feminist Pleasures of Coco Rico's Social Interventions" in *Art and the Artist in Society*, edited by José Jiménez-Justiniano, Elsa Luciano Feal, and Jane Elizabeth Alberdeston (Newcastle upon Tyne: Cambridge Scholars Publishing, 2013), 125–6.

24 The New York Public Library, Performing Arts Division, Billy Rose Theatre Collection [hereafter NYPL BRTC], MWEZ+n.c. 25,998 Freaks – circus clippings, Gahan Wilson, "Freaks: From Legend into Flesh and Blood," April 1966.

25 Paul Rutherford, "Made in America: The Problem of Mass Culture in Canada," in *The Beaver Bites Back: American Popular Culture in Canada*, ed. David H. Flaherty and Frank E. Manning (Montreal: McGill-Queen's University Press, 1993), 260–80.

26 Tom Shakespeare, *Disability Rights and Wrongs* (New York: Routledge, 2006).

27 Geoffrey Reaume, *Remembrance of Patients Past: Patient Life at the Toronto Hospital for the Insane, 1870–1940* (Toronto: Oxford University Press, 2000).

28 Garland-Thomson, *Extraordinary Bodies*; and Russell Shuttleworth, Nikki Wedgwood, and Nathan J. Wilson, "The Dilemma of Disabled Masculinity," *Men and Masculinities* 15, no. 2 (June 2012): 174–94.

29 Titchkosky, *Reading and Writing Disability Differently*, and Robert McRuer, *Crip Theory: Cultural Signs of Disability and Queerness* (New York: New York University Press, 2006).

30 Nadja Durbach, *Spectacle of Deformity: Freak Shows and Modern British Culture* (Berkeley: University of California Press, 2010), 17–19. For a

critique of Durbach's perspective on disability, which informs my work, see Geoffrey Reaume, "Representing Freaks," review of Nadja Durbach, *Spectacle of Deformity: Freak Shows and Modern British Culture*, H-Disability, H-Net Reviews, July 2010.

31 I note here, however, the work of Robert McRuer in reclaiming "crip" as both a personal and theoretical intervention. See McRuer, *Crip Theory*, introduction.

32 Robert Bogdan, *Freak Show: Presenting Human Oddities for Amusement and Profit* (Chicago: University of Chicago Press, 1988), 146.

33 The literature is too numerous to list in its entirety. For examples, see Max Rusid, *Sideshow: Photo Album of Human Oddities* (New York: Amjon, 1975); Daniel Mannix, *Freaks: We Who Are Not as Others* (New York: Juno, 1999); Francine Hornberger, *Carny Folk: The World's Weirdest Sideshow Acts* (New York: Citadel Press, 2004); and Marc Hartzman, *American Sideshow: An Encyclopedia of History's Most Wondrous and Curiously Strange Performers* (New York: Jeremy P. Tarcher/Penguin, 2005).

34 For example, A.W. Stencell, *Girl Show: Into the Canvas World of Bump and Grind* (Toronto: ECW Press, 1999); and Stencell, *Circus and Carnival Ballyhoo*.

35 Leslie Fiedler, *Freaks: Myths and Images of the Secret Self* (New York: Simon and Schuster, 1978).

36 Garland-Thomson, "Introduction," 4.

37 Bogdan, *Freak Show*; and Garland-Thomson, *Extraordinary Bodies*.

38 Garland-Thomson, "Introduction," 11.

39 All Freak Shows Banned by CNE," *Toronto Star*, 17 August 1973, A2; and C. Morrison, letter to the editor, "Can Girl Be in Another Freak Show?" *Globe and Mail*, 23 August 1973, 7.

40 Rachel Adams, *Sideshow U.S.A.: Freaks and the American Cultural Imagination* (Chicago: University of Chicago Press, 2001), 2. See also Thomas Fahy, *Freak Shows and the Modern American Imagination* (New York: Palgrave Macmillan, 2006) for another study of freaks and American literature.

41 Andrea Stulman Dennett, *Weird and Wonderful: The Dime Museum in America* (New York: New York University Press, 1997), 318. M. Alison Kibler repeats Stulman Dennett's conclusion, despite having evidence to the contrary. See "Performance and Display," in *A Companion to American Cultural History*, ed. Karen Halttunen (Malden, MA: Blackwell, 2008), 316.

42 Angus McLaren, *Our Own Master Race: Eugenics in Canada, 1885–1945* (Toronto: McClelland and Stewart, 1990).

43 Durbach, *Spectacle of Deformity*, 171–7, 179–80.

44 Lara Campbell, *Respectable Citizens: Gender, Family and Unemployment in Ontario's Great Depression* (Toronto: University of Toronto Press, 2009), 58;

Nancy Christie, *Engendering the State: Family, Work and Welfare in Canada* (Toronto: University of Toronto Press, 2000); and Christopher Dummitt, *The Manly Modern: Masculinity in Postwar Canada* (Vancouver: University of British Columbia Press, 2007), chap. 3.
45 Nicholas, *The Modern Girl*.
46 David A. Gerber, "The 'Careers' of People Exhibited in Freak Shows: The Problem of Volition and Valorization," in Garland-Thomson, *Freakery*, 38–54.
47 Gerber, "The 'Careers' of People Exhibited in Freak Shows," 45.
48 Ellen Samuels, "Examining Millie and Christine McKoy: Where Enslavement and Enfreakment Meet," *Signs* 37, no. 1 (Autumn 2011): 53–81.
49 See, for example, Franca Iacovetta and Wendy Mitchinson, *On the Case: Explorations in Social History* (Toronto: University of Toronto Press, 1998).

1 Monsters and Freaks

1 *Billboard*, 19 April 1919, 47.
2 Paul Semonin, "Monsters in the Marketplace: The Exhibition of Human Oddities in Early Modern England," in *Freakery: Cultural Spectacles of the Extraordinary Body*, ed. Rosemarie Garland-Thomson (New York: New York University Press, 1996), 76–7.
3 Mark V. Barrow, "A Brief History of Teratology to the Early Twentieth Century," *Teratology* 4, no. 2 (1971): 119–21; and Ambroise Paré, *On Monsters and Marvels*, trans. Janis L. Pallister (Chicago: University of Chicago Press, 1995).
4 Dudley Wilson, *Signs and Portents: Monstrous Births from the Middle Ages to the Enlightenment* (London: Routledge, 1993).
5 A.W. Bates, *Emblematic Monsters: Unnatural Conceptions and Deformed Births in Early Modern Europe* (Amsterdam: Rodopi, 2005), 145–8.
6 Bates, *Emblematic Monsters*, 11, 28.
7 Robert Bogdan, *Freak Show: Presenting Human Oddities for Amusement and Profit* (Chicago: University of Chicago Press, 1990), 25.
8 Philip K. Wilson, "Eighteenth-Century 'Monsters' and Nineteenth-Century 'Freaks': Reading the Maternally Marked Child," *Literature and Medicine* 21, no. 1 (2002): 4, 6.
9 Bates, *Emblematic Monsters*, 147–8, 151.
10 Ibid., 148.
11 In the early twentieth century, collections of either real or faked fetuses in various stages of development would find a new life on the sideshow displayed as "Pickled Punks."

Notes to pages 25–7

12 Michel Foucault, *The Order of Things*, 2nd ed. (London: Routledge, 2005).
13 Michael Hagner's idea and use of "scholarly places" can be found translated from the original German in Birgit Stammberger, "Monstrous Bodies in Rudolf Virchow's Medical Collection in Nineteenth-Century Germany," in *Exploring the Cultural History of Continental European Freak Shows and "Enfreakment,"* ed. Anna Kérchy and Andrea Zittlau (Newcastle upon Tyne: Cambridge Scholars Publishing, 2012), 131.
14 Wilson, "Eighteenth-Century 'Monsters,'" 7.
15 Stammberger, "Monstrous Bodies," 110; Andrea Zittlau, "Enfreakment and German Medical Collections," in Kérchy and Zittlau, *Exploring the Cultural History*, 162; and Wilson, "Eighteenth-Century 'Monsters,'" 11.
16 Peter de Bolla, *The Education of the Eye: Painting, Landscape and Architecture in Eighteenth-Century Britain* (Stanford, CA: Stanford University Press, 2003).
17 Tony Bennett, "The Exhibitionary Complex," *new formations* 4 (1988): 73–102.
18 Michel Foucault, *Discipline and Punish: The Birth of the Prison*, trans. Alan Sheridan (New York: Vintage, 1977), chap. 1.
19 Bennett, "The Exhibitionary Complex," 73.
20 Hunt took on the name Signor Farini as a means to make his show identity more exotic. According to Shane Peacock, Hunt took on the name Farini after the dictator of Modena, Italy, whose name made world papers (and most importantly for Hunt his local *Port Hope Guide*) in 1859 in the wake of the Austro-Italian War. See Shane Peacock, *The Great Farini: The High Wire Life of William Hunt* (Toronto: Penguin Canada, 1996), 49. We could contrast this appropriation of an ethnic identity to make Hunt "exotic" with the actual discriminatory treatment of Italian immigrants in Canada later in the century and throughout the twentieth.
21 Bennett, "The Exhibitionary Complex," 96.
22 Leonore Davidoff and Catherine Hall, *Family Fortunes: Men and Women of the English Middle Class, 1780–1850* (Chicago: University of Chicago Press, 1987).
23 Heather McHold, "Even as You and I: Freak Shows and Lay Discourse on Spectacular Deformity," in *Victorian Freaks: The Social Context of Freakery in Britain*, ed. Marlene Tromp, 21–36 (Columbus: Ohio University Press, 2008), 23.
24 Ibid., 27, 29.
25 Ibid., 22, 26–7. I use the term midget here – and throughout the book – as it was the historical language used at the time to refer to people of small stature. I recognize its offensiveness today and as such also use more

appropriate terms like little people or people of small stature. I have avoided the term dwarfism, despite its current medical usage, since the term historically was often used to differentiate between proportionate and disproportionate peoples of small stature, and the cultural meanings tied to dwarfism historically were very different. For more on the appropriate use of language see Little People of America FAQ, http://www.lpaonline.org/faq-#Definition (accessed 15 May 2013). For historical definitions of midget and dwarf as they were used on the twentieth-century sideshows see *Howard Y. Barry Presents Singers' Midgets in a New Streamline Novelty: A Midget Circus Review* (n.p. n.d., circa 1940s).

26 Wilson, "Eighteenth-Century 'Monsters,'" 14–15.
27 A.H. Saxon, *P.T. Barnum: The Legend and the Man* (New York: Columbia University Press, 1989), 74.
28 Eric Fretz, "P.T. Barnum's Theatrical Selfhood and the Nineteenth-Century Culture of Exhibition," in Garland-Thomson, *Freakery*, 102–3.
29 Benjamin Reiss, "P.T. Barnum, Joice Heth and Antebellum Spectacles of Race," *American Quarterly* 51, no. 1 (1999): 78–107. See also Benjamin Reiss, *The Showman and the Slave: Race, Death, and Memory in Barnum's America* (Cambridge, MA: Harvard University Press, 2001).
30 Saxon, *P.T. Barnum*, 74–5.
31 The phrase "social engagement" is taken from Marlene Tromp and Karyn Valerius's description of the Feejee Mermaid. Marlene Tromp with Karyn Valerius, "Introduction: Toward Situating the Victorian Freak," in Tromp, *Victorian Freaks*, 9.
32 Lennard J. Davis, *Enforcing Normalcy* (London: Verso, 1995), 91–2. Historian Nadja Durbach makes a similar observation on the connection between disability and race in the freak show. See her article, "On the Emergence of the Freak Show in Britain," *BRANCH: Britain, Representation and Nineteenth-Century History*, ed. Dino Franco Felluga. Extension of *Romanticism and Victorianism on the Net*, http://www.branchcollective.org/?ps_articles=art_emergence_of_the_freak (accessed 12 March 2015).
33 Saxon, *P.T. Barnum*, 99.
34 For more on microcephaly, see http://www.mayoclinic.org/diseases-conditions/microcephaly/basics/definition/con-20034823 (accessed 5 January 2014).
35 Bogdan, *Freak Show*, 97.
36 Rosemarie Garland-Thomson, "Introduction: From Error to Wonder," *Freakery*, 1–22; Janet M. Davis, *The Circus Age: Culture and Society under the American Big Top* (Chapel Hill: University of North Carolina Press, 2002), 113–38; Rachel Adams, *Sideshow U.S.A.: Freaks and the American Cultural*

Imagination (Chicago: University of Chicago Press, 2001), 31; and Durbach, "On the Emergence of the Freak Show in Britain," 2.
37 Christopher A. Vaughan, "Ogling Igorots: The Politics and Commerce of Exhibiting Cultural Otherness, 1898–1913," in Garland-Thomson, *Freakery*, 219–33.
38 Adams, *Sideshow U.S.A.*, chap. 1; and Hartmut Lutz, Alootook Ipellie, and Hans-Ludwig Blohm, *The Diary of Abraham Ulrikab: Text and Context* (Ottawa: University of Ottawa Press, 2005).
39 Linda Frost, *Never One Nation: Freaks, Savages, and Whiteness in U.S. Popular Culture, 1850–1877* (Minneapolis: University of Minnesota Press, 2005), 6.
40 Anne Fausto-Sterling, "Gender, Race, and Nation: The Comparative Anatomy of 'Hottentot' Women in Europe, 1815–1817," in *Deviant Bodies: Critical Perspectives on Difference in Science and Popular Culture*, ed. Jennifer Terry and Jacqueline Urla (Indianapolis: Indiana University Press, 1995), 19–38; and Bernth Lindfors, "Hottentot, Bushman, Kaffir: Taxonomic Tendencies in Nineteenth-Century Racial Iconography," *Nordic Journal of African Studies* 5, no. 2 (1996): 1–28.
41 Lutz, Ipellie, and Blohm, *The Diary of Abraham Ulrikab*, xvii, 12–13, 21, 31. For a narrative of the events, see J. Garth Taylor, "An Eskimo Abroad, 1880: His Diary and Death," *Canadian Geographic* 101, no. 5 (1981): 38–43. In 1874, Hagenbeck had staged a group of Sami people as an ethnographic exhibit. They had to live as though unobserved, as the aim was to bring their authentic way of being to German audiences, without the theatrical trappings of false backdrops or staging. In doing so, Hagenbeck shifted the freak display to seem more respectable and scientific, while making his own intentions seem benign. See Anna Kérchy and Andrea Zittlau, "Introduction," in Kérchy and Zittlau, *Exploring the Cultural History*, 7–8.
42 Lutz, Ipellie, and Blohm, *The Diary of Abraham Ulrikab*, 29.
43 Kenn Harper, *Give Me My Father's Body: The Life of Minik, The New York Eskimo* (Frobisher Bay, NWT: Blacklead Books, 1986), 32–3, 35–6. Peary makes a brief mention of this in his book *Nearest the Pole: A Narrative of the Polar Expedition of the Peary Arctic Club in the S.S. Roosevelt, 1905–1906* (London: Hutchinson, 1907), 376.
44 Harper, *Give Me My Father's Body*, 221.
45 Rosalyn Poignant, *Professional Savages: Captive Lives and Western Spectacle* (New Haven, CT: Yale University Press, 2004), 1–3.
46 Cynthia Eagle Russett, *Sexual Science: The Victorian Construction of Womanhood* (Cambridge, MA: Harvard University Press 1989), 7.
47 Bennett, "The Exhibitionary Complex," 96.

48 Peter Stallybrass and Allon White, *The Politics and Poetics of Transgression* (London: Methuen, 1986), 42.
49 Anne McClintock, *Imperial Leather: Race, Gender and Sexuality in the Colonial Contest* (New York: Routledge, 1995); Bennett, "The Exhibitionary Complex," 94–5; and Walden, *Becoming Modern in Toronto*.
50 Barbara Larsen, "Introduction," in *The Art of Evolution: Darwin, Darwinisms, and Visual Culture*, ed. Barbara Larsen and Fae Brauer (Lebanon, NH: Dartmouth College Press, 2009), 7–8.
51 On Pastrana see Rosemarie Garland-Thomson, *Extraordinary Bodies: Figuring Physical Disability in American Culture and Literature* (New York: Columbia University Press, 1997), 70–8; and Rebecca Stern, "Our Bear Women, Ourselves: Affiliating with Julia Pastrana," in Tromp, *Victorian Freaks*, 200–34. Garland-Thomson notes the close connection between Pastrana's display, including pieces of her embalmed body after her death, and that of Sarah Bartman.
52 Saxon, *P.T. Barnum*, 98–9.
53 See Poignant, *Professional Savages*; Vaughn, "Ogling Igorots"; and Adams, *Sideshow U.S.A.*
54 Adams, *Sideshow U.S.A.*, 28.
55 On the American Museum, see Andrea Stulman Dennett, *Weird and Wonderful: The Dime Museum in America* (New York: New York University Press, 1997), chapter 2.
56 David Nasaw, *Going Out: The Rise and Fall of Public Amusements* (New York: Basic Books, 1993), 15.
57 Stulman Dennett, *Weird and Wonderful*, 36.
58 For local histories of dime museums, see, for example, John Sturm, "Detroit's Wonderland Dime Musee," *Chronicle: The Quarterly Magazine of the Historical Society of Michigan* 24, no. 3 (1988): 4–6, 14; Walker Rumble, "A Showdown of 'Swifts': Women Compositors, Dime Museums, and the Boston Typesetting Races of 1886," *New England Quarterly* 71, no. 4 (1998): 615–28; and Larry Widen, "Milwaukee's Dime Museum," *Milwaukee History* 8, no. 1 (1985): 24–34.
59 Bogdan, *Freak Show*, 35; and Frank Cullen with Florence Hackman and Donald McNeilly, *Vaudeville, Old and New: An Encyclopedia of Variety Performers in America* (New York: Routledge, 2006), 312.
60 Walden, *Becoming Modern in Toronto*, 253.
61 Yvan LaMonde, *The Social History of Ideas in Quebec, 1760–1896*, trans. Phyllis Aronoff and Howard Scott (Montreal: McGill-Queen's University Press, 2013), 407. A description of some freak performers working at the Dupuis-Leonard Museum appears in *Billboard*, 14 March 1931, 51.

62 Gerald Lenton-Young, "Variety Theatre," in *Early Stages: Theatre in Ontario, 1800–1914*, ed. Ann Saddlemyer, (Toronto: University of Toronto Press, 1990), 191–3; and Cullen with Hackman and McNeilly, *Vaudeville, Old and New*, 886.
63 Lenton-Young, "Variety Theatre," 191.
64 Walden, *Becoming Modern in Toronto*, 253–4.
65 Stulman Dennett, *Weird and Wonderful*, 85.
66 Elspeth Heaman, *The Inglorious Arts of Peace: Exhibitions in Canadian Society during the Nineteenth Century* (Toronto: University of Toronto Press, 1999), 131.
67 Walden, *Becoming Modern in Toronto*, 254–5.
68 Durbach, "On the Emergence of the Freak Show in Britain," 2.
69 Walden, *Becoming Modern in Toronto*, 261.
70 Bogdan, chapter 2 of *Freak Show*; and Davis, *The Circus Age*, 13.
71 For overviews in Ontario, see Lenton-Young, "Variety Theatre," 171–6; and David Gardner, "Variety," in *Later Stages: Essays in Ontario Theatre from the First World War to the 1970s*, ed. Ann Saddlemyer and Richard Plant (Toronto: University of Toronto Press, 1997), 122–7.
72 Janet Miron, *Prisons, Asylums, and the Public: Institutional Visiting in the Nineteenth Century* (Toronto: University of Toronto Press, 2010), 123–5.
73 Ibid., 124.
74 Of course, this did not mean that there was no conflict or controversy. See Walden, *Becoming Modern in Toronto*; Heaman, *The Inglorious Arts of Peace*; and Jane Nicholas, "'A Figure of a Nude Woman': Art, Popular Culture, and Modernity at the Canadian National Exhibition, 1927," *Histoire sociale/Social History* 41, no. 82 (2008): 313–44.
75 Walden, *Becoming Modern in Toronto*, 279.
76 Ibid., 156–7.
77 Heaman, *The Inglorious Arts of Peace*, 251.
78 Bogdan, *Freak Show*, 48.
79 On the Chicago World's Fair, see Robert Rydell, *All the World's a Fair: Visions of Empire at American International Expositions, 1876–1916* (Chicago: University of Chicago Press, 1987), chap. 2; and Bogdan, *Freak Show*, 49–51.
80 Bogdan, *Freak Show*, 51.
81 Heaman, *The Inglorious Arts of Peace*, 250; and Walden, *Becoming Modern in Toronto*, 256.
82 Heaman, *The Inglorious Arts of Peace*, 250.
83 Guy Scott, *Country Fairs in Canada* (Toronto: Fitzhenry and Whiteside, 2005), 60.
84 Stanley Appelbaum, *The Chicago World's Fair of 1893: A Photographic Record* (New York: Dover, 1980), 95.

85 See, for example, Jerry Holtman [pseud.], *Freak Show Man: Uncensored Memoirs of Harry Lewiston – The Incredible Scoundrel* (Los Angeles: Holloway House, 1968) [hereafter cited as Lewiston, *Freak Show Man*].
86 Kathy Peiss, *Cheap Amusements: Working Women and Leisure in Turn-of-the-Century New York* (Philadelphia: Temple University Press, 1986).
87 Bennett, "The Exhibitionary Complex," 76.

2 The Carnival State

1 Wm. Judkins Hewitt, "Chautauquaized Carnivals: Or Vice-Versa?" *Billboard*, 22 March 1919, 199.
2 Ibid., 199.
3 Loo and Strange describe the period from 1919 to 1939 as one of "widening the net" in regard to moral regulation and the Canadian state. See Tina Loo and Carolyn Strange, *Making Good: Law and Moral Regulation in Canada, 1867–1939* (Toronto: University of Toronto Press, 1997).
4 John Thurston, "Scenes from the Midway: One Hundred Years of Outdoor Amusement," unpublished manuscript, 10. My thanks to Dr Thurston for sharing his work with me.
5 Jack Mosher, "Carnival King," *Maclean's*, 15 July 1941, 14, 29; "Jimmie Sullivan Directs Wallace Bros. Make-Ready," *Billboard*, 4 April 1953, 64.
6 Conklin was sold to a US company in 2004, although a smaller company remains in operation in Canada today. See http://www.conklinshows.com/.
7 Penny Tennenhouse, "E.J. Casey Retiring," *Winnipeg Free Press*, 25 June 1965.
8 Both carried freak exhibits. See, for example, "Wallace Canadian Get under Way," *Billboard*, 1 June 1935, 50; "Parade Helps Lynch at Halifax Opener; Midway Attractive," *Billboard*, 10 June 1939, 41, 43; "Bill Lynch Opens Early to Battle Cool Weather," *Billboard*, 22 June 1946, 57; "Shows 'Flood' Canadian Spots," *Billboard*, 23 August 1947, 55; "Lynch Set for Halifax Date," *Billboard*, 16 April 1949, 80; and "Back at Home Base: Jimmie Sullivan Directs Wallace Bros. Make Ready," *Billboard*, 4 April 1953, 64.
9 Joe McKennon, *A Pictorial History of the American Carnival*, vol. 1 (Sarasota: Carnival Publishers of Sarasota, 1972), 67.
10 William Lindsay Gresham, "The World of Mirth," *Life* magazine, 13 September 1948 (newspaper clipping from Circus World Museum [hereafter CWM], Carnival Collection, box 3).
11 Patrick C. Easto and Marcello Truzzi, "Towards an Ethnography of the Carnival Social System," *Journal of Popular Culture* 6 (1973): 553.
12 Quoted in ibid.

13 Thurston, "Scenes from the Midway," 8.
14 McKennon, *A Pictorial History of the American Carnival*, 1:78–9. See also Stencell, *Circus and Carnival Ballyhoo*, chap. 1. Clarence A. Wortham was born in Texas in 1882 and established a carnival in 1910. By 1922, he owned two large carnivals and held the contracts for the CNE in 1921 and 1922, as well as the lucrative western Canada "A" fairs in 1922. Wortham died later that year. McKennon, *A Pictorial History of the American Carnival*, 2:36.
15 McKennon, *A Pictorial History of the American Carnival*, 1:75, 89–90.
16 Library and Archives Canada [hereafter LAC], RG 76, vol. 594, file 841690, part 3, confidential letter from Thomas Gilley, Division Commission, to A.L. Jolliffe, Commissioner of Immigration, 18 July 1924.
17 These consolidations occurred earlier in the twentieth century as well. For example, Rubin Gruberg owned a midway in 1916, and after partnered (in name only) with W.S. Cherry to established the Rubin and Cherry Shows. The Rubin and Cherry Shows occasionally held the contracts for the midway at the CNE in the 1920s and early 1930s as well as the Pacific National Exhibition (Vancouver) in the early 1940s. McKennon, *A Pictorial History of the American Carnival*, 2:53; "RC Vancouver Take Is Heavy," *Billboard*, 13 September 1941, 30, 60.
18 McKenzie Porter, "Queen of the Midway," *Maclean's*, 1 October 1949, 60. See also "Conklins Get Big Business at Winnipeg," *Billboard*, 18 June 1949, and "Conklins Bale It at Winnipeg as Cele Clicks," *Billboard*, 25 June 1949, 63.
19 Lou Dufour with Irwin Kirby, *Fabulous Years: Carnival Life, World's Fairs, and Broadway* (New York: Vintage Press, 1977), 122.
20 It was the carnivals' ability to make a profit that lead to increasing oversight, professionalization, and surveillance in the 1970s. In the early 1970s the Royal American Shows (RAS), which sometimes played under the title Royal Canadian Shows, came to the attention of the RCMP and the Department of National Revenue. Both agencies were concerned by the suitcases of cash being freely carried from Canada into the United States. The RCMP believed that the money was from "skimming" – carnival operators pocketing a small portion of each transaction. It had long proven difficult to oversee carnivals in regard to revenues and taxes. Constant travel, including border crossings, and dealing in cash meant that auditing books was difficult. A lengthy investigation led to the 1978 public inquiry in Alberta by Justice Laycraft. Royal American Shows became the key target of the investigation due their size and prominence as well as the limited resources of the task force made up of members of the RCMP and the Department of National Revenue. Interestingly, members of the Royal American Show testified to a rumour that the RCMP had been

bribed with $50,000 by a competing carnival company to investigate RAS. Allegedly, the investigation was to try to ensure the Western circuit would go to the Conklin shows. Justice Laycraft dismissed this accusation as "completely unfounded and irresponsible." Overall, however, the inquiry led to the end of the RAS in Canada, the establishment of Alberta Gaming Commission, and also the end of some of the long-standing informal practices by carnivals. See James H. Laycraft, *Royal American Shows Inc. and Its Activities in Alberta: Report of a Public Inquiry of the Commission of Inquiry into the Affairs and Activities in the Province of Alberta of Royal American Shows Inc.* (Edmonton, AB: n.p., 1978), B-8 [cited hereafter as Laycraft inquiry]. When the Laycraft report and the issues it investigated led to the demise of the Royal American Shows' popularity in Western Canada, Conklin filled the hole. See also Angus, "Midway to Respectability."

21 David J. Skal and Elias Savada, *Dark Carnival: The Secret World of Tod Browning – Hollywood's Master of the Macabre* (New York: Anchor Books, 1995).
22 McKennon, *A Pictorial History of the American Carnival*, 1:67.
23 "Up Canada Way," *Billboard*, 4 November 1922, 92.
24 McKennon, *A Pictorial History of the American Carnival*, 1:108.
25 Photograph of the Conklin show The Naked Truth. Author's personal collection.
26 University of South Florida, Digital Libraries Collection, Showman's Oral History Project, interview with Joanne Wilson and Trudy Strong by Andrew T. Huse.
27 Easto and Truzzi, "Towards an Ethnography of the Carnival Social System," 552–3; McKennon, *A Pictorial History of the American Carnival*, 1:19. Carnivals could also include circuses. See, for example, "Jacobs Circus to Tour with Conklin Shows," *Billboard*, 7 March 1942, 29. McKennon states that circuses could not include carnivals.
28 Lewiston, *Freak Show Man*, 240. On damage to property, see City of Saskatoon Archives [hereafter CSA], 1200-0140 City Commissioner Files, letter from City Clerk to City Commissioner, 6 June 1934; letter from Commissioner to Chief Constable, 7 June 1934; and letter from Chief Constable to City Commissioner, 9 June 1934, 1069–1067 (3); letter from City Commissioner to Chief Constable, 7 June 1934; letter from City Clerk to City Commissioner, 6 June 1934, and 1067–1063 (2); letter from City Clerk to Parks Superintendent, 25 June 1935. In 1934, the city council decided that the circus (Al. G. Barnes Circus) would be responsible for "seeing that this block is left in as clean a condition after the circus as when you found it." See letter from City Clerk to Ed F. Maxwell, 11 May 1934.

29 Ramsey Cook, *The Regenerators: Social Criticism in Late Victorian English Canada* (Toronto: University of Toronto Press, 1985), Valverde, *The Age of Soap, Light, and Water*; Marcel Martel, *Canada the Good: A Short History of Vice since 1500* (Waterloo, ON: Wilfrid Laurier University Press, 2014).
30 T. Jackson Lears, *No Place of Grace: Antimodernism and the Transformation of American Culture, 1880–1920* (Chicago: University of Chicago Press, 1991), 18.
31 Carnivals tended not to be union organized, and workers with large circuses like Ringling Bros did not engage in organized labour resistance until the end of the 1930s. Toronto's Labour Men may then have been objecting to the entertainment or the labour practices. "Freaks on Midway Objected to by Labor Men," *Globe*, 5 September 1913, 2.
32 Joe McKennon, *A Pictorial History of the American Carnival*, 1:80.
33 "Freaks Are Barred from Entering Canada," *Globe*, 29 June 1915, 6. In the United States, the idea that society needed to be protected from the disabled extended in some jurisdictions extended to merely seeing people who were deemed to be disabled and/or disfigured. So-called ugly laws, with explicit or implicit references to "exploitative" freak shows, were enacted in a number of American jurisdictions in the late nineteenth and early twentieth centuries, including the states of Pennsylvania, Michigan, California, and Florida, and the cities of Chicago and New York. While some scholars have implied that the legislation was effective in helping end the sideshow, this seems more coincidental than deliberate. Legislation is theoretical unless exercised through enforcement. Chicago's ugly law, for example, was enacted in 1881, two years before the Chicago Columbian Exposition, credited with inventing the modern midway. Much of the ugly laws' focus was on street beggars, but the display of the extraordinary body for profit was something that had the potential to collapse the categories of "beggar" and "freak." Both, people argued, were offensive for the public to witness – an argument that resonated with calls for legislation to ban the shows in Ontario and other Canadian jurisdictions in the 1920s. Yet, as Susan M. Schweik notes, the permeable borders between the two did not render the displays entirely similar. Begging was part of the survival street economy that relied on invoking feelings of pity in passersby. She argues that freaks may have been exploited but were not as precariously situated as beggars. See Susan M. Schweik, *The Ugly Laws: Disability in Public* (New York: New York University Press, 2009), and Garland-Thomson, *Extraordinary Bodies*.
34 City of Vancouver Archives [hereafter CVA], S-1002, box 524 C-6, folder 1 Bulletins 1913–1924, Vancouver Exhibition – Bulletin no. 8, p. 52.

35 F. Beverly Kelley, *It Was Better Than Work* (Gerald, MO: Patrice Press, 1982), 164.
36 CSA, 1069-1062 (3) Licensing, 1931, letter to Frank Miley from City Clerk, 29 July 1931. LAC, RG 76, vol. 594, file 841690, part 3. This is also true of regulations for moving pictures in the period. As Cynthia Comacchio argues, regulation of movies, especially those designed to "protect" youth from their influence, largely failed. See Comacchio, *The Dominion of Youth*, 167–8.
37 Bryan Palmer, *Working Class Experience: Rethinking the History of Canadian Labour, 1800–1991*, 2nd ed. (Toronto: McClelland and Stewart, 1992), 216.
38 Comacchio, *The Dominion of Youth*, and Mary Vipond, "Canadian Nationalism and the Plight of Canadian Magazines in the 1920s," *Canadian Historical Review* 58, no. 1 (March 1977): 43–63.
39 Maria Tippet, *Making Culture: English-Canadian Institutions and the Arts before the Massey Commission* (Toronto: University of Toronto Press, 1990), 7.
40 Vipond, "Canadian Nationalism and the Plight of Canadian Magazines in the 1920s," 43–63.
41 On taste and class, see Pierre Bourdieu, *Distinction: A Social Critique of the Judgement of Taste* (Cambridge, MA: Harvard University Press, 1987), 66.
42 McKennon, *A Pictorial History of the American Carnival*, 1:47.
43 Coates and McGuiness, *Pride of the Land*, 28–9.
44 Ibid., 30.
45 Archives of Ontario [hereafter AO], Attorney General's Files, Office of the Attorney General, RG 4-32, file 1636.
46 AO, Attorney General's Files, Circuses and Travelling Shows, 1919–1921, RG 23-26-20, file 1.57.
47 AO, Attorney General's Files, Circuses and Travelling Shows, 1919–1921, RG 23-26-20, file 1.57.
48 Strange, *Toronto's Girl Problem*, and Valverde, *The Age of Light, Soap and Water*.
49 AO, Attorney General's Files, Circuses and Travelling Shows, 1919–1921, RG 23-26-20, file 1.51, letter from Joseph E. Rogers to W.R. Whatley, 7 August 1920. See also David C. Jones, *Midways, Judges, and Smooth-Tongued Fakirs: The Illustrated Story of Country Fairs in the Prairie West* (Saskatoon: Western Producer Prairie Books, 1983), 51–3.
50 AO, RG 56-1-1-36, Travelling Shows, 1913–1933, resolutions of the Brantford Chamber of Commerce, Oshawa Board of Trade, the Chamber of Commerce of the City of Bellville, the Galt Board of Trade, Chatham Chamber of Commerce, and the Sarnia Chamber of Commerce.
51 AO, RG 56-1-1-36, Travelling Shows, 1913–1933, resolutions of the Galt Board of Trade and the Chatham Chamber of Commerce.
52 See, for example, "Halifax Objects to American Amusements," *Billboard*, 25 April 1931, 48; "Lynch Wings at Moncton," *Billboard*, 11 June 1932, 70;

"St. John Still in Carnival Fold," *Billboard*, 20 February 1937, 49; and "Winnipeg Votes on Annual," *Billboard*, 27 September 1947, 47, 59.
53 AO, RG 56-1-1-36, memorandum from Joseph E. Rogers to Peter Smith, Provincial Treasurer, 27 January 1921, and letter to Peter Smith, Provincial Treasurer, 8 March 1921.
54 CSA, D5W-111-625, License Inspector – Circuses, letter from W. Rise to City Commissioner, 28 June 1927.
55 "Boosters Try to Sell Plan," *Billboard*, 27 September 1947, 47, 59.
56 Loo and Strange, "The Travelling Show Menace."
57 Loo and Strange, *Making Good*, 103.
58 "On to Toronto!" *Billboard*, 18 November 1922, 7.
59 "The Clean-Up Wins at Toronto Meeting," *Billboard*, 9 December 1922, 6.
60 Ibid.
61 W.D. Van Volkenberg, "Out in the Open," *Billboard*, 5 October 1929.
62 LAC, RG 17, vol. 3197, box 1, file 150 (2), letter from S.S. Savage to W.R. Motherwell, 9 April 1930.
63 Laycraft inquiry, B-2. For more on gambling, carnivals, and agricultural fairs, see Suzanne Morton, *At Odds: Gambling and Canadians, 1919–1969* (Toronto: University of Toronto Press, 2003).
64 LAC, RG 17, vol. 3197, box 1, file 150 (1), letter from W. Chisholm to Isabel Cummings and excerpt from *Printer's Ink*, 17 May 1923.
65 Nicholas, "A Figure of a Nude Woman."
66 Loo and Strange, *Making Good*, 145, and Martel, *Canada the Good*, 91.
67 Walden, *Becoming Modern in Toronto*; Rydell, *All the World's a Fair*; and Nicholas, "A Figure of a Nude Woman."
68 "Carnivals Are Essential to the Fairs," *Billboard*, 13 October 1928, 70.
69 Canadian National Exhibition Archives [hereafter CNEA], Auditor's Report, Midway File 1919.
70 *Billboard*, 29 March 1930, 124.
71 H.W. Waters, *History of Fairs and Expositions: Their Classification, Functions and Values* (London, ON: Reid Bros, 1939), 127.
72 Ibid., 127–8.
73 CVA, Am 281 S-10-1, box 524-E-3, folder 2, Vancouver Exhibition Association Bulletin no. 23, 1932, p. 6, and Vancouver Exhibition Association Bulletin no. 24, 1933.
74 CVA, Am 281 S-10-1, box 524-E-3, folders 1–4, Vancouver Exhibition Association Bulletin no. 32, 1941, pp. 4, 7; Pacific National Exhibition Bulletin no. 39, 1948, p. 11; Pacific National Exhibition Bulletin no. 41, 1950, pp. 6, 8.
75 CVA, Am 281 S-10-1, box 524-E-3, folder 4, Pacific National Exhibition Bulletin no. 43, 1952, p. 9.

76 Coates and McGuiness, *Pride of the Land*, 130, 62.
77 Mary Ellen Kelm, *A Wilder West: Rodeo in Western Canada* (Vancouver: University of British Columbia Press, 2012), 110.
78 The League was the professional association for show owners. A Canadian chapter was established in 1958, with Patty Conklin as president. The history is detailed at the Showmen's League of America – Canadian Chapter website at http://www.showmensleague.ca/public/about/. A first-person account of being at one of the League's meetings when the circuits were being bid on can be found in Coates and McGuiness, *Pride of the Land*, 130–1. Most of the League's records were destroyed in a fire in 2001 (see http://www.showmensleague.org/) and the organization encourages researchers to rely on the records in *Billboard* magazine.
79 Angus, "Midway to Respectability," 136n34.
80 Herb Dotten, "Canada's B Goes Long Term," *Billboard*, 29 January 1949, 64.
81 These circuits are described in various issues of *Billboard* magazine. See also Angus, "Midway to Respectability," 119–20 and 136n33; James Gray, *Brand of Its Own: The Hundred Year History of the Calgary Exhibition and Stampede* (Saskatoon: Western Producer Prairie Books, 1985), 33; Wetherell with Kmet, *Useful Pleasures*, 311; and MacEwan, *Agriculture on Parade*, 173–5. A brief history of the Western Fair Association, which is still operating today, can be found at https://www.fairsnet.org/about-wfa/about-wfa.
82 See, for example, "Conklin Repeats in Prairie Loop; Sullivan Gets B," *Billboard*, 31 January 1942, 30; and "Canada A Circ to Conklin," *Billboard*, 1 February 1941, 29.
83 Herb Dotten, "Canada's B Goes Long Term," *Billboard*, 29 January 1949.
84 McKennon, *A Pictorial History of the American Carnival*, 2:106–7.
85 Bob Goldsack, *Johnny's Here: A History of the Johnny J. Jones Exposition* (Nashua, NH: Midway Museum Publications, 1990), 22.
86 *Billboard*, 23 August 1919, 60.
87 The circus was an amalgamation of two (now iconic) American railway circuses: Ringling Bros and Barnum and Bailey. The Barnum and Bailey Circus was born when P.T. Barnum and James A. Bailey merged their respective circuses in 1881. Under that operation, Bailey, after Barnum's death in 1891, operated two large circuses: the Greatest Show on Earth and (former competitor) the Adam Forepaugh & Sells Brothers circus. As the latter's name implies, it too was the product of a merger. The Ringling Bros began to dominate the American circus when Barnum and Bailey did an extensive tour of Europe between 1897 and 1902. The Ringling Bros was owned and operated by the five Ringling brothers

of Baraboo, Wisconsin. The biographies of the Ringling Bros resonated with the popular American cultural narrative of the self-made man. The brothers were five of eight children born to German immigrants, who decided to start their own circus after one visited their hometown. From 1869, the brothers began piecing together live shows and eventually became one of the biggest names in circus history. Unlike many other circuses and carnivals, the Ringlings policed their circus carefully and ensured there was no gambling, graft, or drinking. By 1900, they were known as a "Sunday School" show, a reputation that marked them as respectable, wholesome, and clean purveyors of amusements. By 1904, the companies had agreed to go separate routes to avoid directly competing with each other. After Bailey's death in 1906, the Ringling Bros bought out his circuses in 1907. They maintained them as separate operations until 1919, when they merged to become the Ringling Bros and Barnum and Bailey Circus. Although the circus fell into hard times in the 1930s, it persisted and continues to offer shows today. Janet M. Davis, *The Circus Age Culture and Society under the American Big Top* (Chapel Hill: University of North Carolina Press, 2002), 41, 60–1; and Gene Plowden, *Circus Press Agent: The Life and Times of Roland Butler* (Caldwell, ID: Caxton Printers, 1984), chaps. 1 and 2.

88 "Rain Cuts Attendance at Ottawa Exhibition," *Billboard*, 30 September 1922, 85.
89 "Conklin Show Gets Going," *Billboard*, 15 May 1937, 52.
90 "Twister Hits RAS Midway," *Billboard* 31 July 1937, 48, 59.
91 Scott, *Country Fairs in Canada*, 84.
92 CVA, S-1002, box 524 C-6, folder 1, Bulletins 1913–1924, Vancouver Exhibition – Bulletin no. 8, p. 51.
93 CVA, S-1002, box 524 C-6, folder 1, Bulletins 1913–1924, Vancouver Exhibition – Bulletin no. 8, p. 51.
94 "Fair Managers, Local Politicians, and Local Fixers Are to Blame," *Billboard*, 7 October 1922, 79.
95 CVA, PNE Archives, Am 281 S-6, box 596, folder 10, Pacific Coast Amusement Co Ltd #1 1919–1929.
96 CVA, Pacific National Exhibition Archives, Am 281 S-6, box 596, folder 8, Old Exhibition Contracts, 1925–1941.
97 Laycraft inquiry. See also Coates and McGuiness, *Pride of the Land*, 184.
98 Pacific National Exhibition Annual Calendar of Events, 1949. Author's personal collection.
99 Mosher, "Carnival King," 31.

100 "Conklins Make Five-Year Pact with Exhibition in Sherbrooke," *Billboard*, 26 February 1944, 29; "Four Ontario Fairs Sign Conklin Shows," *Billboard*, 24 February 1945, 42; and "5-Year Winnipeg Pact of Conklin," *Billboard*, 12 May 1945, 36.
101 "Conklins Operating Rides in Three Parks," *Billboard*, 9 June 1945, 47.
102 "Conklins in Toronto 5 Years" *Billboard*, 30 November 1946, 52, 64; "Conklin Tips Plans with 10-Yr. Pacts" *Billboard*, 6 February 1946, 51.
103 See, for example, "Conklin Away to Good Start" *Billboard*, 13 May 1939, 42, 46; and "Hamilton Gives Conklin Largest Opener in Years," *Billboard*, 11 May 1940, 55.
104 "Independent Midway for CNE," *Billboard*, 12 December 1936, 50.
105 North American Carnival Museum and Archives [hereafter NACMA], Jack Ray Red Press Release, ca 1940s.
106 "Halligan Returns to Conklin," *Billboard*, 7 February 1942, 30.
107 "Conklin Loop Kickoff Strong," *Billboard*, 10 July 1943, 30, 33.
108 See "Brydon Building New Org for CNE," and "Brydon Faces Busiest Year; In at Little Rock, Memphis," *Billboard*, 21 June 1947, 53, and 24 April 1948, 53.
109 "Grandstand Cuts into CNE Midway to Put Takes under '47"; "Spending Does Brodie," *Billboard*, 18 September 1948, 75.
110 LAC, RG 17, vol. 3197, box 1, file 150-2-(1) and (2), Department of Agriculture files, Program for Fete Nationale Jacques Cartier, Program for the Quebec Exposition Provencale.
111 Lewiston, *Freak Show Man*, 217.
112 Ibid., 218. On the 1937 polio epidemic and the CNE, see Christopher J. Rutty, "The Middle Class Plague: Epidemic Polio and the Canadian State," *Canadian Bulletin of Medical History* 13, no. 2 (1996): 289–91. On the Toronto epidemic in 1937, see also Heather MacDougall, *Activists and Advocates: Toronto's Health Department, 1883–1983* (Toronto: Dundurn, 1990), 147–50.
113 "A Midway by Any Other Name Still Gets Its Quota of Fans," *Globe and Mail*, 30 August 1937, 31.
114 Ward Hall, *Struggles and Triumphs of a Modern Day Showman: An Autobiography* (Sarasota, FL: Carnival Publishers of Sarasota, 1981), 32–3.
115 "Conklin Gets Ripley Units for Canada," *Billboard*, 13 February 1954, 64.
116 *Billboard*, 30 April 1955, 61.
117 Communication on and between these partners can be found in AO, RG 23-26-20, file 1.11, Circuses and Travelling Shows, 1913–1917, and file 1.39, Circuses and Travelling Shows, 1919, and AO, RG 56-1-1-36, Travelling Shows, 1913–1933, memorandum to Dr. J.D. Monteith, Provincial

Treasurer, regarding Windsor District Maccabees Border Cities Charity, 9 November 1926. Sideshows sometimes broadcast these partnerships: see "Everybody Loves Circus," newspaper clipping, North American Carnival Museum and Archives (NACMA), Conklin Scrapbook, 1930; "Attractions at Conklin Shows," newspaper clipping, NACMA, Conklin Scrapbook, 1942; and "Stars of Sideshows to Help Red Cross"; newspaper clipping, NACMA, Conklin Scrapbook, 1942. For secondary material on sideshows in Ontario, see Scott, *A Fair Share*, 119.
118 Scott, *Country Fairs in Canada*, 61. The still-popular Shrine Circus, of course, also fits this model.
119 "A City Given Up to Noise and Joy," *Toronto Daily Star*, 18 August 1908, 7.
120 *Billboard*, 19 April 1919, 43, and 10 December 1921, 136. The report was referring to the Great War Veterans' Association, which operated from 1917 to 1925. *Billboard* was the largest and most popular of the trade publications for circuses, sideshows, and carnivals at the time.
121 AO, RG 23-26-20, box 1, file 39: see letters from H. Carrington, 5 March 1920, and the reply, 6 March 1920; letter from H.O. Wright, 3 February 1920, and reply, 6 February 1920; and letter from D.E. MacIntyre, 30 April 1920, and reply, 3 May 1920. That summer, however, the OPP fielded some complaints about the show. Further, the tabloid *Jack Canuck* printed a highly critical article with the title "Crooks' Carnival Plagues Ontario." The subtitle pointed a finger at the OPP, stating: "Aggregation of Gamblers and Vile Shows, Endorsed by Provincial Police, Spoils Suckers in Provincial Tows – Chiefs of Police Condemn Outfit, Which Some of Them Close Up." See *Jack Canuck*, 31 July 1920.
122 "Canadian Victory Shows," *Billboard*, 6 May 1922, 82.
123 Gambling and girl shows with rumours of prostitution seem to have come under the most scrutiny. See *Jack Canuck*, 31 July 1920, and the correspondence in AO, RG 23-26-20, box 1, file 39.
124 See AO, RG 56-1-1-36, Travelling Shows, 1913–1933, letter to W.H. Price from J.D. Monteith, 3 August 1926, and letter to J.D. Monteith from W.H. Price, 7 October 1926.
125 "Amusement Tax Again Reduced," *Hamilton Spectator*, 3 September 1927, 29.
126 "New Customs Tax in Canada Affects Carnivals, Circuses," *Billboard*, 15 February 1941, 29.
127 LAC, RG 76, vol. 594, file 841690, part 3, letter from James Healy to unnamed District Superintendent of immigration, 16 June 1955.
128 CSA, Bylaw 1286, 20 December 1920, Bylaw 2648, 4 December 1939, Bylaw3186, 14 August 1950, and Bylaw 1667, revision, 16 August 1926.

129 Davis, *The Circus Age*, 21; Goldsack, *Johnny's Here*, 13; and McKennon, *A Pictorial History of the American Carnival*, 2:91.
130 Provincial Archives of New Brunswick [hereafter PANB], New Brunswick Acts, 1923, An Act Respecting Circuses and Travelling Shows, 1923, and Revised Statues of New Brunswick, 1927, The Theatres Act, 1926.
131 "Canada Eases Tariff Burden on Shows from United States," *Billboard*, 3 May 1947, 52.
132 CSA, D5W-VI-503, Licensing-Fee-Circuses (1914), letter from H.L. Jordan, City Solicitor, to Andrew Leslie, City Clerk, 2 July 1914; D5W-VI-293, Bylaws-Licensing-Circuses (1926), letter from License Inspector to City Commissioner, 17 June 1926, City Council Minutes, 12 July 1915 and 23 June 1952. When the months of the ban changed in 1954 it was announced in *Billboard*. See "Saskatoon Bans Traveling Shows," *Billboard*, 10 April 1954.
133 Quoted in Scott, *Country Fairs in Canada*, 77–8.
134 AO, RG 23-26-20, box 1, file # 1.50, Circuses and Travelling Shows 1920–1921, William Hicks to Joseph E. Rogers, 4 November 1920.
135 AO, RG 23-26-20, box 1, file 1.15, correspondence between Rogers and John Kent, Managing Director of the Canadian National Exhibition.
136 Dave Robeson, *Al G. Barnes: Master Showman As Told by Al G. Barnes* (Caldwell, ID: Caxton Printers, 1935), 272–3.
137 Gresham, "The World of Mirth." See also Jones, *Midways, Judges, and Smooth-Tongued Fakirs*, 55.
138 "Eastern Canada Biz Soars," *Billboard*, 13 September 1947, 74b.
139 Laycraft inquiry, C-1 and C-2.
140 Laycraft inquiry, C-24. My emphasis.
141 Lewiston, *Freak Show Man*.
142 CSA, D5W-VI-587, Licensing-Business, letter from Fred A Morgan to C.J. Yorath, City Commissioner, 9 January 1917, and letter from A. Leslie to Fred. A Meigan, 16 January 1917.
143 CSA, 1200-0291-001, Report No. 11-1930 of the Standing Committee adopted at the meeting of Council held June 9, 1930, and Report No. 22-1930 of the Commissioner adopted at the meeting of Council held August 4, 1930.
144 LAC, RG 76, vol. 594, file 841690, part 3, letter from minister of immigration and colonization to Rev. J.H. Edmison, 20 June 1921.
145 LAC, RG 76, vol. 594, file 841690, part 3, letter from Division Commissioner of Immigration to A.L. Jolliffe, Commissioner of Immigration, Ottawa, 18 July 1924.
146 LAC, RG 76, vol. 110, file 553:45:CD, letter from A.L. May, regional director to Officers-in-Charge, Central District. The letter provides a copy

of another letter to the operators of Amusements of America regarding their planned trip to the Central Canada Exhibition, 1966, 13 June 1966.
147 McKennon, *A Pictorial History of the American Carnival*, 2:122.
148 LAC, RG 76, vol. 594, file 841690, part 3, Circular to Immigration Inspectors-in-Charge from Assistant Division Commissioner, 6 August 1924.
149 LAC, RG 76, vol. 594, file 841690, part 3, letter from A.E. Skinner, Acting Commissioner to F.C. Blair, Secretary of the Department of Immigration and Colonization, 22 September 1922, Board of Enquiry Minutes, 20 September 1922, letter from F.C. Blair, Secretary of the Department of Immigration and Colonization, to Frank A. Cook, Ringling Bros. Circus, 6 October 1922, and letter from Frank A. Cook to F.C. Blair, 16 October 1922.
150 AO, RG 23-26-20, box 1, file 35, letter from Robert M. Matheson, 24 August 1917. Emphasis in the original.
151 AO, RG 23-26-20 box 1, file 35, letter dated 7 September 1917.
152 LAC, RG 76, vol. 110, file 553:45: CD, letter from A.L. May, regional director to Officers-in-Charge, Central District.
153 Coates and McGuiness, *Pride of the Land*. On carnivals closing and consolidating in the 1930s, see McKennon, *A Pictorial History of the American Carnival*.

3 The Carnival Business in Canada

1 Dufour with Kirby, *Fabulous Years*, 88.
2 T. Jackson Lears, *No Place of Grace: Antimodernism and the Transformation of American Culture, 1880–1920* (Chicago: University of Chicago Press, 1991), 18.
3 Ibid., 18.
4 Goldsack, *Johnny's Here*, 8.
5 When Jones died in 1930, his widow took up the reins. In 1933, the show ended up broke and stranded in Virginia and was eventually bailed out by a friend. The show continued under Jones's name until the 1950s, although it was diminished and, in Canada, failed to compete with other carnivals shows. McKennon, *A Pictorial History of the American Carnival*, 2:22–4, and 1:128.
6 Goldsack, *Johnny's Here*, 38.
7 See, for example, the advertisement in ibid., 49.
8 Patty Conklin's life has not yet received the attention it deserves from biographers. John Thurston is completing a biography of the Conklin company in a forthcoming book. It promises to have the most complete

and thorough biography. The history of Conklin's life is cobbled together from the following sources: Thurston, "Scenes from the Midway"; "History of Conklin Shows," *ConklinShows.com*, http://www.conklinshows.com/history/index.html; "The Life and Times of Patty Conklin," originally televised by CBC, video posted on *ConklinShows.com*, http://www.conklinshows.com/history/life-and-times-1.html; "Telescope: Patty Conklin," CBC video, 22:42, http://www.cbc.ca/archives/entry/telescope-patty-conklin; and McKennon, *A Pictorial History of the American Carnival*, 2:11–12. See also Mosher, "Carnival King,"; and Herb Dotten, "Close Ups: Contrasting Conklins Are Alike in Amazing Ability to Make $$," *Billboard*, 9 July 1949, 51, 103.

9 According to Conklin's son, Jim Conklin, Conklin and his brother were adopted by Jim Conklin (Sr) in 1920 for business reasons. Nonetheless, the Renker men became Conklins and, at least to the public, they presented themselves as a family. When Mrs Conklin fell ill in 1931, *Billboard* described her simply as Patty and Frank's mother. "Mrs. Conklin III," *Billboard*, 14 February 1931, 56. In a 1941 *Maclean's* article the adoption is not mentioned at all. See Mosher, "Carnival King," 14.

10 Mosher, "Carnival King," 29–30. When Jim Conklin (Sr) died, the two brothers kept going. In 1924, they bought into Speed Garrett's show, which was renamed the Conklin and Garrett Shows. They began in Kelowna and headed east with a show that included freaks, gambling, and rigged games. By the end of the 1920s, Conklin was so successful working western Canada that he bought out Garrett. Indeed, the Conklins seem to have been a formidable team. By most accounts, Patty Conklin was charismatic and well-trained by Jim Conklin in the practice of "fixing" shows – that is, bribing police and politicians to allow gambling, girl shows, or freaks, which would otherwise be morally offensive to some community members. Frank Conklin's reputation was as a tough character but "genial" and "hard to annoy." In 1931, Conklin met and married Nanaimo-born Edith Bell. They were a handsome and glamorous couple. In 1933, his son Jim was born. At the age of four, Jim was sent to boarding school. The decade was one of personal success but professional challenges. Conklin survived two bankruptcy scares by using cheap labour. Significantly, Conklin never missed payroll – always paying out wages to his employees – which made his organization exceptional in the boom-and-bust world of the travelling carnival, where employees were sometimes left stranded.

11 "The Life and Times of Patty Conklin," CBC.

12 "Conklin New League Head," *Billboard*, 15 December 1934, 44.

13 Goldsack, *Johnny's Here*, 49. Emphasis in the original.
14 Gresham, "The World of Mirth," 143.
15 McKennon, *A Pictorial History of the American Carnival*, 1:11.
16 Thomas Dunk, *It's a Working Man's Town: Male Working-Class Culture*, 2nd ed. (Montreal and Kingston: McGill-Queen's University Press, 2003), chapters 5 and 6.
17 Belisle, *Retail Nation*, chapter 3.
18 Monty Pilling, "'Glitter City' also Carries Tailor, Fireman, Smithie," *Winnipeg Free Press*, 27 June 1952, 8.
19 "Behind the Glittering Tinsel" *Winnipeg Free Press* 16 July 1955.
20 Gresham, "The World of Mirth."
21 Kelm, *A Wilder West*, chapter 3.
22 Goldsack, *Johnny's Here*, 49.
23 F.H. Bee, Jr, "Modern Carnivals," *Billboard*, 27 August 1932, 40, 43; W.R. Hirsch, "The Fair and the Carnival," *Billboard*, 3 December 1932, 32, 36; William J. Hilliar, "The Carnival Business Needs a Moses," *Billboard*, 3 December 1932, 41; "The Future of the Carnival," *Billboard*, 25 August 1934, 41–2; and Ben Krause, "My Idea of How to Put the Carnival on a Higher Plane," *Billboard*, 13 April 1935, 41.
24 Belisle, *Retail Nation*, 85.
25 Robert H. Thompson, *Boyhood Memories of Saskatoon in the 1930s* (Victoria: n.p., 1987), 25–6.
26 Davis, *The Circus Age*, 81.
27 NACMA, Conklin scrapbook, 1942, "Crowds Watch Circus 'Go Up.'"
28 NACMA, Conklin scrapbook, 1937, "Large Sums Will Be Spent Here." While this statement reflected good PR, it also contained some truth. As Becki Ross's work reveals in regard to burlesque in post–Second World War Vancouver, morally questionable amusements supported local industry and workers, including local newspapers. This is in addition to the state apparatus discussed in chapter 2. See Becki L. Ross, *Burlesque West: Showgirls, Sex, and Sin in Postwar Vancouver* (Toronto: University of Toronto Press, 2009), 20–1.
29 J.W. (Patty) Conklin, "Midway Design Important," *Billboard*, 27 March 1948, 6. See also "Paved Midways Probability in Post-War Era," *Billboard*, 9 June 1945, 48, and J.W. (Patty) Conklin, "Paved Midways Pay Off," *Billboard*, 1 December 1945, 18–19.
30 NACMA Conklin scrapbook, 1938, unidentified newspaper clippings of advertisement, "Some of Ripley's Oddities Displayed," and "African Pin-Head Unusual Sight at Carnival," *Hamilton Spectator*, 18 April 1938.
31 James G. Gardiner, "Canadian Fairs and the War," *Billboard*, 29 November 1941, 8–9.

32 See the CNE Archives online, http://www.cnearchives.com/q3.htm#12.
33 J.W. (Patty) Conklin, "Fair for Britain," *Billboard*, 26 December 1942, 34, and Leonard Traube, "Conklin in Terrific Click," *Billboard*, 29, 34, 55.
34 The advertisement was noteworthy and appeared as part of an article in *Billboard* magazine. "Conklin Publicity Ties in with War; 12 Cars This Year," *Billboard*, 24 June 1944, 34.
35 NACMA, Conklin scrapbooks, 1941.
36 Waters, *History of Fairs and Expositions*, 127–9.
37 On Conklin's expansion of the audience from small children through to seniors see Mosher, "Carnival King," 30.
38 NACMA Conklin scrapbook, 1942, newspaper clipping "At the Fair: Odd Items Gleaned around the Grounds" *Regina Leader Post*, 27 July 1942.
39 Scott, *Country Fairs in Canada*, 62.
40 Joseph T. Bradbury, "The Coop and Lent Circus," *Bandwagon* 3, no. 3 (May–June 1959): 3–14. All of the schedules in this section were found in the licence applications for these shows, as well as in *Billboard*, where show owners announced their routes, successes, and challenges.
41 Bradbury, "The Coop and Lent Circus." Conklin once explained that he did not have animals as part of his carnival because he did not want to own anything that ate during the winter off-season. "The Life and Times of Patty Conklin," CBC.
42 *Billboard*, 15 January 1927, 80.
43 "Conklin Starts CNE Work at Toronto," *Billboard*, 14 August 1937, 48; and "Longest Jump?" *Billboard*, 20 June 1942, 28. See also "Wallace Show, Canada, Ends Biggest Year," *Billboard*, 26 October 1946, 56; and "E.J. Casey's 3 Units Home after Playing 111 Fair Dates," *Billboard*, 8 November 1947, 56.
44 J.W. Conklin, "Carnival Problems in Western Canada," *Billboard*, 5 December 1931, 54.
45 Route cards in AO, RG 23-26-20, box 1, file 1.34 and file 1.36. In some smaller communities like Brandon, Manitoba, and Lethbridge, Alberta, they only opened for the afternoon.
46 AO, RG 23-26-20, box 1, file 1.41, Polack Bros. "Big Twenty Show," application for travelling show licence, 1920.
47 Scott, *Country Fairs in Canada*, 62.
48 LAC, RG 76, vol. 594, file 841690, part 3, letter from Frank A. Cook to N.R. Little, Commissioner of Immigration, Eastern Division and Route Card.
49 "Western Canada," *Billboard*, 26 August 1922, 79.
50 "E.J. Casey Shows Carnival Circuit Schedule," *E.J. Casey: From Solider to Showman*, virtual exhibit by NACMA, http://www.virtualmuseum.ca/sgc-cms/histoires_de_chez_nous-community_memories/pm_v2.php?id=record_detail&fl=0&lg=English&ex=00000843&hs=0&rd=248708#.

51 "Conklin to Have All-Steel Train," *Billboard*, 10 March 1934, 44.
52 "Conklin Shows Have Long Season; Mostly in Ontario," *Billboard*, 10 June 1933, 52.
53 *Billboard*, 15 May 1937, 55.
54 Coates and McGuiness, *Pride of the Land*, 114; McKennon, *A Pictorial History of the American Carnival*, 1:147; "Canada Special Train-Car Ban Includes Shows," *Billboard*, 22 May 1943, 3, 33; Conklin's Bow Has Top Gate," *Billboard*, 1 July 1944, 34; and "Conklin Will Move on 12 Cars Again," *Billboard*, 5 May 1945, 34.
55 "Casey Tours Canada B Circ with 4-Car Rail Show," *Billboard*, 3 July 1943, 30, 33; and "Conklin, Casey to Repeat," *Billboard*, 29 January 1944, 33. See also *E.J. Casey: From Solider to Showman*.
56 *E.J. Casey: From Solider to Showman*.
57 LAC, RG 30, vol. 13184, file 8310-21, 1958–1960, letter from George Barnum to Donald Gordon, 13 November 1963.
58 Mosher, "Carnival King," 14.
59 Davis, *The Circus Age*, 67.
60 Ibid., 63–7.
61 Marcel Horne, *Annals of the Firebreather* (Toronto: P. Martin Associates, 1973), 18.
62 Ibid., 65
63 Ibid., 34.
64 David, *The Circus Age*, 69.
65 Mosher, "Carnival King," 14.
66 "PNE Midway Zone Shrugs Off Rain," *Billboard*, 29 August 1960, 59.
67 Hazel Elves, *It's All Done with Mirrors: A Canadian Carnival Life* (Victoria, BC: Sono Nis Press, 1977), 17.
68 Ibid., 45, 79.
69 McKennon, *A Pictorial History of the American Carnival*, 1:160–1.
70 Hall, *Struggles and Triumphs*, 8.
71 Horne, *Annals of the Firebreather*, 34.
72 "Lewiston Loses 15 Teeth when Walloped by Snake," *Billboard*, 5 July 1947, 86.
73 "E.J. Casey Marking 13th Year on Road; Mishaps Verify It," *Billboard*, 24 August 1946, 56, 99; and "Casey Grosses for '48 Tie '47; Expenses Soar," *Billboard*, 20 November 1948, 66.
74 "E.J. Casey Marking 13th Year on Road; Mishaps Verify It," 56.
75 Christopher Dummitt, The Manly Modern: Masculinity in Postwar Canada. Vancouver: University of British Columbia Press, 2007; and Elves, *It's All Done with Mirrors*, 79. See also Davis, *The Circus Age*, 68. In preparation for the New York World's Fair, an effort was made to rely on union labour for the freak shows and the Ringling Bros. operation was

unionized to varying degrees between the late 1930s and the 1950s. In reaction, Ringling substantively cut back its operation and the number of employees. On the New York World's Fair and the brief threat to unionize freak performers, see Dufour with Kirby, *Fabulous Years*, 123. On Ringling, see Davis, *The Circus Age*, 79–80 and 229. Freaks themselves were only once rumoured to have threatened to organize in the United States in the 1930s, although circus historian Janet Davis remains suspicious about whether the threat of a Sunday Order of the Protective Order of Prodigies was anything more than a brief publicity stunt. Davis, *The Circus Age*, 80–1.

76 Davis, *The Circus Age*, 68.
77 Easto and Truzzi, "Towards an Ethnography of the Carnival Social System," 561.
78 Horne, *Annals of the Firebreather*, 25.
79 Ibid., 3.
80 Ibid, 35.
81 AO, RG 23-26-20 box 1, file 39, letter from the superintendent of the OPP to Rev. T. Albert Moore, 5 August 1920.
82 Elves, *It's All Done with Mirrors*, 43.
83 Horne, *Annals of the Firebreather*, 25, 66, 68.
84 Elves, *It's All Done with Mirrors*, 83.
85 Horne, *Annals of the Firebreather*, 74. See also Lewiston, *Freak Show Man*, 115–23.
86 AO, RG 23-26-20, box 1, file 1.13, letter from A.W. Vale to Inspector of Provincial Police, 19 September 1914; RG 23-26-20, box 1, file 1.35, letter from R.M Matheson to Chief of Provincial Police, 24 August 1917; and RG 23-26-20, box 1, file 1.37, letter from J.C. Pevril to Mr. Elliott, 25 August 1917.
87 Elves, *It's All Done with Mirrors*, 118–20.
88 *Fort William Daily Times Journal*, 1 August 1969; and LAC, RG 76, vol. 110, file 553:45:CD.
89 Steve Koptie, "After This, Nothing Happened: Indigenous Academic Writing and Chickadee Peoples' Words," *First Peoples Child and Family Review* 4, no. 2 (2 November 2009): 149. Koptie also notes that "my Mohawk mother ran off with a man whose family owned a travelling carnival" even though his grandfather wanted his children to have nothing "to do with residential school or 'carnies.'" My thanks to Steve Koptie for sharing his scholarship with me.
90 McKenzie Porter, "Queen of the Midway," *Maclean's*, 1 October 1949, 8. For examples of her shows, see *Billboard*, 22 September 1945, 45; 3 July 1948, 76; and 10 May 1952, 65.

91 AO, RG 23-26-20, box 1, file 1.7, Police Report, 20 June 1914.
92 I have assigned the woman a pseudonym here. This letter was part of the documents I requested from the Archives of Ontario under the Freedom of Information and Protection of Privacy Act. In the original letter, her name had been blacked out in accordance with the legislation. In subsequent documentation, her name appeared. AO, RG 23-26-20, box 1, file 1.43, Circuses and Travelling Shows, 1919–1921, letter from unknown woman to the Chief of Police, Toronto, 16 August 1920.
93 AO, RG 23-26-20, box 1, file 1.43, Circuses and Travelling Shows, 1919–1921, letter from Superintendent of the OPP to Mrs G Brown, 23 August 1920.
94 AO, RG 23-26-20, box 1, file 1.51, letter from Frank Whit to Joseph Rogers, Chief of the Ontario Provincial Police, 15 September 1920, and letter from Rogers to Whit, 18 September 1920.
95 Strange, *Toronto's Girl Problem*, 136.
96 Truth and Reconciliation Commission of Canada, *Final Report of the Truth and Reconciliation Commission of Canada*, vol. 1: Summary: Honouring the Truth, Reconciling for the Future (Toronto: James Lorimer, 2015), 1. Hereafter cited as TRC, *Final Report*.
97 On running away from residential schools see TRC, *Final Report*, 118–120.
98 Joan Sangster, *Regulating Girls and Women: Sexuality, Family and the Law in Ontario, 1920–1960* (Toronto: Oxford University Press, 2001), 151–2; Myers, *Caught*, 143; and Myers, "The Voluntary Delinquent: Parents, Daughters, and the Montreal Juvenile Delinquents' Court in 1918," *Canadian Historical Review* 80, no. 2 (June 1999): 242–68.
99 Comacchio, *The Dominion of Youth*, 53.
100 Frank Conlon, "Co-Eds Carnival Stars," *Winnipeg Free Press*, 7 July 1956.
101 NACMA scrapbook, 1942, unidentified newspaper clipping, "Former Waterloo Girl 'Eats' Fire for a Living and Loves It."
102 Easto and Truzzi, "Towards an Ethnography of the Carnival Social System," 559–60.
103 Jim Christy, "Chalk One for the Bland and Boring," *Globe and Mail*, 24 August 1977, A12.
104 Garland-Thomson, *Extraordinary Bodies*, 24.
105 Geoffrey Reaume, "Not Profits, Just a Pittance: Work, Compensation, and People Defined as Mentally Disabled in Ontario, 1964–1990," in *Mental Retardation in America: A Historical Reader*, ed. S. Noll and J.W. Trent (New York: New York University Press, 2004,) 466–93.
106 C. Hailock [pseud.], letter to the editor, "The Exhibition of Freaks," *Globe*, 5 March 1930, 4.

107 Down's syndrome, although not part of freak show exhibitions, is an excellent example of this conflation. Until the mid-1960s Down's was more commonly known as mongolism, due to atavistic beliefs that reflected common racial hierarchies. Donald Wright, *Downs: The History of Disability* (Oxford: Oxford University Press, 2011), 83.
108 Ena Chadha, "'Mentally Defectives' Not Welcome: Mental Disability in Canadian Immigration Law, 1859–1927," *Disability Studies Quarterly* 28, no. 1 (Winter 2008): http://dsq-sds.org/article/view/67/67; and Wright, *Downs*, 101.
109 CNEA, Official Catalogue and Programme, 1934, 6.
110 William Lindsay Gresham, *Monster Midway: An Uninhibited Look at the Glittering World of the Carny* (New York: Rinehart, 1948), 101.
111 Ward Hall, *My Very Unusual Friends* (Gibsonton: Ward Hall, 1991).
112 Elves, *It's All Done with Mirrors*.
113 Dolly Dimples [pseud. for Celesta Geyer], *The Greatest Diet in the World* (Orlando, FL: Chateau, 1968). Another edition appeared as Geyer and Roen, *Diet or Die*. Both were simultaneously published in Canada by George. J. McLeod, Toronto. All references are from *Diet or Die*. Geyer, *Diet or Die*, 15.
114 "Sideshow People," *Toronto Daily Star*, 24 July 1934, 4.
115 This was the defence frequently invoked, for example, in the 1968 debates over the banning of freak show performers under the age of eighteen in North Carolina that erupted in the trade magazine *Amusement Business*. CWM vertical files, sideshows.
116 Patricia T. Rooke and R.L. Schnell, *Discarding the Asylum: From Child Rescue to the Welfare State in English Canada, 1800–1950* (Latham, MD: University Press of America, 1983), chapter 10; and Harvey G. Simmons, *From Asylum to Welfare: The Evolution of Mental Retardation Policy in Ontario from 1831–1980* (Downsview, ON: National Institute on Mental Retardation, 1982), chapter 8.
117 Quoted in Bogdan, *Freak Show*, 95.
118 "Freaks" and "Freaks to Order," *Billboard*, 23 November 1901, 5, and 22 February 1903, 2; and "The Astonishing Ormsby Quadruplets as They Appeared, Happy and Vigorous, at the Age of One Year," *Pittsburgh Press*, 12 January 1908, 37.
119 "Freaks to Order," *Billboard*, 1 February 1902, 3.
120 *Billboard*, 5 December 1914 and 5 July 1919. Old Home Weeks were popular events in small towns in Ontario in the interwar years. They functioned as tourist events and acts of commemoration. See Françoise Noël, "Old Home Week Celebrations as Tourism Promotion and

Commemoration: North Bay, Ontario, 1925 and 1935," *Urban History Review / Revue d'histoire urbaine* 37, no 1 (fall 2008): 36–47.
121 *Billboard*, 5 January 1959, 52.
122 University of California Santa Barbara [hereafter UCSB], Special Collections, Toole-Stott Circus Collection, PA Mss 14, box 42, unbound scrapbook, ca late 1920s–1930s, newspaper clipping, "Hidden Tragedies of the People of Never-Never Land," *Sunday Chronicle*.
123 Hall, *My Very Unusual Friends*.
124 Mannix, *Freaks*, 97.
125 *Billboard*, 5 December 1914, 5 July 1919, 7 February 1942. Conklin had contracted the freak show out to Jack Halligan that year. This practice would continue with the Conklin carnival.
126 *Billboard*, 7 February 1942. A beef-trust revue was a common sideshow name for fat shows, where grossly obese people would either sit or perform dances or shows for audiences.
127 Geyer, *Diet or Die*, 116–21.
128 NACMA, Conklin scrapbook, 1939, newspaper clipping, "580 Pounds of Cheerful Woman Likes Show Life."
129 Elves, *It's All Done with Mirrors*.
130 Geyer, *Diet or Die*.
131 Lewiston, *Freak Show Man*, 25.
132 "No More Rubes," *Time*, 29 September 1958.
133 Elves, *It's All Done with Mirrors*, 19.
134 *Billboard*, 14 March 1914, 39.
135 Joe Nickell, *Secrets of the Sideshow* (Lexington: University Press of Kentucky, 2005), 322–6; and Thurston, "Scenes from the Midway," 30.
136 Hall, *Struggles and Triumphs*, 62.
137 Robert Thomas Allen, "Mermaids Made to Measure," *Maclean's*, 1 June 1950, 16, 34–5.
138 Shane Peacock, "Africa Meets the Great Farini," in *Africans on Stage: Studies in Ethnological Show Business*, ed. B. Lindfors (Bloomington: Indiana University Press, 1999), 86–7.
139 "Circus Glossary – Lot Lingo," *White Tops*, August–September 1939, 12.
140 Interview with James Gibson, "Working the Sideshow at the Canadian National Exhibition, 22 July 2008, Peer Street, Niagara Falls. Recorded by K.E. Lyn and transcribed by K.E. Lyn and Natalie Przbyl. Virtual Museum of Canada, http://www.virtualmuseum.ca/sgc-cms/histoires_de_chez_nous-community_memories/pm_v2.php?id=record_detail&fl=0&lg=English&ex=00000659&rd=179154.
141 Bernth Lindfors, "Ethnological Show Business: Footlighting the Dark Continent," in *Freakery*, 217.

142 Davis, *The Circus Age*, 70–1.
143 Chadha, "'Mentally Defectives' Not Welcome."
144 Jones, *Midways, Judges, and Smooth-Tongued Fakirs*, 55–6; and AO, RG 4-32, file 1898, no. 1171, Attorney General's Files on King v. Clark, 1903.
145 Gresham, *Monster Midway*, 101.
146 Lewiston, *Freak Show Man*, 7–13.
147 Ibid., 222–3.
148 For another tale of abuse of a freak show performer see Neil Parson, *Clicko: The Wild Dancing Bushman* (Chicago: University of Chicago Press, 2010).
149 For the legal records of the case brought against the Ringling Bros. by Willie and George Muse, see State Records Central Repository, Richmond, VA, box 196, 1928–1929.
150 "Passing of a Famous Novelty: Death of the World's Ugliest Woman," *World's Fair*, 30 December 1933, http://www.nfa.dept.shef.ac.uk/history/worlds_fair/extracts/1931-1940.html
151 "Ugliest Woman upon Earth Possessed Beautiful Soul," *Globe*, 23 August 1924.
152 Gresham, "World of Mirth."
153 Ibid.
154 Hall, *My Very Unusual Friends*, 39.
155 Lara Campbell, *Respectable Citizens: Gender, Family, and Unemployment In Ontario's Great Depression* (Toronto: University of Toronto Press, 2009). Mothers' allowances in some provinces were the exception, but as Little argues, they were also a form of moral regulation. See Margaret Little, *No Car, No Radio, No Liquor Permit: The Moral Regulation of Single Mothers in Ontario, 1920–1996* (Don Mills, ON: Oxford University Press, 1998).
156 The case of Simon Metz is frequently used to espouse the positive qualities of sideshow work, but the evidence is paltry. Metz was a child when he was first exhibited by Pete Kortes, but the heydays of his performances were in the 1920s and 1930s. Metz was exhibited as "Schlitzie." How Kortes came to have Metz in his care is unclear, as are most details of his life before the sideshow. Metz was born with microcephaly and performed as a pinhead. He dressed in women's clothing and had his hair cut to accentuate the shape of his skull. His performances consisted of standing on stage, speaking simple sentences, and sometimes reacting to the taunts or calls from the audience. Some sources suggest that Metz dressed and performed as a woman because he was incontinent and dresses made it easier for his caretakers. Metz's performances sometimes caused discomfort among some audience members. Ward Hall recalls Metz's repetition of overheard conversations,

saying that audience members would take a couple of minutes before realizing "they were listening to the incoherent rambling of an idiot before nervously glancing around and embarrassingly moving away."

Eventually Metz passed from Kortes to another American showman named George Surtees, who allegedly willed Metz to his daughter. According to most documentation, Surtees's daughter institutionalized Metz in Los Angeles in the 1960s. The common sideshow narrative positions the institutionalization of Metz as negative, and according to most of those sources, he was "saved" by Sam Alexander, an American-born showman who ran a popular Canadian sideshow company. Alexander heard of Metz's institutionalization from an employee, Bill Unks, who also worked the sideshows as a sword swallower, and recognized Metz. Hall's *My Very Unusual Friends* includes the following often-repeated description: "Bill called Sam Alexander, whose show the Surtees and Schlitzie had been with. Sam called the institution authorities advising them of Schlitzie's background. When psychiatrists had finished their evaluation, they suggested the state make Schlitzie a ward of Sam Alexander. The doctor stated that with Schlitzie's advanced age, if she were institutionalized and deprived of the affection of the showpeople and attention of the public she wouldn't live six months."

Hall's defence of the exhibition of pinheads, and Schlitzie in particular, is illuminating: "I would no longer exhibit anyone mentally deficient, due to the criticism of those who would not understand the improvement in the quality of life such as a person would receive in a freak show environment, as opposed to confinement in an institution. I have no doubt that Schlitzie enjoyed the trips to Hawaii, Venezuela, Puerto Rico, Mexico, Canada, etc. ... This with the same delight and exuberance of a small child. Once having been rescued from the locked away existence of early childhood, Schlitzie had a comfortable, happy existence for the rest of her eighty plus years."

The narrative of Alexander's "rescue" of Metz was a great public relations move for sideshows wanting to reveal their allegedly benevolent care of people whom normal society ostensibly threw away. Metz's voice is missing from the historical record. For more on Metz see, for example, Hornberger, *Carny Folk*, 128–131, and Hartzman, *American Sideshow*, 210–11. One sideshow historian has suggested that Metz was born in Montreal and sold from the institution he was placed in by his mother to a sideshow. See Ari Roussimoff, "The Freaks of 'Freaks Uncensored,'" http://www.roussimoff.com/freaks_bios.htm. Simon Metz is the basis for the character Pepper on *American Horror Story: Asylum*: see

Solvej Schou, "Best of 2012 (Behind the Scenes): Naomi Grossman on Being Cast, Transformed into Pepper on 'American Horror Story: Asylum,'" *Entertainment Weekly*, 4 December 2012, http://www.ew.com/article/2012/12/04/american-horror-story-asylum-naomi-grossman. The quotes from Hall can be found in Hall, *My Very Unusual Friends*, 22–3.

157 Brigham A. Fordham, "Dangerous Bodies: Freaks Shows, Expression, Exploitation," *UCLA Entertainment Law Review* 14, no. 207 (2007): 208–45.

158 Andrew J. Bakner, "Side Show Attractions," *Bandwagon*, November-December 1973, 38

4 The Twentieth-Century Freak Show

1 "Army of Exhibition Toilers Welcomes Midnight Hour," *Globe*, 4 September 1924, 12.

2 Wendy Mitchinson, *The Nature of Her Body: Women and Their Doctors in Victorian Canada* (Toronto: University of Toronto Press, 1991); and Mona Gleason, *Small Matters: Canadian Children in Sickness and Health, 1900–1940* (Montreal: McGill-Queen's University Press, 2013).

3 Bogdan, *Freak Show*, 94–6.

4 Ibid., 97.

5 Ibid., 116.

6 Nadja Durbach, "'Skinless Wonders': *Body Worlds* and the Victorian Freak Show," *Journal of the History of Medicine and Allied Sciences* 69, no. 1 (2012): 41.

7 Ibid., 42. This argument is further elaborated in her book *Spectacle of Deformity*, 38–46.

8 Roy Porter, *Flesh in the Age of Reason: The Modern Foundations of Body and Soul* (New York: W.W. Norton, 2003).

9 On modernity and the expert, see Mona Gleason, *Normalizing the Ideal: Psychology, Schooling, and the Family in Postwar Canada* (Toronto: University of Toronto Press, 1999).

10 For two examples, see Tracy Penny Light, "Consumer Culture and the Medicalization of Women's Roles in Canada, 1919–39," and Kristin Hall, "Selling Lysol as a Household Disinfectant in Interwar North America," both in *Consuming Modernity: Gendered Behaviour and Consumerism before the Baby Boom*, ed. Cheryl Krasnick Warsh and Dan Malleck (Vancouver: University of British Columbia Press, 2013), 34–54.

11 Cynthia Comacchio, *Nations Are Built of Babies: Saving Ontario's Mothers and Children, 1900–1940* (Montreal: McGill-Queen's University Press, 1998); James Opp, *The Lord for the Body: Religion, Medicine, and Protestant

Notes to pages 119–22

Faith Healing in Canada, 1880–1930 (Montreal: McGill-Queen's University Press, 2005); and Wendy Mitchinson, *Body Failure: Medical Views of Women, 1900–1950* (Toronto: University of Toronto Press, 2013).

12 Comacchio, "Mechanomorphosis," 35–67.
13 Lennard J. Davis, "Constructing Normalcy," in *The Disability Studies Reader*, 3rd ed., ed. Lennard J. Davis (New York: Routledge, 2010), 3, 7–12. See also his *Enforcing Normalcy*, chap. 2.
14 Adolphe Quetelet, *A Treatise on Man and the Development of His Faculties*, first English translation (1842; reprint, New York: Burt Franklin, 1968), 5.
15 Garabad Eknoyan, "Adolphe Quetelet (1796–1874) – The Average Man and Indices of Obesity," *Nephrology Dialysis Transplantation* 23 (2008): 47.
16 Quetelet, *A Treatise on Man*, x. Emphasis in the original.
17 Davis, *Enforcing Normalcy*, 24.
18 Garland-Thomson, introduction to *Freakery*, 4.
19 Garland-Thomson, *Extraordinary Bodies*, 75.
20 Lillian E. Cranton, *The Victorian Freak Show: The Significance of Disability and Physical Differences in 19th-Century Fiction* (Amherst, NY: Cambria Press, 2010), 32–4.
21 Rosemarie Garland-Thomson, "Integrating Disability, Transforming Feminist Theory," *NWSA Journal* 14, no. 3 (Autumn 2002): 10.
22 George M. Gould and Walter L. Pyle, *Anomalies and Curiosities of Medicine* (1896; reprint, Philadelphia: W.B. Saunders, 1901), 2. Page numbers are from the e-Gutenberg edition.
23 Barrow, "A Brief History of Teratology to the Early 20th Century," 119–29.
24 Ibid., 123–5.
25 Catherine Gallagher and Thomas Laqueur, "Introduction," in *The Making of the Modern Body: Sexuality and Society in the Nineteenth Century* (Berkeley: University of California Press, 1987), vii.
26 H.E. Thelander, letter to the editor, *Journal of the American Medical Association* 187, no. 8 (February 1964): 621. This letter is in line with a wider cultural shift – sparked by mothers and the children themselves – to cast off the cloak of shame and to challenge the pressures of institutionalization for disabled children beginning in the 1950s. Two classic first-person accounts are Pearl S. Buck, *The Child Who Never Grew: A Memoir* (New York: Woodbine House, [1950] 1992); and Dale Evans Rogers, *Angel Unaware* (Westwood, NJ: Fleming H. Revell, 1953).
27 Quoted in Lisa Kochanek, "Reframing the Freak: From Sideshow to Science," *Victorian Periodicals Review* 30, no. 3 (1997): 228.
28 R.J. Bean, "The Etiology of Embryonic Deformities," *Canadian Medical Association Journal* (June 1926): 652–6.

29 "Hypertelorism with Remarks upon Anomalies in General," *Canadian Medical Association Journal* (January 1925): 81.
30 Cynthia Comacchio, "'The Rising Generation': Laying Claim to the Health of Adolescents in English Canada, 1920–70," *Canadian Bulletin of Medical History* 19 (2002): 139–78.
31 Gleason, *Small Matters*, 29.
32 A.R. Colón with P.A. Colón, *Nurturing Children: A History of Pediatrics* (Westport, CT: Greenwood, 1999), 187–8.
33 Gleason, *Small Matters*, 24.
34 Ibid., 120–1.
35 Nic Clarke, "Sacred Daemons: Exploring British Columbian Society's Perceptions of 'Mentally Deficient' Children, 1870–1930," *BC Studies* 144 (Winter 2004–5): 61–89.
36 P.W. Head, "Thoracopagus Monster Delivered by Caesarean Section," *Canadian Medical Association Journal* (April 1931): 547–8.
37 H. Beattie, "A Case of Anencephalous Monster," *The Lancet* (17 December 1904): 1712–13.
38 Kirsten Ostherr, *Medical Visions: Producing the Patient through Film, Television, and Imaging Technologies* (Oxford: Oxford University Press, 2013), 224; and College of Physicians of Philadelphia and Laura Lindgren, eds, *Mutter Museum Historic Medical Photographs* (New York: Blast Books, 2007).
39 J.E. Jospehson and K.B. Waller, "Anencephaly in Identical Twins," *Canadian Medical Association Journal* (July 1933): 34–7.
40 AO, F 677 MU 2853, Memoirs of Clifford Hugh Smylie, 198. My thanks to Whitney Wood for sharing with me this evidence from her own project.
41 Richard T. Caesar, "Case of Amelus or Limbless Monster," *British Medical Association Journal* (9 March 1889): 525; "Case of Amelus or Limbless Monster," *British Medical Association Journal* (8 June 1889): 1289; "A Limbless Monster," *British Medical Association Journal* (19 January 1889): 147; E. Child, "A Case of Maternal Impression," *The Lancet* (7 November 1868): 599; H.J. Clemens, "Case of Triplets, with Monstrosity," *The Lancet* (15 October 1887): 755; John S. Beale, "Monstrosity and Maternal Impressions," *The Lancet* (3 November 1860); R.B. Jessup, "Monstrosities and Maternal Impressions," *Journal of the American Medical Association* (13 October 1888): 519–20; Jacob Schneck, "A Child without Arms or Legs, Maternal Impressions," *Journal of the American Medical Association* (12 March 1892): 314–5; and W.F. Batman, "Maternal Impressions," *Journal of the American Medical Association* (14 November 1896): 1031–2. For a lengthy critical essay on maternal impressions, see J.M. Fort, "Do Maternal

Impressions Affect the Foetus in Utero?" *Journal of the American Medical Association* (20 April 1889): 541–7.

42 E.T. Shelly, *Journal of the American Medical Association* (4 April 1903); F. Anson Evans, letter to the editor, "Maternal Impression," *Journal of the American Medical Association* (30 May 1903): 1519; E.T. Shelly, "Superstition in Teratology with Special Reference to the Theory of Impressionism," *Journal of the American Medical Association* (26 January 1907): 308–11; Emile Aronson, letter to the editor, "Superstition in Teratology," *Journal of the American Medical Association* (February 1907): 625; J.W. Robinson, letter to the editor, "Maternal Impressions," *Journal of the American Medical Association* (9 March 1907): 876.

43 Cawas Homi, "A Case of Phocomelus," *The Lancet* (17 July 1920): 128.

44 On the continuation of maternal impressions in twentieth-century in Canada, see Wendy Mitchinson, *Giving Birth in Canada, 1900–1950* (Toronto: University of Toronto Press, 2002), 105, 111–13, and 143–7. Paternal impressions also make an appearance in Gould and Pyle's *Anomalies and Curiosities* and a 1907 article by a Canadian-trained nurse who relies heavily on the same evidence consolidated in the previously mentioned work. Telegony, or the alleged influence of a woman's previous mates on subsequently produced children, also had some credit among nineteenth-century physicians and scientists and is also mentioned in both works. See Gould and Pyle, *Anomalies and Curiosities*, and Menia S. Tye, "Prenatal Influences," *American Journal of Nursing* 7, no. 5 (February 1907): 362–7.

45 For more on Lionel, see Hornberger, *Carny Folk*, 138; and Nickell, *Secrets of the Sideshow*, 156.

46 For Howard's pamphlet, see CWM, File Howard (Lobster Boy), pamphlet.

47 "Circus and Museum Freaks – Curiosities of Pathology," *Scientific American*, 28 March 1908.

48 Garland-Thomson, *Extraordinary Bodies*, 75. Under these conditions, conjoined twins Millie-Christine McKoy, who were born into slavery in the United States and bought and sold even after the Emancipation Proclamation, were subject to repeated medical examinations in the 1850s and 1860s. In the 1850s, they toured British North America, although it remains unclear which, if any, Canadian physicians examined them. If they did not, it broke the typical pattern of Millie-Christine's exhibition, which was physical examination by a doctor, publication of the doctor's findings of the legitimacy and rarity of their body, and finally, paid public exhibition. After years of invasive examination, Millie-Christine McKoy refused all medical examinations except one after they were freed. Doctors'

responses varied from disappointment to incredulity. One reported that "despite all our insistence, it was impossible for us to observe the most secret parts of the body."

Another well-studied example is Julia Pastrana. In the 1850s, hirsute woman Julia Pastrana found herself the subject of similar medical examinations and publications. Pastrana was born in 1834 in an Indigenous tribe in Mexico. For unknown reasons, she had been abandoned as a child and worked in the governor of Sinaloa's home until discovered by an American showman. Pastrana was exhibited in the 1850s under a variety of descriptive titles, including the Bear Woman, the Baboon Lady, and the Ugliest Woman in the World. Pastrana's exhibition at a variety of locations, including Boston's Horticultural Hall in 1855, garnered a lot of popular and professional attention. A "certificate" of her authenticity was issued a year earlier by a Dr Alex B. Mott, and published testimonials and descriptions of her body's "freakishness" exist from other physicians and naturalists. An 1857 issue of British Medical Association Journal *The Lancet* published Dr J.Z. Laurence's detailed account of her body. Gould and Pyle's book includes an entry on Pastrana, of which Garland-Thomson concludes, "The entertainment discourse parades its collaboration with medicine in Pastrana's exhibition, whereas the medical discourse suppresses the fact that doctors were actually attending the shows to examine Pastrana." Pastrana died in Moscow, Russia, while giving birth to a son, who died within hours of birth. Pastrana's mummified remains toured with a circus in the United States as recently as 1972. More recently, in 2013, the University of Oslo in Norway returned Pastrana's remains to Mexico for burial. On the McKoys see Samuels, "Examining Millie and Christine McKoy,"Sarah E. Gold, "Millie-Christine McKoy and the American Freak Show: Race, Gender, and Freedom in the Postbellum Era, 1851–1912," *Berkeley Undergraduate Journal* 23, no. 1 (2010): 5–6; Joanne Martell, *Millie-Christine: Fearfully and Wonderfully Made* (Winston-Salem, NC: John F. Blair, 2000); and Linda Frost, "Introduction," *Conjoined Twins in Black and White* (Madison: Wisconsin University Press, 2009), 8–11. On Pastrana see, Rosemarie Garland-Thomson, "Making Freaks: Visual Rhetorics and the Spectacle of Julia Pastrana," in *Thinking the Limits of the Body*, ed. Jeffrey Jerome Cohen and Gail Weiss (Albany: State University of New York Press, 2003), 129–43; Garland-Thomson, *Extraordinary Bodies*, 70–8; Rebecca Stern, "Our Bear Women, Ourselves"; Charles Wilson, "An Artist Finds a Dignified Ending for an Ugly Story," *New York Times*, 11 February 2013, http://www.nytimes.com/2013/02/12/arts/design/julia-pastrana-who-died-in-1860-to-be-buried-in-mexico.html?pagewanted=all&_r=0; and

"World's 'Ugliest Woman' Julia Pastrana Buried 153 Years On," *BBC News*, http://www.bbc.com/news/world-latin-america-21440400.

49 CWM, Small Collections, Libbera, Jean and Jacques, "Life Story and Facts about Jean and Jacques Libberra Joined Together Twins."
50 "Anencephalous Monsters," *British Medical Association Journal* (15 June 1912: 1376.
51 Sir John Bland-Sutton, "On a Parasitic Foetus," *The Lancet* (7 January 1928): 24.
52 The celebration of the heroic surgery to separate conjoined twins, even if it costs one of the twins their lives, is ongoing. It ignores that some conjoined twins, like Millie-Christine McKoy, see themselves not as two separate people but one or sometimes something different. Alice Domurat Dreger has challenged the idea that a normal body is a single body. See her book *One of Us: Conjoined Twins and the Future of Normal* (Boston, MA: Harvard University Press, 2005).
53 "Human Oddities and Freaks," *British Medical Association Journal* (26 January 1935): 167.
54 Mark Murphy, "Serviceable and Congenial," *New Yorker*, 9 May 1942, 40.
55 John Lentz, "How Medical Progress Has Hastened the Passing of the Side Show," *Today's Health*, March 1964, retrieved from the Disability History Museum digital collection, 5 March 2015.
56 CWM, Small Collections, Miss Gabriel, "My Life's History."
57 "Pygopagus Marriage," *Time*, 16 July 1934.
58 Frost, *Conjoined Twins in Black and White*, 11–12. By Frost's own admission, the copies of Daisy and Violet's autobiography she has republished were from a poor copy of the original that appeared in the American tabloid *American Weekly*. I have used both her reprinted version and a copy of *American Weekly* found in CWM, Small Collections, Daisy and Violet Hilton.
59 CWM, Small Collections, Daisy and Violet Hilton, newspaper clipping from Cincinnati paper, 1926.
60 CWM, Small Collections, Daisy and Violet Hilton, newspaper clippings.
61 Currently, the University of Maryland Medical Center puts contemporary survival rates of conjoined twins between 5 per cent and 25 per cent, with a majority of conjoined twins being stillborn or surviving less than a day. See http://www.umm.edu/programs/conjoined-twins/facts-about-the-twins.
62 James A. Rooth, "The Brighton United Twins," *The British Medical Association Journal*, 23 September 1911.
63 "Intimate Loves and Lives of the Hilton Sisters," in Frost, *Conjoined Twins in Black and White*, 134–5. Yet it must be noted that not all medical patients felt this way about examinations or the photographs taken of them. In her

memoir *Autobiography of a Face*, Lucy Grealy recalled: "Curiously, those sterile, bright photos are easy for me to look at. For one thing, I know that only doctors look at them, and perhaps, I'm even slightly proud that I'm such an interesting case, worthy of documentation. Or maybe I do not really think it is me sitting there; Case 3, figure 6-A." Lucy Grealy, *Autobiography of a Face* (New York: Houghton Mifflin, 1994), 12. My thanks to Patricia Jasen for sharing this reference with me.

64 A fuller discussion of this case in regard to ethics and photography can be found in Jane Nicholas, "A Debt to the Dead? Ethics, Photography, History, and the Study of Freakery," *Histoire sociale / Social History* 47, no. 93 (May 2014): 139–55.
65 Wadlow's case is discussed here in regard to medicine, but he never performed in Canada.
66 Frederic Fadner, *The Gentleman Giant: The Biography of Robert Pershing Wadlow* (Boston: Bruce Humphries, 1944), 35.
67 Ibid., 148–50.
68 Charles D. Humberd, "Giantism: Report of a Case," *Journal of the American Medical Association* 108, no. 7 (1937): 545.
69 Fadner, *The Gentleman Giant*, 152–60.
70 Garland-Thomson, *Extraordinary Bodies*, 75.
71 Tye, "Prenatal Influences," 364.
72 The New York Public Library, Manuscripts and Archives Division, Astor, Lenox, and Tilden Foundations [hereafter NYPL], New York World's Fair 1939/1940, Central Files, P1 637, file 9 Freaks A–K (1939), letter from Marc Wallace, 7 November 1938.
73 Clarke, "Sacred Daemons."
74 Rosemarie Garland-Thomson, *Staring: How We Look* (Oxford: Oxford University Press, 2009), 29.
75 Alice Domurat Dreger, "Jarring Bodies: Thoughts on the Display of Unusual Anatomies," *Perspectives in Biology and Medicine* 43, no. 2 (Winter 2000): 170.
76 Foucault, *The Birth of the Clinic*.
77 Patient agency is a well-developed theme in Mitchinson's work. See, for example, her *The Nature of Their Bodies: Women and Their Doctors in Victorian Canada* (Toronto: University of Toronto Press, 1991); and *Giving Birth in Canada*.
78 CWM, Small Collections, Johnny Eck pamphlet, "Facts concerning Johnny Eck."
79 Skal and Savada, *Dark Carnival*, 167.
80 CNEA, Canadian National Exhibition Official Catalogue and Programme, 1938.

81 CWM, Ringling Bros. and Barnum and Bailey Route Books, 1943, 1944, 1946, 1947, 1948, 1949, and 1950.
82 CWM, Small Collections, Frieda K. Pushnik, pamphlet, "Freda K. Pushnick Photo and Story."
83 Lewiston, *Freak Show Man*, 242–243.
84 NACMA Conklin Scrapbook 1942, newspaper clipping "At the Fair: Odd Items Gleaned around the Grounds," *Regina Leader Post*, 27 July 1942.
85 NACMA, Conklin scrapbook 1942, "Saskatoon Girl in Midway Show."
86 Paul K. Longmore, *Telethons: Spectacle, Disability, and the Business of Charity* (New York: Oxford University Press, 2016), chapter 7.
87 NACMA, Conklin Scrapbook, pamphlet and photograph of sideshow front.
88 NACMA, Conklin Scrapbook, unidentified newspaper clipping, "Even Nature Makes Mistakes; See Them at Conklin Shows."
89 Dufour with Kirby, *Fabulous Years*, 61–3.
90 Dufour with Kirby, *Fabulous Years*, 171–2. For a discussion of a similar medical display, see Valerie Minnett, "Public Body, Private Health: *Mediscope*, the Transparent Woman, and Medical Authority, 1959," in *Contesting Bodies and Nation in Canadian History*, ed. Patrizia Gentile and Jane Nicholas (Toronto: University of Toronto Press, 2013), 286–304.
91 CWM, Small Collections, Jeanie and Al Tomaini, pamphlet.
92 CWM, Carnival Collection, box 1, Beckman and Gerety Shows.
93 NACMA, Conklin Scrapbook, newspaper clipping from an unidentified Regina newspaper, "At the Fair: Odd Items Gleaned from the Grounds," 27 July 1942.
94 NACMA, Conklin Scrapbook, newspaper clipping from an unidentified paper, "Attractions at Conklin Shows."
95 Hartzman, *American Sideshow*, 230.
96 Herb Dotten, "America's Favorite R.E. Dick Best's Circus Sideshow," *Billboard*, 24 November 1956, 92.
97 Jean Shaw, "Carnival Hobbies," *Globe and Mail*, 7 September 1951, 17.
98 "Born without Arms, Uses Feet," *Fort William Daily Times Journal*, 3 August 1957.
99 "History of the Conklin Shows," http://conklinshows.com/history/index.html. Bernard and Barry had travelled in Ontario in the 1940s. See "Bernard-Barry Gets Away in Fine Weather," *Billboard*, 17 May 1947, 53.
100 CWM, Carnival Collection, box 1, Bernard Shows of Canada.
101 Jacalyn Duffin, *History of Medicine: A Scandalously Short Introduction*, 2nd ed. (Toronto: University of Toronto Press, 2010), 117–18; and Cheryl Krasnick Warsh, *Prescribed Norms: Women and Health in Canada and the United States since 1800* (Toronto: University of Toronto Press, 2010), 197.

102 Veronica Strong-Boag, "Today's Child: Preparing for the 'Just Society' One Family at a Time," *Canadian Historical Review* 86, no. 4 (December 2005): 693.
103 I use the term "colonized" here and throughout to reflect the widespread and multidirectional process of colonization but note that people who were the targets of such processes continually and actively resisted colonization.
104 Barrington Walker, "Following the North Star: Black Canadians, IQ Testing, and Biopolitics in the Work of H.A. Tanser, 1939–2008," in Gentile and Nicholas, *Contesting Bodies and Nation in Canadian History*, 56–64.
105 TRC, *Final Report*.
106 Douglas C. Baynton, "Disability and the Justification of Inequality in American History," in *The New Disability History*, edited by Paul K. Longmore and Lauri Umansky (New York: New York University Press, 2002), 33–57.
107 NACMA, Jay Ray Red Press Release, 1940s.
108 CNEA, Official Catalogue Canadian National Exhibition, 1932, 40.
109 CNEA, Midway Photographs, G. Hollies photograph of Ubangi Savages.
110 "Disc-Lipped Savages," *White Tops*, December 1929, 1.
111 NACMA, Conklin scrapbook,1937 newspaper clipping "Scribe Holds Mummy Heads as Jungle Drums Mutter."
112 NACMA, Conklin scrapbook 1938 "Dancers, Firewalkers, Wild Animals and Rides Feature Midway at Fair."
113 NACMA, Lew Dufor scrapbook, undated photograph.
114 Ralph F. Hartman, "Unusual Circus Features," *White Tops*, November – December 1961, 47.
115 NACMA, Conklin Scrapbook, 1937.
116 The presentation was neither unique nor out of line with historical developments percolating over almost a century. When white colonialists discovered the Central Africa Forest People in 1865, they understood them to be among the most different, savage, and primitive peoples in the world. Anthropological studies continued, and in the 1930s the people were described as being without language, monkey-like, and without civilized habits like bathing. By the 1930s, the "scientific" discovery was also entertainment. That the so-called Pigmies would shun modern white society and embrace proximity to lions rendered them less human, more animal. Darwinism, eugenics, and colonial science remained popular in the twentieth century. Sideshows sought to profit and in doing so engaged the discourses of colonization and racialized science, but also set up their own trade in people. That colonial science and entertainment

should mix is unsurprising in the racialized exhibits of pygmies, wildmen, and savages on the sideshows. See C. Kidd, "Inventing the 'Pygmy': Representing the 'Other,' Presenting the 'Self,'" *History and Anthropology* 20, no. 4 (December 2009): 402–4.

117 Peter Geller, *Northern Exposures: Photographing and Filming the Canadian North, 1920–45* (Vancouver: University of British Columbia Press, 2004), 89.

118 NACMA, Conklin Scrapbook, 1937, unidentified newspaper clipping, "Eskimo Buys Refrigerator!" and "Refrigerator Is Sold to Eskimo at C.N.E."

119 NACMA, Conklin Scrapbook, 1937, unidentified newspaper clipping, "Sweltering Days of August Getting C.N.E. Eskimos Down."

120 Joy Parr, *Domestic Goods: The Material, the Moral and the Economic in the Postwar Years* (Toronto: University of Toronto Press, 1999), 247.

121 NACMA, Conklin Scrapbook, 1937, unidentified newspaper clipping, "Refrigerator Is Sold to Eskimo at C.N.E." See also the unidentified newspaper clipping, "Surrounded by Igloos and Snow, Huskies Puzzled by Hot Weather."

122 NACMA, Conklin Scrapbook, 1938, unidentified newspaper clipping, "Telegram Reporter at C.N.E. Radios Interviews to Office."

123 Geller, *Northern Exposures* 118.

124 CNEA, Official Souvenir Catalogue and Programme, 1931, 43. The Florida Seminole Indian Village was also a part of the Worth of Mirth Shows in Ottawa in 1936. See "World of Mirth Makes Record," *Billboard*, 12 September 1936, 46.

125 Mikaëla M. Adams, "Savage Foes, Noble Warriors, and Frail Remnants: Florida Seminoles in the White Imagination, 1865–1934," *Florida Historical Quarterly* 87, no. 3 (Winter 2009): 422.

126 CNEA, Official Catalogue, 1931, 45.

127 Patsy West, *The Enduring Seminoles: From Alligator Wrestling to Ecotourism* (Gainesville: University of Florida Press, 1998).

128 NACMA, Conklin Scrapbook, 1937, newspaper clipping, "Indian's Life Seen at C.N.E. in True Form," and "C.N.E. Indian Play Late but Fine Entertainment."

129 Walden, *Becoming Modern in Toronto*, 170.

130 Ian Radforth, *Royal Spectacle: The 1860 Visit of the Prince of Wales to Canada and the United States* (Toronto: University of Toronto Press, 2004); and Paige Raibmon, "Theatres of Contact: The Kwakwaka'wakw Meet Colonialism in British Columbia and at the Chicago's World's Fair," *Canadian Historical Review* 81, no. 2 (June 2000): 157–90.

131 Tina Loo, "Dan Cranmer's Potlatch: Law as Coercion, Symbol, and Rhetoric in British Columbia," *Canadian Historical Review* 73, no. 2 (1992): 141–3.
132 Raibmon, "Theatres of Contact," 189.
133 Michael David McNally, "The Indian Passion Play: Contesting the Real Indian in Song of Hiawatha Pageants, 1901–1965," *American Quarterly* 58, no. 1 (March 2006): 131–2.
134 NACMA, Conklin Scrapbook, 1937, newspaper clipping, "Young Indians Plan to Wed," and "Cupid Shoots Heap Big Dart at Indian Tableau at 'Ex.'"
135 NACMA, Conklin Scrapbook, 1937, newspaper clipping, "Ojibways Cancel Wedding Minister not Available."
136 NACMA, Conklin Scrapbook, 1937, newspaper clipping, "These Things Too Darn Hot Says Bride of Indian Garb," and also "Indian Bride and Groom Received in Tribal Style."
137 NACMA, "These Things Too Darn Hot."
138 Davis, *Enforcing Normalcy*, 2.
139 Ibid., 91–2, 99.

5 Not Just Child's Play

1 John Bland-Sutton, "A Lecture on the Psychology of Conjoined Twins: A Study of Monsterhood," *British Medical Journal* 1, no. 3548 (5 January 1929): 1–4.
2 Bogdan, *Freak Show*, 149.
3 For one description of the period under study here, see Diana Serra Cary's *What Ever Happened to Baby Peggy? The Autobiography of Hollywood's Pioneer Child Star* (New York: St Martin's Press, 1996), a critical autobiography about children working in the film industry. See also Viviana Zelizer, *Pricing the Priceless Child: The Changing Social Value of Children* (New York: Basic Books, 1985), 92–6.
4 Mary Jo Maynes, "Age as a Category of Historical Analysis: History, Agency, and Narratives of Childhood," *Journal of the History of Childhood and Youth* 1, no. 1 (Winter 2008): 114–24; and Kristine Alexander, "Can the Girl Guide Speak?" *Jeunesse: Young Peoples, Texts, Cultures* 4, no.1 (2012): 132.
5 Cynthia Comacchio, Janet Golden, and George Weisz, "Introduction: Healing the World's Children," in *Healing the World's Children: Interdisciplinary Perspectives on Child Health in the Twentieth Century*, ed. Cynthia Comacchio, Janet Golden, and George Weisz (Montreal: McGill-Queen's University Press, 2008), 3.

6 Zelizer, *Pricing the Priceless Child*.
7 Chen, *Tending the Gardens of Citizenship*, chap. 3.
8 Myers, *Caught*, 21.
9 Comacchio, *The Dominion of Youth*, 163.
10 Ibid., chap. 6.
11 Jones, *Midways, Judges, and Smooth-Tongued Fakirs*, 64.
12 Thompson, *Boyhood Memories of Saskatoon in the 1930s*, 25.
13 Ibid., 26–7.
14 MacEwan, *Agriculture on Parade*, 187.
15 Neil Sutherland, *Growing Up: Childhood in English Canada from the Great War to the Age of Television* (Toronto: University of Toronto Press, 1997), 176–7.
16 On the development and solidification of youth culture in the period, especially in relation to commercial amusements, see Comacchio, *The Dominion of Youth*.
17 "New Record Reached as 203,000 Children Throng Great Fair," *Globe*, 27 August 1924.
18 "Kiddies Revel on Own Day at District Fair," *Fort William Daily Times Journal*, 16 August 1927.
19 Ben Krause, "My Idea of How to Put the Carnival on a Higher Plane," *Billboard*, 13 April 1935, 41.
20 "Big Biz for Polack at Vancouver, B.C.," *Billboard*, 14 May 1938, 38.
21 Gresham, *Monster Midway*, 31.
22 NACMA, Jack Ray Red Press Release, circa 1940s.
23 See, for example, "Moves for Better Convoying of Foreign Acts Going to Canada," *Billboard*, 5 December 1931, 64; and J.W. (Patty) Conklin, "Patty Conklin: Kiddie Dimes Better Quarters; Gate-Ride Combination Helps," *Billboard*, 7 April 1956, 85.
24 Gresham, *Monster Midway*, 32. See also "Potent Kids Show Formed by Ringling," *Billboard*, 19 April 1952, 62.
25 "Children Get Big Thrill Trying out Facsimile," *Globe and Mail*, 29 August 1939, 1.
26 "Newsboys Think Johnny J. Jones Real Swell Guy," *Fort William Daily Times Journal*, 13 August 1926.
27 "Barnes Circus Gives Really Great Show," *Vancouver Sun*, 8 June 1927, 4. See also "Orphans Will See This," *Vancouver Sun*, 7 June 1927, 6.
28 "Sun Newsboys at Nanaimo See Circus," *Vancouver Sun*, 12 May 1927, 3.
29 For examples of these types of appeals to children, see CNEA, CNE catalogues from 1920s–1960s. Young Canada Day became Children's Day in 1935. See also *Fort William Daily Times Journal*, 28 August 1923, 18 August 1930, 3 August 1940, 2 August 1952, and 9 August 1962. On newsboys'

work during the Depression, see Campbell, *Respectable Citizens*, 93–4. On the orphans, see NACMA, Conklin Scrapbook, 1941, newspaper clippings.
30 "Johnny J. Jones Exposition," *Billboard*, 26 August 1922, 102.
31 Elves, *It's All Done with Mirrors*, 9, 13.
32 Gleason, *Small Matters*; and Strong-Boag, *Fostering Nation?*
33 Chen, *Tending to the Garden*, 7.
34 John Bullen, "Hidden Workers: Child Labour and the Family Economy in Late Nineteenth-Century Urban Ontario," in *Canadian Working Class History: Selected Readings*, edited by Laurel Sefton MacDowell and Ian Radforth (Toronto: Canadian Scholars' Press, 1992), 273.
35 Neil Sutherland, "'We Always Had Things to Do': The Paid and Unpaid Work of Anglophone Children between the 1920s and the 1960s," *Labour/Le travail* 25 (Spring 1990): 105–41.
36 Gleason, *Normalizing the Ideal*. For organizers and audiences of the New York World's Fair in 1940, the sideshow may have reinforced the message of one of the most popular main exhibits: "the typical American family." Historian Robert Rydell argues that the display of forty-eight families selected through state contests was driven by eugenicist principles. In addition to expressing a desire for families consisting of "parents and two children," the questionnaire produced by the fair for local judges "included 'racial origins' as one of the categories to be considered." Robert Rydell, *World of Fairs: The Century-of-Progress Expositions* (Chicago: University of Chicago Press, 1993), 56–7.
37 As Valverde notes, Ontario was influential in developing welfare and social services because of its size and financial resources. Mariana Valverde, "Representing Childhood: The Multiple Fathers of the Dionne Quintuplets," in *Regulating Womanhood: Historical Essays on Marriage, Motherhood and Sexuality*, ed. Carol Smart (New York: Routledge, 1993), 120.
38 Veronica Strong-Boag, "'Children of Adversity': Disabilities and Child Welfare in Canada from the Nineteenth to the Twenty-First Century," *Journal of Family History* 32, no. 4 (October 2007): 422.
39 Strong-Boag, *Fostering Nation?* 56–7.
40 Ibid., 57.
41 In the 1970s, disability rights activists and scholars questioned the presentation, and especially the use of "pity," in such displays. For an overview, see Beth A. Haller, "Telethons," in *Encyclopedia of Disability*, ed. Gary L. Albrecht (Thousand Oaks, CA: Sage, 2006), 1545–7.
42 Veronica Strong-Boag, "'Forgotten People of All the Forgotten': Children with Disabilities in English Canada from the Nineteenth Century to the New Millennium," in *Lost Kids: Vulnerable Children and Youth in*

Twentieth-Century Canada and the United States, ed. Mona Gleason, Tamara Myers, Leslie Paris, and Veronica Strong-Boag (Vancouver: University of British Columbia Press, 2009), 40–1.

43 LAC, RG 29, vol. 990 499-3-6, part 1, Address of Wm. F. Macklaier, Q.C. to Dinner Meeting of the Cerebral Palsy Section of the Canadian Council for Crippled Children and Adults, Winnipeg, 8 April 1960.

44 Karen Balcom, *The Traffic in Babies: Cross-Border Adoption and Baby-Selling between the United States and Canada, 1930–1972* (Toronto: University of Toronto Press, 2011), 4–5. One case was the dramatic story of Americans George and Willie Muse that took place when their mother accused the Ringling Bros. of kidnapping the boys and, in 1927, sued the show after reclaiming the boys when the circus was in town. The story is partially documented in court records from Virginia. George Muse, identified in the proceedings as Georgie Muse, "an infant under the age of twenty-one years," was suing for fifty thousand dollars on the grounds that he was forcibly taken at the age of nine by a Mr Stokes. After a period of time, which Muse could not be precise about, the boys were traded to Herman Shelton, a manager for the Ringling Bros. The filing by George accused Shelton of forcing them to work against their will as freaks. The filing argues that the Muses were "slaves" who, upon recognizing their mother in the crowd at the performance in 1927, left the stage and "escaped from the clutches" of the circus manager. The manager and the Ringling Bros. were further accused of not paying the Muse brothers "one single, solitary, red penny for their services; that all they have obtained during their four and one-half years work for the said principal defendant has been their board and very little clothing." Neither could read or write, and George at least was under the legal age of majority. Being poor and Black with intellectual delays meant that the Muse brothers were especially vulnerable to exploitation and had no access to appropriate legal remedy. Allegedly, the case also involved some physical conflicts between some of the show people and members of the community. Showman Al Barnes described the context succinctly: "There was some trouble before the case was settled." While the suit was quashed on a technicality, it did provide the opportunity to publicly draw attention to their treatment, and when they returned to work for the same company, they were paid. In 1933, the brothers appeared as Eko and Iko, "Peculiar People," and four years later as "Eko and Iko Ministers from Dahomey." They would perform until their retirement in 1961. State Records Centre Repository, Richmond, VA, box #196 1928–1929, Georgie Muse v. Ringling Brothers and Barnum and Bailey Combined Shows, Incorporated and Herman Shelton, Manager of

the Business of Said Principal Defendant and the Officers, Agents, and Employees of the Said Principal Defendant in the City of Richmond, VA, Motion to Quash Attachment, 27 October 1927 and Robeson, *Al G. Barnes*, 276–7. See also Beth Macy and Jen McCaffery, "The Stuff of Legend," *Roanoke Times*, in CWM Small Collections, "Eko and Iko." For a fuller account of their lives, see Beth Macy, *Truevine: Two Brothers, A Mother's Quest, and a Kidnapping: A True Story of the Jim Crow South* (New York: Little, Brown, 2016).

45 Martell, *Millie-Christine*; Frost, "Introduction," *Conjoined Twins in Black and White*, 8–11; and Peacock, "Africa Meets the Great Farini," 85.
46 CWM, Small Collections, Waino and Plutano.
47 LAC, R 219-29-4-E, Correspondence with Canadian and British Government Departments, files "Missing armless Indian boy lent for Exhibition" and "Whereabouts of armless Indian boy, loaned for exhibition purposes."
48 Hall, *My Very Unusual Friends*, 45.
49 Nickell, *Secrets of the Sideshows*, chap. 6.
50 Strong-Boag, *Finding Families, Finding Ourselves*, chap. 1.
51 Ibid., xiii.
52 Parr, *Labouring Children*.
53 Strong-Boag, *Finding Families, Finding Ourselves*, 186–7; Balcom, *The Traffic in Babies*.
54 NYPL, New York World's Fair 1939/40 Central Files, P1 630, box 540, file 3, letter from Mrs Ed Orbeck, dated 9 February 1939.
55 See, for example, NYPL, file 9, "P1 637 Freaks A–K" (1939), letters dated 28 March 1939, 22 July 1939, 28 July 1939, and 11 March 1939.
56 NYPL, New York World's Fair 1939/40 Central Files, file 9 "P1 637 Freaks A–K (1939).
57 Clarke, "Sacred Daemons"; Geertje Boschma, "A Family Point of View: Negotiating Asylum Care in Alberta, 1905–1930," *Canadian Bulletin for Medical History* 25, no. 2 (2008): 376–8.
58 Reaume, *Remembrance of Patients Past*, 23–4.
59 WPA is an acronym for the Works Progress Administration, a federal program of relief which generated jobs for the unemployed through public works development that ranged from infrastructure to the arts.
60 NYPL, file 9 "P1 637 Freaks A–K" (1939), letter dated 23 April 1939.
61 NYPL, file 9 "P1 637 Freaks A–K" (1939), letter dated 26 June 1939.
62 NYPL, file 9 "P1 637 Freaks A–K" (1939), letter dated 7 November 1938.
63 Martin S. Pernick, *The Black Stork: Eugenics and the Death of "Defective" Babies in American Medicine and Motion Pictures since 1915* (New York:

Oxford University Press, 1996). The issue of euthanizing also comes up in the case of conjoined twins Millie-Christine McKoy. Millie contracted tuberculosis and died in 1912. The attending physician, after consulting with other doctors and the state governor, euthanized Christine with massive doses of opiates. It is unclear if he consulted Christine. See Martell, *Millie-Christine*, 269.

64 Jessa Chupik and Donald Wright, "Treating the 'Idiot' Child in Early 20th-Century Ontario" *Disability and Society* 21, no. 1 (January 2006): 87.
65 NYPL, file 9 "P1 637 Freaks A–K" (1939), letter from Dr Frank Monaghan, Director of Research, 29 May 1939.
66 *Billboard*, 19 March 1910. 94. Webb's obituary appeared in various newspapers, including the *New York Times*, 20 July 1938.
67 NACMA, Conklin Scrapbook, 1940s, newspaper clipping.
68 "Miracle Operation Proves Successful," *Winnipeg Free Press*, 10 February 1944, 1.
69 NACMA, Conklin scrapbook, pamphlet.
70 NACMA, Conklin scrapbook, photograph.
71 William Good, "Surgery Makes Him One," *Winnipeg Tribune*, 10 February 1944, 1, 11. According to Pierre Berton, the Dionne quintuplets were of interest to more than one sideshow promoter. Pierre Berton, *The Dionne Years: A Thirties Melodrama* (New York: W.W. Norton, 2007), 59.
72 McKennon, *A Pictorial History of the American Carnival*, 2:11.
73 Sutherland, *Growing Up*, 114.
74 Gender differences are important to note here. Girls often worked at home, helping their mothers with domestic duties including the care of younger siblings, or moved into cities for factory, retail, or domestic work depending on class and race. Boys, Campbell notes, were less likely to be kept at home with their mothers except "in some cases a combination of poverty, illness, and lack of clothing kept boys home to help their mothers." See Campbell, *Respectable Citizens*, 95.
75 James Struthers, *The Limits of Affluence: Welfare in Ontario, 1920–1970* (Toronto: University of Toronto Press, 1994).
76 Cynthia Comacchio, *The Infinite Bonds of Family: Domesticity in Canada, 1850–1940* (Toronto: University of Toronto Press, 1999), 113.
77 NACMA, Conklin Scrapbook, newspaper clipping.
78 "Miracle Operation Proves Successful," *Winnipeg Free Press*, 10 February 1944, 1.
79 NACMA, Conklin Scrapbook, newspaper clippings.
80 On informal adoption on the sideshows from a largely uncritical perspective, see Nickell, *Secrets of the Sideshows*, chap. 6, and Hall, *Struggles*

and Triumphs. On adoption and children with disabilities, see Strong-Boag, *Fostering Nation?*

81 NACMA, Conklin Scrapbook, 1935, *carte de visite*.
82 "'Patty' Conklin Urges Paved Midway at Fair," *Fort William Daily Times Journal*, 8 August 1944.
83 NYPL, New York World's Fair 1939/40, Central Files, P1 637, box 547, file 8, Freaks (1940), letter from J.B. Goyer, 1 March 1940.
84 The so-called girl shows reveal the issues. See Stencell, *Girl Show*.
85 AO, RG 23-20-20 box 1, file 38, Circuses and Travelling Shows, 1918–1920, letter dated 30 August 1920. Under the current privacy legislation in Ontario, the names of the girls and their chaperone were removed.
86 NACMA, Conklin Scrapbook, newspaper clipping, "Surgeon Removes 'Parasitic Twin,' Boy Now Normal."
87 William Good, "Surgery Makes Him One," *Winnipeg Tribune*, 10 February 1944, 1, 11.
88 Ibid.
89 The quotation appears in a number of newspapers using reports from the Associated Press (AP). These include "Parasitic Twin Cut from Youth: Clinic Performs Operation Formerly Held Fatal," *Deseret News*, 11 February 1944; "'Siamese Twin' Cut from Boy," *Eugene Register-Guard*, 11 February 1944; and "Boy Normal after Partial Twin Removed from Body," *Free Lance-Star*, 11 February 1944.
90 A.W. Stencell reports that Ernie worked behind the scenes at various shows in the 1950s before becoming a banker. See Stencell, *Circus and Carnival Ballyhoo*, 272.
91 See, for example, "Parasitic Twin Severed from Body of Boy, 12: Extra Arms, Legs, and Liver Removed; Winnipeg Youth Now Reported Normal," *Pittsburgh Post-Gazette*, 11 February 1944; "Knife Gives Normal Life to Partial Twin," *Palm Beach Post*, 11 February 1944; "Boy Normal after Partial Twin Removed from Body," *Free Lance-Star*, 11 February 1944; and "Surgery Makes Him One: Through with Sideshows Now, Young Defort Is Happy at School," *Winnipeg Tribune*, 10 February 1944.
92 Sally Mennill and Veronica Strong-Boag, "Identifying Victims: Child Abuse and Death in Canadian Families," *Canadian Bulletin of Medical History* 25, no. 2 (2008): 316.
93 Leroy Ashby, *Endangered Children: Dependency, Neglect and Abuse in American History* (New York: Twayne, 1997).
94 Mennill and Strong-Boag, "Identifying Victims," 316–17; and Lori Chambers, *The Legal History of Adoption in Ontario, 1921 to 2014* (Toronto: University of Toronto Press, 2017).

95 LAC, RG 29, vol. 990, 449-3-6 pt. 3, Report of the National Executive Director, Canadian Council for Crippled Children and Adults, Reports of the Year's Activities 1959–1960.
96 LAC, RG 29, vol. 990 449-2-14, Abstract of "Mongolism, Working Paper on Mental Retardation," 2.
97 Janet Read and Luke Clements, "Demonstrably Awful: The Right to Life and the Selective Non-Treatment of Disabled Babies and Young Children," in *Disabled People and the Right to Life: The Protection and Violation of Disabled People's Most Basic Human Rights*, ed. Luke Clements and Janet Read (London and New York: Routlege, 2008), 152–4.

6 The Spectacularization of Small and Cute

1 James Brough with Annette, Cecile, Marie, and Yvonne Dionne, *We Were Five: The Dionne Quintuplets' Story from Birth through Girlhood to Womanhood* (New York: Simon and Schuster, 1965), 10.
2 Bennett, "The Exhibitionary Complex."
3 Garland-Thomson, *Staring*, 173.
4 Mona Gleason, "Size Matters: Medical Experts, Educations, and the Provision of Health Services to Children in Early to Mid-Twentieth Century English Canada," in Comacchio, Golden, and Weisz, *Healing the World's Children*, 178.
5 For historical definitions of "midget" and "dwarf" as they were used on the sideshows, see *Howard Y. Barry Presents Singers' Midgets in a New Streamline Novelty: A Midget Circus Review* (n.p., n.d [circa the 1940s]).
6 Veronica Strong-Boag, "Intruders in the Nursery: Childcare Professionals Reshape the Years One to Five, 1920–1940," in *Childhood and Family in Canadian History*, ed. Joy Parr (Toronto: McClelland and Stewart, 1982), 160–78; Valverde, "Representing Childhood, 119–46; and the Winter 1994 issue of the *Journal of Canadian Studies* on the Dionnes.
7 Gary S. Cross, *The Cute and the Cool: Wondrous Innocence and Modern American Children's Culture* (New York: Oxford University Press, 2004), 51.
8 Lori Merish, "Cuteness and Commodity Aesthetics: Tom Thumb and Shirley Temple," in Garland-Thomson, *Freakery*, 188.
9 Merish, "Cuteness and Commodity Aesthetics," 194. Emphasis in the original.
10 Ibid., 187–8.
11 Ibid.
12 John F. Kasson, *The Little Girl Who Fought the Depression: Shirley Temple and 1930s America* (New York: W.W. Norton, 2014), 156.

13 The general pattern for dolls followed from lady dolls to baby dolls to teen dolls from the late nineteenth to the mid-twentieth century. The dolls available to Canadian girls, including homemade ones, remained diverse. See Jacqueline Reid-Walsh and Claudia Mitchell, "Mapping a Canadian Girlhood Historically through Dolls and Doll-Play," in *Depicting Canada's Children*, ed. Loren Lerner (Waterloo, ON: Wilfrid Laurier University Press, 2009), 113. For some Canadian examples in regard to food advertising, see Cheryl Krasnick Warsh, "Vim, Vigour, and Vitality: 'Power' Foods for Kids in Canadian Popular Magazines, 1914–1954," in *Edible Histories, Cultural Politics: Towards a Canadian Food History*, ed. Franca Iacovetta, Valerie J. Korinek, and Marlene Epp (Toronto: University of Toronto Press, 2012), 387–408.
14 Cross, *The Cute and the Cool*, 69–70.
15 Belisle, *Retail Nation*; and Cynthia Wright, "'Feminine Trifles of Vast Importance': Writing Gender into the History of Consumption," in *Gender Conflicts: New Essays in Women's History*, ed. Franca Iacovetta and Mariana Valverde (Toronto: University of Toronto Press, 1992).
16 Valverde, *The Age of Light, Soap and Water*; Strange, *Toronto's Girl Problem*; Lindsey McMaster, *Working Girls in the West: Representations of Wage-Earning Women* (Vancouver: University of British Columbia Press, 2008); and Nicholas, *The Modern Girl*.
17 Patricia Jasen, *Wild Things: Nature, Culture, and Tourism in Ontario, 1790–1914* (Toronto: University of Toronto Press, 1995); and Mark Moss, *Manliness and Militarism: Educating Young Boys in Ontario for War* (Don Mills, ON: Oxford University Press, 2001).
18 Moss, *Manliness and Militarism*, 56–7.
19 Jane Nicholas, "Scales of Manliness: Masculinity and Disability in the Displays of Little People as Freaks in Ontario, 1900s–1950s," in *Masculinities in Canadian History*, ed. Robert Rutherdale and Peter Gossage (Vancouver: University of British Columbia Press, forthcoming).
20 Stewart, *On Longing*, 111.
21 Quoted in Richard Howells and Michael M. Chemers, "Midget Cities: Utopia, Utopianism, and the *Vor-schein* of the 'Freak' Show," *Disability Studies Quarterly* 25, no. 3 (Summer 2005): n.p.
22 See, for example, "Big Little Man," *Fort William Daily Times Journal*, 14 August 1935.
23 Bogdan, *Freak Show*, chap. 6.
24 Quoted in ibid., 149.
25 Ibid., 152.
26 Women with small stature giving birth was of interest to physicians as well. For example, see James W. McClaran, "Cesarean [sic] Section on a

True Dwarf," *Journal of the American Medical Association*, 2 August 1924, 356–7.
27 Bogdan, *Freak Show*, 157–9.
28 Gary Cross, "Crowds and Leisure: Thinking Comparatively across the 20th Century," *Journal of Social History* 39, no. 3 (Spring 2006): 637.
29 *Billboard*, 14 February 1920, 91; and 17 January 1920, 75.
30 NACMA, Conklin Scrapbook, 1930, newspaper clipping, "Everybody Loves Circus"; NACMA newspaper clipping Conklin Scrapbook, 1935, *Victoria Daily Times*, "Versatile Dwarf Circus Feature."
31 NACMA, Conklin Scrapbook, 1938.
32 NACMA, Conklin Scrapbook, 1942, newspaper clipping, *Fort William Daily Times Journal* 9 August 1941; CNEA, Official Catalogue and Programme, 1938, 18; 1939, 16; and 1941, 18.
33 Merish, "Cuteness and Commodity Aesthetics," 196.
34 Little people were prohibited from membership within the Screen Actors Guild until 1970. Bogdan, *Freak Show*, 163.
35 See, for example, CWM, Carnival Collection, box 2, Johnny J. Jones Exposition, and box 3, Little People Troupes; CNEA, General Photo Collection, COI file 214, G. Hollies. One group performing in the 1950s called themselves the Hollywood Midget Revue. See the *Fort William Daily Times Journal*, 11 August 1953.
36 Beth M. Adelson, "Dwarfs: The Changing Lives of Archetypical 'Curiosities' – Echoes of the Past," *Disability Studies Quarterly* 25, no. 3 (Summer 2005).
37 Robert W. Marks, "Midget Mystery," *Maclean's*, 1 October 1944, 18.
38 Ibid.
39 "Newsboys Think Johnny J. Jones Real Swell Guy," *Fort William Daily Times Journal*, 13 August 1926.
40 Bogdan has their performance dates ending in 1935. See Bogdan, *Freak Show*, 162. In the 1940s, a promotional booklet was published as *Howard Y. Barry presents Singers' Midgets in a New Streamline Novelty: A Midget Circus Revue* (n.p, n.d. [circa the 1940s]).
41 CWM, Carnival Collection, box 3, World of Mirth, 1955.
42 CNEA, General Photo Collections, COI file 214, G. Hollies.
43 "How Do Midgets Dress? A Peep in the Wardrobe" *Globe*, 26 August 1924, 16.
44 Marks, "Midget Mystery," 22.
45 "Midway Midget Has Large Thirst," *Toronto Daily Star*, 8 September 1927, 3.
46 CWM, Carnival Collection, box 3, World of Mirth, 1959.
47 Lewiston, *Freak Show Man*.
48 Stewart, *On Longing*, 124.

49 CWM, Carnival Collection, box 3, World of Mirth, 1955.
50 Gleason, *Small Matters*, 14.
51 C.G. Sturtevant, "Super Freaks of the Sideshow: Part II," *White Tops*, April–May 1936, 4–6.
52 Quoted in Berton, *The Dionne Years*, 68.
53 See, for example, S.R. Foster and William Carson, "A Case of Quintuple Pregnancy," *The Lancet*, 21 July 1923, 120; Dennis Vinrace, letter to the editor, "Survival of Quadruplets," *The Lancet*, 17 January 1920, 78; Norma Ford and Gioacchino Caruso, "Two Unrecorded Cases of Quintuplet Births, Canadian and Italian," *Canadian Medical Association Journal*, October 1938, 333–5; and "Siamese Twins Born," *Globe*, 30 January 1931, 16. The Dionnes were certainly the most financially successful, despite the fact that little of their earnings trickled down to them. On the Dionnes and finances, see Brough et al., *We Were Five*, 253.
54 NYPL, New York World's Fair 1939/40, Central Files, P1 630, file 4, letter from Major Roullett, dated 3 April 1939; file 5, letter from Lourene Pulfrey to John Krimsky, dated 28 January 1939; file 12, letter from T.W. Youngblood, undated; box 540, file 1, confirmation of telephone message and letter from John Krimsky, Acting Director Department of Entertainment, dated 8 February 1938.
55 NYPL, New York World's Fair 1939/40, Central Files, P1 630, file 12, letter from Arthur Bourassa, 1 December 1938, and file 13, letter from Frank Delbridge, 3 December 1938.
56 Susan J. Pearson, "'Infantile Specimens': Showing Babies in Nineteenth-Century America," *Journal of Social History* (Winter 2008): 346.
57 For examples of baby contests, see "Asbury Park Picks Baby Miss America," *New York Times*, 1 September 1927, 10; "1,000 Babies Parade at Atlantic City," *New York Times*, 9 September 1926, 9; "500 Babies Parade at Atlantic City," *New York Times*, 8 September 1927, 17; "500 Babies March in Shore Parades," *New York Times*, 4 September 1927, 12; "Walter Wicks Wins at Boys' Baby Show," *Toronto Daily Star*, 19 September 1927, 26; "Baby Contest Will Attract Many Entries," *Vancouver Sun*, 4 June 1927, 2.
58 On the Baby Peggy contest, see, for example, AO, 17–1, Original Newspaper Collection, *News Mirror*, 31 May 1924, 15, 22; and 14 June 1924, 23. Baby Peggy later changed her name to Diana Serra Cary and published a highly critical autobiography about children working in the film industry. See Cary, *What Ever Happened to Baby Peggy*.
59 Strong-Boag, "Intruders in the Nursery"; and Comacchio, *Nations Are Built of Babies*.
60 "Babies Purr and Gurgle with Delight," *Globe*, 7 September 1920, 5.

61 Alexandra Minna Stern, "Beauty Is Not Always Better: Perfect Babies and the Tyranny of Paediatric Norms," *Patterns of Prejudice* 36, no. 1 (2002): 77.
62 Fred J. Collins, "Make the People Smile," *Billboard*, 22 March 1919, 32.
63 Gerald E. Thomson, "'A Baby Show Means Work in the Hardest Sense': The Better Baby Contests of the Vancouver and New Westminster Local Councils of Women, 1913–1929," *BC Studies* 128 (Winter 2000–1): 5–6.
64 "Roma Holland Prize Baby, Quickly Stars in Movies," *Evening Telegram*, 6 September 1927, 24; and *Hamilton Spectator*, 6 September 1927, 1.
65 Alarmingly racist representations existed, like one photograph from the late nineteenth century in the United States that showed a number of black toddlers under the description "Alligator Bait." Robin Bernstein, "Childhood as Performance," in *The Children's Table: Childhood Studies in the Humanities*, ed. Anna Mae Duane (Athens: University of Georgia Press, 2013), 209–10.
66 Thomson, "'A Baby Show Means Work in the Hardest Sense.'"
67 LAC, RG 10, file no. 600178, Blackfoot Agency – Correspondence Regarding Child Welfare, letter from G. H. Gooderham, 30 March 1926.
68 LAC, RG 10, file no. 600178, Blackfoot Agency – Correspondence Regarding Child Welfare, letter from Gooderham, 14 August 1926.
69 Strong-Boag, "Intruders in the Nursery"; Little, *No Car, No Radio*; Comacchio, *Nations Are Built of Babies*.
70 Strong-Boag, *Fostering Nation?* 116–21; and Franca Iacovetta, *Gatekeepers: Reshaping Immigrant Lives in Cold War Canada* (Toronto: Between the Lines, 2006).
71 Jeffrey P. Baker, *The Machine in the Nursery: Incubator Technology and the Origins of Newborn Intensive Care* (Baltimore: Johns Hopkins University Press, 1996), 86.
72 Ibid., 103–5.
73 Ibid., 103.
74 This included the 1939 and 1940 World's Fairs in New York.
75 Berton, *The Dionne Years*, 59; and Dufour with Kirby, *Fabulous Years*, 83.
76 "Dionne Babies Become Wards," *Montreal Gazette*, 27 July 1934, 1, 9.
77 Dufour with Kirby, *Fabulous Years*, 82–3.
78 Brough et al., *We Were Five*, 39.
79 "Change of Diet Is Beneficial to Quintuplets," *Globe*, 1 June 1934; and "Order Obtained for Guardians of Dionne Babes," *Globe*, 27 July 1934. See also "Mrs. Ovila [sic] Dionne and Quintuplets May See Chicago," *Montreal Gazette*, 1 June 1934, 1; "Quintuplets Still Thriving," *Montreal Gazette*, 2 June 1934, 1; and "Quintuplets' Trip to Chicago Banned," *Montreal Gazette*, 4 June 1934, 7.

80 For an overview, see Valverde, "Representing Childhood," 123–4.
81 "61,000 CNE 8 Days' Gain," *Billboard*, 7 September 1935, 60.
82 AO, Premier Mitchell F. Hepburn Press Clippings, Dionne Case, 1934–36, "Dionnes Irk Mr. Hepburn," *Border Cities Star*, 9 February 1935.
83 "Dionne Bill," *Globe*, 12 March 1935, 2.
84 On the weight gain and loss see the reporting by the *Montreal Gazette* for the month of July 1934. After August 1934, the paper reported on the weight more sporadically for a year. On the milk provided see "RVH Mile for Dionne Big Five" and "Eldest Quintuplet Now Four Pounds," *Montreal Gazette* 14 July 1934, 1, 9.
85 Cynthia Wright, "They Were Five: The Dionne Quintuplets Revisited" *Journal of Canadian Studies* 29, no. 4 (Winter 1994): 5–14.
86 A.E. Fulford, "Quintuplets' Act Draws Thousands," *Montreal Gazette*, 29 July 1935, 9.
87 Valverde, "Representing Childhood," 129.
88 Berton, *The Dionne Years*, 158. On infants feeling the stare, see Garland-Thomson, *Staring*, 17.
89 Bogdan, *Freak Show*. Garland-Thomson also notes the importance of the spiel given by an "expert," the related promotion material like pamphlets, the costuming and theatrics of the display, and the photographs in the making of sideshow exhibits. See her essay, "Introduction," in *Freakery*, 7.
90 Pearson, "'Infantile Specimens,'" 362.
91 Berton, *The Dionne Years*, 68.
92 AO, F 4392-58, B236444, St Lawrence Starch Company Fonds, Dionne Quintuplet Files.
93 Brough et al., *We Were Five*, 255.
94 Françoise Noël, *Family and Community Life in Northeastern Ontario: The Interwar Years* (Montreal: McGill-Queen's University Press, 2009), 52, 195.
95 Brough et al., *We Were Five*, 55; and Strong-Boag, "Intruders in the Nursery," 177.
96 LAC, MG 31 J18, Louise de Kiriline fonds, Letters to Hillevid de Flach, 28 September 1937.
97 Berton, *The Dionne Years*, 186.
98 "Retirement of Quints Predicted by Dafoe," *Globe and Mail*, 6 December 1938, 1.
99 "Artistic Career Seen for Quints," *Globe and Mail*, 1 August 1939.
100 "Club Initiates Dafoe as 'Doctor of Litters,'" *Globe and Mail*, 13 April 1939.
101 The history in this paragraph is from Berton, *The Dionne Years*; Strong-Boag, "Intruders in the Nursery"; Valverde, "Representing Childhood";

as well as the newspaper clippings in AO, RG 3-14, B 308107, box 407 Mitchell F. Hepburn Press Clippings, Dionne Case.
102 Denyse Baillargeon, *Babies for the Nation: The Medicalization of Motherhood in Quebec, 1910–1970* (Waterloo, ON: Wilfrid Laurier University Press, 2009), 63.
103 Valverde, "Representing Childhood." See also Comacchio, *The Infinite Bonds of Family*, 137. The quints' reintegration with their birth family was difficult, and decades later the three surviving quints wrote a book alleging sexual abuse at the hands of their father. See Jean-Yves Soucy, *Family Secrets: The Dionne Quintuplets' Autobiography* (New York: Berkley Books, 1997).
104 Berton, *The Dionne Years*, 191.
105 Comacchio, *The Dominion of Youth*, chap. 1. The problems were made clear in the debates over beauty contests in the period. See Jane Nicholas, *The Modern Girl*, chap. 4.
106 Fadner, *The Gentleman Giant*, 95–6.
107 Kasson, *The Little Girl Who Fought the Depression*, 150.
108 Durbach, *Spectacle of Deformity*, 171.

Epilogue: "I guess it really is all over"

1 Jim Christy, "Chalk One for the Bland and Boring," *Globe and Mail*, 24 August 1977, A12.
2 Ibid.
3 Only a photograph of a fat performer called "Dora" was accessible to me in the archives. CNEA, photo collection, Midway, "Dora 'the fat woman,' CNE Midway Side Show during Conklin's Antique Carnival, 1978."
4 Dufour with Kirby, *Fabulous Years*, 164.
5 In the academic literature this is exemplified in Fiedler, *Freaks*. See also Adams, *Sideshow U.S.A.* for an excellent discussion on the book.
6 See, for example, Wendy Michener, "Movies: A Touching, Honestly Terrifying Film," *Globe and Mail*, 16 February 1968.
7 Garland-Thomson, introduction, *Extraordinary Bodies*.
8 Tod Browning, *Freaks*, Metro-Goldwyn-Mayer, 1932.

Bibliography

Repositories

Archives of Ontario
Canadian National Exhibition Archives
Circus World Museum
City of Saskatoon Archives
City of Toronto Archives
City of Vancouver Archives
Galt Museum and Archives
Library and Archives Canada
The New York Public Library Manuscripts and Archives Division. Astor, Lenox, and Tilden Foundations
The New York Public Library Performing Arts Division. Billy Rose Theatre Collection
North American Carnival Museum and Archives
Provincial Archives of New Brunswick
State Archives of Florida
State Records Cental Repository, Richmond, Virginia
University of California Santa Barbara Archives
University of South Florida, Digital Libraries Collection, Showman's Oral History Project

Published Primary Sources – Newspapers, Periodicals, Journals, and Trade Publications

* Fully cited in notes

Bandwagon
Billboard

British Medical Association Journal
Canadian Medical Association Journal
Fort William Daily Times Journal
Globe [*Globe and Mail*]
Hamilton Spectator
Jack Canuck
Journal of the American Medical Association
The Lancet
Maclean's
Montreal Star
Toronto Daily Star [*Toronto Star*]
White Tops
Winnipeg Free Press

Published Primary Sources – Books and Articles

Brough, James, with Annette, Cecile, Marie, and Yvonne Dionne. *'We Were Five:' The Dionne Quintuplets' Story from Birth through Girlhood to Womanhood.* New York: Simon and Schuster, 1965.

Buck, Pearl S. *The Child Who Never Grew: A Memoir.* New York: Woodbine House, [1950] 1992.

Cary, Diana Serra. *Whatever Happened to Baby Peggy? The Autobiography of Hollywood's Pioneer Child Star.* New York: St Martin's Press, 1996.

"Circus and Museum Freaks – Curiosities of Pathology." *Scientific American*, 28 March 1908.

Dufour, Lou, with Irwin Kirby. *Fabulous Years: Carnival Life, World's Fairs, and Broadway.* New York: Vintage Press, 1977.

Elves, Hazel. *It's All Done with Mirrors: A Canadian Carnival Life.* Victoria, BC: Sono Nis Press, 1977.

Fadner, Frederic. *The Gentleman Giant: The Biography of Robert Pershing Wadlow.* Boston: Bruce Humphries, 1944.

Frost, Linda. *Conjoined Twins in Black and White: The Lives of Millie-Christine McKoy and Daisy and Violet Hilton.* Madison: University of Wisconsin Press, 2009.

Geyer, Celesta "Dolly Dimples." *The Greatest Diet in the World.* Orlando: Chateau Publishing, 1968.

Geyer, Celesta "Dolly Dimples," and Samuel Roen. *Diet or Die: The Dolly Dimples Weight Reducing Plan.* New York: F. Fell, 1968.

Good, William. "Surgery Makes Him One," *Winnipeg Tribune*, 10 February 1944, 1, 11.

Gould, George M., and Walter L. Pyle, *Anomalies and Curiosities of Medicine*. Philadelphia: W.B. Saunders, 1901 [1896].
Gray, Spalding. *In Search of the Monkey Girl*. New York: Aperture, 1982.
Gresham, William Lindsay. *Monster Midway: An Uninhibited Look at the Glittering World of the Carny*. New York: Rinehart, 1948.
– "The World of Mirth." *Life Magazine*, 13 September 1948.
Hall, Ward. *My Very Unusual Friends*. Gibsonton: Ward Hall, 1991.
– *Struggles and Triumphs of a Modern Day Showman: An Autobiography*. Sarasota, FL: Carnival Publishers of Sarasota, 1981.
Holtman, Jerry [pseud. for Harry Lewiston]. *Freak Show Man: Uncensored Memoirs of Harry Lewiston – the Incredible Scoundrel*. Los Angeles, CA: Holloway House, 1968.
Horne, Marcel. *Annals of the Firebreather*. Toronto: Peter Martin Associates, 1973.
Howard Y. Barry Presents Singers' Midgets in a New Streamline Novelty: A Midget Circus Revue (n.p, n.d circa 1940s).
Kelley, F. Beverly. *It Was Better Than Work*. Gerald, MO: Patrice Press, 1982.
Laycraft, James H. "Royal American Shows Inc. and Its Activities in Alberta: Report of a Public Inquiry of the Commission of Inquiry into the Affairs and Activities in the Province of Alberta of Royal American Shows Inc." Edmonton, AB: n.p., 1978.
Lentz, John. "How Medical Progress Has Hastened the Passing of the Side Show." *Today's Health*, March 1964, retrieved from The Disability History Museum digital collection, 5 March 2015.
Lutz, Hartmut, Alootook Ipellie, and Hans-Ludwig Blohm. *The Diary of Abraham Ulrikah: Text and Context*. Ottawa: University of Ottawa Press, 2005.
Murphy, Mark. "Serviceable and Congenial." *New Yorker*, 9 May 1942.
"No More Rubes," *Time*, 29 September 1958.
Pare, Ambroise. *On Monsters and Marvels*. Translated by Janis L. Pallister. Chicago: University of Chicago Press, 1995.
"Passing of a Famous Novelty: Death of the World's Ugliest Woman." *World's Fair*, 30 December 1933. https://www.sheffield.ac.uk/nfca/researchandarticles/wf1931-1940.
Peary, Robert. *Nearest the Pole: A Narrative of the Polar Expedition of the Peary Arctic Club in the S.S. Roosevelt, 1905–1906*. London: Hutchinson, 1907.
"Pygopagus Marriage" *Time*, 16 July 1934.
Quetelet, Adolphe. *A Treatise on Man and the Development of His Faculties* (First Translated Edition). Translated by Robert Knox. New York: Burt Franklin, 1968.
Robeson, Dave. *Al G. Barnes: Master Showman as Told by Al G. Barnes*. Caldwell, ID: Caxton Printers, 1935.

Rogers, Dale Evans. *Angel Unaware*. Westwood, NJ: Fleming H. Revell, 1953.
Thompson, Robert H. *Boyhood Memories of Saskatoon in the 1930s*. Victoria: n.p., 1987.
Tye, Menia S. "Prenatal Influences." *American Journal of Nursing* 7, no. 5 (February 1907): 362–7.
Waters, H.W. *History of Fairs and Expositions: Their Classification, Functions and Values*. London, ON: Reid Bros., 1939.
Wilson, Charles. "An Artist Finds a Dignified Ending for an Ugly Story," *New York Times*, 11 February 2013. http://www.nytimes.com/2013/02/12/arts/design/julia-pastrana-who-died-in-1860-to-be-buried-in-mexico.html?pagewanted=all&_r=0.
"World's 'Ugliest Woman' Julia Pastrana Buried 153 Years On." *BBC News*. http://www.bbc.com/news/world-latin-america-21440400.

Published Secondary Sources

Adams, Mikaëla M. "Savage Foes, Noble Warriors, and Frail Remnants: Florida Seminoles in the White Imagination, 1865–1934." *Florida Historical Quarterly* 87, no. 3 (Winter 2009): 404–35.
Adams, Rachel. *Sideshow U.S.A.: Freaks and the American Cultural Imagination*. Chicago: University of Chicago Press, 2001.
Adelson, Beth M. "Dwarfs: The Changing Lives of Archetypical 'Curiosities' – and Echoes of the Past." *Disability Studies Quarterly* 25, no. 3 (Summer 2005). http://dsq-sds.org/article/view/576/753.
Alexander, Kristine. "Can the Girl Guide Speak?: The Perils and Pleasures of Looking for Children's Voices in Archival Research." *Jeunesse: Young Peoples, Texts, Cultures* 4, no. 1 (Summer 2012): 132–45.
Angus, Fiona. "Midway to Respectability: Carnivals at the Calgary Stampede." In *Icon, Brand, Myth: The Calgary Exhibition and Stampede*, edited by Max Foran, 111–46. Edmonton: Athabasca University Press, 2008.
Appelbaum, Stanley. *The Chicago World's Fair of 1893: A Photographic Record*. New York: Dover Publications, 1980.
Ashby, Leroy. *Endangered Children: Dependency, Neglect and Abuse in American History*. New York: Twayne Publishers, 1997.
Baillargeon, Denyse. *Babies for the Nation: The Medicalization of Motherhood in Quebec, 1910–1970* Translated by W. Donald Wilson. Waterloo, ON: Wilfrid Laurier University Press, 2009.
Baker, Jeffrey P. *The Machine in the Nursery: Incubator Technology and the Origins of Newborn Intensive Care*. Baltimore: Johns Hopkins University Press, 1996.

Balcom, Karen A. *The Traffic in Babies: Cross-Border Adoption and Baby-Selling between the United States and Canada, 1930–1972*. Toronto: University of Toronto Press, 2011.

Barrow, Mark V. "A Brief History of Teratology to the Early 20th Century." *Teratology* 4, no. 2 (1971): 119–29.

Bates, A.W. *Emblematic Monsters: Unnatural Conceptions and Deformed Births in Early Modern Europe*. Amsterdam: Rodopi, 2005.

Baynton, Douglas C. "Disability and the Justification of Inequality in American History." In *The New Disability History*, edited by Paul K. Longmore and Lauri Umansky, 33–57. New York: New York University Press, 2002.

Belisle, Donica. "Crazy for Bargains: Inventing the Irrational Female Shopper in Modernizing English Canada." *Canadian Historical Review* 92, no. 4 (December 2011): 581–606.

Belisle, Donica. *Retail Nation: Department Stores and the Making of Modern Canada*. Vancouver: University of British Columbia Press, 2011.

Bennett, Tony. "The Exhibitionary Complex." *new formations* (Spring 1988): 73–100.

Bernstein, Robin. "Childhood as Performance." In *The Children's Table: Childhood Studies in the Humanities*, edited by Anna Mae Duane, 203–12. Athens: University of Georgia Press, 2013.

Berton, Pierre. *The Dionne Years: A Thirties Melodrama*. Toronto: McClelland and Stewart, 1977.

Bogdan, Robert. "Charles B. Tripp." In *American National Biography: Supplement 2*, edited by Mark C. Carnes, 558–9. Oxford: Oxford University Press, 2005.

– *Freak Show: Presenting Human Oddities for Amusement and Profit*. Chicago: University of Chicago Press, 1988.

Boschma, Geertje. "A Family Point of View: Negotiating Asylum Care in Alberta, 1905–1930" *Canadian Bulletin for Medical History* 25, no. 2 (2008): 367–89.

Bourdieau, Pierre. *Distinction: A Social Critique of the Judgement of Taste*. Cambridge, MA: Harvard University Press, 1987.

Bradbury, Bettina. "The Fragmented Family: Family Strategies in the Face of Death, Illness, and Poverty, Montreal, 1860–1885. " In *Childhood and Family in Canadian History*, edited by Joy Parr, 109–28. Toronto: McClelland and Stewart, 1982.

Bullen, John. "Hidden Workers: Child Labour and the Family Economy in Late Nineteenth-Century Urban Ontario." In *Canadian Working Class History: Selected Readings*, edited by Laurel Sefton MacDowell and Ian Radforth, 269–87. Toronto: Canadian Scholars' Press, 1992.

Butler, Judith. *Undoing Gender*. New York and London: Routledge, 2004.
Campbell, Lara. *Respectable Citizens: Gender, Family, and Unemployment in Ontario's Great Depression*. Toronto: University of Toronto Press, 2009.
Chadha, Ena. "'Mentally Defectives' Not Welcome: Mental Disability in Canadian Immigration Law, 1859–1927." *Disability Studies Quarterly* 28, no. 1 (Winter 2008). http://dsq-sds.org/article/view/67/67.
Chambers, Lori. *The Legal History of Adoption in Ontario, 1921 to 2014*. Toronto: University of Toronto Press, 2016.
Chen, Xiaobei. *Tending the Gardens of Citizenship: Child Saving in Toronto, 1880s–1920s*. Toronto: University of Toronto Press, 2005.
Christie, Nancy. *Engendering the State: Family, Work, and Welfare in Canada*. Toronto: University of Toronto Press, 2000.
Chupik, Jessa and Donald Wright. "Treating the 'Idiot' Child in Early 20th-Century Ontario." *Disability and Society* 21, no. 1 (January 2006): 77–90.
Clarke, Nic. "Sacred Daemons: Exploring British Columbian Society's Perceptions of 'Mentally Deficient' Children, 1870–1930." *BC Studies* 144 (Winter 2004/5): 61–89.
Clément, Dominique. *Canada's Rights Revolution: Social Movements and Social Change, 1937–82*. Vancouver: University of British Columbia Press, 2008.
Coates, Kenneth, and Fred McGuiness. *Pride of the Land: An Affectionate History of Brandon's Agricultural Exhibitions*. Winnipeg: Peguis Publishers, 1985.
College of Physicians of Philadelphia and Laura Lindgren, eds. *Mutter Museum Historic Medical Photographs*. New York: Blast Books, 2007.
Colón, A.R., with P.A. Colón. *Nurturing Children: A History of Pediatrics*. Westport, CT: Greenwood Press, 1999.
Comacchio, Cynthia. *The Dominion of Youth: Adolescence and the Making of Modern Canada, 1920 to 1950*. Waterloo, ON: Wilfrid Laurier University Press, 2008.
– *The Infinite Bonds of Family: Domesticity in Canada, 1850–1940*. Toronto: University of Toronto Press, 1999.
– "Mechanomorphosis: Science, Management, and 'Human Machinery' in Industrial Canada, 1900–45." *Labour/Le Travail* 41 (Spring 1998): 35–67.
– *Nations are Built of Babies: Saving Ontario's Mothers and Children, 1900–1940*. Montreal and Kingston: McGill-Queen's University Press, 1998.
– "'The Rising Generation': Laying Claim to the Health of Adolescents in English Canada, 1920–70." *Canadian Bulletin of Medical History* 19 (2002): 139–78.
Comacchio, Cynthia, Janet Golden, and George Weisz. "Introduction: Healing the World's Children." In *Healing the World's Children: Interdisciplinary Perspectives on Child Health in the Twentieth Century*, edited by Cynthia

Comacchio, Janet Golden, and George Weisz, 3–13. Montreal and Kingston: McGill-Queen's University Press, 2008.

Cook, Ramsey. *The Regenerators: Social Criticism in Late Victorian English Canada*. Toronto: University of Toronto Press, 1985.

Copp, Terry. *The Anatomy of Poverty: The Condition of the Working Class in Montreal, 1897–1929*. Toronto: McClelland and Stewart, 1974.

Cranton, Lillian E. *The Victorian Freak Show: The Significance of Disability and Physical Differences in 19th-Century Fiction*. Amherst, NY: Cambria Press, 2010.

Cross, Gary S. "Crowds and Leisure: Thinking Comparatively across the 20th Century." *Journal of Social History* 39, no. 3 (Spring 2006): 631–50.

– *The Cute and the Cool: Wondrous Innocence and Modern American Children's Culture*. New York: Oxford University Press, 2004.

Cullen, Frank, with Florence Hackman and Donald McNeilly. *Vaudeville, Old and New: An Encyclopedia of Variety Performers in America*. London and New York: Routledge, 2006.

Davidoff, Lenore, and Catherine Hall. *Family Fortunes: Men and Women of the English Middle Class, 1780–1850*. Chicago: University of Chicago Press, 1987.

Davis, Janet M. *The Circus Age: Culture and Society under the American Big Top*. Chapel Hill: University of North Carolina Press, 2002.

Davis, Lennard J. "Constructing Normalcy: The Bell Curve, the Novel, and the Invention of the Disabled Body in the Nineteenth Century." In *The Disability Studies Reader*, 3rd ed., edited by Lennard J. Davis, 3–16. New York: Routledge, 2010.

– *Enforcing Normalcy: Disability, Deafness, and the Body*. London: Verso, 1995.

de Bolla, Peter. *The Education of the Eye: Painting, Landscape and Architecture in Eighteenth-Century Britain*. Stanford, CA: Stanford University Press, 2003.

Dennett, Andrea Stulman. "The Dime Museum Freak Show Reconfigured as Talk Show." In *Freakery*, edited by Rosemarie Garland-Thomson, 315–26. New York: New York University Press, 1996.

– *Weird and Wonderful: The Dime Museum in America*. New York: New York University Press, 1997.

Domurat Dreger, Alice. "Jarring Bodies: Thoughts on the Display of Unusual Anatomies." *Perspectives in Biology and Medicine* 43, no. 2 (Winter 2000): 161–72.

– *One of Us: Conjoined Twins and the Future of Normal*. Boston: Harvard University Press, 2005.

Duffin, Jacalyn. *History of Medicine: A Scandalously Short Introduction*. 2nd ed. Toronto: University of Toronto Press, 2010.

Dummitt, Christopher. *The Manly Modern: Masculinity in Postwar Canada*. Vancouver: University of British Columbia Press, 2007.

Dunk, Thomas. *It's a Working Man's Town: Male Working-Class Culture*. 2nd ed. Montreal and Kingston: McGill-Queen's University Press, 2003.

Durbach, Nadja. "On the Emergence of the Freak Show in Britain." *BRANCH: Britain, Representation and Nineteenth-Century History*, edited by Dino Franco Falluga. Extension of *Romanticism and Victorianism on the Net*. http://www.branchcollective.org/?ps_articles=art_emergence_of_the_freak.

– "'Skinless Wonders': *Body Worlds* and the Victorian Freak Show." *Journal of the History of Medicine and Allied Sciences* 69, no. 1 (2012): 38–67.

– *Spectacle of Deformity: Freak Shows and Modern British Culture*. Berkeley: University of California Press, 2010.

Easto, P.C., and M. Truzzi. "Towards an Ethnography of the Carnival Social System." *Journal of Popular Culture* 6, no. 3 (Spring 1973): 550–66.

Eknoyan, Garabad. "Adolphe Quetelet (1796–1874) – The Average Man and Indices of Obesity." *Nephrology Dialysis Transplantation* 23 (2008): 47.

Fahy, Thomas. *Freak Shows and the Modern American Imagination: Constructing the Damaged Body from Willa Cather to Truman Capote*. New York: Palgrave Macmillan, 2006.

Fausto-Sterling, Anne. "Gender, Race, and Nation: The Comparative Anatomy of 'Hottentot' Women in Europe, 1815–1817." In *Deviant Bodies: Critical Perspectives on Difference in Science and Popular Culture*, edited by Jennifer Terry and Jacqueline Urla, 19–48. Indianapolis: Indiana University Press, 1995.

Fiedler, Leslie. *Freaks: Myths and Images of the Secret Self*. New York: Simon and Schuster, 1978.

Finkel, Alvin, and Margaret Conrad. *History of the Canadian Peoples*, vol. 2. Toronto: Pearson, 2002.

Fordham, Brigham A. "Dangerous Bodies: Freaks Shows, Expression, and Exploitation." *UCLA Entertainment Law Review* 14, no. 2 (2007): 207–45.

Foucault, Michel. *The Birth of the Clinic* London: Tavistock, 1973.

– *Discipline and Punish: The Birth of the Prison*. New York: Vintage, 1977.

– *The Order of Things*. 2nd ed. London and New York: Routledge, 2005.

Fretz, Eric. "P.T. Barnum's Theatrical Selfhood and the Nineteenth-Century Culture of Exhibition." In *Freakery*, edited by Rosemarie Garland-Thomson, 97–107. New York: New York University Press, 1996.

Frost, Linda. "Introduction: Peculiar Intimacies." In *Conjoined Twins in Black and White: The Lives of Millie-Christine McKoy and Daisy and Violet Hilton*, edited by Linda Frost, 3–39. Madison: University of Wisconsin Press, 2009.

– *Never One Nation: Freaks, Savages, and Whiteness in U.S. Popular Culture, 1850–1877*. Minneapolis: University of Minnesota Press, 2005.

Gallagher, Catherine, and Thomas Laqueur. "Introduction." In *The Making of the Modern Body: Sexuality and Society in the Nineteenth Century*, edited by

Catherine Gallagher and Thomas Laqueur, vii–xv. Berkeley: University of California Press, 1987.
Gardner, David. "Variety." In *Later Stages: Essays in Ontario Theatre from the First World War to the 1970s*, edited by Ann Saddlemyer and Richard Plant, 121–223. Toronto: University of Toronto Press, 1997.
Garland-Thomson, Rosemarie. *Extraordinary Bodies: Figuring Physical Disability in American Culture and Literature*. New York: Columbia University Press, 1997.
– ed. *Freakery: Cultural Spectacles of the Extraordinary Body*. New York: New York University Press, 1996.
– "Integrating Disability: Transforming Feminist Theory." *NWSA Journal* 14, no. 3 (Autumn 2002): 1–32.
– "Introduction: From Wonder to Error – A Genealogy of Freak Discourse in Modernity." In *Freakery: Cultural Spectacles of the Extraordinary Body*, edited by Rosemarie Garland-Thomson, 1–20. New York: New York University Press, 1996.
– "Making Freaks: Visual Rhetorics and the Spectacle of Julia Pastrana." In *Thinking the Limits of the Body*, edited by Jeffrey Jerome Cohen and Gail Weiss, 129–44. Albany: State University of New York Press, 2003.
– *Staring: How We Look*. New York: Oxford University Press, 2009.
Geller, Peter. *Northern Exposures: Photographing and Filming the Canadian North, 1920–1945*. Vancouver: University of British Columbia Press, 2004.
Gerber, David A. "The 'Careers' of People Exhibited in Freak Shows: The Problem of Volition and Valorization." In *Freakery*, edited by Rosemarie Garland-Thomson, 38–54. New York: New York University Press, 1996.
Gleason, Mona. *Normalizing the Ideal: Psychology, Schooling, and the Family in Postwar Canada*. Toronto: University of Toronto Press, 1999.
– "Size Matters: Medical Experts, Educations, and the Provision of Health Services to Children in Early to Mid Twentieth Century English Canada." In *Healing the World's Children: Interdisciplinary Perspectives on Child Health in the Twentieth Century*, edited by Cynthia Comacchio, Janet Golden, and George Weisz, 176–203. Montreal and Kingston: McGill-Queen's University Press, 2008.
– *Small Matters: Canadian Children in Sickness and Health, 1900–1940*. Montreal and Kingston: McGill-Queen's University Press, 2013.
Gold, Sarah E. "Millie-Christine McKoy and the American Freak Show: Race, Gender, and Freedom in the Postbellum Era, 1851–1912." *Berkeley Undergraduate Journal* 21, no. 1 (2010): 1–45.
Goldsack, Bob. *Johnny's Here: A History of the Johnny J. Jones Exposition*. Nashua, NH: Midway Museum Publications, 1990.

Gomall, Lucian. "The Feminist Pleasures of Coco Rico's Social Interventions." In *Art and the Artist in Society*, edited by José Jiménez-Justiniano, Elsa Luciano Feal, Jane Elizabeth Alberdeston, 119–32. Newcastle Upon Tyne: Cambridge Scholars Publishing, 2013.

Gray, James. *A Brand of Its Own: The Hundred Year History of the of the Calgary Exhibition and Stampede*. Saskatoon: Western Producer Prairie Books, 1985.

Grosz Elizabeth. *Volatile Bodies: Toward a Corporeal Feminism*. Indianapolis: Indiana University Press, 1994.

Hall, Kristin. "Selling Lysol as a Household Disinfectant in Interwar North America." In *Consuming Modernity: Gendered Behaviour and Consumerism before the Baby Boom*, edited by Cheryl Krasnick Warsh and Dan Malleck, 55–76. Vancouver: University of British Columbia Press, 2013.

Haller, Beth A. "Telethons." In *Encyclopedia of Disability*, edited by Gary L. Albrecht, 1545–7. Thousand Oaks, CA: Sage, 2006.

Harper, Kenn. *Give Me My Father's Body: The Life of Minik, The New York Eskimo*. Frobisher Bay: Blacklead Books, 1986.

Hartzman, Marc. *American Sideshow: An Encyclopedia of History's Most Wondrous and Curiously Strange Performers*. New York: Jeremy P. Tarcher/Penguin, 2005.

Heaman, Elsbeth. *The Inglorious Arts of Peace: Exhibitions in Canadian Society during the Nineteenth Century*. Toronto: University of Toronto Press, 1999.

Hornberger, Francine. *Carny Folk: The World's Weirdest Sideshow Acts*. New York: Citadel Press, 2004.

Howells, Richard, and Michael M. Chemers. "Midget Cities: Utopia, Utopianism, and the *Vor-schein* of the 'Freak' Show." *Disability Studies Quarterly* 25, no. 3 (Summer 2005). http://dsq-sds.org/article/view/579/756.

Iacovetta, Franca. *Gatekeepers: Reshaping Immigrant Lives in Cold War Canada*. Toronto: Between the Lines, 2006.

Iacovetta, Franca, and Wendy Mitchinson. *On the Case: Explorations in Social History*. Toronto: University of Toronto Press, 1998.

Jasen, Patricia. *Wild Things: Nature, Culture, and Tourism in Ontario, 1790–1914*. Toronto: University of Toronto Press, 1995.

Jones, David C. *Midways, Judges, and Smooth-Tongued Fakirs: The Illustrated Story of Country Fairs in the Prairie West*. Saskatoon: Western Producer Prairie Books, 1983.

Kasson, John F. *The Little Girl Who Fought the Depression: Shirley Temple and 1930s America*. New York: W.W. Norton, 2014.

Kelm, Mary Ellen. *A Wilder West: Rodeo in Western Canada*. Vancouver: University of British Columbia Press, 2012.

Kerchy, Anna, and Andrea Zittlau. "Introduction." In *Exploring the Cultural History of Continental European Freak Shows and "Enfreakment*," ed. Anna Kerchy and Andrea Zittlau, 1–19. Newcastle upon Tyne: Cambridge Scholars Publishing, 2012.

Kibler, M. Alison. "Performance and Display." In *A Companion to American Cultural History*, edited by Karen Halttunen, 311–26. Malden, MA: Blackwell, 2008.

Kidd, C. "Inventing the 'Pygmy': Representing the 'Other,' Presenting the 'Self.'" *History and Anthropology* 20, no. 4 (December 2009): 395–418.

Kochanek, Lisa. "Reframing the Freak: From Sideshow to Science." *Victorian Periodicals Review* 30, no. 3 (1997): 227–43.

Koptie, Steve. "After This, Nothing Happened: Indigenous Academic Writing and Chickadee Peoples' Words." *First Peoples Child and Family Review* 4, no. 2 (2 November 2009): 144–51.

LaMonde, Yvan. *The Social History of Ideas in Quebec, 1760–1896*. Translated by Phyllis Aronoff and Howard Scott. Montreal and Kingston: McGill-Queen's University Press, 2013.

Larsen, Barbara. "Introduction." In *The Art of Evolution: Darwin, Darwinisms, and Visual Culture*, edited by Barbara Larsen and Fae Brauer, 1–17. Lebanon, NH: Dartmouth College Press, 2009.

Lears, T. Jackson. *No Place of Grace: Antimodernism and the Transformation of American Culture, 1880–1920*. Chicago: University of Chicago Press, 1991.

Lenton-Young, Gerald. "Variety Theatre." In *Early Stages: Theatre in Ontario, 1800–1914*, edited by Ann Saddlemyer, 166–213. Toronto: University of Toronto Press, 1990.

Lindfors, Bernth. *Africans on Stage: Studies in Ethnological Show Business*. Bloomington: Indiana University Press, 1999.

– "Hottentot, Bushman, Kaffir: Taxonomic Tendencies in Nineteenth-Century Racial Iconography." *Nordic Journal of African Studies* 5, no. 2 (1996): 1–28.

Little, Margaret. *No Car, No Radio, No Liquor Permit: The Moral Regulation of Single Mothers in Ontario, 1920–1996*. Toronto: Oxford University Press, 1998.

Loo, Tina. "Dan Cranmer's Potlatch: Law as Coercion, Symbol, and Rhetoric in British Columbia." *Canadian Historical Review* 73, no. 2 (1992): 125–65.

Loo, Tina, and Carolyn Strange. "The Travelling Show Menace: Contested Regulation in Turn-of-the-Century Ontario." *Law and Society Review* 29, no. 4 (1995): 639–67.

– *Making Good: Law and Moral Regulation in Canada, 1867–1939*. Toronto: University of Toronto Press, 1997.

MacDougall, Heather. *Activists and Advocates: Toronto's Health Department, 1883–1983*. Toronto: Dundurn Press, 1990.

MacEwan, Grant. *Agriculture on Parade: The Story of the Fairs and Exhibitions of Western Canada*. Toronto: Thomas Nelson and Sons, 1950.

Macy, Beth. *Truevine: Two Brothers, A Mother's Quest, and a Kidnapping: A True Story of the Jim Crow South*. New York: Little, Brown, 2016.

Mannix, Daniel. *Freaks: We Who Are Not as Others*. New York: Juno Books, 1999.

Martel, Marcel. *Canada the Good: A Short History of Vice since 1500*. Waterloo, ON: Wilfrid Laurier University Press, 2014.

Martell, Joanne. *Millie-Christine: Fearfully and Wonderfully Made*. Winston-Salem: John F. Blair, 2000.

Maynes, Mary Jo. "Age as a Category of Historical Analysis: History, Agency, and Narratives of Childhood." *Journal of the History of Childhood and Youth* 1, no. 1 (Winter 2008): 114–24.

McClintock, Anne. *Imperial Leather: Race, Gender and Sexuality in the Colonial Contest*. New York and London: Routledge, 1995.

McHold, Heather. "Even as You and I: Freak Shows and Lay Discourse on Spectacular Deformity." In *Victorian Freaks: The Social Context of Freakery in Britain*, edited by Marlene Tromp, 21–36. Columbus: Ohio University Press, 2008.

McKennon, Joe. *A Pictorial History of the American Carnival*, vols 1 and 2. Sarasota: Carnival Publishers of Sarasota: 1972.

McLaren, Angus. *Our Own Master Race: Eugenics in Canada, 1885–1945*. Toronto: McClelland and Stewart, 1990.

McMaster, Lindsey. *Working Girls in the West: Representations of Wage-Earning Women*. Vancouver: University of British Columbia Press, 2008.

McNally, Michael David. "The Indian Passion Play: Contesting the Real Indian in Song of Hiawatha Pageants, 1901–1965." *American Quarterly* 58, no. 1 (March 2006): 105–36.

McRuer, Robert. *Crip Theory: Cultural Signs of Disability and Queerness*. New York: New York University Press, 2006.

Mennill, Sally, and Veronica Strong-Boag. "Identifying Victims: Child Abuse and Death in Canadian Families" *Canadian Bulletin of Medical History* 25, no. 2 (2008): 311–33.

Merish, Lori. "Cuteness and Commodity Aesthetics: Tom Thumb and Shirley Temple." In *Freakery: Cultural Spectacles of the Extraordinary Body*, edited by Rosemarie Garland-Thomson, 185–203. New York: New York University Press, 1996.

Minnett, Valerie. "Public Body, Private Health: *Mediscope*, the Transparent Woman, and Medical Authority, 1959." In *Contesting Bodies and Nation in Canadian History*, edited by Patrizia Gentile and Jane Nicholas, 286–304. Toronto: University of Toronto Press, 2013.

Miron, Janet. *Prisons, Asylums, and the Public: Institutional Visiting in the Nineteenth Century*. Toronto: University of Toronto Press, 2010.

Mitchinson, Wendy. *Body Failure: Medical Views of Women, 1900–1950*. Toronto: University of Toronto Press, 2013.

– *Giving Birth in Canada, 1900–1950*. Toronto: University of Toronto Press, 2002.

– *The Nature of Their Bodies: Women and Their Doctors in Victorian Canada*. Toronto: University of Toronto Press, 1991.

Morton, Suzanne. *At Odds: Gambling and Canadians, 1919–1969*. Toronto: University of Toronto Press, 2003.

– *Ideal Surroundings: Domestic Life in a Working-Class Suburb in the 1920s*. Toronto: University of Toronto Press, 1995.

Moss, Mark. *Manliness and Militarism: Educating Young Boys in Ontario for War*. Don Mills: Oxford University Press, 2001.

Myers, Tamara. *Caught: Montreal's Modern Girls and the Law, 1869–1945*. Toronto: University of Toronto Press, 2006.

– "The Voluntary Delinquent: Parents, Daughters, and the Montreal Juvenile Delinquents' Court, 1918." *Canadian Historical Review* 80, no. 2 (June 1999): 242–68.

Nasaw, David. *Going Out: The Rise and Fall of Public Amusements*. New York: Basic Books, 1993.

Nicholas, Jane. "'A Figure of a Nude Woman': Art, Popular Culture, and Modernity at the Canadian National Exhibition, 1927." *Histoire sociale / Social History* 41, no. 82 (November 2008): 313–44.

– "A Debt to the Dead? Ethics, Photography, History and the Study of Freakery." *Histoire sociale / Social History* 47, no. 93 (May 2014): 141–57.

"Scales of Manliness: Masculinity and Disability in the Displays of Little People as Freaks in Ontario, 1900–1950s." In *Masculinities in Canadian History*, edited by Robert Rutherdale and Peter Gossage. Vancouver: University of British Columbia Press, forthcoming.

– *The Modern Girl: Feminine Modernities, the Body, and Commodities in the 1920s*. Toronto: University of Toronto Press, 2014.

Nickell, Joe. *Secrets of the Sideshows*. Lexington: University Press of Kentucky, 2005.

Noël, Françoise. *Family and Community Life in Northeastern Ontario: The Interwar Years*. Montreal and Kingston: McGill-Queen's University Press, 2009.

– "Old Home Week Celebrations as Tourism Promotion and Commemoration: North Bay, Ontario, 1925 and 1935." *Urban History Review / Revue d'histoire urbaine* 37, no 1 (Fall 2008): 36–47.

O'Connor, Erin. *Raw Material: Producing Pathology in Victorian Culture*. Durham, NC: Duke University Press, 2000.

Opp, James. *The Lord for the Body: Religion, Medicine, and Protestant Faith Healing in Canada, 1880–1930.* Montreal and Kingston: McGill-Queen's University Press, 2005.

Ostherr, Kirsten. *Medical Visions: Producing the Patient Through Film, Television, and Imaging Technologies.* Oxford: Oxford University Press, 2013.

Palmer, Bryan. *Working Class Experience: Rethinking the History of Canadian Labour, 1800–1991.* 2nd ed. Toronto: McClelland and Stewart, 1992.

Parr, Joy. *Domestic Goods: The Material, the Moral and the Economic in the Postwar Years.* Toronto: University of Toronto Press, 1999.

– *Labouring Children: British Immigrant Apprentices to Canada, 1869–1924.* Montreal and Kingston: McGill-Queen's University Press, 1980.

Peacock, Shane. "Africa Meets the Great Farini." In *Africans on Stage: Studies in Ethnological Show Business*, edited by B. Lindfors, 81–106. Bloomington: Indiana University Press, 1999.

– *The Great Farini: The High-Wire Life of William Hunt.* Toronto: Viking, 1995.

Pearson, Susan J. "'Infantile Specimens': Showing Babies in Nineteenth-Century America." *Journal of Social History* 42, no. 2 (Winter 2008): 341–70.

Peiss, Kathy. *Cheap Amusements: Working Women and Leisure in Turn-of-the-Century New York.* Philadelphia: Temple University Press, 1986.

Penny Light, Tracy. "Consumer Culture and the Medicalization of Women's Roles in Canada, 1919–39." In *Consuming Modernity: Gendered Behaviour and Consumerism before the Baby Boom*, edited by Cheryl Krasnick Warsh and Dan Malleck, 34–54. Vancouver: University of British Columbia Press, 2013.

Pernick, Martin S. *The Black Stork: Eugenics and the Death of "Defective" Babies in American Medicine and Motion Pictures since 1915.* New York: Oxford University Press, 1996.

Piva, Michael. *The Conditions of the Working Class in Toronto, 1900–1921.* Ottawa: University of Ottawa Press, 1979.

Plowden, Gene. *Circus Press Agent: The Life and Times of Roland Butler.* Caldwell, ID: Caxton Printers, 1984.

Poignant, Rosalyn. *Professional Savages: Captive Lives and Western Spectacle.* New Haven, CT: Yale University Press, 2004.

Porter, Roy. *Flesh in the Age of Reason: The Modern Foundations of Body and Soul.* New York: W.W. Norton, 2003.

Radforth, Ian. *Royal Spectacle: The 1860 Visit of the Prince of Wales to Canada and the United States.* Toronto: University of Toronto Press, 2004.

Raibmon, Paige. "Theatres of Contact: The Kwakwaka'wakw Meet Colonialism in British Columbia and at the Chicago's World's Fair." *Canadian Historical Review* 81, no. 2 (June 2000): 157–90.

Read, Janet, and Luke Clements. "Demonstrably Awful: The Right to Life and the Selective Non-Treatment of Disabled Babies and Young Children." In *Disabled People and the Right to Life: The Protection and Violation of Disabled People's Most Basic Human Rights*, edited by Luke Clements and Janet Read, 148–75. New York and London: Routledge, 2008.

Reaume, Geoffrey. "Not Profits, Just a Pittance: Work, Compensation, and People Defined as Mentally Disabled in Ontario, 1964–1990." In *Mental Retardation in America: A Historical Reader*, edited by S. Noll and J.W. Trent, 466–93. New York: New York University Press, 2004.

– *Remembrance of Patients Past: Patient Life at the Toronto Hospital for the Insane, 1870–1940*. Toronto: University of Toronto Press, 2000.

Reid-Walsh, Jacqueline, and Claudia Mitchell. "Mapping a Canadian Girlhood Historically through Dolls and Doll-Play." In *Depicting Canada's Children*, edited by Loren Lerner, 109–29. Waterloo, ON: Wilfrid Laurier University Press, 2009.

Reiss, Benjamin. "P.T. Barnum, Joice Heth and Antebellum Spectacles of Race." *American Quarterly* 51, no. 1 (March 1999): 78–107.

– *The Showman and the Slave: Race, Death, and Memory in Barnum's America*. Cambridge, MA: Harvard University Press, 2001.

Rooke, Patricia T., and R.L. Schnell. *Discarding the Asylum: From Child Rescue to the Welfare State in English-Canada, 1800–1950*. Latham, MD: University Press of America, 1983.

Ross, Becki L. *Burlesque West: Showgirls, Sex, and Sin in Postwar Vancouver*. Toronto: University of Toronto Press, 2009.

Rumble, Walker. "A Showdown of 'Swifts': Women Compositors, Dime Museums, and the Boston Typesetting Races of 1886." *New England Quarterly* 71, no. 4 (December 1998): 615–28.

Rusid, Max. *Sideshow: Photo Album of Human Oddities*. New York: Amjon Publishers, 1975.

Russett, Cynthia Eagle. *Sexual Science: The Victorian Construction of Womanhood*. Cambridge, MA: Harvard University Press 1989.

Rutherford, Paul. "Made in America: The Problem of Mass Culture in Canada." In *The Beaver Bites Back: American Popular Culture in Canada*, edited by David H. Flaherty and Frank E. Manning, 260–80. Montreal and Kingston: McGill-Queen's University Press, 1993.

Rutty, Christopher J. "The Middle Class Plague: Epidemic Polio and the Canadian State." *Canadian Bulletin of Medical History* 13, no. 2 (1996): 277–314.

Rydell, Robert. *All the World's a Fair: Visions of Empire at American International Expositions, 1876–1916*. Chicago: University of Chicago Press, 1987.

– *World of Fairs: The Century-of-Progress Expositions.* Chicago: University of Chicago Press, 1993.
Samuels, Ellen. "Examining Millie and Christine McKoy: Where Enslavement and Enfreakment Meet." *Signs* 37, no. 1 (Autumn 2011): 53–81.
Sangster, Joan. *Regulating Girls and Women: Sexuality, Family, and the Law in Ontario, 1920–1960.* Don Mills, ON: Oxford University Press, 2001.
Saxon, A.H. *P.T. Barnum: The Legend and the Man.* New York: Columbia University Press, 1989.
Schweik, Susan M. *The Ugly Laws: Disability in Public.* New York: New York University Press, 2009.
Scott, Guy. *Country Fairs in Canada.* Markham, ON: Fitzhenry and Whiteside, 2005.
Scott, Guy. *A Fair Share: A History of Agricultural Societies and Fairs in Ontario, 1792–1992.* Peterborough: Ontario Association of Agricultural Societies, 1992.
Semonin, Paul. "Monsters in the Marketplace." In *Freakery*, edited by Rosemarie Garland-Thomson, 69–81. New York: New York University Press, 1996.
Shakespeare, Tom. *Disability Rights and Wrongs.* New York and London: Routledge, 2006.
Shildrick, Margarit. *Embodying the Monster: Encounters with the Vulnerable Self.* Thousand Oaks, CA: Sage, 2002.
Shuttleworth, Russell, Nikki Wedgwood, and Nathan J. Wilson. "The Dilemma of Disabled Masculinity." *Men and Masculinities* 15, no. 2 (June 2012): 174–94.
Simmons, Harvey G. *From Asylum to Welfare: The Evolution of Mental Retardation Policy in Ontario from 1831–1980.* Downsview, ON: National Institute on Mental Retardation, 1982.
Skal, David J., and Elias Savada. *Dark Carnival: The Secret World of Tod Browning – Hollywood's Master of the Macabre.* New York: Anchor Books, 1995.
Soucy, Jean-Yves. *Family Secrets: The Dionne Quintuplets' Autobiography.* New York: Berkley Books, 1997.
Stallybrass, Peter, and Allon White. *The Politics and Poetics of Transgression.* London: Methuen, 1986.
Stammberger, Birgit. "Monstrous Bodies in Rudolf Vichow's Medical Collection in Nineteenth-Century Germany." In *Exploring the Cultural History of Continental European Freak Shows and "Enfreakment,"* edited by Anna Kérchy and Andrea Zittlau, 129–49. Newcastle Upon Tyne: Cambridge Scholars Publishing, 2012.

Stencell, A.W. *Circus and Carnival Ballyhoo: Sideshow Freaks, Jabbers, and Blade Box Queens.* Toronto: ECW Press, 2010.
– *Girl Show: Into the Canvas World of Bump and Grind.* Toronto: ECW Press, 1999.
Stern, Alexandra Minna. "Beauty Is Not Always Better: Perfect Babies and the Tyranny of Paediatric Norms." *Patterns of Prejudice* 36, no. 1 (2002): 68–78.
Stern, Rebecca. "Our Bear Women, Ourselves: Affiliating with Julia Pastrana." In *Victorian Freaks: The Social Context of Freakery in Britain*, edited by Marlene Tromp, 200–34. Columbus: Ohio University Press, 2008.
Stewart, Susan. *On Longing: Narratives of the Miniature, the Gigantic, the Souvenir, the Collection.* Baltimore: Johns Hopkins University Press, 1984.
Strange, Carolyn. *Toronto's Girl Problem: The Perils and Pleasures of the City, 1880–1930.* Toronto: University of Toronto Press, 1995.
Strong-Boag, Veronica. "'Children of Adversity': Disabilities and Child Welfare in Canada from the Nineteenth to the Twenty-First Century." *Journal of Family History* 32, no. 4 (October 2007): 413–32.
– *Finding Families, Finding Ourselves: English Canada Confronts Adoption from the 19th Century to the 1990s.* Toronto: Oxford University Press, 2006.
– "'Forgotten People of all the Forgotten': Children with Disabilities in English Canada from the Nineteenth Century to the New Millennium." In *Lost Kids: Vulnerable Children and Youth in Twentieth-Century Canada and the United States*, edited by Mona Gleason, Tamara Myers, Leslie Paris, and Veronica Strong-Boag, 33–50. Vancouver: University of British Columbia Press, 2010.
– *Fostering Nation? Canada Confronts Its History of Childhood Disadvantage.* Waterloo, ON: Wilfrid Laurier University Press, 2011.
– "Intruders in the Nursery: Childcare Professionals Reshape the Years from One to Five, 1920–1940." In *Childhood and the Family in Canadian History*, edited by Joy Parr, 160–78. Toronto: McClelland and Stewart, 1982.
– "Today's Child: Preparing for the 'Just Society' One Family at a Time." *Canadian Historical Review* 86, no. 4 (December 2005): 673–99.
Struthers, James. *The Limits of Affluence: Welfare in Ontario, 1920–1970.* Toronto: University of Toronto Press, 1994.
Sturm, John. "Detroit's Wonderland Dime Musee." *Chronicle: The Quarterly Magazine of the Historical Society of Michigan* 24, no. 3 (1988): 4–14.
Sutherland, Neil. *Growing Up: Childhood in English Canada from the Great War to the Age of Television.* Toronto: University of Toronto Press, 1997.
– "'We always had things to do': The Paid and Unpaid Work of Anglophone Children between the 1920s and the 1960s." *Labour/Le Travail* 25 (Spring 1990): 105–41.
Taylor, J. Garth. "An Eskimo Abroad, 1880: His Diary and Death" *Canadian Geographic*, October/November 1981, 38–43.

Thompson, John Herd, with Allen Seager. *Canada 1922–1939: Decades of Discord*. Toronto: McClelland and Stewart, 1986.

Thomson, Gerald E. "'A Baby Show Means Work in the Hardest Sense': The Better Baby Contests of the Vancouver and New Westminster Local Councils of Women, 1913–1929." *BC Studies* 128 (Winter 2000–1): 5–36.

Thurston, John. "Scenes from the Midway: One Hundred Years of Outdoor Amusement." Unpublished manuscript.

Tippet, Maria. *Making Culture: English-Canadian Institutions and the Arts before the Massey Commission*. Toronto: University of Toronto Press, 1990.

Titchkosky, Tanya. *Reading and Writing Disability Differently: The Textured Life of Embodiment*. Toronto: University of Toronto Press, 2007.

Tromp, Marlene, with Karyn Valerius. "Introduction: Toward Situating the Victorian Freak." In *Victorian Freaks: The Social Context of Freakery in Britain*, edited by Marlene Tromp, 1–18. Columbus: Ohio University Press, 2008.

Valverde, Mariana. *The Age of Light, Soap, and Water: Moral Reform in English Canada, 1885–1925*. 2nd ed. Toronto: University of Toronto Press, 2008.

– "Representing Childhood: The Multiple Fathers of the Dionne Quintuplets." In *Regulating Womanhood: Historical Essays on Marriage, Motherhood and Sexuality*, edited by Carol Smart, 119–46. New York and London: Routledge, 1993.

Vaughan, Christopher A. "Ogling Igorots: The Politics and Commerce of Exhibiting Cultural Otherness, 1898–1913." In *Freakery: Cultural Spectacles of the Extraordinary Body*, edited by Rosemarie Garland-Thomson, 219–33. New York: New York University Press, 1996.

Vipond, Mary. "Canadian Nationalism and the Plight of Canadian Magazines in the 1920s." *Canadian Historical Review* 58, no. 1 (March 1977): 43–65.

Walden, Keith. *Becoming Modern in Toronto: The Industrial Exhibition and the Shaping of a Late Victorian Culture*. Toronto: University of Toronto Press, 1997.

Walker, Barrington. "Following the North Star: Black Canadians, IQ Testing, and Biopolitics in the Work of H.A. Tanser, 1939–2008." In *Contesting Bodies and Nation in Canadian History*, edited by Patrizia Gentile and Jane Nicholas, 56–64. Toronto: University of Toronto Press, 2013.

Warsh, Cheryl Krasnick. *Prescribed Norms: Women and Health in Canada and the United States since 1800*. Toronto: University of Toronto Press, 2010.

– "Vim, Vigour, and Vitality: 'Power' Foods for Kids in Canadian Popular Magazines, 1914–1954." In *Edible Histories, Cultural Politics: Towards a Canadian Food History*, ed. Franca Iacovetta, Valerie J. Korinek, and Marlene Epp, 387–408. Toronto: University of Toronto Press, 2012.

West, Patsy. *The Enduring Seminoles: From Alligator Wrestling to Ecotourism*. Gainesville: University Press of Florida, 1998.

Wetherell, Donald G., with Irene Kmet. *Useful Pleasures: The Shaping of Leisure in Alberta, 1896–1945*. Regina, SK: Canadian Plains Research Center, 1991.

Widen, Larry. "Milwaukee's Dime Museum." *Milwaukee History* 8, no. 1 (1985): 24–34.

Wilson, Dudley. *Signs and Portents: Monstrous Births from the Middle Ages to the Enlightenment*. London and New York: Routledge, 1993.

Wilson, Philip K. "Eighteenth-Century 'Monsters' and Nineteenth-Century 'Freaks': Reading the Maternally Marked Child." *Literature and Medicine* 21, no. 1 (2002): 1–25.

Wright, Cynthia. "'Feminine Trifles of Vast Importance': Writing Gender into the History of Consumption." In *Gender Conflicts: New Essays in Women's History*, edited by Franca Iacovetta and Mariana Valverde, 229–60. Toronto: University of Toronto Press, 1992.

– "They were five: The Dionne Quintuplets Revisited." *Journal of Canadian Studies* 29, no. 4 (Winter 1994): 5–10.

Wright, Donald. *Downs: The History of Disability*. Oxford: Oxford University Press, 2011.

Zelizer, Viviana A. *Pricing the Priceless Child: The Changing Social Value of Children*. New York: Basic Books, 1985.

Zittlau, Andrea. "Enfreakment and German Medical Collections." In *Exploring the Cultural History of Continental European Freak Shows and "Enfreakment,"* edited by Anna Kérchy and Andrea Zittlau, 129–49. Newcastle Upon Tyne: Cambridge Scholars Publishing, 2012.

Internet Sites

Historical information on the E.J. Casey Shows has been documented online at the Virtual Museum:

"E.J. Casey Shows Carnival Circuit Schedule." *E.J. Casey: From Solider to Showman*, virtual exhibit by NACMA. http://www.virtualmuseum.ca/sgc-cms/histoires_de_chez_nous-community_memories/pm_v2.php?id=record_detail&fl=0&lg=English&ex=00000843&hs=0&rd=248708#

Some information on the CNE's history was formally available online. The site is no longer available. http://www.cnearchives.com.

Information about the professional organization The Showmen's League is available on two sites: http://www.showmensleague.org and http://www.showmensleague.ca.

Information on the Western Fairs Association: http://www.westernfairs.org/default.aspx.

Information on "conjoined twins" framed by a biomedical understanding of the body is available at: http://www.umm.edu/conjoined_twins/facts.htm.

Information on historical and contemporary terminology regarding people of small stature is accessible though the Little People of America organization: http://www.lpaonline.org/faq-#Definition.

A brief history of the Conklin shows is available at: http://www.conklinshows.com.

Information about the history of the Conklin shows, including old television episodes were formerly available through the CBC archives. http://www.cbc.ca/archives/.

Information on microcephaly framed by a biomedical understanding of the body is available at: http://www.mayoclinic.org/diseases-conditions/microcephaly/basics/definition/con-20034823.

Fiction

Grealy, Lucy. *Autobiography of a Face*. New York: Houghton Mifflin, 1994.
Susan Swan, *The Biggest Modern Woman in the World*. Toronto: LO&D, 1983.

Film

Browning, Tod. *Freaks*. Metro-Goldwyn-Mayer, 1932.

Index

Note: Spelling of names in carnival sources is inconsistent. The most common spellings have been used throughout the text and the index for ease of identification.

Abyssian Pigmies, 142–3
acceptance within carnival community, 96–7, 103–5
Adams, Rachel, 16, 33
admission prices, 48
"adoption," sideshow, 161–2
agricultural fairs: about, 58; establishment of own midways, 38; as freak show venue, 35; gambling exemption for, 57
Al G. Barnes Circus: in Saskatoon, 218n28; in Vancouver, 156
Alberta: carnival regulation in, 70; public inquiry into bribery, 72–3
Alexander, Sam (sideshow owner), 3, 16, 66, 67, 106, 237n156
Alter, Helen (show woman), 108
Alter, Lew (showman), 108
American culture, concern over, 51–2, 55
American Museum of Natural History, 31
Amusements of America (1966), 76

Anomalies and Curiosities of Medicine (Gould and Pyle), 120–1, 242m48
anthropology. *See* ethnological shows
antisemitism, 53
Appelbaum, Stanley, 38
asylum tourism (19th-century), 36
"Aztec Children," 29

baby contests, 184–5, 186–90
Baby Peggy (Peggy-Jean Montgomery), 150, 187, 258n58
Bacon, Francis, 25
Badgett quadruplets, 185–6
Baillargeon, Denyse, on Dionne quintuplets, 198
Bakner, Andrew J., on freak show employment, 113–14
Balcom, Karen, on trafficking of babies, 160
bans and protests, 49–58
Barnes, Al G. (showman): on bribes, 72; on Muse brothers case, 251n43. *See also* Al G. Barnes Circus

Barnum, P.T., 27–9, 33–4; Tom Thumb and, 149, 178–9
Barnum's American Museum, influence of, 33–7, 40
Bartholomew Fair, 23
Bartman, Sarah ("Hottentot Venus"), 30, 214n51
Bates, A.W., 24
Bayly, Edward (deputy attorney general), 55
Beattie, H. ("A Case of Anencephalous Monster"), 124
beauty culture, 17, 112–13, 180–1, 184. *See also* "ugly laws"; baby contests; cuteness
Beckman and Gerety Carnival, 138
Bee, F.H. Jr, on carnival business practices, 83
beef-trust revues, 107, 235n126
Bejano, Emmitt ("Alligator-Skinned Man"), 150, 161
Bejano, Johnny (showman), 161
Belisle, Donica, 95
Bell, Edith (wife of Patty Conklin), 228n10
Belleville, Ontario, 55, 66, 97
Belmont Park (Montreal), 66, 106
Bennett, Tony, 9, 25, 26, 31, 41
Bergen, Frank (World of Mirth owner), 80, 82
Bernard and Barry Shows of Canada, 139
Bertram Mills shows (England), 106, 128–9
Best, Dick (sideshow operator), 139
Bevans, Mary Ann ("Ugliest Woman in the World"), 17, 112–13
Bill Lynch Shows, 44
Billboard, advertisements in, 61, 108, 166

Billboard, articles in: 1930s, on future of carnivals, 82; on baby shows, 188; on banning carnivals, 47; on bans and protests, 55–7; on carnival's educational value, 155; on circuit bidding results, 60–1; on Dionne family, 192; on effect of war, 86; on effects of weather, 62; on fair association hypocrisy, 63; on financial success of carnivals, 58–9; on Johnny J. Jones midgets, 180; on regulation of carnivals, 42; on taxes and tarriffs, 69, 70; on touring, 89–90, 91
Billboard, want ads in, 68, 92–3, 105–6, 107
Birtle, Manitoba, 124
Bland-Sutton, Sir John: on conjoined twins, 128, 149
Blazek, Rosa and Josepha (conjoined twins), 121
Boas, Franz, 30–1
Bob Hermine's Midgets, 183
Bob Morton Circus, 69
body parts, display of, 214n51
Bogdan, Robert (sociologist): on freak presentation strategies, 29, 117, 138; *Freak Show* (book), 15; on Midway Plaisance, 38; on viewing disability, 14
Border Cities Star (Windsor, Ontario), on Dionne quintuplets, 192
Bourassa family (St Barnabe, Quebec), 186
Boyd, A.B. (police officer), 99
Brandon Agricultural Exhibition, 76, 154
Brandon, Manitoba: deportation case in, 75–6; opposition to carnivals in, 52–3; on tour route, 90

Brantford Expositor, 86
Brantford, Ontario, 51, 53, 55, 89–90, 99
Brenner, Josephine (fire eater), 101
bribes, 53, 71–3, 217–18n20
British Columbia Amusements Company, 63–4
British Medical Association Journal, 124, 129, 131
Brown and Dyer Shows, 99–100
Brown, Mrs G. (pseudonym, mother of runaway), 99–100
Browning Amusement Company (Salem, Oregon), 64–5
Browning, Tod (filmmaker), 136, 203, 204
Brydon, Ray Marsh, 67
Buddy, Grant (child fairgoer), 154

cabinets of curiosities, 24–5, 33
Calgary: Conklin at Stampede, 62; police bribes in, 72
Callander, Ontario. *See* Dionne quintuplets
Canada Carnival Company, 106
"Canada's Fattest Boy," 69
Canadian Council for Crippled Children and Adults, 159, 173
Canadian Council on Child Welfare, 159, 187
Canadian Lakehead Exhibition (Fort William, Ontario), 98
Canadian Medical Association Journal, on anomalies, 122, 124
Canadian National Exhibition: attendance during polio epidemic, 67; Conklin Shows at, 65–6; Grace McDaniels at, 113; Johnny J. Jones Freak Show at, *45*; Second World War relocation of, 86; "Ubangi savages" at, *143*; World's Fair Freaks at, *39*
Canadian National Railway, 89, 94
Canadian Victory Shows, 68–9
"Captured by Cannibals" (1919 show), 22
carnies. *See* carnival workers
Carnival Managers Association of America, 50
carnival workers, *85*: seasonal and short-term, 101; violence among, 98–9; work ethic of, 95–6
carnivalesque gaze, 11
carnivals: as businesses, 43, 60, 81–8; compared with circuses, 35, 48; as family, 81–82, 96–9, 108; as fundraisers, 68–9; locals and, 97; opposition to, 49–58; personified as feminine, 81
Carrington, H. (Army and Navy Veterans), 68
Cartier Centenary Celebration, 106
Cartier, Jacques, 30
Casey, E.J. *See* E.J. Casey Shows
censorship, 42, 70, 72. *See also* moral and social reform
Centennial Exposition (Philadelphia, 1876), 37
Central Canada Exhibition, 62, 76, 82, 155
Century of Progress Exposition (Chicago), 137–8, 174, 189, 191
"Century of the Child," 151–2
charitable profit-sharing, 68–9
Chatham, Ontario, 55, 140
Chautauqua, 42
Chicago: Century of Progress Exposition, 137–8, 174, 189, 191; Elks' partnerships with carnivals, 68; Midway Plaisance, 37–8;

World's Columbian Exposition (1893), 30–1, 37–8, 120
child labour, 156–8, 167–8
child welfare discourse: child welfare institutions, 187; sociocultural conditions and, 157–8, 169; vis-à-vis child performers, 17, 170
child-friendly zones, at Conklin fairs, 155–6
childhood, modern concept of, 153–4, 174
children: as carnival attendees, 151–7, *152*; carnival pricing for, 48, 149, 155; as freak show workers, 157–66, *152*; newsboys and orphans, 156–7. *See also* youth culture
children with disabilities: display of, 24; offering of by parents and others, 162–6, 169–70, 185–6; trafficking of, 159–61, 251n43; welfare systems and, 158–9, 162
children, runaway, 99–101
Childrens' Day (CNE), 67
Chisholm, William (James Fisher Company Ltd.), 57
Christy, Jim (*Globe and Mail*), on demise of the midway, 201
church opposition to carnivals, 73–4. *See also* moral and social reform
circuits, 59–62
Circus Saints and Sinners Club, 196, 197
circuses: Clyde Beatty Circus, 35; compared with carnivals, 35, 48. *See also* Coop and Lent Circus; James Patterson Trained Wild Animal Show and Gollmar Brothers Circus; Ringling Brothers
Clarke, Nic, on childhood disability, 123, 133
clinical gaze, 11, 134–5
Clyde Beatty Circus, 35
Coates, Kenneth, 76
Col. Hope's "Freaks of Nature," 69
Comacchio, Cynthia (historian), 151–2
Coney Island: baby show at, 189; midget show at, 179
Congress of Fat People, 107; Johnny J. Jones shows, *45*; S.W. Brundage, 107
Congress of Freaks (Ringling & Barnum and Bailey), 126
Conklin and Garrett Shows, 156, 228n10
Conklin Shows: accusations of bribery against, 217–18n20; awarded C-class circuits, 61; history of, 43–4, 216n6, 235n125; midget shows at, 180; response to moral scrutiny, 47
Conklin Shows (1920s), circuits, 61
Conklin Shows (1930s): CNE contract, 61, 65–6; setback in Hamilton, 61
Conklin Shows (1940s): censors in Quebec City, 72; CNE contract, 66; "pinheads" at, 141; public relations, 66, 84–7; setback in Calgary, 61; size of, 94; subcontracting of sideshows, 66–7
Conklin Shows (1970s), Conklin's Antique Carnival, 202
Conklin, Frank: about, 80, 228n9, 228n10; on carnivals' benefiting communities, 84

Conklin, Jim (Sr), 228n9, 228n10
Conklin, Patty ("King of the Carnival"): about, 48, 80, 222n78, 227–8n8, 228n9, 228n10, 230n40; attempts to display Dionne quintuplets, 65–6; awarded long-term contracts, 65–6; on Ernie Defort, 169; "Patty Conklin's code," 87
consumer culture: cuteness and, 175, 176–7; emergence of, 49, 153–4; exhibitionary complex and, 203–4; influence on carnivals, 40, 77, 150, 155, 175, 200
consumer gaze, 11, 134
contracts: between carnivals and independent sideshows, 65–8; between local operators and carnivals, 62–5; between sideshow owners and performers, 107 (*see also* income, of sideshow performers)
Coop and Lent Circus, 88–9; 1916 tour map, *89*
Cooper, Roy (showman), 96
corpses, display of, 24–5, 28, 242n48
Couney, Martin (physician), 189–90
Country Gentleman, The (magazine), 57
Croll, David (Ontario minister of public welfare), 65–6, 192
cross-border travel: along tour routes, 90–1; objections to, 55; personnel issues, 98–9; racialization in, 111; regulation of, 69–70, 73–7
Cross, Gary, 176, 179–80
Crystal Beach (Fort Erie), 66
Cummings, Isabel (secretary to minister of agriculture), 57

cuteness, 176–7, 199–200
Cuvier, Georges, 30

Dafoe, Dr Allan, 190, 192–3, 195–6, *197*
Darling of New York, The (film), 187
Darwin, Charles, 32, 122
Darwinism, 246n115
Darwinism, social, 122
Davis, Hiram and Barney (Waino and Plutano, "Wild Men of Borneo"), 37, 160
Davis, Lennard, 28–9, 103, 119, 148
de Kiriline, Louise (Dionne quintuplets' nurse), on Dr Allan Dafoe, 195–6
de Leon, Jose ("Armless Wonder"), 139
deception: in ethnological shows, 29, 33, 109–11, 141–8; fake freak show performers, 108–9; Feejee Mermaid, 28; in medically themed shows, 138; through exoticism and aggrandizing, 117; in midget shows, 178–9, 182
Defort, Ernie ("Ernie-Len"), 137, 166–71, *167*
dehumanization of sideshow performers: disabled performers, 102–3; Inuit performers, 145; microcephalic performers, 112, 141; racialized Others, 29, 32, 142–3, *143*
de-institutionalization, 105
Dennett, Andrea Stulman (historian), 16, 34
Department of Immigration and Colonization, 44–5, 74–5, 112. *See also* cross-border travel
deportation of carnival employees, 75–6

Depression, effects of, 46–7, 92–3, 95, 109–10, 160, 167–8, 190, 199
Des monstres et des prodigies (Ambroise Paré), 24
deviations from the norm, Quetelet on, 119–120
difference, categorization of, 31–3
dime museums, 33–5, 106
Dionne quintuplets, 174–5, 190–8, *194*, 260n84, 261n103; Chicago Century of Progress Exposition and, 191; Conklin and, 65–6; New York World's Fair and, 162, 185, 196; *We Were Five*, 174
Dionne, Elzire, 185, 192
Dionne, Oliva, 174, 190–2, 196
disability: acquired vs. congenital, 17, 124; conflation of race and, 28–9, 102–3, 137, 141, 148; overcoming, as sideshow theme, 138–9; social process of determining, 119
Discipline and Punish: The Birth of the Prison (Foucault), 25–6
"Disc-Lipped Savages," 141–2
Division of Child Welfare, 187
Domurat Dreger, Alice, on the medical gaze, 134
Donnacona (Iroquoian chief), 30
Dotten, Herb, on circuit bidding, 60
Drewer, Doc, treatment of microcephalic performers, 112
Dufferin Park (Toronto), 61
Dufour and Rogers Shows, 45–6, 162
Dufour, Lou (showman), 45–6, 66, 108–9, 137–8, 142, 191, 203
Dummit, Christopher, on risk and masculinity, 96
Durbach, Nadja (historian), 13, 17, 37, 117–18, 200

E.J. Casey Shows, 44, 56, 91–2, 93, 95
Eagle, Nate: as midget manager, 182; on public health initiatives, 129; on sexuality of midgets, 184
Eastern Townships Agricultural Association, Conklin Shows at, 66
Eck, Johnny ("The Only Living Half Boy"), 135–6
economic factors: in sideshow employment, 112–14; in sideshow employment of children, 133, 150, 162–4, 168, 186, 203
Edmison, Rev J.H., 73–4
Eko and Iko (George and Willie Muse), 67, 251n43
Elks, Benevolent and Protective Order of: gambling regulation and, 57; hosting children at circus, 156; partnerships with carnivals, 68, 73
Elves, Hazel (sideshow manager): about, 95; on acceptance within sideshow community, 104; on carnival workers, 95, 96, 97, 98; on children in sideshows, 157; on Frank Hall (her father), 108; on girl show performers, 97–8
Emo, Ontario, 92
Ernie-Len. *See* Defort, Ernie ("Ernie-Len")
"Eskimoland" (CNE, 1937), 143–5, *144*
ethnological shows, 22, 28–33, 37–8, 140–8
eugenics: baby contests and, 184–5, 188; Dionne quintuplets and, 185; medical profession and, 122–3, 125; racialized performers and, 141–8; United States Eugenics Record Office, 178. *See also* race; racialization

eugenics, effects of: on the disabled, 16–17; on immigration law, 50, 103, 219n33; on sideshows, 116, 139–40
exhibitionary complex, modern: about, 3–4, 9, 25–6; Barnum and, 27–8; consumer culture and, 203–4; cuteness in, 174
exhibitionary culture: about, 8; anthropology and, 31–2; flexibility of, 40; middle-class identity and, 33–7, 52; rise of, 8–9, 22–3; role of extraordinary bodies in, 40–1, 102, 118; world's fairs and, 37–40
"extraordinary bodies," about, 14, 40–1

fakes. *See* deception
family, carnivals as, 81–2, 96–9, 108
Far Quhr Shriner's Club (Stratford), 69
Farini (William Hunt), 26, 109, 160, 211n20
Farini, Krao, 27, 29, 32, 94, 150
Fausto-Sterling, Anne, 30
"feeble-mindedness," 103, 125
Feejee Mermaid, 28
Fees: informal, 71–3; licensing, 69–71
fetuses, display of, 108–9
fictionalized narratives, in ethnological shows, 33, 109–11, 141–8
Fiedler, Leslie, on freaks, 15
Fleming, J.E. (immigration official), 99
Fort Erie, Ontario, 66
Fort William Daily Times Journal, 169
Fort William, Ontario, 90, 98–9, 139, 155, 156

Foucault, Michel, 8–9, 25–6, 134
freak show. *See* sideshow (freak show)
Freak Show (Bogdan), 15
freak show performers. *See* sideshow (freak show) performers
Freaks (1932 film, Browning), 136, 203, 204
Freaks (1978 book, Fiedler), 15
freaks of nature vs. freaks of culture, 15
"Frog Girl Side Show," 139
Frolexland (Conklin), 107, 146
Frost, Linda, on racialized performances, 29
fundraisers, sideshows as, 68–9

"gaffed freaks," 108
Galt, Ontario, 55
Galton, Francis (eugenicist), 122
gambling, 40: 1922 clean fair resolution, 56–7; at agricultural fairs, 57; controversy over, 49–50, 52, 63
Garland-Thomson, Rosemarie: coining of term "enfreakment," 15; coining of term "extraordinary bodies," 14; on the consumer gaze, 134; on disability, 4, 102; on feminist theory, 13; on the modern body, 10; on trajectory of freak shows, 15–16
Garrett, Speed, 228n10
Gawley, Andrew, 138–9
Gayway. *See* Skid Way (also Skid Road, PNE)
gazes, types of, 11, 134–5
Geller, Peter, 145
Gerber, David A. (historian): on empathy, 18; on social context, 17

Geyer, Celesta (fat lady), 104, 107, 108
Gibson, James (black performer), 109–11, *110*
Gilly shows, 48
girl performers, *54*
girl shows: 1922 clean fair resolution, 56–7; controversy over, 47, 52–3, 63, 225n123; legality of, 73; Lewiston's, 73, 98; profitability of, 67. *See also* bans and protests
Gizeh Temple Patrol (Vancouver), 155
Gleason, Mona (historian), 116, 123, 175, 184
Globe and Mail: on demise of midway, 200; on Dionne quintuplets, 191, 196; on midget shows, 183; on midway attendance, 67, 155; on sideshow bans, 50; on sideshow workers, 112–13, 115, 139
Godsell, Philip, 143–4
Golden, Janet (historian), 151
Goldsack, Bob (Johnny J. Jones biographer), 79
Good, William *(Winnipeg Tribune)*, 171
Gould, George M. (physician), 120–1
Government of Ontario, regulating exhibit of Dionne quintuplets, 174, 191–3
Goyer, J.B. (Montreal), 169–70
Grand Trunk Railroad, 89
Graubart, Julius (microcephalic performer), 112
Great War Veterans' Association, 225n120; support for carnivals, 47, 68

Great Wortham Shows, 62
Greater Sheesley Shows, 71, 97
Gresham, William Lindsay: on child-friendly zones, 156; on Frank Bergen, 80–1; on sideshow performers, 104, 112
Growing Up (Sutherland), 154
Gruberg, Rubin (showman), 44, 58–9, 217n17
Guelph, Ontario, 93
Guilford, W.S., 58
Guise Bagley, J.G. (lawyer), 53

Hagenbeck, Carl (animal collector), 30, 213n41
Hailock, C., on 1930 Toronto freak show, 102–3
Hale, Walter (Conklin press representative), 66
Halifax, child labour in, 158
Hall, Frank (carnival worker), 95
Hall, Ward (showman), 66; on Betty Lou Williams, 104; on Emmitt Bejano, 161; as juvenile carnival worker, 95; on Simon Metz, 236–7n156; on successful venues, 67–8
Halligan, Jack (showman): on Dolly Reagan, 137; sideshow at Fair for Britain, 86; World's Fair Freaks, *39*, 66, 107, 137
Hamilton Spectator, 85–6
Hamilton, Ontario: carnival fundraiser in, 68; carnival PR in, 85–6; child labour in, 158; Lewiston's shows, 73; setbacks for Conklin shows, 62
"Handsome Johnny Webb," 166
Hanlan's Point amusement park (Toronto), 35

hard work, ethos of, 95–6. *See also* self-made man, cultural narrative of
Head, P.W. (physician), 124
Healy, James (Hospitals Tax Branch), 69
Heaman, Elspeth (historian), on cultural impact of sideshows, 38
Hepburn, Mitchell (Ontario premier), 192
Hess, Julian (physician), 190
Heth, Joice (sideshow performer), 28
Hewitt, Wm. Judkins, 42
"Hey, Rube," 21, 97
Hicks, William (Greater Sheesley Shows), 71
Hill, Harry (carnival worker), 98
Hilton, Daisy and Violet (conjoined twins), 61, 130–1, 150
History of Fairs and Expositions (Waters), 59, 87
Homi, Cawas (physician), on phocomelus monster, 126
Hootchie Cootchie dancers, 38, 52
Horne, Marcel, 94, 95–8
Hospital for Sick Children (Toronto), 123, 193
Howard the Lobster Boy, 126
Hughes, Elwood (CNE general manager), 65–6
Humberd, Charles (physician), Robert Wadlow and, 132
Hunt, William. *See* Farini

immigration law (Canadian and American), 73–5. *See also* cross-border travel, regulation of
income, of sideshow performers, 107–8, 109–14, 136
Indian Act (1895), 147

Indigenous children: in baby contests, 189; runaway, 100
Indigenous peoples, display of, 140–8. *See also* ethnological shows
Ingalls, Clyde (Ringling Bros. recruiter), on finding and staging freaks, 105, 106
institutionalization: of disabled children, 158–159; freak show as alternative to, 103, 105, 107, 129, 162–4. *See also* de-institutionalization; welfare
International Association of Fairs and Expositions, 56–7
International Longshoreman's Association, support for carnivals, 47
Inuit peoples, display of: Chicago (1893), 30–1, 37; Eskimoland, CNE, 143–5, *144*; Germany, 30
Inuit performers: Abraham Ulrikab, 30; Minik, 31
It's All Done with Mirrors (Elves), 157

Jack Halligan's Side Show (Fair for Britain), 86
Jacobsen, Adrian (trader in ethnographic peoples), 30
James Patterson Trained Wild Animal Show and Gollmar Brothers Circus, 73, 90; 1917 tour map, *91*
Jay, Hugh E. (Old Home Week), 106
Johnny J. Jones shows: at CNE (1913), *45*; at CNE (1919), 61; child performers with, 170; Congress of Fat People, *45*; Johnny Eck in, 135–6; Mary Ann Bevans in, 113; midget shows in, 180; octopus for, 109; size of, 45, 70, 74

Johnson, Martin, 22
Johnston, Archie, 109
Jones, Johnny Jenkins ("Mighty Monarch of All Tented Shows"), 44, 156; life of, 79–80. *See also* Johnny J. Jones shows
Jones, Merle (child fairgoer), 154
Jones, Yvonne and Yvette (conjoined twins), 150
Josephson, J.E. (Dep't of Physiology, Queen's University), on anencephalic twins, 125
Journal of the American Medical Association, 121–2, 124, 132, 239n26

Kagong, Grace (Indigenous performer), 147–8
Kapuskasing, Ontario, 92
Kay, Ellen, "Century of the Child" declaration, 151–2
Kelley, F. Beverly (Ringling Bros. publicist), on immigration restrictions, 51
Kelso, J.J. (Office of Neglected and Dependent Children), 170
Kempe, C. Henry, 172–3
Kiki and Bobo (microcephalic performers), 112
Kingston, Ontario, 36, 66
Koptie, Steve, 99, 232n88
Kortes, Pete (showman), 66–7, 236–7n156
Krao. *See* Farini, Krao
Krause Great Shows, 155

labour, performative. *See* performative labour
Laloo (asymmetrically conjoined twin), 26, 128
Lancet, The, 124, 190, 242n48

Lauther, Carl (showman), 61, 161
Lauther, Percilla ("Monkey Girl"), 61, 150, 161
Laycraft, Justice James H., 72–3, 217–18n20
Leamington, Ontario, 66
Lears, Jackson, on the self-made man, 79
Les Marechal Midgets, 180, 182
Lethbridge and District Exhibition, 85
Levitt-Brown-Huggins Shows, size of entourage (1924), 74
Lewiston, Harry (showman): accident, 96; child performers and, 112; Conklin and, 66, 67, 73; sexual exploitation by, 98; Quebec Exposition Provencale, 67; Rubin and Cherry Shows, 67; selling Bibles, 108; on trickery, 136
Libbera, Jean and Jacques (conjoined twins), 127–8
LIFE exhibition (Lou Dufour), 137–8
Linderman, Max, 98
Lindfors, Bernth, 30, 111
Lindsay, Ontario, 66
Linnaeus, Carl, 25
Lionel the Lion-Faced Boy, 32, 126
Lions Club, 85
Little Egypt Hootchie Cootchie dancer, 38
London, Ontario, 73
Lucas, Charles (Darkest Africa), 67

MacEwan, Grant (child fairgoer), 154
Macklaier, William F. (Canadian Council for Crippled Children and Adults), 159
Maclean's: on midgets, 181–2; on "Queen of the Midway," 45; on sideshow deception, 109

Magri, Count Primo, 179
Marco, Dottie (Godmother of the Midway), 101, 201
Marks, Robert (*Maclean's*), on midgets, 181–2, 183
masculinity, discourses of: modernity and, 176–7; carnival ideology and, 79–81, 95–6. *See also* self-made man, cultural narrative of
Masse family (Exeter, Ontario), 186
maternal impressions, 23, 51, 126, 241n44
Matheson, Robert M. (Crown prosecutor), 75–6
McDaniels, Grace, 112–13
McGuiness, Fred, 76
McHold, Heather, 27
McKennon, Joe (historian), 52, 81
McKoy, Millie-Christine (conjoined twins), 160, 241–2n48, 243n52
McNally, Michael David, on Indigenous performances, 147
McRuer, Robert, 13
medical gaze, 134–5
medical journals, reports on extraordinary bodies, 122, 124–5
medical professionals: relationships with individual performers, 129–33; relationships with sideshows, 127–9
medical science, discourse of: in baby contests, 187; defining childhood, 184; defining the normal body, 116–17, 118–26; in Dionne display, 194–5; reshaping the sideshow, 127–9, 133–40 (*see also* science, modern)
Meigan, Fred A. (agent), 73
Merish, Lori, on cuteness, 176
Metz, Simon ("Schlitzie"), 236–8n156

Meyerding, Dr Henry W., 171
microcephaly, 29, 112, 236–8n156. *See also* "pinheads"
middle-class bias: in baby contests, 187, 189. *See also* masculinity, discourses of; racialization; whiteness
middle-class identity, exhibitionary culture and, 33–7, 52
middle-class values: in midget shows, 183–4; in moral and social reform, 10, 42, 49, 50, 55, 157
Midget City, CNE, 61, *181*
Midget City, Coney Island, 179
midget shows, 177–84; midgets and dwarfs compared, 178; paternalism in, 182
midget shows, specific: Midget Village (Conklin), 180; Nate Eagle's Midgets, 184; Singer Midgets, 180, 182; Tiny Town Revue Midgets, The (Conklin), 180; Tom Thumb, 121, 149, 176, 178–9; Weeny Teeny Tiny Town (Conklin), 180
Midway Plaisance (Chicago), 37
Minik (Inuit performer), 31
Miron, Janet, 36
Miss Gabriel ("The Only Half-Lady by Birth"), 130
"Missing Link, the," 32
Mitchinson, Wendy, 116, 126
"Monkey Girl" (Percilla Lauther), 61, 150, 161
"Monkey Girl" (Pookie), 3, 4, 16, 17, 19, 21, 171, 202, 203
monsters and monstrosities: early perceptions of, 23–5; modern explanations for, 124–5 (*see also* teratology); use of terms, 121–2

Montgomery, Peggy-Jean (child film star Baby Peggy), 150, 187, 258n58
Montreal: ads for shows in, 106; Belmont Park, 66, 106; child labour in, 158; dime museums in, 34; pediatrics in, 123
Montreal Gazette, on Dionne quintuplets, 193
moral and social reform, 42, 49–58
Motherwell, W.R. (federal minister of agriculture), 57
movies, as competition, 47
multiple births, 185–6; Ormsby quadruplets, 106. *See also* Dionne quintuplets
Munro, Keith (Dionne quintuplets' manager), 195
Muse, George and Willie (Eko and Iko), 67, 251n43
Musee Theatre (Toronto), 34

Naked Truth, The (Conklin show), 47
Nanaimo, BC, 156
Nanook of the North (film), 145
Nanson, Jean (show woman), 45, 99
Nate Eagle's Midgets, 184
"Nature's Mistakes," *134*; medical discourse and, 133–40
Neiss, Victor J. (Canadian Victory Shows), 68
New Brunswick, regulation in, 70
New York Medical Journal, on "circus and museum freaks," 127
New York State Fair, letter of offer to, 169–70
New York World's Fair: baby show at, 189; Dionne quintuplets and, 162, 185, 196; eugenicist principles and, 250n35; letters of offer to, 133, 159–60, 162–6, 185–6; sideshow profits at, 46
newsboys, 156–7
Niagara Falls, Ontario, 138
"normal," definition of, 120
normal body, the: Adolphe Quetelet on, 119–20; exhibitionary culture and, 41; medical definitions of, 118–26; origins of concept, 8, 115–18; race, gender, and age of, 8, 116, 140; sculptures of (1893), 120
normality, cuteness and, 184–5, 186–90

O'Connor, F.P. (senator), 65–6
Ontario Association of Agricultural Societies, 60
Ontario Fairs Convention, 71
Ontario government, regulating exhibit of Dionne quintuplets, 174, 191–3
Ontario Provincial Police: bribes, 71–2; interventions, 75–6, 97, 98–9, 100
Orbeck, Mrs. (mother of albino sons), 162–3
order of things; freak shows as, 26–7; search for, 23, 25; white bourgeois, 27 (*see also* white supremacy)
Oriental Dancing Dolls, 69
Origin of Species (Darwin), 32
Orlando, Florida, 180
Ormsby quadruplets, 106
orphans, 156–7
Oshawa, Ontario, 55
Ottawa, Ontario: child labour in, 158; Polack Bros. in, 90, 155; World of Mirth in, 62, 82, 247n123
overcoming disability, as sideshow theme, 138–9

Pacific National Exhibition (Vancouver): midway crowd at, 1940, *46*; "Nature's Mistakes" (1940), *134*; securing a carnival company, 62–3; Siamese twin show banned (1917), 50; Skid Road Attractions (1919), *64*; Skid Way, 59, 62, 63–4, 65; Wagner Carnival at (1960), 95
Pantages Theatre, 187
Paré, Ambroise, 24
partnerships with local organizations, 68–9, 85–6, 155, 156
Pastrana, Julia ("Bear Woman," "Baboon Lady"), 32, 214n51, 242n48
paternal impressions, 241n44
paternalism: in carnival management, 58, 81–3, 87–8, 98, 108; vis-à-vis Indigenous peoples, 145; vis-à-vis midgets, 182. *See also* self-made man, cultural narrative of
"Patty Conklin's code," 87
Pearl, Jolly (fat lady), 107, 108
Pearson, Susan J. (historian), on American baby shows, 186, 194
Peary, Robert, 31
pediatrics, development of, 123
performative labour: by children, 150, 157–66; freak shows as, 102–3, 114
performers and physicians, relationship between, 129–33
Pete Kortes's No. 1 Side Show unit, Look at Life, 66
Peterborough, Ontario, 53, 96
Philadelphia, Centennial Exposition (1876), 37
physicians and performers, relationship between, 129–33

"pickled punk" shows, 108–9, 137–8
Pilling, Monty (*Winnipeg Free Press*), 81–2
"pinheads," 29, 85–6, 105, 108, 112, 141
"pit shows," 48
Pither, R.J.N. (Indian agent), 160–1
Polack Bros. Circus: 1920 tour, 90, *92*; children's pricing, 155; at PNE, 59; size of, 44, 70; in Toronto, 61; touring schedule, 90
polio, 1937 epidemic, 67
Pookie ("Monkey Girl"), 3, 4, 16, 17, 19, 21, 171, 202
Port Arthur, Ontario, 155
Port Loring, Ontario, 125
poverty. *See* economic factors
premature infants, display of, 189–90
Prince Albert, Saskatchewan, 89
Princess Beatrice Hospital (London), 128–9
Princess Corita and her midget ballet, 69
Princess Ha-Ha the Aztec Wonder, 61
profitability: of Dionne quintuplets' display, 196; of sideshows, 38, 40, 58–9, 66, 76–7, 109, 114, 167, 201–2
promotional pamphlets and souvenirs: about, 107–8, 169; examples of, *126*, *127–8*, *130*, *136*, *137*, *138*, *139*, *186*, *194*
protests and bans, 49–58
public health initiatives, effect of on potential performers, 129
public relations, 83–7; 1922 IAFE resolution as, 56–7; carnivals and child welfare, 156, 169; Patty Conklin and, 66, 169

Pushnik, Frieda (armless, legless woman), 136, 150
Pyle, Walter L. (physician), 120–1

Quebec City, censors at Conklin sideshow, 72; child labour in, 158
Quetelet, Adolphe (statistician), on normalcy, 119–20
Quintland, 174, 193–8

Race: conflation of disability and, 28–9, 102–3, 137, 141, 148; cuteness and, 176, 187, 188; science and, 28, 32–3
racialization: in ethnological shows, 22, 28–33, 37–8, 109–11, 116, 117, 141–8; in immigration laws, 74–5, 111; in medically themed shows, 137, 187. *See also* dehumanization of sideshow performers; Indigenous peoples, display of; white supremacy
rail travel, 89–94
Rainy River, Ontario, 92
raree shows, 40
Raucci, Celia ("Fat Woman" Winsome Winnie), 107
Reagan, Dolly (The Ossified Lady), 106–7, 137
Reaume, Geoffrey (historian), 13, 164
Red Cross, 68, 187
Regina Leader Post, 87
Regina, Saskatchewan, 99, 136–7
regulation of carnivals: moral, 42, 49–58; state, 69–77
Reiss, Jonathan (historian), on Joice Heth's autopsy, 28
Rendezvous Park (Winnipeg), 93
Renker, Joe. *See* Conklin, Patty ("King of the Carnival")

respectability: of baby and midget shows, 177, 184; of dime museums, 33–5; responsibility for, 63; through charitable activities, 68–9, 156; through ideal of childhood, 170; through medical discourse, 128, 135; of world's fairs, 39–40, 49–50, 106. *See also* bans and protests; moral and social reform
Ringling Bros.: 1922 clean fair resolution and, 56–7; in Canada, 35; deportation fees and, 75; runaways with, 99; size of, 70, 91; unionization and, 219n31, 231–2n74
Ringling Bros. and Combined Barnum and Bailey Circus: 1922 tour map, 93; about, 222–3n87; in Canada, 51; Congress of Freaks, 126; freak recruitment and production at, 105, 106, 129; independence of, 61–2; sued for kidnapping, 251n43
Ringling Bros., performers with: "Disc-Lipped Savages," 141–2; Frieda Pushnik, 136; George and Willie Muse, 251n43; Krao, 94; Robert Wadlow, 131–3, 198–9
Ripley's Believe It Or Not, 68, 139
Riverdale Park (Toronto), 86
Robinson and Company Dime Museum (Toronto), 34
Rockwood, Ontario, 125
Rogers, Joseph E. (OPP superintendent), 53, 55, 68–9
Rooth, James A. (physician), on Hilton twins, 131
Roullett, Major, 186
Routhier, Father Daniel (parish priest), 191

Royal American Shows, about: as family, 81–2; public inquiry into practices, 72, 202, 217–18n20; in Saskatoon, 62, 83–4; skimming by, 46; temporary Canadianization of, 44; in West Kildonan, 56

Royal American Shows, performers: Betty Lou Williams (conjoined twin), 104, 139; Jose de Leon ("Armless Wonder"), 139

Royal Canadian Shows, 44, 217–18n20

Royal Victoria Maternity Hospital (Montreal), 193

Rubin and Cherry Shows: at CNE, 58–9, 103, 217n17; Harry Lewiston (showman) at, 67; at PNE, 217n17; size of entourage (1924), 45, 74

runaway children, 99–101

Rydell, Robert (historian), 250n35

Saint-Hilaire, Isidore, 120, 121

Samuels, Ellen, 18

Sandwell, Bernard K., on American popular culture, 52

Sargeant, Dudley (anthropologist), 120

Sarnia, Ontario, 51

Saskatoon: Al G. Barnes Circus in, 218n28; child attendees in, 154; Royal American Shows in, 62, 83–4; travelling show regulation in, 55, 70, 71, 73

Saskatoon Exhibition, 71

Sault Ste Marie, Ontario, 53

Saxon, A.H. (Barnum biographer), 27

scheduling and logistics, 88–94

science, modern: categorizing difference through, 28, 31–3; exhibitionary culture and, 23, 25–7, 36, 127–9, 133–40

Second World War: amusement as patriotism, 86–7; labour shortages during, 95; travel restrictions during, 93; use of CNE grounds during, 86

self-made man, cultural narrative of, 79–81, 223n87. *See also* masculinity, discourses of

"Seminoles, Village of" (CNE, 1931), 145–6

Serpentine, the girl without bones, 61

sexual abuse and exploitation, 98, 100, 261n103

sexuality: child performers and, 169–70; in midget shows, 176, 184; in racialized performances, 22, 143; target of moral reformers, 49 (*see also* girl shows)

Shildrick, Margarit, 20

Shoal Lake, Manitoba, 92

Showmen's League of America, 50, 60, 67, 80, 222n78

Shriners, 68, 69, 156

sideshow (freak show) performers: acting as "Zulus," 109–11, *110*; contracts and earnings, 107–8, 109–14; cultural production of, 15, 105–7; declining availability of, 108; fake, 108–9; income of, 107–8, 109–14, 136; physicians and, 129–33; search for, 105–7

Sideshow U.S.A. (Adams), 16

sideshows (freak shows): defined, 7; origins of, 23–31; relationship with medical profession, 127–9; subcontracting of, 65–8; as workplaces, 102–3, 114

Singer Midgets, 180, 182
Singer, Leo (showman), 180, 182
Skid Road Attractions (1919), 64
Skid Way (also Skid Road, PNE), 59, 62, 63–4, 65
"skimming," 46, 217–18n20
Skinner, Kate (mother of Hilton twins), 130, 133
Smylie, Clifford Hugh (physician), on anencephalic monster, 125
Smythe, Fred (Ringling manager), on public health initiatives, 129
social Darwinism, 122
social reform. See moral and social reform
sociocultural factors and exhibitionary culture, 25–6, 33–7, 115, 169
Song of Hiawatha pageants, 147
Spear, Ivan (showman), Dionne quintuplets and, 190–1
St Boniface, Manitoba, 92
St Vital, Manitoba, 56
staging, of sideshow performers, 105–6, 213n41; medical discourse in, 137, 138, 140
staring, 11, 104, 135
state regulation: of carnivals, 69–77; of Dionne quintuplets exhibit, 191–3
Stern, Alexandra Minna, 187
Stewart, Susan, 7, 178
stillborn children, display of, 24
Stratford, Ontario, 69
Strathroy, Ontario, 106
Stratton, Charles Sherwood. See Tom Thumb
Strong, Trudy (circus performer), 48
Strong-Boag, Veronica, on disabled children, 158–9

subcontracting of sideshows, 65–8
Sullivan, Jimmie, 60–1
"Sunday School" shows, 40, 57, 223n87
Sunnyside Park (Toronto), 66
Surtees, George (showman), 237n156
Sutherland, Neil, on child fairgoers, 154–5
Swan, Anna (giantess), 27

Tambo (Australian Aboriginal boy), 30
Tanser, H.A. (school superintendent), 140
taxation of carnivals, 69–70
telegony, 241n44
Temple, Shirley, 150, 199
teratology, 25, 121–3, 124–6
Thelander, H.E. (physician), on use of term "monster," 121–2, 239n26
Thomas Shows, 98–9
Thompson, Robert (child fairgoer), 154
Thompson, Robert (Saskatoon), 83–4
Thurston, John, 43
ticket prices, 48
Timmins, Ontario, 92
Tiny Town Revue Midgets, The (Conklin), 180
Titchkosky, Tanya, 13
Tom Thumb, General (Charles Sherwood Stratton), 121, 149, 176, 178–9
Tomaini, Al and Jeanie ("Giant and Half-Girl"), 138
Toronto: censorship in, 42; child labour in, 158; dime museums in, 34; pediatrics in, 123; Dufferin Park, 61; Sunnyside Park, 66. See also Canadian National Exhibition

Toronto Industrial Exhibition, 35, 38, 146
Toronto's Baby Peggy contest, 187
touring conditions, 94–5
trafficking, of children with disabilities, 159–61, 251n43
travel and transportation, 43–4, 88–95. *See also* circuits
Tripp, Charles ("Armless Wonder"), 27
twins, conjoined, about: Bland-Sutton on, 128, 149; contemporary survival rates, 243n61; surgical separation of, 128, 142, 243n52
twins, conjoined, specific: Betty Lou Williams, 104, 139; Chang and Eng, 121; Daisy and Violet Hilton, 61, 130–1, 150; Defort, Ernie ("Ernie-Len"), 137, 166–71, *167*; Jean and Jacques Libbera, 127–8; Laloo, 26, 128; Millie-Christine McKoy, 160, 241–2n48, 243n52; Rosa and Josepha Blazek, 121; Yvonne and Yvette Jones, 150
Tye, Menia (nurse), on infant with spina bifida, 133

"Ubangi Savages" (CNE), 141–2, *143*
"ugly laws," 50, 219n33
Ulrikab, Abraham (Inuit performer), 30
United States Eugenics Record Office, 178
University of Toronto Faculty of Medicine, pediatric department, 123

Valverde, Mariana, 170, 193, 250n36
Vancouver: children at carnivals in, 156; Pacific National Exhibition, *46*, 59, *64*, *134*; Siamese twin show banned (1917), 50
Vancouver Exhibition Association, 63–5
Victorian Order of Nurses, 187
"Village of Seminoles" (CNE, 1931), 145–6
Violence, among carnival workers, 98–9
Virchow, Rudolf, 25

Wadlow, Robert (giant), 131–3, 198–9
Wagner Carnival, 95
Wahbunosa, John (Indigenous performer), 147–8
Walden, Keith: on modern urban culture, 8; on social hierarchies, 36
Wallace Bros. All-Canadian Shows, 44, 61
Wallace, Marc (physician), on child without arms or legs, 133
Wallers, K.B. (physician), on anencephalic twins, 125
War Measures Act, 50
Warner, Hanford (showman), 160
Warren, Lavinia (wife of Tom Thumb), 178–9
Waters, H.W., 59, 87
We Were Five (Dionne quintuplets), 174
Weeny Teeny Tiny Town (Conklin), 180
Weisz, George (historian), 151
Welfare: attitudes toward, 105, 114, 168, 169; disabled children and, 158–9, 162; HBC and Inuit peoples, 145
Welland, Ontario, 68
West Algoma Agricultural Association Fair, 155

West Kildonan, Manitoba, 56, 66
West, Patsy, 146
Western Association of Exhibitions, 60
Western Fair Association, 59–60
"What Is It?" racialized shows, 32–3
Whatley, W.R. (OPP), 53
Whit, Frank (brother of runaway), 100
White Tops, 81; on Hilton twins, 131; on multiple births, 185; on quasi-ethnological shows, 141–2; term "Zulu" in, 109
whiteness: in concepts of childhood, 157–8, 187, 199; in concepts of cuteness, 176, 179; sideshows as legitimation for, 140–8 (*see also* ethnological shows). *See also* racialization
"Wild Men of Borneo" (Hiram and Barney Davis), 37, 160
Williams, Betty Lou (conjoined twin), 104, 139
Wilson, Gahan, on gaze, 11
Wilson, Joanne (circus performer), 48
Windsor, Ontario, 93
Winnipeg: circuit bidding at, 60–1; opposition to carnivals in, 52; Rendezvous Park, 93; travelling show regulation in, 55–6. *See also* E.J. Casey Shows

Winnipeg Free Press, on carnival as family, 81–2
Winnipeg Tribune (orphans' picnic), 156
Witts World Famous Show, 53
Wizard of Oz, The (1939 film), 180
World at Home Shows (Polack Bros.), 44, 61, 70, 75
World of Mirth magazine, 184
World of Mirth Shows, 62, 82, 104, 113, 155, 183, 247n123
World's Columbian Exposition (Chicago, 1893), 30–1, 37–8, 120
World's Fair Freaks (Halligan), 66, 107, 137; at CNE, 39
world's fairs, 37–40
World's Famous Shows, 100
World's Smallest Home (CNE), 183
Wortham, Clarence A., 44, 217n14; Great Wortham Shows, 62
Wright, Cynthia, on Quintland, 193

Youngblood, T.W., 185–6
youth culture, 150, 154–5, 179–80

Zahorsky, John (physician), 189–90
Zelizer, Viviana, on childhood, 153
"Zulus," freak show performers as, 109–11

www.ingramcontent.com/pod-product-compliance
Lightning Source LLC
Chambersburg PA
CBHW020355080526
44584CB00014B/1024